Dan Xu (Editor)

Plurality and Classifiers across Languages in Chin

Trends in Linguistics Studies and Monographs

Volume 255

Plurality and Classifiers across Languages in China

Edited by
Dan Xu

DE GRUYTER
MOUTON

ISBN 978-3-11-048534-9
e-ISBN 978-3-11-029398-2
ISSN 1861-4302

Library of Congress Cataloging-in-Publication Data
A CIP catalog record for this book has been applied for at the Library of Congress.

Bibliographic information published by the Deutsche Nationalbibliothek
The Deutsche Nationalbibliothek lists this publication in the Deutsche Nationalbibliografie;
detailed bibliographic data are available in the Internet at http://dnb.dnb.de.

© 2012 Walter de Gruyter GmbH, Berlin/Boston
Typesetting: RoyalStandard, Hong Kong
Printing and binding: Hubert & Co. GmbH & Co. KG, Göttingen
♾ Printed on acid-free paper
Printed in Germany

www.degruyter.com

Table of contents

Preface

Quantification is one of the most basic notions for human beings, and consequently it is one of the most commonly marked notions in languages. It is indicated with different devices, phonological, morphological, syntactic, and others. In this book, quantification will be observed and studied from three different perspectives: synchronic, diachronic and typological. Several topics are studied in the book, with a focus on plurality. The book will take advantage of recent results from research on quantification in languages of China to deal with more concrete and more targeted subjects, such as relationships between plurality and classifiers, plurality and reduplication, plurality expressions in non-Han languages, and plurality concepts in child language acquisition.

This book originated from a project awarded by the French ANR, *Quantification and Plurality* ANR-06-BLAN0259, then by the IUF (University Institute of France). Without their substantial financial support, this book could not have been completed. The editor expresses her sincere gratitude to these institutions. The authors are from France, Germany, Norway, China, Hongkong and the United States. Thanks to collective research and to the contribution of each scholar, the book progressively took shape and became what it is today. Completion of the project is actually marked by the publication of two books: one was published in China, *Liàng yǔ fùshù de yánjiū* 量与复数的研究 ([Quantification and plurality] 2010), and the second (the present book) is being published in Europe. In the research, as well as in the editing work, my colleagues have helped me in one way or another and have given me pertinent remarks and useful advice. The editor's thanks also go to Murielle Fabre who did the formatting work for this volume, which is time-consuming labor. Many thanks also to Marie-Claude Paris and Jingqi Fu for helping me with checking work. Undoubtedly, all faults are mine.

Dan Xu
Paris
September 2012

Dan Xu
Introduction
Plurality and Classifiers across languages
of China[1]

1 Background

Plurality has drawn the attention of scholars (Sanches [1971] 1973; Greenberg 1972, 1988; Lü 1984; Dryer 1989, 1992; Bisang 1993, Heide 1995, Ortmann 2000, Comrie 2008, Xu 2010, among others) for several decades. Papers on plurality have most often discussed it in terms of numeral classifiers and the absence of obligatory plural marking. But numeral classifiers and plural marking are not the only strategies for grammatical quantification; reduplication is a third device for quantification. In fact, plural marking, numeral classifiers and reduplication constitute the main means of quantification marking in the domain of grammar. There are many more lexical devices for expressing quantification, but this book is interested in grammatical systems. The present introduction will first concentrate on the typological correlation between the three different strategies for quantification, as well as some general issues. In the second section, it will address individual devices for quantification in Chinese, concentrating on plurality and reduplication, which have been studied less frequently than classifiers. The third part will go beyond Chinese and will present a short typology of how quantification is expressed in the other languages of China. A description of how the book is organized will conclude this introduction.

Languages in which all three strategies of quantification are marked obligatorily are rare, while languages lacking all of them are even less frequent (see Chapter 2 in this volume). It is important to distinguish two notions here, co-occurrence and co-existence. I refer to the co-existence of three devices (plural markers, reduplication and classifiers) instead of their co-occurrence, which is

---

1 This book is one of the outcomes related to the ANR projects *Quantification et Pluralité ANR-06-BLANO259* and *Space and Quantification* (IUF). We express our gratitude for their financial support. Our thanks also go to the anonymous reviewer for his/her constructive comments on the Introduction and to all participants who have provided their contribution to the present volume.

My debts to Walter Bisang are numerous. He has given me not only effective support and help but also very useful suggestions for this Introduction.

Finally thanks to Craig Baker for his help with proofreading.

impossible in most languages. They are correlated in expressing quantity: if one is present and obligatory, the other two are often absent or optional. This also assumes that in human languages, quantification has to be explicitly or implicitly indicated by different means. If a language does not possess obligatory plural marking, it tends to exploit reduplication as a grammatical device. In this sense, plural marking and reduplication are comparable in syntax. More concretely, one or the other is frequently attested in the nominal structures of human languages.

Reduplication often co-exists with classifiers in Mainland Southeast Asian languages. This is one of the characteristics of this linguistic area (Enfield 2005). In fact, two patterns are found in languages: obligatory plural marking on the one hand vs. reduplication-classifier marking on the other. Reduplication is rarely obligatory (even though it is fully productive in many languages, cf. Rubino 2005) and adds specific semantics to plurality. For that reason, it can easily co-exist with the numeral-classifier systems of Chinese and Mainland Southeast Asian languages.

Even though the mutual exclusion of numeral classifiers and obligatory plural marking has often been discussed in typological work since Sanches ([1971] 1973) and Greenberg (1972), the theory is not as water-tight as is often claimed. Even Greenberg (1972) does not treat this correlation as having no exceptions. Some publications, especially a monograph on Japanese by P. Downing (1996), have pointed out that the correlations between plurality and classifiers must be more widely investigated and better described, since counterexamples exist. Based on Japanese data, Downing (1996: 28) indicates that "the language [Japanese] possesses not only numeral classifiers, but several plural markers which may appear with nouns which are accompanied by classifiers as well." Bisang (in this volume) also shows potential counterexamples with data on Northern Kam and Weining Ahmao.

Reduplication and the occurrence of numeral classifiers are compared much less in the literature. In contemporary Chinese, plural marking and reduplication are not obligatory, while classifiers are when using numerals. One device cannot co-occur with the others as is illustrated by the following examples:

(1) 人们,　　　人人,　　　　　五个人
　　rén men　 *rén rén*　　　 *wǔ ge rén*
　　person-PL, person-person, five-CL-person
　　'people, everybody/people, five people'

(2) *人人们,　　　　*五个人们
　　rén rén men　　 *wǔ ge rén men*
　　person-person-PL, five-CL-person-PL

In fact, Chinese seems to have become a nominal classifier language not as early as has been believed, and the order "numeral + classifier + noun" won as a dominant order only after the 10th century AD (Wu 2006). This means that Old Chinese was not a classifier language for a long time. It is thus interesting to investigate how plurality marking developed during the periods when classifiers were not obligatory (see Feng in this volume). Plural markers in contemporary Chinese are obviously based on word plurality (one of the categories of plurality denoted by Dryer [1989]), while Old and Middle Chinese used other means (Xu 2010). In Chinese, nouns and verbs can be reduplicated to express plurality, pluractionality, distributivity, etc. Not all nouns can be reduplicated, and not all reduplicated nouns indicate plurality. Also, productive reduplication is relatively new in Chinese, and very few examples can be found in Old Chinese and Middle Chinese. In modern Mandarin Chinese, nouns cannot be freely reduplicated. Not as many nouns can be reduplicated (such as 人人 *rénrén* 'everyone', 天天 *tiāntiān* 'everyday') as adjectives and verbs. Classifiers, like nouns, can be repeated indicating distributivity:

(3) 人人,　　年年
     rénrén,　*niánnián*
     'everyone, every year'

(4) 个个,　　张张
     gègè,　*zhāngzhāng*
     'every one, every piece (of paper)'

(5) 家家户户
     jiājiāhùhù
     'each family'

Example (3) is often cited to show noun reduplication in Chinese. In fact, this is far less productive than adjective or verb reduplication. Temporal words such as 年 *nián* 'year' can be reduplicated. In (4), classifiers are reduplicated to express distributivity. In general, classifiers can be reduplicated when the context is clear. Example (5) shows that some reduplicated words have been completely lexicalized. These examples are abundant and we shall pass over them here. One thing is clear: distribution/distributivity is in fact another way to express plurality; and without a concept of collectivity in which plurality is implied, the expression "everyone" is not tenable.

Quantification and many other grammatical phenomena are better described and studied in Indo-European languages because comparative methods have been established by European scholars since the 19th century. The investigation of the languages of China seems to lag far behind. The linguistic situation in China is also more complex, since more languages from more families are involved. The languages of China consist of the Han languages (Mandarin and at least nine other Sinitic languages), and the Han are surrounded by different ethnic groups and languages. It is thus important and necessary to study the Han languages as well as the non-Han languages of China. Since European languages tend to have obligatory plural marking and lack numeral classifiers, and since they use reduplication less productively and less frequently (cf. Rubino 2005) than many languages of China, a better understanding of the quantification strategies in the languages of China will certainly enrich our comprehension of human language and thought. In addition, the study of Chinese and the other languages spoken in China will have its impact on the study of other language families. The languages of China deserve more investigation, especially the non-Han languages, because many of them remain unknown or poorly studied.

Plurality is "an area that has been rather neglected, especially in typological work" (Dryer 1989: 888); and "A clearer understanding of the diachronic origin (or origins) of plural words is necessary in order to better understand their synchronic properties." (Dryer 1989). This book tries to remedy the general lack of information on grammatical quantification in the languages of China by providing papers by scholars who have been working in these fields for a long time and have made important contributions to the study of the languages in China. A book edited by Li Jinfang and Hu Suhua (2005) observes non-Han languages of China and studies classifiers. In a recent book *Liàng yǔ fùshù de yánjiū* 量与复数的研究 ([Quantification and plurality], Dan Xu [ed.], 2010) which has been published as a companion to the present volume, seventeen authors (two papers are written by co-authors) give their contributions to these problems. The authors of these two books do not overlap, and the first one was written in Chinese while the present one is in English. These two books aim to review Chinese and some non-Han languages in depth to better understand the correlation between plurality and classifiers.

2 Devices for marking quantity in Chinese[2]

Chinese is one of the languages that does not require plural marking in noun phrases (see Feng Shengli and Harbsmeier in this volume for Old Chinese). Plurality is expressed in the clause by numerous adverbs, or indicated in nominal

---

2 Studies on the origin and development of the plurality suffix -*men* in Chinese can be found in the sister book *Quantification and Plurality* (2010) mentioned earlier.

phrases by numerals, adjectives or noun modifiers (Paris in this volume). Plurality in Chinese is not obligatorily expressed by a morpheme or several morphemes as in Indo-European languages, but by abundant adjunct words. Thus, Chinese seems to follow Greenberg's (1972) universal even though the complementary distribution of obligatory plural markers and numeral classifiers has been challenged by more recent data (see Bisang, this volume).

Chinese differs from morphologically rich languages, but might have used morphology for expressing quantification in its early history. Eventually, plural words (lexical items) became prominent. Though contemporary Chinese does not have obligatory marking of every NP for plurality, it possesses some adverbs to indicate plurality (see Lee in this volume), such as 都 *dōu* 'all', 皆 *jiē* 'all', 全 *quán* 'all', etc. The list was much longer in Middle Chinese: 都 *dōu*, 皆 *jiē*, 全 *quán*, 並 *bìng*, 盡 *jìn*, 具/俱 *jù*, 悉 *xī*, 咸 *xián*, 總 *zǒng*, 舉 *jǔ*, etc. (see also Meisterernst in this volume). It seems that the Chinese language prefers marking plurality in the VP to marking it in the NP.

In previous studies on plural marking in Chinese, scholars have focused on the plural marker *men* which is only applicable to noun phrases with the feature [+human] and it is not obligatory especially in the object position. In Early Old Chinese (11th–5th centuries BC), some words like 眾 *zhòng*, 群 *qún*, 諸 *zhū*, marked plural meaning in the prenominal position. Only 余 *yú* was a postnominal plural word. These prenominal plural words became lexicalized later (see also Meisterernst in this volume) and some postnominal plural words like 曹 *cáo*, 輩 *bèi*, 等 *děng* took over the function of plural marking. Due to its postnominal position, *yú* survived and continued to express plural meaning. There is no major debate among scholars about the status of these plural words which are not full-fledged plural markers. The real plural marker *men* evolved during the Song Dynasty (960–1279 AD). From diachronic data, Dan Xu (2009a) suggests that the emergence of postnominal plural marking is correlated with the development of classifiers which moved from the postnominal position to the prenominal position, while plural marking did the reverse (see also Jang-Ling Lin and Alain Peyraube in this volume). In this book, authors will observe the relationship between plural marking and classifiers from different angles to better understand the problem. The investigation will not be limited to Chinese, but will extend to other languages spoken in China in order to work with different perspectives on this topic.

Reduplication is a frequent phenomenon in Asian and African languages (for example, Malay in Indonesia, Lepcha in India, Lomongo in the Congo, Amharic in Ethiopia, Malagasy in Madagascar, Yoruba in Western Africa, etc.). It can indicate a variety of concepts such as plurality, distributivity, iteration, and intensity (cf. Rubino 2005 for a more exhaustive list). One of its meanings in Chinese is that of the diminutive. In this case, it has to be considered as a morphological device by which the iconic function of repeating phonological material has a symbolic meaning (see detailed analysis of Dan Xu in this volume). Some reduplicated nouns express an intimate meaning[3]; again these nouns are not very prevalent and are often found in adult-child dialogue.

When adjectives are reduplicated, the degree of the adjective's quality is, in general, intensified. But the intensification interpretation is not always present in contemporary Chinese: for example, color perception can be subjective and variable, therefore adjectives describing color are prone to subjective interpretation. More precisely, reduplicated adjectives, in the beginning, were iconically motivated to emphasize degree. Some of them can emphasize the subjective perception of the author (see Montaut 2009); thus the diminutive interpretation is possible. The ABB type of reduplication is very well-developed in contemporary Chinese. Cheng Xiangqing (1992: 95) points out that the ABB form began to become more prevalent in the Tang Dynasty (618–907 AD). This phenomenon can also be seen in Modern Hindi. Singh (2005: 268) reveals that in some cases, a reduplicated adjective can express an emphatic distribution if the noun is plural, while the same word can signify an "approximation" in other cases. Compare his two examples:

(6) *hariiharii*
    green green (leaves)
    'very green (leaves)'

(7) *hariiharii saarii*
    green green sari
    'a greenish sari'

These examples suggest that the subjective interpretation of colors is frequent in languages, and the subjectivity plays a key role in favoring the evolution of the plus-degree towards the minus-degree. However diachronic examples of Chinese ABB confirm that at the beginning of its development, reduplication marked the plus degree in an iconic way. When this device is full-fledged, it can become a morphological device, losing its initial meaning. In fact, reduplicated verbs marking diminutive meaning in Chinese illustrate this change well. More concretely speaking, in the first stage, they generally indicate emphasis, reinforcement and the plus-degree, while in the second stage, they almost always express diminutive meaning and the minus-degree. Here are some examples:

---

3 For example: 勺勺 *sháoshao* 'spoon', 兜兜 *dōudou* 'pocket', 包包 *bāobao* 'bag'.

(8) 看看, 想想, 说说, 走走
    kànkan,   *xiǎngxiang,* *shuōshuo,*   *zǒuzou*

    'to take a look, to think a bit, to say something, to take a walk'

In the above examples from contemporary Chinese, the reduplicated verbs mean "to go to do something a little bit, to try". The grammatical meaning "unaccomplished, atelic, imperfective, short duration action" is in fact an interpretation of the new status of the reduplicated part: it indicates the future. Reduplicated verbs are not compatible with the past tense, adverbs implying the past, or elements indicating accomplishment. An aspect marker [+accomplish] *le* has to be inserted between the two parts if one wishes to express the past, a telic action. Again, I think that some contemporary non-iconic meanings have to progressively lose their initial iconic signification. Now we will illustrate this point of view with some diachronic examples:

(9) 看看似相识 (孟浩然 *Mèng Hàorán*, 689–740 AD)

    kànkàn sì   xiāngshí

    see see like be acquainted

    'Seeing each other, it seems that we are acquainted.'

(10) 望望不见君 (李白 *Lǐ Bái*, 701–762 AD)

    wàngwàng bú   jiàn jūn

    look look NEG see you

    'I am looking and looking but I cannot see you'

In these sentences, the reduplicated verbs intensify the continuance of the action in repeating the same verb. The iconic meaning is clear. According to Cheng Xiangqing (1992) and Liu Xiaonong's separate descriptions (1992) and to Wang Ying's (1996: 234) studies, reduplicated verbs from before or during the Tang never indicated diminutive meaning. All of them express high frequency, augmented quantity, continuance, and so on. It is interesting to note that in modern Yangzhou (located in Jiangsu Province) dialect, reduplicated verbs have kept the iconic meaning indicating high frequency of the action (Zhu Jingsong cited by Wang Ying 1996: 240), in contrast with Mandarin Chinese.

How did these iconically motivated reduplicated verbs lose their initial meaning and become non-iconic, i.e. morphological devices, in Mandarin Chinese? Again diachronic data and contemporary dialects provide us with complementary evidence. I believe that the rise and the merger of the patterns V1 (V2) *kàn* 'see' (try to do something) and V*yī* 'one' V (do something once) caused reduplicated verbs to lose their iconic meaning. Cai Jinghao (1990) and Wu Fuxiang (1995) provide a diachronic study of V1 (V2) *kàn*. Wu indicates that V *yī* 'one' V (do something once) is found in the Song and may come from "V + Numeral + classifier" in which the verbal classifier was copied from the same verb. Observe some examples:

(11) 可去拜一拜，作别一声。
      (碾玉观音 *Niǎn yù Guānyīn* 12th–13th centuries)

      kě qù bài yí bài   *zuòbié   yì   shēng*
      can go worship one once, bid-farewell one sound

      'You can worship them and bid them farewell.'

(12) 掀起帘子看一看 (碾玉观音 *Niǎn yù Guānyīn*)

      xiānqǐ liánzi   kàn yí kàn
      raise   curtain look-one-look

      'When he raised the curtain and took a look inside...'

In these cases, the verbal classifiers already express a short duration action meaning "once". In contemporary Chinese the reduplicated verbs VV signifying a diminutive meaning can reincorporate *yī* 'one' between them. All examples cited in (8) can be rewritten as V *yī* 'one' V instead of VV. This suggests that some contemporary instances of VV indicating diminutive meaning came from the V *yī* 'one' V pattern but not directly from iconically motivated ones like (9) and (10). These instances of VV are just the shortened form of "V one V". Another construction also favors the diminutive interpretation of VV: V1 (V2) *kàn* 'look' in which the verb *kàn* 'look' was gradually grammaticalized as a particle indicating a future meaning, since verbs which do not denote perception can be combined with *kàn*, originally meaning 'look'. Here are some examples cited by Wu (2006):

(13) 试尝看 (白居易 *Bái Jūyì*, 772–846 AD)

      shì cháng kàn
      try taste   see

      'Try it'

(14) 收拾看 (祖堂集 *Zǔtángjí*, 10th century)

      shōushi   kàn
      put-in-order see

      'Try to put it in order'

(15) 你猜猜看 (西游记 *Xīyóu Jì*, 16th century)

    nǐ   cāi   cai   kàn

    you guess guess see

    'Try to guess it'

(16) 等我尝尝看 (西游记 *Xīyóu Jì*)

    děng wǒ chángchang kàn

    wait me taste taste   see

    'Let me taste it'

The above sentences also indicate an atelic action expressing "try to do". Even today VV *kàn* exists in Mandarin Chinese, retaining the same meaning. In the construction VV *kàn*, the verb *kàn* 'see' has undergone a process of grammaticalization, evolving from a full verb to a grammatical element, and finally became completely optional. Example (15) is already entirely similar to today's Mandarin Chinese in which the particle *kàn* can be omitted.

The rise and development of these two constructions, which originally indicated a one-time, attempted action, facilitated replacing iconically motivated verb reduplication. In other words, these constructions' shortened form VV coincided with the reduplicated verbs indicating high degree and intensification. The latter did not survive in Mandarin Chinese and gave way to newly arisen constructions which took the VV form but modified the initial meaning.

This hypothesis can be indirectly confirmed by contemporary dialect data (Cao Zhiyun, ed. 2008). Except for Mandarin in the Northeast (Heilongjiang, Jilin, Liaoning, Hebei, Shanxi and Shandong) and dialects in the South (concentrated in Guangzhou and Hainan), most dialects lack the VV form and use another construction to express a short time action or a diminutive meaning: V 一下 *yíxià* 'once'. This construction coexists with VV in Beijing Mandarin indicating a diminutive meaning or a short duration action. These facts suggest that contemporary VV in the North with minus-degree meaning comes from other constructions, but does not imply that reduplicated V was not iconic at the initial stage. Diachronic data in Chinese shows us that some contemporary instances of reduplication may have originally come from other constructions, and sometimes a modern reduplicated form signifying diminution is the residue of an ancient non-reduplicated form.

3 Plural typology in languages of China

Three types of plurality are attested in China's non-Han languages (Dan Xu in this volume):

(a) Tibeto-Burman type;
(b) Hmong-Mien (Miao-Yao), Tai and Austro-Asian type;
(c) Altaic type.

Some languages such as Mandarin share some characteristics with the first and second types. In other words, they actually belong to a mixed type. Their plural marking is applicable to nouns (not obligatory) and pronouns (obligatory)[4].

(a) Tibeto-Burman type
In this group, all languages, except the Bai language (see Jingqi Fu in this volume), have an OV word order, and classifiers. Differences in plural marking are seen in this group. For example, in the Tibetan, Yi (see Hongyong Liu and Yang Gu in this volume), and Jingpo subgroups, plural marking exists and is sensitive, in most cases, to human or animate features of the noun, such as in Baima, Lahu, Naxi, Rouruo and Dulong. The Qiang group, belonging to the same family as these languages, behaves in a different manner: almost half of the plural markers use the same form for animate or non-animate noun phrases.

(b) Hmong-Mien (Miao-Yao), Tai and Austro-Asian type
The Hmong-Mien (Miao-Yao), Tai and Austro-Asian languages form the second group. All languages in this group have a VO word order and classifiers, but the plural marker is not widely used. In most languages of China, plural markers are found after an NP, while in some languages in this group such as Mulao, Dai (Dehong), Bunu and Jiongnai, plural markers can be put before NPs when NPs refer to parental terms (Sun, Huang and Hu 2007). It is clear that this kind of plural marker is not widespread, but it still merits attention. Geographically, these languages are sprinkled around the south of China and do not present a coherent region like Tibeto-Burman or Altaic languages. This also partly explains why they often present Chinese language features despite being genetically distant or unrelated. For the same reason, some of these languages show typologically rare plural-marking systems which are expressed morphologically on the classifier (cf. Bisang in this volume on Kam and Weining Ahmao).

(c) Altaic type
In this type, plural markers are rather well developed and classifiers are absent (except some languages such as Salar, Korean, and Manchu). In these languages

---

4 The plural marking for noun and pronoun is not always the same. For example in the Shixing language, the marking is distinct (Dan Xu 2009b).

the use of the plural marker does not depend on the semantic feature [+animate] and all nouns can be marked by plural suffixes. However, the plural marker is not always obligatory as in European languages. The Salar, Korean, and Manchu languages employ classifiers due to influence from the Chinese language. Geographically they have been surrounded by Chinese languages for centuries and language contact has been very intense. The evidence for this contact-induced change is that classifiers are not yet obligatory in Salar, Korean, or Manchu, and the word order of numeral and noun is not fixed. For these reasons, we suppose that classifiers do not present a significant feature for this type of language, even though some of them have begun to develop classifiers due to long contact with Chinese languages.

It is clear that the Sinitic languages have VO order like type (b) and use classifiers like (a) and (b). It is important to notice that in groups (a) and (b), almost all languages (42/44) use reduplication devices and all of them employ classifiers. This fact confirms our hypothesis that reduplication and classifiers form one pattern with regard to plural marking. Additionally, in languages using classifiers, plural markers are often distinct in that they are sensitive to the feature [animate].

4 Organization of the book

In this volume, quantification will be observed and studied from different perspectives. The book studies several topics focusing on plurality. Based on the present results of research on quantification, different chapters deal with concrete and targeted subjects such as relations between plurality and classifiers, plurality and reduplication, expression of plurality in non-Han languages, and plurality concepts in child language acquisition.

The papers are divided into three sections. The first one takes a typological perspective and consists of two papers in which correlations between different types of quantification are discussed. Bisang deals with the correlation between the presence of numeral classifiers and the non-obligatoriness of plural marking as claimed by Greenberg (1972); Xu describes reduplication in its interaction with plural marking and numeral classifiers. The second section deals with numeral classifiers and their diachronic development in Mandarin Chinese (Feng) and Early Southern Min (Lin and Peyraube). The expression of plurality is the topic of the third section. It starts with the expression of plurality in the history of Chinese, first in its semantic form in classical Chinese (Harbsmeier), then in the form of the marker 諸 zhū from Han to Wei Jin Nanbeichao Chinese (Meisterernst). Both of these papers are looking at the domain of nouns. This also applies to the next two papers on the use of 不同 *bùtóng* 'different' (Paris) and the expression of plurality in the pronominal system of Bai (Fu). The paper by Liu and Gu is dedicated to the expression of plurality in the domain of the verb. Finally, Lee's paper looks at the acquisition of quantification by three-year-old children.

4.1 Correlations between different types of quantification

Chapter 1, "Numeral classifiers with plural marking. A challenge to Greenberg" by Walter Bisang, starts out with data on Northern Kam and Weining Ahmao, in which numeral classifiers obligatorily mark number. These findings are problematic to Greenberg's (1974: 25) universal claim that "[n]umeral classifier languages generally do not have compulsory expression of nominal plurality, but at most facultative expression." Even though plural marking is not fully obligatory in these languages, the fact that there are processes of grammaticalization which support a classifier system that carries obligatory information on number shows the weakness of Greenberg's claim. After a discussion of the diachronic language-internal processes that produced the classifier systems of Northern Kam and Weining Ahmao, the paper will offer some general observations concerning the status of implicational universals. It supports Newmeyer's (2005) view that typological generalizations must be seen as "holistic" in the sense that there is only an indirect correlation between implicational universals and rules, constraints and the properties of constructions in individual languages.

Chapter 2, "Reduplication in languages: A case study of languages of China" by Dan Xu, deals with reduplication from a typological perspective. Reduplication is broadly attested in human languages, especially in the Southern Hemisphere. In languages where reduplication and classifiers are found extensively, plural marking is not well-developed, and is sensitive to the semantic feature [+human]. The more plural marking is developed, such as in Indo-European languages and Altaic languages, the less this semantic feature is required. The more a language possesses developed plural-marking morphology, the less it needs reduplication and classifiers. Reduplication is iconically motivated. Positive degree constitutes its core meaning. Reduplication with negative meaning characterizes the grammaticalization process from icon to symbol.

4.2 Numeral classifiers and their diachronic development

Chapter 3, "The Syntax and Prosody of Classifiers in Classical Chinese," is written by Shengli Feng, who scrutinizes what mechanism might have triggered the rise of classifiers in Chinese. Based on Borer's theory of nominal structure (2005: 95), the author notes a parallelism between light verbs and light nouns, i.e. classifiers. Plural marking and classifiers are in fact two sides of the same coin. Given the theory presented here, the author argues that pre-Archaic Chinese, though possessing neither plurality nor classifiers as traditionally observed, actually had some lexical markers that served to individualize nouns, which may confirm the hypothesis that there is no language which has neither a plural morphology nor a classifier system. It is further argued that the emergence of classifiers in Late Archaic Chinese, though syntactically licensed, was prosodically motivated, and in turn, constitutes a sub-case of a typological change from the synthetic characteristics of Pre-Archaic Chinese (before 1000 BC) to the analytical characteristics of Post-Archaic Chinese, around the time of the Eastern Han (25–220 AD).

Chapter 4, "Individuating Classifiers in Early Southern Min (14th–19th centuries)" by Lin Jang-Ling and Alain Peyraube, analyzes the evolution of the nature and function of the individuating classifiers in Southern Min from the 14th c. to the 19th c. The paper is a comparative analysis of different versions of *Lao Qida* (15th–18th c.), which represents a Chinese Northern dialect and several versions of *Li Jing Ji* (16th–19th c.), an opera in Southern Min dialect. The authors conclude that the classifiers used in the Southern Min documents are more diversified than those seen in the Northern Chinese of the same period. Furthermore, the occurrences of classifiers found in the former are more numerous than those attested in the latter. The hypothesis of cyclic change of classifiers put forward by Peyraube (1998) obviously seems to be less evident in the southern dialects than in the northern ones.

4.3 The expression of plurality

Chapter 5, "Plurality and the subclassification of nouns in Classical Chinese" by Christoph Harbsmeier, provides a survey of the role of the semantic categories "plural" and "singular" in Classical Chinese, an uninflected language which does not generally use explicit markers for the plural. Harbsmeier gives a meticulous analysis of commonly used words in classical Chinese revealing their singular/plural meaning, which has often been ignored by readers and even by researchers. The author's work is inspired by the Danish linguist Otto Jespersen, who, in his historical grammar of English, elaborated a subclassification of English nouns that can provide inspiration for a proper treatment of the subclassification of nouns in Chinese historical grammar.

Chapter 6, "Number in Chinese: a diachronic study of the case of 諸 *zhū* from Han to Wei Jin Nanbeichao Chinese" by Barbara Meisterernst, discusses the syntactic and semantic constraints of the plural word *zhū*. The author indicates that semantically the function of *zhū* is to refer to a well-defined plural set of items, and that syntactically, *zhū* has to be analyzed as an adjective rather than a determiner since it can combine with determiners such as demonstratives and personal pronouns. Using the Animacy Hierarchy framework, Meisterernst shows that personal pronouns, which are situated at the top of the Animacy Hierarchy, are not compatible with *zhū*. *Zhū* underwent an important extension from [+animate] [+human] to [−animate]. According to the data from the Wei Jin Nanbeichao (220–589 AD) periods, and especially from the early 5th century Buddhist text *Gaoseng Faxian zhuan*, the author concludes that pluralization obviously was not the only function of *zhū*, at least during that period.

Chapter 7, "*Bu-tong* 'different' and nominal plurality in Mandarin Chinese" by Marie-Claude Paris, studies a pair of two Mandarin (apparent) synonyms — 不同 *bùtóng* 'different' and 不一样 *bù yíyàng* 'different'. Although their meaning seems at first sight to be equivalent, *bùtóng* and *bù yíyàng* actually behave very differently, both at the syntactic and at the semantic levels. While they can be substituted for each other in some cases, in other cases they cannot; hence their difference is established. *Bù yíyàng* can only be used as a scalar relative predicate or as a predicate modifier, whereas *bùtóng* can function both as an absolute predicate and as a noun determiner. This paper concludes that (i) plurality and number constitute two different markings, whose distribution is not complementary in Mandarin and that (ii) *bùtóng* can, in some contexts, be labeled a 'redundant' plurality marker.

Chapter 8, "Plurality in the pronominal paradigms of Bai dialects" by Jingqi Fu, investigates plurality in Bai, a Sino-Tibetan language whose linguistic affiliation is debatable. Examining how plurality and case are expressed in the pronominal paradigms of Bai dialects, she proposes to derive the plural pronouns, possessive and objective pronouns by a complex form of pronoun base followed by an ending: plural morpheme, possessive and locative markers respectively, contrary to the analysis where the inflected plural is independently derived via vowel inflection. In doing so, she accounts for the different forms of plural pronouns by the differences in the plural endings across dialects. She also investigates how plural formation interacts with case (objective, subjective and genitive). This account is consistent with the general characteristic of Bai of being a non-inflected language and puts Bai on a par with other Tibeto-Burman languages which developed the objective case later.

Chapter 9, "Frequentative Aspect and Pluractionality in Nuosu Yi" by Hongyong Liu and Yang Gu, explores plurality's relationship with frequentative aspect. Nuosu Yi belongs to the Tibeto-Burman language group and possesses three different means to encode a frequentative event: by using a preverbal temporal adverb, a postverbal frequentative aspect marker (like the West Greenlandic suffix "-tar"), or by both of them co-occurring in the same sentence. The authors propose a unified way to explain these three different means. Following Van Geenhoven (2004, 2005), the authors argue that the Nuosu Yi frequentative aspect marker is a pluractional operator, but the preverbal adverb is not. Because of semantic overlap between the preverbal adverb and the frequentative aspect marker, the authors study in detail the semantic and syntactic constraints on the non/co-occurrence of these two markers in Nuosu Yi.

Chapter 10, "Quantificational structures in three-year-old Chinese-speaking children" by Thomas Hun-tak Lee, investigates the realizations of existential quantification, universal quantification, negation and modals in children's language. The experiments are performed on Mandarin-speaking and Cantonese-speaking children from one and a half to three and a half years of age. Cognitive structures relative to these quantifications are explored. The standard quantificational structures have been much expanded to describe restricted quantification, binding of sets and predicates, questions and various kinds of modality. Based on rich data on child language, the author makes some remarks on how the logical operators are realized in Chinese, providing evidence for these operators. Lee's data show that existential quantification occurs earlier than universal quantification.

This book is expected to have an impact on the study of linguistic typology, language contact, and patterns of the evolution (grammaticalization, lexicalization) of languages and linguistic areas. More and more linguists are realizing that forming conclusions on patterns in general linguistics without a better understanding of Chinese and languages of China is risky and dubious. This volume may also provide useful material for cognitive sciences and anthropology. Typological studies require a solid description of Chinese and the languages of China. Investigation of quantification in diachronic Chinese and non-Han languages will offer general linguists a schema complementary to other languages of the world.

References

Andler, Daniel. 2004. Reprint. *Introduction aux sciences cognitives* [Introduction to cognitive sciences]. Paris: Editions Gallimard, 1992.

Behr, Wolfgang. 2006. "Homosomatic juxtaposition" and the problem of "syssemantic" (*huì yì*) characters. In *Ecriture chinoise. Données, usages et représentations* [Chinese writing, data, use and representations], Françoise Bottéro and Redouane Djamouri (eds.), 75–114. Paris: EHESS/CRLAO.

Bisang, Walter. 1993. Classifiers, Quantifiers and Class Nouns in Hmong. *Studies in Languages* 17: 1–51.

Borer, Hagit. 2005. *In Name Only*. Oxford: Oxford University Press.

Bybee, Joan, Perkins Revere and Pagliuca William. 1994. *The Evolution of Grammar*. Chicago/London: University of Chicago Press.

Cai, Jinghao. 1990. Chongtan yuzhuci 'kan' de qiyuan [Again on the origin of the particle kan], *Zhongguo Yuwen* 1: 75–76.

Cao, Zhiyun (eds.). 2008. *Hanyu fangyan ditu ji* [Chinese dialects Atlas]. Beijing: Commercial Press.

Carlson, Robert. 1991. Grammaticalization of Postpositions and Word Order in Senufo Languages. In *Approaches to Grammaticalization*, Elizabeth Closs Traugott and Bernd Heine (eds.), vol. II: 201–223. Amsterdam/Philadelphia: John Benjamins Publishing Company.

Chao, Yuen Ren. 1968. *A Grammar of Spoken Chinese*. Berkeley/Los Angeles: University of California Press.

Chen, Chusheng. 2004. *Jinwen changyong zidian* [Dictionary of inscriptions on bronze in common use]. Xi'an: Shanxi renmin chubanshe.

Cheng, Xiangqing. 1992. Bianwen fuyinci yanjiu [dissyllabic words in the Bianwen]. In *Sui Tang Wudai hanyu yanjiu* [Studies of Chinese in the Sui, Tang and Wudai], Cheng Xiangqing (ed.), 1–132. Jinan: Shandong Jiaoyu chubanshe.

Clark, Herbert H. 1973. Space, Time, Semantics and the Child. In *Cognitive Development and the Acquisition of Language*, Timothy E. Moore (ed.), 27–63. New York/London: Academic Press.

Comrie, Bernard. 2008. The Areal Typology of Chinese: Between North and Southeast Asia. In *Chinese Linguistics in Leipzig* CLE 2, Redouane Djamouri, Barbara Meisterernst and Rint Sybesma (eds.), 1–21. Paris: EHESS/CRLAO.

Corbett, Greville. 2000. *Number*. Cambridge: Cambridge University Press.

Croft, William. 1990. *Typology and Universals*. Cambridge: Cambridge University Press.

Dai, Qingxia. 1990. Yimianyu de jiegou zhuci [The grammatical markers in Tibeto-Burman languages]. In *Zangmian yuzu yuyan yanjiu* [Research on Tibeto-Burman languages], 83–97. Beijing: Minzu chubanshe.

Downing, Pamela. 1996. *Numeral Classifier Systems: The case of Japanese*. Amsterdam/Philadelphia: John Benjamins Publishing Company.

Dryer, Matthew. 1989. Plural words. *Linguistics* 27: 865–895.

Dryer, Matthew. 1992. The Greenbergian word order correlations. *Language* 68 (1): 81–138.

Dryer, Matthew. 2003. Word order in Sino-Tibetan languages from a typological and geographical perspective. In *The Sino-Tibetan languages*, Graham Thurgood and Randy J. LaPolla (eds), 43–55. London/New York: Routledge.

Enfield, Nick J. 2005. Areal Linguistics and Mainland Southeast Asia. *Annual Review of Anthropology* 34: 181–206.

Feng, Chuntian. 1991. *Jindai hanyu yufa wenti yanjiu* [Grammatical studies in Modern Chinese]. Jinan: Shandong jiaoyu chubanshe.

Greenberg, Joseph. 1972. Numeral classifiers and substantival number: problems in the genesis of a linguistic type. *Language Universals* 9: 1–39.

Greenberg, Joseph. 1974. Numeral classifiers and substantival number: problems in the genesis of a linguistic type. In *Proceedings of the 11th International Congress of Linguistics, Bologna – Florence, Aug–Sept 1972, Bologna 1974*: 17–37. (Reprinted in Greenberg 1990: 16–93).

Greenberg, Joseph. 1988. The first person inclusive dual as an ambiguous category. *Studies in Language* 12: 1–18.

Greenberg, Joseph. 1990. On language. In *Selected writings of Joseph H. Greenberg*, Denning, K. and S. Kemmer (eds.). Stanford: Stanford University Press.

Guo, Pan. 2004. *Hanyu sheshu wenti yanjiu* [Studies on numbers in Chinese]. Beijing: Zhonghua shuju.

Guo, Wengao. 1995. 'Yu' qianzhi yu shuci de yongfa. ['Yu' used before numbers]. *Zhongguo Yuwen* 5: 367–368.

Hagège, Claude. 2010. *Adposition*. Oxford: Oxford University Press.

Haiman, John. 1980. The Iconicity of grammar: Isomorphism and motivation. *Language* 56 (3): 515–540.

Haiman, John (ed.). 1985. *Iconicity in Syntax*. Amsterdam/Philadelphia: John Benjamins Publishing Company.

Heide, Wegener. 1995. The German plural and its acquisition in the light of markedness theory. In *The Development of Morphology Systematicity. A Cross-Linguistic Perspective*, Hanna Pishwa and Karl Maroldt (eds), 247–261. Tübingen: Gunter Narr.

Heine, Bernd and Tania Kuteva. 2002. *World lexicon of grammaticalization*. Cambridge: University of Cambridge.

Heine, Bernd, Ulrike Claudi and Friederike Hünnemeyer. 1991. From Cognition to Grammar-Evidence from African Languages. In *Approaches to grammaticalization*, Elizabeth Closs Traugott and Bernd Heine (eds.), Volume 1: 149–187. Amsterdam/Philadelphia: John Benjamins Publishing Company.

Hopper, Paul J. and Sandra A. Thompson. 1980. Transitivity in grammar and discourse. *Language* 56: 251–299.

Iljic, Robert. 2001. The problem of the suffix-*men* in Chinese grammar. *Journal of Chinese Linguistics* 29 (1): 11–68.

Jiang, Lansheng. 1995. Shuo "mo" yu "men" tongyuan ["Mo" and "men" have the same origin] *Zhongguo Yuwen* 3: 180–190.

Li, Jinfang and Suhua, Hu. 2005. *Han Zang yuxi liangci yanjiu* [Studies on classifiers in Sino-Tibetan]. Beijing: Zhongyang Minzu daxue chubanshe.

Li, Yanhui and Yuzhi, Shi. 2000. Hanyu liangci xitong de jianli yu fushu biaoji "men" de fazhan [The establishment of the classifier system and the development of the plural marker "men"]. *Dangdai yuyanxue* 2: 27–36.

Liu, Xiaonong. 1992. Tang Wudai ci dieyin chutan [Preliminary study of reduplicated sounds in Tang and Wudai]. In *Sui Tang Wudai hanyu yanjiu* [Studies of Chinese in Sui, Tang and Wudai], Cheng Xiangqing (ed.), 440–471. Jinan: Shandong Jiaoyu chubanshe.

Lü, Shuxiang and Jiang Lansheng. 1985. *Jindai hanyu zhidaici* [Demonstratives and pronouns in Modern Chinese]. Shanghai: Xuelin chubanshe.

Lü, Shuxiang. 1984. *Hanyu yufa lunwenji* [Collected papers on Chinese grammar]. Beijing: Commercial Press.

Ma, Guoquan. 1979. Liang Zhou tongqi mingwen shuci liangci chutan [A preliminary study on numerals and classifiers in bronze inscriptions during the Eastern and Western Zhou]. *Gu wenzi yanjiu* 1: 126–136.

Mei, Tsu-lin. 1986. Guanyu jindai hanyu zhidaici [About demonstratives and pronouns in Modern Chinese]. *Zhongguo Yuwen* 6: 401–412.

Montaut, Annie. 2009. Réduplication et constructions en écho en hindi/ourdou [Reduplication and echo constructions in Hindi/Urdu]. *Faits de Langue/Les Cahiers* 1: 9–44.

Newmeyer, Frederick J. 2005. *Possible and probable languages: A generative perspective on linguistic typology*. Oxford: Oxford University Press.

Ortmann, Albert. 2000. Where plural refuses to agree: Feature unification and morphological economy. *Acta Linguistica Hungarica*, Volume 47: 249–288.

Peyraube, Alain. 1998. On the History of Classifiers in Archaic and Medieval Chinese. In *Studia Linguistica Serica*, Benjamin K. Tsou (ed.), 39–68. Hong Kong: City University of Hong Kong.

Peyraube, Alain and Wiebusch Thekla. 1993. Le rôle des classificateurs nominaux en chinois et leur évolution historique: un cas de changement cyclique [The role of nominal classifiers in Chinese and their historical development: a case of cyclical change]. *Faits de langues* 2: 47–57.

Rubino, Carl. 2005. Order of subject, object and verb. In *The world atlas of language structures*, Martin Haspelmath, Matthew S. Dryer, David Gil and Bernard Comrie (eds.). Oxford: Oxford University Press.

Sagart, Laurent. 1999. *The Roots of Old Chinese*. Amsterdam/Philadelphia: John Benjamins Publishing Company.

Sanches, Mary. 1973. Numeral classifiers and plural marking : an implicational universal. *Language Universals* 11: 1–22.

Singh, Rajendra. 2005. Reduplication in Modern Hindi and the theory of reduplication. In *Grammar, Comparative and general–Reduplication*, Bernard Hurch (ed.), 263–281. Berlin/ New York: Mouton de Gruyter.

Sun, Hongkai. 2001. Lun Zangmian yuzu zhong de qiangyuzhi yuyan [On the Qiangic branch of the Tibeto-Burman languages]. *Languages and linguistics* 2: 1, 157–181.

Sun, Hongkai, Huang Xing and Hu Zengyi (eds). 2007. *Zhongguo de yuyan* [Languages in China]. Beijing: Commercial Press.

Svorou, Soteria. 1993. *The Grammar of Space*. Amsterdam/Philadelphia: John Benjamins Publishing Company.

Tsou, Benjamin. 1976. The structure of nominal classifier systems. In *Austroasiatic Studies*, Philip N. Jenner, Laurence C. Thompson, and Stanley Starosta (eds.), Part II: 1215–1247. Honolulu: University of Hawaii Press.

Talmy, Leonard. 2000a. How Language Structures Space. *Toward a Cognitive Semantics*, Volume 1: 177–254. Cambridge/Massachusetts: Massachusetts Institute of Technology Press.

Talmy, Leonard. 2000b. A Typology of Event Intergration. *Toward a Cognitive Semantics*, Volume 2: 213–288. Cambridge/Massachusetts: Massachusetts Institute of Technology Press.

Van Geenhoven, Veerle. 2004. For-adverbials, frequentative aspect, and pluractionality. *Natural Language Semantics* 12: 135–190.

Van Geenhoven, Veerle. 2005. Atelicity, pluractionality and adverbial quantification. In *Perspectives on Aspect*, Henk Verkuyl, Henriëtte de Swart and Angeliek van Hout (eds.), 107–124. Netherlands: Springer.

Wang, Ying. 1996. Tangshi zhong de dongci chongdie [Reduplicated verbs in Tang poetry], *Zhongguo Yuwen* 3: 233–234, 240.

Wang, Huayun. (preprint). *Fushu ciwei "men" de laiyuan* [Origin of the plural suffix -men].

Wu, Fuxiang. 1995. Changshitai zhuci "kan" de lishi kaocha [Diachronic examination of the tentative aspect particle "kan"]. *Yuyan yanjiu* 2: 161–166.

Wu, Fuxiang. 2006. Wei Jin Nanbeichao shiqi hanyu mingliangci fanchou de yufahua chengdu [Degree of grammaticalization of nominal classifiers during the Wei Jin Nanbeichao periods]. In *Linguistic Studies in Chinese and Neighboring Languages: Festschrift in Honor of Professor Pang-Hsin Ting on His 70th Birthday. Language and Linguistics Monograph Series Number W-6*: 553–571.

Xing, Fuyi. 1960. Lun "men" he "zhuwei" zhilei bingyong [On the coexistence of "men" he "zhuwei"]. *Zhongguo Yuwen* 6: 289, 292.

Xu, Dan. 1994. Guanyu hanyu li dongci + X + didianci de juxing [On the V + X + locative pattern in Chinese]. *Zhongguo Yuwen* 3: 180–185.

Xu, Dan. 2006. *Typological change in Chinese syntax*. Oxford: Oxford University Press.

Xu, Dan. 2009a. Cong Zhanguo zonghengjia shu kan Xi Han chuqi fushu gainian de biaoda [Plurality in Chinese during the early Han as seen in the Zhanguo zonghengjia shu], *Lishi yuyanxue yanjiu*, Volume 2. Beijing: Commercial Press.

Xu, Dan. 2009b. Xiayou Shixingyu de mouxie tedian [Some syntactic features of Down-river Shixing]. *Minzu Yuwen*, 1: 25–42.

Xu, Dan. 2010. Cong yuyan leixing kan hanyu fushu xingshi de fazhan [The development of plurality from a typological perspective]. In: Dan Xu (ed.), *Liang yu fushu de yanjiu* [Quantification and plurality], 90–112. Beijing: Shangwu yinshuguan.

Xu, Dan (ed.). 2008. *Space in Languages of China: Cross-linguistic, synchronic and diachronic perspectives*. Dordrecht: Springer.

Xu, Dan (ed.). 2010. *Liang yu fushu de yanjiu* [Quantification and plurality]. Beijing: Shangwu yinshuguan.

Xu, Dan, and Fu Jingqi. 2012. *Classifiers and some typological considerations. To appear in Breaking down the barriers: Interdisciplinary studies in Chinese linguistics and beyond.* (Language and Linguistics Monograph Series) Taipei: Institute of Linguistics, Academia Sinica.

Xu, Zhongshu (ed.). 1989. *Jiaguwen zidian* [Dictionary of bone inscriptions]. Chengdu: Sichuan cishu chubanshe.

Zhang, Meilan. 2001. *Jindai Hanyu houzhui xingrongci* [Suffixed adjectives in Modern Chinese]. Guiyang: Guizhou jiaoyu chubanshe.

Zhao, Jie. 1989. *Xiandai Manyu yanjiu* [Study on Contemporary Mandchou], Beijing: Minzu chubanshe.

I Correlations between different types of quantification

Walter Bisang

1 Numeral classifiers with plural marking. A challenge to Greenberg

Abstract: Classifiers of Northern Kam languages show a clear distinction between singular and plural. Classifiers in Weining Ahmao do the same but they not only inflect for number (singular vs. plural) but also for definiteness and size (Gerner and Bisang 2008). The cooccurence of systematic number marking and numeral classifiers casts some doubt on Greenberg's (1974) universal on the incompatibility of numeral classifiers with obligatory plural marking. This paper will show how language internal processes of grammaticalization can produce structures which seem to be typologically rare or even impossible. Since these processes are characterized by the interaction of various levels of grammar (at least phonetics/ phonology, morphology, syntax, semantics), the paper also shows that a typology that singles out individual levels of grammar is doomed to failure.

Keywords: numeral classifiers, numeral classifiers in Niger-Congo languages, obligatory plural marking, mass/count distinction, (in)definiteness, classifier inflection, typological universals

1 Introduction: The compatibility of numeral classifiers with number marking on the noun

1.1 The general assumption

Numeral classifiers are an important areal feature of East and mainland Southeast Asian languages. In most languages belonging to this area, nouns can only be counted if they are combined with a numeral classifier. Thus, a Chinese noun like *xìn* 'letter' must occur with its classifier *fēng* (1a) in the context of counting and with some other operations of quantification, otherwise (1b) the construction is ungrammatical. The same applies to the Thai noun *còtmǎay* 'letter' with its classifier *chabàp* in (2):

(1) a. *sān* **fēng** *xìn*   b. **sān*   *xìn*
         three CL   letter   three   letter
         'three letters'   *I.M.*: 'three letters'

(2) *Thai*

    a. *còtmǎay* **sǎam** *chabàp*   b. **còtmǎay* **sǎam**
       letter   CL   three   letter   three
       'three letters'   *I.M.*: 'three letters'

The classical explanation for examples like (1) and (2) and for the existence of numeral classifiers in general was given by Greenberg (1974, also cf. Sanches and Slobin 1973), who claims a universal implicational relation between numeral classifiers and the lack of obligatory plural marking:

> Numeral classifier languages generally do not have compulsory expression of nominal plurality, but at most facultative expression
> (Greenberg 1974: 25).

1.2 Numeral classifiers are compatible with number marking on the noun

Even though Greenberg's (1974) universal claim had and still has an important impact on typological research in numeral classifier systems, it does not apply universally. Greenberg (1974) himself is aware of this when he adds the adverb 'generally' to his above implicational universal and thus signals that there may be exceptions. And indeed, there are exceptions. Aikhenvald (2000: 100) points out in her compendium of classification systems that there are even quite a few languages all over the world in which numeral classifiers and obligatory number marking coexist. Aikhenvald (2000: 100) mentions South Dravidian languages, Nivkh (Paleosiberian isolate), some Algonquian languages, some South American languages (Tucano, North Arawak) and various languages "which combine numeral classifiers with noun class systems." Since it is not possible to illustrate each language in a short paper like this, only the last type of languages will be briefly discussed. This type is represented in some Bantoid languages (Niger-Congo: Benue-Congo) with their noun class system as one of their genetic characteristics. Since many noun classes of these languages consist of pairs of obligatory prefixes in which one stands for singular and the other for plural, number is firmly integrated into the system. If a language of this type with its inbuilt singular/plural distinction additionally has numeral classifiers the implicational universal claimed by Greenberg (1974) is automatically violated. One of the languages in which this is the case is Ejagham, a language spoken in the Cross River Basin in Nigeria and Cameroon (Watters 1981). This language has nineteen noun classes. Twelve of them are double class, i.e., they consist of a singular marker and a plural marker. In the case of noun class 3/6 for long thin objects and for natural objects, the singular prefix (class 3) is *N-* and the plural prefix (class 6) is *a-* as in *ǹ-čɔ̌g* 'pestle' vs. *à-čɔ̌g* 'pestles' (Watters 1981: 294).

In addition to these noun classes, Ejagham has five numeral classifiers which are derived from nouns and have their own noun-class prefixes. One of them is the classifier *Ǹ-sûm* (singular)/*à-sûm* (plural) of noun class 3/6 for "any fruit or root which is long" (Watters 1981: 310). As can be seen from (3) on the overall structure of the noun phrase, the numeral classifier takes the initial position of the noun phrase:

(3)   CL GEN-LINK N NUM

The genitive linker (GEN-LINK) between the classifier and the noun is controlled by the noun class of the classifier (CL). The numeral, which is situated at the end of the construction[1], also agrees with the class of the classifier. In the following example, the noun *-tǝbὲ* 'okra pod', which belongs to noun class 9/14 (singular: *Ǹ-tǝbὲ*; plural: *ɔ̀-tǝbɛ* Watters 1981: 300) is presented in combination with the numerals *-d* 'one' and *-báᶦὲ* 'two'. As can be seen, the head noun and the classifier are both marked for number:

(4)   The classifier *Ǹ-sûm* (sg.)/*à-sûm* in *Ejagham*

   a. *Ǹ-sûm*   *ì*   *Ǹ-tǝbɛ̂*   *yǝ̂-d*

      NCL3:SG-CL:fruit GEN-LINK NCL9:SG-okra.pod NCL3:SG-one

      'one okra pod'

   b. *à-sûm*   ˊ   *ɔ̀-tǝbɛ̂*   *á-báᶦὲ*

      NCL6:PL-CL:fruit GEN-LINK NCL14:PL-okra.pod NCL6:PL-two

      'two okra pods'   (Watters 1981: 310)

The numeral classifier system of Ejagham is not pervasive. As Watters (1981: 313) points out, "most nouns do not use a classifier when being enumerated, but for the various types of nouns listed above, e.g. seeds, grains, kernels, nuts, long fruits and roots, round fruits and roots, clusters of fruits, plants, trees and vegetables a classifier is generally required".

---

1 The structure of the classifier construction in Ejagham additionally contradicts Greenberg's (1974: 31) claim that the classifier and the numeral must form a continous constituent. As can be seen from (3) and (4), word order in the classifier construction of Ejagham is [CL-N-NUM]. While classifiers form a coherent unit with the numeral in East and mainland Southeast Asian languages, they establish a more coherent relation with the noun to be counted in Ejagham and other Niger-Congo languages. In Ejagham, this can be seen from the genitive-linker, which agrees with the classifier and creates a head-modifier relation between the classifier and the classified noun. The coherence between the numeral and the classifier is maintained by the agreement relation as it is controlled by the class-membership of the classifier.

There are other Niger-Congo languages in which the numeral-classifier system is pervasive, i.e., each count noun needs to have a classifier in the context of enumeration. One language of this type is Kana, another Cross River language spoken in the South of Nigeria, which has lost the Bantu noun class system (Ikoro 1994, 1996):[2]

(5) *Kana*

    a. *bàὲ bēὲ   ŋwíí*
        two CL:fruit child
        'two children'

    b. *tāà té   ítòbtòb*
        three CL:tree motorcycle
        'three motorcycles' (Ikoro 1996: 91–92)

Even if the use of classifiers is limited to certain semantic domains in Ejagham, the combination of obligatory number marking and numeral classifiers remains a challenge to Greenberg's (1974) claim. This challenge may be mitigated to a certain extent if it turns out that fully pervasive systems of numeral classifiers are limited to those Niger-Congo languages in which the obligatory opposition of singular vs. plural reflected in the noun-class system has vanished (see Section 4).

In spite of a considerable amount of counter-evidence against Greenberg's implicational claim from various languages and areas across the globe, there hasn't been much counter-evidence from the area of East and mainland Southeast Asia. More recent research on Northern Kam (Gerner 2006) and on Weining Ahmao (Gerner and Bisang 2008, 2009, 2010) shows that there is evidence against this universal claim even in the isolating languages of that area. In fact, the few instances of morphology that developed in these two languages are concerned with the morphophonological form of the classifier and – what is even more remarkable – with the emergence of singular/plural-distinctions that are marked on the classifier itself. As will be shown in the next section, classifier morphology is the result of fusion with other words or markers which lose their syntactic independence. Such processes are not limited to the development of classifier inflection, they are also attested in other domains of grammar. One of

---

2 As can be seen from (5), Kana does not violate the word-order constraints claimed by Greenberg (1974: 31) (cf. endnote 1). Its word order is [NUM-CL-N]. In spite of this, the fusion between CL and N is higher than between NUM and CL. There is a genitive linker in the form of a floating low tone which takes the final syllable of the head of the construction, i.e., the classifier (CL) followed by the noun (N) as its dependent. Thus, the form *bēὲ* 'CL:fruit' in (5a) is a combination of [*bēē* plus low tone]. In the case of *té* 'CL:tree' in (5b), the low tone does not show any effects.

them is discussed by Fu (in this volume) on the integration of plural markers into pronominal paradigms of Bai. It is needless to say that the integration of plural marking into the morphophonology of classifiers or pronominal systems considerably weakens Greenberg's universal claim.

The paper is organized as follows: Section 2 presents the classifier systems of Northern Kam (see Subsection 2.1) and Weining Ahmao (see Subsection 2.2). Section 3 describes the factors that operate against Greenberg's (1974) universal claim. It will turn out that none of these factors are associated with cognitive motivations that are generally mentioned in linguistic typology. A short conclusion in section 4 will take up the discussion of the validity of typological generalizations where there are various factors that potentially undermine them.

2 The data from Northern Kam and Weining Ahmao

2.1 Number-sensitive numeral classifiers in Northern Kam

Northern Kam belongs to the Kam-Tai branch of the Kadai language family.[3] Like most of the other East and mainland Southeast Asian languages, Northern Kam is an isolating language. There is only one exception, and that exception shows up in the numeral-classifier system. Since this is nicely described by Gerner (2006), I will only summarise his findings in the present subsection.

Numeral classifiers in Northern Kam show a regular morphophonological contrast between singular and plural forms. The initial consonant of the singular form is almost always a glide ([w], [j]) or a voiced fricative ([z̠], [ɣ]), while the plural form of classifiers starts with a voiceless stop or a nasal. This distinction is made only in Northern Kam. The numeral classifier system of Southern Kam does not have such a distinction. Since the single classifier form of Southern

---

3 There are two different classifications of this language family. The older one is from Edmondson and Solnit (1988) and distinguishes three subfamilies, i.e., Kam-Tai, Hlai (= Li) and Geyang. In this classification, which is also called the "Kadai hypothesis", Kam-Tai is further divided into Kam-Sui (to which Kam belongs) and Tai. A more recent classification by Chamberlain (1997), which is sometimes dubbed "Tai-Kadai hypothesis", splits Kam-Tai into two independent subbranches and thus distinguishes four subfamilies, i.e., Tai, Kam-Sui, Hlai and Kadai. This classification is known under the heading of "Zhuang-Dong" in the Chinese context. Since Gerner's (2006) comparative analysis of core classifiers in 22 Kam-Tai languages provides supportive evidence for the Kadai hypothesis of Edmondson and Solnit (1988), I adopt this classification. My above description of the genetic situation is from Gerner (2006: 239).

Kam systematically corresponds to the plural form of Northern Kam, the singular form of Northern Kam must be a special, historically derived form which only developed in that language (Gerner 2006: 244–247). The derivational rules are described in detail in Gerner (2006). For that reason, only a few examples will be presented in this paper:

(6) Singular vs. plural form of Northern Kam (Gerner 2006: 244–245)[4]

Derivation			Class meaning	CL:SG	CL:PL
a.	[w]	<– [p]	human	$w\partial u^{45}$	$p\partial u^{45}$
b.	[w]	<– [m]	dual body parts	wan^{55}	man^{55}
c.	[w]	<– [m]	clothes	$w\partial i^{31}$	$m\partial i^{31}$
d.	[j]	<– [ɕ]	entities with handle	jan^{45}	$ɕa\ n^{45}$
e.	[j]	<– [ţ]	1-dim entities	jiu^{22}	$ţiu^{22}$
f.	[ʐ]	<– [n]	3-dim entities	$ʐan^{45}$	nan^{45}
g.	[ɣ]	<– [ʔ]	small diverse range	$ɣa^{55}$	$ʔa^{55}$

As is to be expected from the above description, the singular form of the classifier is used with the numeral i^{45} 'one' in (7a). For numbers greater than one, the plural form is employed in (7b):

(7) *Northern Kam*
(Gerner 2006: 243–244; for the form of the classifier, cf. [5e])

    a. i^{45} **jiu^{22}** na^{45}
        one   CL:SG   river

        'one river'

    b. ham^{11} **$ţiu^{22}$** na^{45}
        three   CL:PL   river

        'three rivers'

Numeral classifiers also occur in [classifier + noun] constructions. In this construction, they mark indefiniteness. The singular form stands for singular indefinite (8a) and (9a), while the plural form expresses plural indefinite in (8b) and (9b):

---

4 The tones are represented by number combinations. The numbers represent relative pitch on a scale from 1 (lowest) to 5 (highest). The first number represents the beginning of the tonal contour, the second number stands for its end.

(8) *Northern Kam*
   (Gerner 2006: 249; for the form of the classifier, cf. [6c])

   a. **wəi**^{31} *tu*^{33} b. **məi**^{31} *tu*^{33}
       CL:SG garment   CL:PL garment

       'a garment'   'garments'

(9) *Northern Kam*
   (Gerner 2006: 249; for the form of the classifier, cf. [6g])

   a. **ɣa**^{55} *hoŋ*^{22} b. **ʔa**^{55} *hoŋ*^{22}
       CL:SG loom   CL:PL loom

       'a loom'   'looms'

In other grammatical contexts, only the plural form of the classifier is used. In the case of the demonstrative construction, the classifier marks singular, even though the plural form is used:

(10) *Northern Kam*
   (Gerner 2006: 251; for the form of the classifier, cf. [6b])

   maŋ^{55} *ta*^{45} *ai*^{33}
   CL:PL eye DEM:this

   'this eye'

The situation as it has been described so far is remarkable in at least two respects. First, it is typologically rare that the plural form provides the basic form from which the singular is derived. Of course, singulative forms are attested in a considerable number of languages but this is usually limited to a subset of nouns. In Northern Kam, the derivation of the singular from the plural is pervasive. Second, the form which explicitly marks plural in the [numeral + classifier]-construction (7b) and in the [classifier + noun]-construction ([8b] and [9b]) marks singular in the demonstrative construction (10). Both of these properties can be accounted for if one looks at the historical development of the number distinction in Northern Kam classifiers.

Based on Shi (1997), Gerner (2006: 244) convincingly argues that the singular/plural-distinction of numeral classifiers developed "when the ancestor classifiers collocated with the numeral *i*^{45} 'one'". The new classifier forms that emerged from the collocation with that numeral were reanalysed as singular forms in contrast to the original form which collocated with all other numerals and did not undergo any morphophonological change. Since this unchanged form occurred with all numerals higher than one, it was only natural to associate this form with plural meaning. Thus, the typologically remarkable situation that the singular is derived from the plural synchronically is due to a morphophonological process of change. Once the distinction of singular vs. plural was established with numerals, it moved into the [classifier + noun]-construction with its indefinite meaning. This scenario is quite plausible if one takes into account that the construction [one + classifier + noun] is used for expressing indefiniteness in a vast number of languages (Dryer 2005). As soon as the [singular classifier + noun]-construction was associated with indefiniteness as a short form of the [one + classifier + noun]-construction, the ancient form of the classifier was reanalysed as a plural indefinite marker in the [plural classifier + noun]-construction.

As can be seen from example (10), the number distinction is not fully grammaticalized through all constructions which take a numeral classifier. In these constructions, the plural classifier is used even though it does not necessarily mean plural. If one takes the plural form as the original form of the classifier it does not come as a surprise that this form occurs in all grammatical contexts in which the singular/plural-distinction remains irrelevant. As I will argue in the remainder of this subsection, the fact that it actually marks singular in the demonstrative construction can be accounted for by a look at Thai as another Kam-Tai language. In Thai, numeral classifiers are optional in the demonstrative construction. If they occur with demonstratives there is a very strong tendency to interpret them as singulative markers (Hundius and Kölver 1983, Becker 2005). Thus, (11a) with no classifier can be singular or plural, while (11b) with a classifier is most likely to be singular:

(11) *Thai*

    a. *rót níi*   b. *rót **khan** níi*
       car this   car CL   this
       'this car/these cars'   'this car'

If one assumes that the situation in Northern Kam was similar to that in Thai before the emergence of number-sensitive classifiers, the occurence of a classifier in the demonstrative construction also triggered a singular interpretation in Northern Kam. Since the singular/plural-distinction did not go beyond the numeral construction and the [classifier + noun]-construction, the original form is still the only option for the demonstrative construction. The seemingly paradoxical case that the form used with plural function in some constructions triggers a singular interpretation in the demonstrative construction can thus be resolved by the argument that there is no other form available for the demonstrative construction and that that form triggers singular interpretation as it did before the singular/plural-distinction took shape.

2.2 Classifier inflection in Weining Ahmao

Weining Ahmao is a Miao language spoken in the Weining County of Western Guizhou. Its classifier system is described since Wang Fushi (1957 [1972])[5] and Wang Deguang (1986, 1987) and it seems to be unparalleled in the world's languages (for more data and the analysis of the inflectional paradigm, see Gerner and Bisang 2008, 2010). Each of its classifiers is inflected for the categories of number (singular vs. plural), reference (definite vs. indefinite) and size (augmentative, medial, small). The forms concerning size also express social deixis in dialogues (not in narratives). Roughly speaking, male speakers use the augmentative form of the classifier, female speakers the medial form and children the diminutive form (for more details, see Gerner and Bisang 2008, 2010). The following table shows how the form of Ahmao classifiers varies within the twelve-slot paradigm determined by these three categories:

Table 1: The inflectional paradigm of classifiers in Weining Ahmao (Gerner and Bisang 2008: 721; Gerner and Bisang 2010: 79)

Gender/Age		Singular		Plural	
Register	Size	Definite	Indefinite	Definite	Indefinite
Male	Augmentative	CVT	C*VT	$ti^{55}\ a^{11}$ CVT'	$di^{31}\ a^{11}$ C*VT'
Female	Medial	Cai^{55}	$C*ai^{213}$	$tiai^{55}\ a^{11}$ CVT'	$diai^{213}\ a^{11}$ C*VT'
Children	Diminutive	Ca^{53}	$C*a^{35}$	$tia^{55}\ a^{11}$ CVT'	$dia^{55}\ a^{11}$ C*VT'

    The definite singular augmentative form with its structure of CVT is the basic form of the classifier. It consists of a consonant (C), a vowel nucleus (V) and a lexically determined tone (T)[6]. Each of these elements can be subject to morphophonological change in the other slots. The symbol C* stands for changes in the properties of the consonant in some classifiers. Depending on the individual classifier, the properties involved are voicing and aspiration to distinguish indefinite from definite classifiers. The vowel quality [ai][7] is characteristic of medial size, while [a] marks diminutive size. Medial-definite forms are typically expressed with [^{55}] tone, medial-indefinite forms exhibit a [^{213}] tone. Diminutive-definite forms display the tones [^{53}] (singular) or [^{55}] (plural) and

---

5 The description of Wang Fushi (1957) slightly differs from the one presented in Gerner and Bisang (2008). Wang Fushi (1957) does not mention the distinction between definite and indefinite augmentative/male forms in the singular (cf. *Tables 1* and *2*).
6 On the notation of tones by the combination of numbers, cf. fn. 2.
7 Wang Fushi (1957) has [ae] instead of [ai].

finally diminutive-indefinite forms are associated with the tones [^{35}] (singular) and [^{55}] (plural) (Gerner and Bisang 2008: 722). The plural forms are characterized by the marker ti^{55}, which undergoes similar changes as the singular classifier forms described in table 1. This marker is followed by a^{11} plus the classifier in its form of C*VT', in which T' indicates that the tone takes a special form at least with some classifiers.

There are some 40 to 50 numeral classifiers in Weining Ahmao. To illustrate how the pattern described above works with a concrete classifier, table 2 shows the inflectional forms of the classifier lu^{55}, one of the most common classifiers which is used with nouns denoting inanimates.

Table 2: The inflectional paradigm of the classifier lu^{55} in Weining Ahmao (Gerner and Bisang 2008: 722)

Gender/Age Register	Size	Singular		Plural	
		Definite	Indefinite	Definite	Indefinite
Male	Augmentative	lu^{55}	lu^{33}	$ti^{55} a^{11} lu^{55}$	$di^{31} a^{11} lu^{55}$
Female	Medial	lai^{55}	lai^{213}	$tiai^{55} a^{11} lu^{55}$	$diai^{213} a^{11} lu^{55}$
Children	Diminutive	la^{53}	la^{35}	$tia^{55} a^{11} lu^{55}$	$dia^{55} a^{11} lu^{55}$

The following example shows how the different classifier forms are used in a text. The text in (12) is a Weining Ahmao version of the well-know fable of the fox and the crow. In the first line, the classifier tu^{44} for animals occurs in its indefinite (medial singular) form, since the noun $a^{33} dy^{33}$ 'fox' is introduced into the text[8]. Later, it is taken up in the corresponding definite form tae^{33}. The noun $nG'ae^{35}$ 'meat', which stands for the cheese in the western version of the fable, is already known from previous context and is thus marked by the definite ($ts'ae^{33}$: singular, medial) form of the classifier. The crow is also marked by the definite (ta^{33}: singular, diminutive) form of the classifier because it has been introduced earlier. Since classifiers also occur in possessive constructions, we find the classifier lu^{55} in its definite (singular, diminutive) form la^{55} on the last line.[9] Possessive constructions have the form [possessor CL$_i$ possessee$_i$], in

---

8 In narratives, the selection of size depends on the real size of the objects described. In (12), the fox is marked by the medial-size form, not by the augmentative form. In principle, the selection of the size form depends on the view of the speaker. If she wants to point out the big size of a given nominal concept she can chose the augmentative form. Since foxes are not extremely big, the use of the medial form corresponds to the default. Once the size of a given element of a narrative is determined, this feature contributes to reference tracking.

9 Wang Fushi (1957) reports a different tone for this classifier form. As can be seen from table 2, the medial definite singular form of lu^{55} is la^{53} in Gerner and Bisang (2008) instead.

which the classifier reflects the properties of the possessee. The definiteness of the possessee a^{33} '$ndʐʻau^{35}$ 'mouth' can be inferred from its inalienable relation to the possessor.

(12) *Weining Ahmao*

    $tʻau^{33}$ i^{55} $mʼa^{35}$ i^{55} **dae^{35}** **a^{33} dy^{33}** $dʻœy^{31}$ $dʻa^{35}$.
    time that there.is one CL:INDEF fox exit come

    tae^{33} **a^{33} dy^{33}** **$ɲi^{55}$** la^{11} ae^{55} $tʂʻae^{55}$ dau^{11}, i^{55} vie^{33} $ɲʻi^{13}$
    CL:DEF fox this also very hungry PF but he

    $nfʻie^{55}$ hi^{33} tau^{33} qu^{55} qa^{55} $ṣi^{33}$ $nʼau^{35}$. $ɲʻi^{13}$ $bʻo^{31}$ **$tsʻae^{33}$**
    look.for not get food anything eat he see CL:DEF

    $nɢʻ_{AE}{}^{35}$ ku^{11} $ɲo^{55}$ $vʼae^{31}$ **ta^{33}** **li^{55} a^{55} la^{55}** **a^{33} '$ndʐʻau^{35}$** i^{55}, …
    meat REL at place CL:DEF crow CL:DEF *mouth* *that*

    'At that time a fox came out. He too became very hungry, but he had been unable to find anything to eat. When he saw the piece of meat in the crow's mouth, …' (Wang Fushi 1957: 106–107; 1972: 161–162)

    The text in (12) is a narrative text. In dialogues as the one in (13) below, the size value of classifiers is additionally associated with social deixis. Thus, male speakers normally use the augmentative forms, female speakers the medial form and child speakers the diminutive form (cf. above). While this is roughly the standard rule, the system is more flexible and can trigger a lot of politeness effects in specific situations. Example (13) presents a dialogue between two male speakers. The first speaker A uses the augmentative form of the classifier lu^{55} as one would expect it of a male speaker. In contrast, the second male speaker B, reacts with the corresponding female form of the classifier (lai^{55}). The reason for this selection is straightforward if one takes into account that speaker B reacts to a compliment. Due to politeness, he opts for being modest and thus selects the female classifier which is associated with lower social status if used by a male speaker:

(13) *Weining Ahmao* (Gerner and Bisang 2008: 728)

    A: $gfii^{31}$ **lu^{55}** $ŋgfia^{55}$ $ɲi^{55}$ zau^{44} ku^{11}.
        2:PL CL:AUG:SG:DEF house DEM:PROX good very
        Male Speaker A: 'Your house is so nice.'

    B: qha^{55} $tsau^{55}$ ku^{55} **lai^{55}** $ŋgfia^{55}$ $ɲi^{55}$.
        NEG:IMP praise 1.SG CL:MED:SG:DEF house DEM:PROX
        Male speaker B: 'Don't praise my house.'

Apart from its inflectional classifiers, Weining Ahmao is basically an isolating language as most other East and mainland Southeast Asian languages. This begs the question of how the inflectional classifier system emerged. Gerner and Bisang (2009: 19–29; 2010: 86–90) suggest a two-stage scenario. The first stage induced the development of the three size distinction. It is characterized by a rebracketing process followed by further processes of erosion. The second stage, which was responsible for the distinctions of definite vs. indefinite, started out from the combination of the numeral i^{55} 'one' with a classifier.

The first stage is based on derivational markers which are used to form augmentatives and diminutives. In the case of Weining Ahmao, these markers are a^{55} $\textipa{n}ie^{53}$ (augmentatives) and ηa^{11} (diminutives). The augmentative marker is related to the noun $\textipa{n}ie^{53}$ 'mother', while the diminutive marker is still present in the noun ηa^{11} $\textipa{z}au^{11}$ 'child'. Both markers can take the initial position of nominal compounds. If these markers are combined with nouns for animals, their initial meaning is still visible – the augmentative marker produces a noun referring to the female gender of animals, while the diminutive marker derives a noun denoting the juvenile members in adult-young animal pairs (14a). If combined with inanimate nouns the two markers express a vague idea of largeness (physically or metaphorically) and smallness, respectively (cf. example [14b]):

(14) *Weining Ahmao* (Gerner and Bisang 2010: 87)

    a.   *mpa*^{44} 'pig, hog' → a^{55} $\textipa{n}ie^{53}$ mpa^{44} 'sow

                                                                 [augmentative, female]'

                          → ηa^{11} mpa^{44} 'piglet

                                                                 [diminutive, child]'

    b.   *tɕa*^{44} 'wind'   → a^{55} $\textipa{n}ie^{53}$ $tɕa^{44}$ 'storm'

                                                                 [augmentative]'

                          → ηa^{11} $tɕa^{44}$ 'breze of wind

                                                                 [diminutive]'

The development of different classifier forms for size started out with a process of reanalysis in which the augmentative and diminutive markers no longer formed a unit with the noun that followed them but were rebracketed into a new unit consisting of the classifier plus the augmentative/diminutive marker:

(15) NUM CL [a^{55} $\textipa{n}ie^{53}$/ηa^{11}–NOUN] → NUM [CL–a^{55} $\textipa{n}ie^{53}$/ηa^{11}] NOUN

After this change of word boundaries, the sequences [CL–a^{55} $\textipa{n}ie^{53}$] and [CL–ηa^{11}] were further reduced through various stages (loss of the nasals $\textipa{n}$ and η, etc.) into [ai] and [a], respectively. The association of the initial augmentative form in [ai] as a marker of medial size has to do with the use of these markers in the social setting between men, women and children (for details, cf. Gerner and Bisang 2009: 13–18). In this context, males used the original classifiers, while the forms in [ai] and [a] basically remained for women and children, respectively. Through this process, the size values of the various forms were redistributed. The original form was associated with augmentative and male speakers, while the forms in [ai] and [a] were downgraded: [ai] was newly associated with medial size and female speakers and [a] became the marker for diminutive size and child speakers. The initial meanings of 'mother' and 'child' might have contributed additionally to this process of redistribtion.

The second stage is based on the function of numeral classifiers as markers of definiteness in the bare-classifier construction [CL + N]. This is illustrated by *ts'ae*^{33} *nɢ'ae*^{35} [CL meat] 'the meat' and *ta*^{33} *li*^{55} *a*^{55} [CL crow] 'the crow' in example (12) from Weining Ahmao. Since Weining Ahmao is accessible only in its contemporary form with its fully-fledged classifier-inflection system, it is not possible to illustrate this stage without the simultaneous integration of size. The vast majority of Miao languages do not express size on the classifier but they use bare-classifier constructions for marking definiteness. One of these languages is Hmong, which will be used to illustrate classifiers as definiteness markers in bare-classifier constructions without the interference of size. In (16), the two nouns *niam* 'wife' and *txiv* 'husband' are introduced in the first sentence and are then taken up with their classifier *tus* as definite NPs in the next sentence:

(16) *Hmong*

    Thaum ub muaj   *ob*   *tug niam txiv.*   ***Tus txiv***   *tuag lawm.*
    Long.ago   there.are   two   CL   wife   husband   CL   husband   die   PFV

    Tus *niam quaj quaj, nrhiav*   *nrhiav*   *tsis*   *tau*   ***tus*** *txiv.*
    CL   wife   cry   cry   look.for   look.for   NEG   get   CL   husband

    'Long ago there were a wife and a husband. The husband died.
    The wife was crying a lot but no mattter how hard she tried
    she was not able to find her husband.'   (Mottin 1980: 200)

Indefinite nouns are marked by the numeral *ib* 'one' as in the Kam language described in subsection 2.1.

(17) *Hmong*

    Ua ciav   *nws pom* **ib**   **lub** *nkauj npuas.*
    suddenly   he   see   one   CL   pigpen

    'Suddenly, he discovered a pigpen.'   (Mottin 1980)

Parallel to the situation in Northern Kam, the classifier changed its form under the influence of the preceding numeral one, which is i^{55} in Weining Ahmao, written ib^{10} in Hmong, and can be reconstructed with a closed syllable as *iet* which became *$i?^{55}$ at a later stage. As is argued by Gerner and Bisang (2009, 2010), it was the interaction of the glottal stop with the classifier in sequences of the type [*$i?^{55}$ CL] which triggered processes such as voicing, aspiration or tonal change in the phonological structure of the classifier.[11] The opposition that was formerly expressed by [CL + N]$_{definite}$ vs. [one + CL + N]$_{indefinite}$ is now reflected by different forms of the classifier itself and can be represented as [CL$_{def}$ + N] vs. [CL$_{indef}$ + N]. Since this opposition was developed in the context of the singular form of [one + CL + N]$_{indefinite}$, the formal distinction was limited to the singular. For expressing the same distinctions (plus the three size distinctions) in the plural, the language followed another strategy.

The opposition between singular and plural is based on some sort of a plural classifier which must have undergone the same changes as the normal classifiers described in table 1. The details of this development need more research. From the look at another Miao language like Hmong, one can clearly say that there are plural classifiers. In Hmong, there is even a distinction between the plural classifiers *cov* and *tej*, which roughly mark definiteness and indefiniteness, respectively. In (18), the definite plural classifier *cov* in line 2 refers to the seven wives (*poj niam*) mentioned before in line 1. The plural classifier *tej* in (19) refers to an unspecified plural number of widows (*poj ntsuag*):

(18) *Hmong*

    Ces ob tug mus txog chaw   *uas Yawm Pus*
    then two CL go to country/place REL Yao Pu

    *muaj xya tus poj niam. Ces **cov** poj niam quaj dheev*   *tias:...*
    have seven CL wife then PL:CL wife cry very.much QUOT

    'Then, the two of them arrived at the country in which Yap Pu had seven wives. The wives cried and said: ...' (Mottin 1980)

---

10 There are no syllables with consonantal codas in Hmong (the nasal η is the only exception). The Latin-based writing system of Hmong thus uses the post-nuclear position for encoding tones by various consonant letters. The consonant -*b*, for instance, represents the high-level tone [^{55}].

11 This process is known as "change in glottal articulation" (Lehmann 1992: 193; also cf. Gerner and Bisang 2009, 2010).

(19) *Hmong*

Kuv niam   tias: *kom kuv tuaj   nrhiav **tej**   poj ntsuag*
I   mother QUOT IMP 2.SG come seek   CL:PL widow

tsev   nyob xwb.
house live   only

'My mother told me: you only frequent houses of widows.'
[During your journey, you shall only ask for hospitality in houses of widows.]   (Mottin 1980)

3 Discussion: Factors that operate against Greenberg's (1974) universal claim

Greenberg's (1974) implicational universal discussed in Subsection 1.1 excludes the cooccurrence of obligatory plural marking and numeral classifiers. From such a strict perspective, the classifier systems of Northern Kam and Weining Ahmao provide no counter-evidence against Greenberg (1974), since the expression of number is still not compulsory in these two languages, i.e., the bare noun alone with no classifier is still sufficient in certain contexts and if it is clear that plurality is meant. This conclusion is certainly correct if one looks at Greenberg's claim from a purely synchronic angle that disregards the historical development of grammatical systems. However, a solid universal claim should not only be observable at the synchronic level but also at the diachronic level. If combinations of properties that are excluded by a universal claim can be tied together in historical processes of language change this casts serious doubt on the solidity of that universal.

In the case of Chinese, the findings from diachronic research basically support the claim that there is a correlation between transnumerality and numeral classifiers (cf. Meisterernst, this volume; Harbsmeier, this volume). The marker *zhū* does not exclusively express plural, it also quantifies over unmarked plural nouns and it expresses referentiality (Meisterernst, this volume). Even the existence of unmarked nouns with plural meaning (Harbsmeier, this volume) is no straightforward argument against the overall transnumeral character of nouns as long as plural nouns are a clearly defined subset of lexicalized plurals of a limited size. Personal pronouns seem to be the only instance in which obligatory plural marking is of some importance (cf. Meisterenst, this volume; also cf. Fu, in this volume, on number in the pronominal system of Bai). But this only affects the highest level of the animacy hierarchy as discussed by Corbett (2000) and thus concerns only a small number of nominals.

The examples of Northern Kam and Weining Ahmao represent a much stronger challenge to Greenberg's universal claim. If it were a rigid universal it should operate against the fusion of number marking with a numeral classifier system. In addition, this development produced a situation on the synchronic level in which the use of a classifier automatically forces the speaker to select a value for number (singular vs. plural). A system in which the use of a classifier entails number marking is additional evidence against the strength of Greenberg's claim. From what has been said so far, one can distinguish two types of languages which are problematic for Geenberg's universal claim:

(i) Languages with numeral classifiers and obligatory plural marking
(ii) Languages in which the use of a classifier obligatorily calls for number marking

Both types are attested in the world's languages. Ejagham as described in section 1 represents a straightforward case of type (i), while Northern Kam and Weining Ahmao stand for type (ii). The processes that favour the emergence of such structures are not uniform. In spite of this, all of them are related in one way or another to the specific grammatical constellations that existed in the languages concerned immediately before the change took place. In the case of Ejagham, it is important to know that its numeral-classifier system is certainly much younger than the noun-class system with its obligatory distinction of singular vs. plural. The noun-class system is genetically well-established in Bantoid languages and belongs to the reconstructed inventory of Proto-Bantoid. If a language with such a noun-class system develops numeral classifiers it does not necessarily lose the property of obligatory number marking and, if that is the case, contradicts Greenberg's (1974) universal claim. Of course, such a combination of properties should not emerge at all if Greenberg's claim would be an absolute universal with no exceptions.

In the case of Northern Kam and Weining Ahmao, the most important motivation for the emergence of inflectional classifiers is of a purely phonetic and phonological character and has nothing to do with cognitive motivations as they are generally discussed in linguistic typology. The whole development was instigated by the numeral 'one' (i^{45} in Northern Kam, i^{55} in Weining Ahmao) and its phonetic influence on the consonant of the numeral classifier, sometimes also on its vowel nucleus and its tonality in Weining Ahmao (see Section 2). Interestingly enough, the functional oppositions associated with the changes on the classifier differ in the two languages. In Northern Kam, the opposition is interpreted in terms of number (singular vs. plural), while it is employed for marking number (singular) and definiteness vs. indefiniteness in Weining Ahmao. The reason for that difference lies again in the specific grammatical constellations immediately before the new systems developed, or, to be more precise, in the grammatical functions of the classifiers before their form was influenced by the numeral 'one'. In Weining Ahmao, the classifier developed its different morphophonological realizations at a time when the classifier was used for marking definiteness. In Northern Kam, the expression of definiteness was certainly not a central function of the classifier. As a consequence, there was little chance for classifiers of Northern Kam to be associated with definiteness, while this was a real option for classifiers in Weining Ahmao. In Weining Ahmao, a second process of reanalysis followed by morphophonological erosion led to the three-way distinction between augmentative/male, medial/female and diminutive/child. Since the distinctions of definite vs. indefinite and singular vs. plural equally operate on all three elements of the size distinction, it is reasonable to assume that size distinction took place first.

4 Conclusion

Functional explanations of the incompatibility of numeral classifiers and obligatory plural marking are based on the assumption that nouns in numeral-classifier languages are transnumeral, i.e., they are not specified for number in the lexicon (Greenberg 1974, Hundius and Kölver 1983, Bisang 1999, 2002). Due to their transnumerality, nouns cannot occur in immediate combination with numerals, they have to be individualized by the numeral classifier which provides them with the necessary conceptual boundaries by which they can be perceived as countable entities. From the perspective of formal semantics, Chierchia (1998a, b) argues that all nouns in Chinese are mass nouns in the sense that they do not make a distinction between sets of atoms and sets of sums of atoms (also cf. Li and Bisang 2012). The denotation of a noun like Chinese *māo* 'cat' includes both the set of atoms of *cats* and the set of sums of atoms of *cats*. As a consequence, mass nouns are inherently plural and do not need additional plural marking. If they have to be counted they have to be atomized, i.e., they have to be singled out as individual atoms by a numeral classifier. However, the analyses and motivations of the type discussed so far are not uncontroversial. Cheng and Sybesma (1999), for instance, argue that there is a mass/count-distinction in the lexical properties of Chinese nouns. The incompatibility of numeral classifiers and number marking is not only reflected in semantic approaches, it is also integrated into syntactic theories. One of them is Borer's (2005) nominal structure. In her theory, plural morphology and numeral classifiers cannot cooccur because they both are dividers and thus express the same function (cf. Feng, this volume).

No matter how appropriate the motivations for the presence of numeral classifiers in a language are in general, the present paper shows that there are various factors that do not depend on transnumerality and the existence of a mass/count-distinction. Thus, it seems rather implausible to argue that all nouns in a Bantoid language such as Ejagham are mass nouns if that language makes a systematic distinction between singular and plural in its noun-class system. In spite of this, the language is about to develop a numeral classifier system. The data from Kana with its fully developed classifier system and its loss of the old noun-class system (cf. example [5]) may support the hypothesis that there is a correlation between transnumerality and the existence of numeral classifiers because the singular/plural distinction associated with the noun-class system has vanished in the course of time. The question is whether the disappearance of the noun-class system is directly linked to the development of a fully-fledged numeral-classifier system. An alternative explanation for this loss comes from phonetics and phonology and is related to the erosion of phonological substance, a process which may well be completely unrelated to transnumerality. A lot of additional research will be needed to understand the emergence of the numeral-classifier systems of Niger-Congo languages.

In East and mainland Southeast Asian languages such as Northern Kam and Weining Ahmao, the singular/plural-distinction developed even if it is plausible to argue that they were transnumeral at least before they integrated number distinctions into their respective classifier systems. From a typological perspective which emphasizes the relevance of whether there is a count/mass-distinction in a language, the shift from a simple classifier system based on transnumeral nouns to a system with number-distinctions which somehow presuppose a count/mass-distinction looks rather great. However, the phonetic process that was ultimately responsible for this shift does not depend at all on that functional motivation.

This leads to the ultimate question of the status of typological universals and their cognitive motivations. The findings of this paper seem to support Dryer's (1997) view that exceptionless universals are extremely rare and that typologists should better spend their time on statistical universals. They also argue rather for what Newmeyer (2005) calls holistic functionalism than for atomistic functionalism. Atomistic functionalism assumes that "[t]here is direct linkage between properties of particular grammars and functional motivations for those properties" (Newmeyer 2005: 174). In contrast, holistic functionalism sees a far more indirect relation between grammars and motivations. As Newmeyer states, "grammars as wholes reflect the 'interests' of language users, but there is no question of parceling out rules, constraints, constructions, and so on of individual grammars and assigning to them a functional motivation"

(Newmeyer 2005: 178). The examples shown in this paper illustrate how individual structures of languages depend on a multitude of individual factors which make universally valid generalizations extremely difficult. Thus, Greenberg's (1974) universal on numeral classifiers is certainly not exceptionless and its linkage to functional motivations can only be an indirect one in the sense of holistic functionalism. If one takes into account the considerable amount of evidence against it and the fact that it does not exclude processes of grammaticalizaton which combine classifiers with plural marking, it is safe to assume that Greenberg's universal claim is a rather week universal.

References

Aikhenvald, Alexandra Y. 2000. *A Typology of Noun Categorization Devices*. Oxford: Oxford University Press.

Becker, Neele. 2005. *Numeralklassifikatoren im Thai*. Ph.D. diss., Department of English and Linguistics, University of Mainz (Germany).

Bisang, Walter. 1993. Classifiers, quantifiers and class nouns in Hmong. *Studies in Language* 17: 1–51.

Bisang, Walter. 1999. Classifiers in East and Southeast Asian languages: counting and beyond. In *Numeral Types and Changes Worldwide*, Jadranka Gvozdanovic (ed.), 113–185. Berlin/ New York: Mouton de Gruyter.

Bisang, Walter. 2002. Classification and the evolution of grammatical structures: a universal perspective. *Sprachtypologie und Universalienforschung* 55: 289–308.

Borer, Hagit. 2005. *In Name Only*. Oxford: Oxford University Press.

Chamberlain, James R. 1997. Tai-Kadai anthropods: A preliminary biolinguistic investigation. In *Comparative Kadai, the Tai Branch*, Jerold Edmondson, Jerold and David Solnit (eds.), 291–326. Dallas: Summer Institute of Linguistics and the University of Texas at Arlington.

Cheng, Lai-Shen Lisa and Rint Sybesma. 1999. Bare and not-so-bare nouns and the structure of NP. *Linguistic Inquiry* 30: 509–542.

Chierchia, Gennaro. 1998a. Reference to kinds across languages. *Natural Language Semantics* 6: 339–405.

Chierchia, Gennaro. 1998b. Plurality of mass nouns and the notion of 'semantic Parameter'. In *Events and Grammar*, Susan Rothstein (ed.), 53–103. Dordrecht: Kluwer Academic Publishers.

Corbett, Greville G. 2000. *Number*. Cambridge: Cambridge University Press.

Dryer, Matthew S. 1997. Why statistical universals are better than absolute universals. *Chicago Linguistic Society* 33: 123–145.

Dryer, Matthew S. 2005. Indefinite articles. In *The World Atlas of Language Structures,* Martin Haspelmath, Matthew S. Dryer, David Gil and Bernard Comrie (eds.). Oxford: Oxford University Press.

Edmondson, Jerold and David Solnit. 1988. Introduction. In *Comparative Kadai: Linguistic Studies Beyond Tai*, Jerold Edmondson and David Solnit (eds.), 1–26. Dallas: Summer Institute of Linguistics and the University of Texas at Arlington.

Feng, Shengli. 2012. The syntax and prosody of classifiers in classical Chinese. *This volume.*

Fu, Jingqi. 2012. Plurality in the pronominal paradigms of Bai dialects. *This volume.*

Gerner, Matthias. 2006. Noun classes in Kam and Chinese Kam-Tai languages: their morpho-syntax, semantics and history. *Journal of Chinese Linguistics* 34: 237–305.

Gerner, Matthias, and Walter Bisang. 2008. Inflectional speaker-role classifiers in Weining Ahmao. *Journal of Pragmatics* 40: 719–731.

Gerner, Matthias, and Walter Bisang. 2009. Inflectional classifiers in Weining Ahmao: mirror of the history of a people. *Folia Linguistica Historica* 30: 1–36.

Gerner, Matthias, and Walter Bisang. 2010. Social-deixis classifiers in Weining Ahmao. In *Rara and Rarissima. Documenting the Fringes of Linguistic Diversity*, Jan Wohlgemuth and Michael Cysouw (eds.), 75–94. Berlin/New York: Mouton de Gruyter.

Greenberg, Joseph H. 1974. Numeral classifiers and substantival number: Problems in the genesis of a linguistic type. In *Proceedings of the 11th International Congress of Linguistics, Bologna – Florence, Aug–Sept 1972*. Bologna. 17–37. Reprinted in Greenberg, 1990: 16–93.

Greenberg, Joseph H. 1990. *On Language. Selected Writings of Joseph H. Greenberg*, ed. by Denning, K. and S. Kemmer. Stanford: Stanford University Press.

Harbsmeier, Christoph. 2012. Plurality and the subclassification of nouns in classical Chinese. *This volume.*

Hundius, Harald, and Ulrike Kölver. 1983. Syntax and semantics of numeral classifiers in Thai. *Studies in Language* 7: 165–214.

Ikoro, Suanu M. 1994. Numeral classifiers in Kana. *Journal of African Languages and Linguistics* 15: 7–28.

Ikoro, Suanu M. 1996. *The Kana language*. Leiden: Research School CNWS.

Lehmann, Winfred P. 1992. *Historical Linguistics. An Introduction*. London: Routledge.

Li, Xuping, and Walter Bisang. 2012. Classifiers in Sinitic languages: From individuation to definiteness marking. *Lingua* 122: 335–355.

Meisterernst, Barbara. 2012. Number in Chinese: a diachronic study of the case of *zhu* from Han to Wei Jin Nanbeichao Chinese. *This volume.*

Mottin, Jean. 1980. *Contes et légendes Hmong Blanc*. Bangkok: Don Bosco Press.

Newmeyer, Frederick J. 2005. *Possible and Probable Languages. A Generative Perspective on Linguistic Typology*. Oxford: Oxford University Press.

Sanches, Mary, and Linda Slobin. 1973. Numeral classifiers and plural marking: an implicational universal. *Working Papers in Language Universals* 11: 1–22.

Shi, Lin. 1997. 侗语汉语语法比较研究 *Dongyu Hanyu yufa bijiao yanjiu* [Dong-Han Comparative Grammar Research]. Beijing: Central University of Nationalities Press.

Wang, Deguang. 1986. 威宁苗语话语材料 *Weining Miaoyu huayu cailiao* [Language material in the Weining dialect of the Miao language]. *Minzu Yuwen* 民族语文 3: 69–80.

Wang, Deguang. 1987. 贵州威宁苗语量词拾遗 *Guizhou Weining Miaoyu liangci shiyi* [Findings on numeral classifiers in the Weining dialect of the Miao language in Guizhou]. *Minzu Yuwen* 民族语文 5: 36–38.

Wang, Fushi. 1957. 贵州威宁苗语量词 *Guizhou Weining Miaoyu liangci* [The classifier in the Weining dialect of the Miao language in Guizhou]. *Yuyan Yanjiu* 语言研究 1957: 75–121. Translated 1972 as: The classifier in the Weining dialect of the Miao language in Kweichou. In *Miao and Yao Linguistic Studies: Selected Articles in Chinese*, Herbert Purnell (ed.), 111–185. Ithaca, NY: Cornell University.

Watters, John Roberts. 1981. A phonology and morphology of Ejagham – with notes on dialect variation. Ph.D Diss., University of California, Los Angeles.

Dan Xu

2 Reduplication in languages: A case study of languages of China[1]

Abstract: Reduplication is widely attested in human languages, especially in the southern hemisphere. This distribution, often complementary with plural markings, is also found in languages spoken in China, which show a correlation between plural marking and reduplication/classifiers: if reduplication and classifiers are found extensively, then plural marking is not developed, and is sensitive to the semantic feature [+human]. The more plural marking is developed, such as in Altaic languages, the less this semantic feature is required. The more a language possesses a developed plural-marking morphology, the less it needs reduplication and classifiers. Subjectivity plays a key role in reduplicated adjectives. Reduplication is iconically motivated. Positive degree constitutes its core meaning. Reduplication with negative meaning characterizes the grammaticalization process from icon to symbol.

Key words: reduplication, iconicity, motivation, plurality, typology

1 Introduction

Reduplication can be defined as proposed by Carl Rubino (2005): "the repetition of phonological material within a word for semantic or grammatical purposes". This definition follows the one formulated by Sapir (1921: 76), that reduplication is "repetition of all or part of the radical element." According to Sapir (1921: 76), reduplications "indicate such concepts as distribution, plurality, repetition, customary activity, increase of size, added intensity, continuance". It is now well known that reduplication is a widely used morphological device in human languages. Due to language typology research, we have access to a vast amount of data from different languages covering almost the whole world. Today a cross-language approach to reduplication is possible and necessary.

For almost one century, the wide distribution and the high frequency of reduplication in languages has drawn the attention of many linguists including Sapir (1921: 76–78) who noticed that in numerous languages such as Chinese,

1 The present work was supported by the grant *'Quantification et Pluralité' ANR-06-BLAN-0259* awarded by the Research Department of the French Government and by the University Institute of France.

Tibetan, Manchu, Somali, Chinook (spoken in the United States), Tsimshian (spoken in Canada and the United States), Ewe (spoken in Togo, Ghana), and so on, "this fundamental function can be quoted from all parts of the globe". Since the 70's, more investigations have been done on this topic. The paper written by Moravcsik (1978) is representative, including numerous examples in diverse languages. Recent research in English on reduplication can be found in the book edited by B. Hurch (2005), which includes twenty-four papers discussing reduplication in the world's languages, and doesn't leave out child language or sign languages. Several Asian languages are also concerned, including Indonesian, Modern Hindi and Japanese. The Chinese language and other languages of China, which widely use the device of reduplication, are absent however. Papers collected by A. Michaud and A. Morgenstern (eds. 2007) show us the current investigations on this subject in France. Besides studies of different language families, the article by M-C. Paris denotes how reduplication is exploited in contemporary Chinese as one of its important morphological means. Since this phenomenon in Chinese and languages of China (which mainly include different language families such as Sino-Tibetan, Altaic, Miao-Yao and Tai) is so common, papers and articles written in Chinese are abundant, but not well-known by linguists outside of China.

In spite of the great variety of languages described by scholars, essential characteristics wonderfully converge into the following meanings which in general denote "increased quantity". A reduplicated noun can indicate:

– Totality:

Lomongo (spoken in Congo-Kinshasa): *wané* 'day', *wané wané* 'the whole day', *nkésa* 'morning', *nkésa nkésa* 'the whole morning' (Ait-Hamou 1979: 19)

– Plurality:

Bontoc Igorot (spoken in Philippines): *anak* 'child', *ananak* 'children' (Sapir 1921: 78). Washo (Indian language of Nevada): *gusu* 'buffalo', *gususu* 'buffaloes' (Sapir 1921: 78). Mantauran (Rukai): *savare* 'jeune homme', *asavasavare* 'jeunes hommes' (Zeitoun 2007: 46)

– Distribution:

Mandarin Chinese: *renren* 'everyone'. Yoruba: *odún* 'year', *odoodún* 'every year' (Ait-Hamou 1979: 23). Hiligaynon (Malayo-Polynesian): *baláy* 'house', *baláy-baláy* 'every house' (Kiyomi 1995: 1152).

A reduplicated verb or adjective can express:

– Intensification:

Fa d'Ambô Creole Portuguese: *féyu* 'ugly', *fé féyu* 'very ugly' (Gulf of Guinea; Post 1998, cited by Rubino 2005: 24). Maya: *zac* 'white', *zazac* 'very white' (Ait-Hamou 1979: 73). Mantauran (Rukai): *ma-poli* 'white', *ma-poli-poli* 'very white' (Zeitoun 2007: 45)

– Repetition of action:
Jamaican Creole English: *biit* 'beat, whip', *biit-biit* 'whip constantly' (Bailey 1966, cited by Rubino 2005: 24).

– Continuity:
Jamaican Creole English: *taak* 'talk', *taak-taak* 'talk continuously' (Bailey 1966, cited by Rubino 2005: 24). Ambrym (Malayo-Polynesian): *mün* 'drink', *mün-mün* 'to keep on drinking' (Kiyomi 1995: 1158).

– Frequency of action:
Mantauran (Rukai): *tamako* 'fumer', *tamakomako* 'fumer souvent' (Zeitoun 2007: 46).

If we summarize the significance of the above functions, the metaphor carried by them is "more of form is more of content" (Lakoff and Johnson 1980: 127). As these authors indicate, form and content are linked in our conceptual system because long words are expected to contain more content. In other words, "linguistic expressions are containers, and their meanings are the *content* of those containers" (Lakoff and Johnson 1980: 127). This metaphor is applicable to most languages of the world, and the generalization can be expressed as follows (Lakoff and Johnson 1980: 128):

> A noun stands for an object of a certain kind.
> More of the noun stands for more objects of that kind.
> A verb stands for an action.
> More of the verb stands for more of the action (perhaps until completion).

Even though exceptions exist in some languages (we will expand on this in section 3), the metaphor established by the mentioned authors seems to be general and universal. Normally speaking, a reduplicated word (noun or verb) increases in the majority of cases the quantity of an entity or of an action.

The present paper is divided into four sections. In Section 1 I will briefly present reduplication devices in the world languages based on WALS (World Atlas of Language Structures). More details will be given in section 2 on reduplication in languages of China. These data are based on different works published in China. Section 3 will deal with the motivation of reduplication in order to understand such a largely distributed morphological process. Concluding remarks will be offered in section 4.

2 Reduplication in world languages

Since the essential function of reduplication consists of increasing quantity in languages, our initial working hypothesis is to compare it with other devices indicating quantity, such as nominal plurality markings and numeral classifier structures. Some scholars such as Greenberg (1972) and Sanches (1973) notice that obligatory plural markings and numeral classifiers do not, in most cases, co-occur in human languages (see also counterexamples by Walter Bisang in this volume). More precisely, languages using classifiers do not possess obligatory plural marking. We will add a new parameter, reduplication, in order to compare these three criteria, because three of them share the function of marking quantity in languages.

Thanks to the authors of WALS, who provided us with a large corpus of precious information[2], we have been given the opportunity of investigating numerous languages, including those which are less well-known and studied.

If we count languages which have obligatory plural marking and reduplication separately, WALS's statistics show 133/291 languages have the first device and 312/368 languages use the second. They also tell us that a reduced number of languages have numeral classifiers: 78/400 languages use this device. However, if these languages do not overlap completely, it is difficult to compare these statistics. Let us look at some statistics provided by WALS about different feature combinations between nominal plurality, numeral classifiers and reduplication. When two features are combined, the available number of languages is considerably decreased. Let us observe the situation in which occurrence of nominal plurality and numeral classifiers are combined in WALS. Just over one hundred languages indicate plurality. Among these languages, 45 have obligatory plural marking, while 43 have optional plural marking. 12 languages only mark human nouns, but the marking is obligatory. The same map shows that most (88) of these languages do not have numeral classifiers. Consequently, the correlation between plural marking and classifiers seems to be confirmed again in a larger corpus. Comparing plural marking and reduplication in a feature combination map, we notice that among 116 languages available in WALS, 91 use reduplication while 25 languages (most of them concentrated in Europe) ignore it. This suggests to us that like plural marking, reduplication constitutes one of the major devices of indicating plurality in human languages. However the statistics cannot be used safely since often the languages presented in WALS do not totally overlap with respect to the three required features. For this reason, I have chosen 61 languages which all are classified with the required three features, i.e. plural marking (PL), reduplication (R) and classifiers (CL) which are available in WALS (see *Table 1*).

First of all, some symbols must be clarified. "+" means that the feature is present and "−" indicates that it is absent. The symbol "±" implies that the

---

2 Language statistics based on the WALS site, November 2009.

Table 1: Distribution of three features based on WALS: PL, R and CL

PL+	PL±	PL−	R+	R±	R−	CL+	CL±	CL−
		Pirahã, Yidiny	Yidiny		Pirahã			Pirahã, Yidiny
		Maybrat Tidore	Maybrat Tidore				Maybrat Tidore	
	Chamorro, Hixkaryana Maricopa		Chamorro Maricopa		Hixkaryana			Chamorro, Hixkaryana Maricopa
	Japanese Mandarin		Mandarin	Japanese		Japanese Mandarin		
	Amele, Kutenai Lango, Tiwi		Amele, Tiwi		Kutenai, Lango			Amele, Kutenai, Lango, Tiwi
	Djingili, Khalkha Ngiyambaa Rapanui, Tagalog, Yawelmani Yoruba		Djingili, Khalkha Ngiyambaa Tagalog, Yawelmani, Yoruba	Rapanui				Djingili, Khalkha, Ngiyambaa Rapanui, Tagalog, Yawelmani Yoruba
	Ainu, Indonesian Khmer		Khmer	Ainu, Indonesian			Ainu, Indonesian, Khmer	
	Garo, Jakaltek Nivkh Vietnamese		Garo, Jakaltek Vietnamese	Nivkh		Garo, Nivkh Jakaltek Vietnamese		
	Mosetén		Mosetén					Mosetén
Mokilese			Mokilese			Mokilese		
Abkhaz, Alamblak, Apurinã, Armenian (Eastern), Basque Chukchi, Cree (Plains), English, Erromangan, Evenki, Finnish, French, Georgian German, Hausa, Hebrew (Modern), Hindi, Hunzib Kanuri, Koromfe, Lezgian, Malayalam, Miya, Quechua (Imbabura), Russian, Swahili Tepehuan (Southeastern), Yimas, Zulu, Zuni			Abkhaz, Alamblak, Chukchi Cree, Georgian Hausa, Hebrew (Modern), Hindi Hunzib, Kanuri Miya, Swahili Yimas	Armenian Erromangan Malayalam Quechua (Imbabura) Tepehuan (South-eastern), Zulu	Apurinã Basque English, Evenki Finnish, French German Koromfe Lezgian Russian, Zuni			Abkhaz, Alamblak, Apurinã, Armenian (Eastern), Basque Chukchi, Cree (Plains) English, Erromangan, Evenki, Finnish, French, Georgian German, Hausa, Hebrew (Modern), Hindi, Hunzib Kanuri, Koromfe, Lezgian, Malayalam, Miya, Quechua (Imbabura), Russian, Swahili Tepehuan (Southeastern) Yimas Zulu, Zuni
Hungarian, Turkish			Hungarian Turkish				Hungarian Turkish	

feature is present but with some constraints such as "optional", "only human nouns", "only full reduplication", etc. Thus the symbol "±" loosely includes different constraints, facilitating broad observation. From Table 1 it can bee seen that languages generally use two of these three devices, and that if they possess the third one, it is often optional and not obligatory. Languages using three of them, such as Mokilese spoken in Micronesia (hundreds of small islands in the western Pacific Ocean), or none of them, like Pirahã (spoken in Brazil), are definitely rare. Within these 61 available languages, 33 of them have plural marking which can apply to all nouns and is always obligatory. It is interesting to see that almost the same proportion, 35 languages, use the device of reduplication to indicate plurality, intensification, etc. Out of 61 languages, 47 do not possess classifiers. Among them, 11 employ obligatory plural marking and completely ignore reduplication, including Basque, English, French, German[3], etc.

Table 1 shows some general tendencies in these languages from around the world:

1. Languages having obligatory plural marking do not possess classifiers (30/33) (see Greenberg 1972 and Sanches 1973). Out of 33 languages with obligatory plural marking, 16 are compatible and 11 are incompatible with reduplication. The rest (the last 6 ones) accept reduplication to some degree.

2. Languages which do not employ obligatory plural marking tend to seek reduplication to compensate the lack. Out of 24 languages using non-strict plural marking, 21 (5 of them only use full reduplication) utilize the device of reduplication. Three languages which do not have plural marking at all use productive reduplication: Yidiny (spoken in Australia), Maybrat (spoken in Indonesia) and Tidore (also spoken in Indonesia).

As I have mentioned in point 1, 11 languages lacking reduplication have obligatory plural marking, while only three languages, Hixkaryana (spoken in Brazil), Kutenai (spoken in the States and Canada), and Lango (spoken in Uganda), do not have reduplication but have a plural system (non-obligatory). In this regard, the real exception is Pirahã (spoken in a hunter-gatherer tribe in Brazil) which possesses neither plural marking nor reduplication and classifiers.

The distribution of reduplication in human languages is impressive, as Carl Rubino (2005: 22) indicates:

---

3 Cases like "very very tall" in English, "noir noir" in French and "Film Film" in German are not taken into account since reduplication is not productive in these languages.

Reduplication can be found in several areas of the world that are genetically quite diverse. One such area is the India subcontinent where reduplicative morphemes can be found in languages spanning several families, e.g. Indo-European, Dravidian, Austro-Asiatic and Tibeto-Burman. The Horn of Africa is yet another area where reduplication plays an important role in various languages of distinct families, e.g. Nilo-Saharan and Afro-Asiatic (Omotic, Cushitic, and Semitic) families [...]

Looking at the maps provided by WALS gives the impression that languages using reduplication devices heavily are distributed in the southern hemisphere and concentrated in a zone including Asia and Australia. Austronesian languages also seem to be incorporated. Abbi (1991, cited by Zhang Min 1997: 39) thinks that reduplication is one of the linguistic areal features of the Indian subcontinent and of Southeast Asia.

Data on languages spoken in China are not provided sufficiently in WALS. They are often less studied or even unattested in the English literature since most research is published in Chinese. They are especially interesting if we compare them with other languages of the world. We will see that they present a different pattern and more complex combinations.

3 Reduplication in languages of China

Our data is based on diverse publications in Chinese. Apart from books and articles on different languages spoken in China, a recent book *Zhongguo de yuyan* [Languages of China], published in 2007 and edited by Sun, Hu and Huang, is also used to compare and complete the information given by other scholars. Sometimes their descriptions and comments are divergent and difficult to reconcile because the authors often used heterogeneous criteria. The "sources" column presents the original reference giving the information seen in corresponding lines, and some comments have been added.

The data is very interesting for general linguistics since most non-Han languages[4] spoken in China are given in *Table 2*. Sino-Tibetan languages (including subgroups such as Tibeto-Burman, Tai and Hmong-Mien), Austro-Asian languages and Altaic languages (with Turkic, Mongolian and Tungusic), are listed in the following table. These rich documents will complete the data offered by WALS in the Asian area.

---

4 Austronesian languages and Indo-European languages are not present in *Table 2* since they are not widespread in Mainland China.

Table 2: Distribution of the features of PL (Plural marking), R (Reduplication) and CL (Classifiers) in languages in China.

Languages	VO/OV	PL	R	CL	Sources
Tibeto-Burman groups of Sino-Tibetan languages					
Tibetan					
瑪曲藏語 *Mǎqū Zàngyǔ*	OV	+ [+H] and [−H] distinct mark	+	+	Zhou, MC. 2003
倉洛語 *Cāngluò yǔ*	OV	+ [+H] and [−H] same mark	+	+	Zhang, JCh. 1986
門巴語 *Ménbā yǔ*	OV	+ [+H] and [−H] same mark	+	+	Lu, ShZ. 2002
白馬 *Báimǎ*	OV	+ [+A]	+	+	*Zhongguo de yuyan* Sun, HK. *et al.* 2007
Yi					
彝語 *Yíyǔ*	OV	not seen	+	+	*Zhongguo de yuyan* Sun, HK., *et al.* 2007
拉祜 *Lāhù*	OV	+ [+H]	+	+	Chang, HE., *et al.* 1986
納西 *Nàxī*	OV	+ [+H]	+	+	He and Jiang 1985
桑孔 *Sāngkǒng*	OV	+ [+H] and [−H] same mark	+	+	Li, YS. 2002
卡卓 *Kǎzhuó*	OV	+ [+H] and [−H] distinct mark	+	+	Mu, ShH. 2003
柔若 *Róuruò*	OV	+ [+H] and [−H] distinct mark	+	+	Sun, HK., *et al.* 2002
白語 *Báiyǔ*	VO	+ [+H] and [−H] distinct mark	+	+	Xu and Zhao 1984

Languages	VO/OV	PL	R	CL	Sources
Jingpo					
獨龍 *Dúlóng*	OV	+ [+H]	+	+	*Zhongguo de yuyan* Sun, HK., *et al.* 2007
蘇龍 *Sūlóng*	OV	+ [+H] and [−H] distinct mark	−	+	Li, DQ. 2004
景頗語 *Jǐngpōyǔ*	OV	+ [+H] and [−H] same mark	+	+	Dai and Jiang 2004
格曼 *Gémàn*	OV	+ [+H] and [−H] distinct mark	+	+	Li, DQ. 2002
阿儂 *Anóng*	OV	+ [+H] and [−H] same mark	+	+	Sun and Liu 2005
Burman					
浪速 *Làngsù*	OV	+ [+H] and [−H] distinct mark	+	+	Dai, QX. 2005
阿昌 *Āchāng*	OV	−	+	+	*Zhongguo de yuyan* Sun, HK. *et al.* 2007
載瓦 *Zǎiwǎ*	OV	+ [+H] and [−H] distinct mark	+	+	*Zhongguo de yuyan* Sun HK. *et al.* 2007
Qiang					
羌語 *Qiāngyǔ*	OV	+ [+H] and [−H] same mark	+	+	Liu, Guangkun 1998
普米 *Pǔmǐ*	OV	+ [A]	+	+	Lu, ShZ. 2001
嘉絨 *Jiāróng*	OV	+ [+H] and [−H] same mark	+	+	Xiang, BL. 2008
史興 *Shǐxīng*	OV	+ [+H] and [−H] distinct mark	+	+	Xu, Dan 2009a
木雅 *Mùyǎ*	OV	+ [+H] and [−H] same mark	+	+	*Zhongguo de yuyan* Sun, HK., *et al.* 2007

Languages	VO/OV	PL	R	CL	Sources
爾礱 *Ěr gōng*	OV	+ [+H] and [−H] same mark	+	+	*Zhongguo de yuyan* Sun, HK., *et al.* 2007
爾蘇 *Ěr Sū*	OV	+ [+H] and [−H] same mark	+	+	*Zhongguo de yuyan* Sun, HK., *et al.* 2007
Tai (Dong-Tai) group					
拉珈 *Lājiā*	VO	−	+	+	Mao, ZW. *et al.* 1982
壯語 (武鳴) *Zhuàngyǔ (Wǔmíng)*	VO	−	+	+	Zhang, Junru. *et al.* 1999
莫話 *Mòhuà*	VO	−	+	+	Yang, TY. 2000
拉基語 *Lājīyǔ*	VO	−	+	+	Li, YB. 2000
標話 *Biāohuà*	VO	−	+	+	Liang and Zhang 2002
木佬 *Mùlǎo*	VO	+ only family members	+	+	Bo, WZ. 2003
布央 *Bùyāng*	VO	−	+	+	Li, JF. 1999
Hmong-Mien (Miao-Yao) group					
苗語 *Miáoyǔ*	VO	−	+	+	Wang, FSh. *et al.* 1985
勉語 *Miǎnyǔ*	VO	−	+	+	Mao, ZW. 2004
布努 *Bùnǔ*	VO	+ only family members	+	+	Mao, ZW. *et al.* 1982
炯奈語 *Jiǒngnài-yǔ*	VO	+ only family members	+	+	Mao and Li 2002
Austro-Asian languages					
克蔑語 *Kèmièyǔ*	VO	−	+	+	Chen, GQ. 2005
莽語 *Mǎngyǔ*	VO	−	+	+	Gao, YQ. 2003
京語 *Jīngyǔ*	VO	−	+	+	Ouyang, *et al.* 1984

Languages	VO/OV	PL	R	CL	Sources
傣語 *Láiyǔ*	VO	–	+	+	Li XL. 1999
布賡 *Bùgēng*	VO	–	+	+	Li, YB. 2005
布興 *Bùxīng*	VO	–	–	+	Gao, YQ. 2004
克木 *Kèmù*	VO	–	+	+	Chen, GQ. 2002
Altaic languages					
Turkic					
撒拉 *Sālā*	OV	+ [+H] and [−H] same mark	+	+[5]	Lin, LY. 1985
哈薩克 *Hāsàkè* Qazaq	OV	+ [+H] and [−H] same mark	? +[6]	–	*Zhongguo de yuyan* Sun, HK. *et al.* 2007 Chen, Xiaoyun 1998
維吾爾 *Wéiwúěr*	OV	+ [+H] and [−H] same mark	±	+	*Zhongguo de yuyan* Sun, HK. *et al.* 2007
Mongolian					
蒙古 *Měnggǔ*	OV	+ [+H] and [−H] same mark	–[7]	–	*Zhongguo de yuyan* Sun, HK. *et al.* 2007
土族 *Tǔzú*	OV	+ [+H] and [−H] same mark	–	–	*Zhongguo de yuyan* Sun, HK. *et al.* 2007
達斡爾 *Dáwòěr*	OV	+ [+H] and [−H] same mark	–	–	*Zhongguo de yuyan* Sun, HK. *et al.* 2007
東鄉 *Dōngxiāng*	OV	+ [+H] and [−H] same mark	–	–	*Zhongguo de yuyan* Sun HK. *et al.* 2007

---

5 According to Lin (1985: 54), classifiers are optional and some of them are loaned from Chinese.

6 In ZGDYY, this problem is not mentioned, while Chen provides abundant examples of reduplication.

7 In interrogative sentences, interrogative particles can sometimes be reduplicated.

Languages	VO/OV	PL	R	CL	Sources
保安 *Bǎo'ān*	OV	+ [+H] and [−H] same mark	−	−	*Zhongguo de yuyan* Sun HK. *et al.* 2007
Tungusic					
錫伯 *Xībó*	OV	+ [+H] and [−H] same mark	−	−	*Zhongguo de yuyan* Sun HK. *et al.* 2007
朝鮮 Korean	OV	+ [+H] and [−H] same mark	−	±	Jin Haiyue 2005
滿語 Manchu	OV	+ [+H] and [−H] same mark	+	±	Wang QF. 2005
鄂溫克 *Èwēnkè*	OV	+ [+H] and [−H] same mark	−	−	*Zhongguo de yuyan* Sun HK. *et al.* 2007

It may be noted that nominal plural marking is very sensitive to the [+Human] or [+Animate] feature in numerous languages spoken in China. The more plural marking is developed, such as in Altaic languages, the less this semantic feature is required. In the south of China, the Tibeto-Burman group presents some contrastive characteristics in the case of Tai, Hmong-Mien groups and Austro-Asian languages: on one side the Tibeto-Burman (TB) group has OV order (except Bai), while the other three (Tai, Hmong-Mien groups and Austro-Asian languages) have VO order. Moreover, plural marking seems more developed in TB than the rest even though the semantic feature [±Human] is important in almost the half of these languages. Plural marking is not formed or is not necessary according to updated reports of Tai, Hmong-Mien groups and Austro-Asian languages. The authors do not always give information about partial vs. full reduplication; this detail is not provided in the Reduplication column in *Table 2*. It is striking that except Altaic, all other languages presented in *Table 2*, i.e. Tibeto-Burman, Tai, Hmong-Mien groups of Sino-Tibetan and Austro-Asian languages, all use reduplication devices and classifiers. Languages which do not possess plural marking systematically appeal to both reduplication and classifiers. In other words, of these languages, none has recourse to just one device, R or CL. This suggests that in non-Han languages spoken in the south of China, reduplication and classifiers are linked or complementary devices in the plural marking system, perhaps due to language contact with the Chinese language, which has both features. This phenomenon is not observed in other languages of the world, since a minority of languages uses classifiers (78/400, see Section 1). Note that 12/61 languages in *Table 1* use both reduplication and classifiers.

Typologically and geographically, languages in China are divided into three types as summarized in *Table 3*. In the north, languages are quite similar to those in Europe, with obligatory plural marking, often ignoring reduplication and classifier devices. In Altaic languages, Manchu (almost extinct) and Korean have assimilated many Chinese loan words, such as classifiers. This phenomenon has also occurred in Salar, in which measure words (these are not real classifiers and exist in all human languages) are often loaned from Chinese. It seems that the Turkic group and Tungusic group are more influenced by the Chinese languages. In the southwest, plural marking exists, as well as reduplication and classifiers, while in the southeast, languages geographically encircled by the Chinese language behave almost like it: plural marking is not developed, but reduplication and classifiers are widely used. The three situations are summarized in *Table 3*:

Table 3: Three types of languages spoken in China

Languages	Altaic lgs	TB lgs	Tai, HM, Austro-A	Chinese
Word-order	OV	OV	VO	VO
Is plural marking devloped?	+	±	−	−
Is reduplication developed?	−	+	+	+
Are classifiers obligatory?	−	+	+	+

If we compare *Table 3* with *Table 1* we will see that plural marking is not only correlated with classifiers but also with reduplication. It is interesting to note that in numerous Austronesian languages, where plural marking does not exist, it is reduplication which indicates the meaning of plural. It is also clear that the more a language possesses a developed plural marking morphology, the less it needs reduplication and classifiers. These last two devices seem to be more appropriate for languages having less-developed or undeveloped plural marking, in order to compensate for the need of expressing quantification.

4 Motivation of reduplication

Iconicity is commonly defined as a similarity between the form of a sign and its meaning. In this section I will use this cognitive approach to explain reduplication. Haiman (1980: 515)[8] proposes and develops two types of iconicity: *imagic iconicity* and *grammatic iconicity*. "An iconic *image* is a single sign which resembles its referent with respect to some characteristics" such as photographs, statues, and onomatopoeic words in languages. He calls *iconic diagram* "a systematic arrangement of signs, none of which necessarily resembles its referent, but whose relationships to each other mirror the relationships of their referents". "The clearest example of such iconicity is that of sequence. Other things being equal, the order of statements in a narrative description corresponds to the order of the events they describe". Within the iconicity of grammar, Haiman distinguishes two types: (a) isomorphism (one sign and one meaning) and (b) motivation (relationships between the word order and the events). In other words, type (a) presents "the correspondence of parts" and type (b) indicates "the correspondence of relations between parts" (Croft 1990: 164). However, as Croft (1990: 171) points out, the distinction between *isomorphism* and *iconic motivation* is not always clear because of the choice of these terms. Givón (1985: 188) thinks that the distinction between *isomorphic* and *diagrammatic* "is arbitrary and not supported by traditional usage, neither in the 'hard' sciences nor in philosophy." I will use Haiman's "grammatic iconicity" adopting the terms of Givón (1985), who distinguishes *icon* and *symbol* as two extreme points on a scale forming a continuum. This gradual scale is necessary and more appropriate to the analysis of reduplication, thus allowing some reduplicated words to be classified as an intermediate stage.

Reduplication is one of the iconically motivated grammatical devices, since "the structure of language directly reflects some aspect of the structure of reality." (Haiman 1980: 515). In previous sections, I stated that plural marking is relative to reduplication in human languages. Haiman (1980: 528) also classified these two grammatical means as iconically motivated: "it is universally assumed that markedness is iconically motivated" as Greenberg (cited by Haiman) points out:

> There is no language in which the plural does not have some non-zero allomorphs, whereas there are languages in which the singular is expressed only by zero.

It is not surprising that marking of plural occurs more frequently than singular since, in general, the singular is much more recurrent in discourse than the plural. Reduplication is a marked device in languages. It constitutes, apart from other functions, one of the forms of plural, complementary with plural marking. Similarly, reduplication is also iconically motivated and is impressively

---

8 Haiman has developed two types of "iconicity" put forth by Peirce (1932).

widespread in human languages, and its meaning is strikingly common. In most cases, reduplication expresses an increasing quantification, but in some cases it can indicate a diminution of the meaning. This case may present counterexamples to iconicity. In fact, the origin of reduplication is iconically motivated, and when reduplication becomes a *morphological means* (a more abstract item), the diminutive meaning is possible in some languages.

The topic of the relationships between a language and the way of expressing it was already dealt with by Greek philosophers (Pierre Swiggers, 1993: 22) In the *Cratyle* it is written that the sound *r* makes some words more expressive. Chan (1996, cited by Zhang Min, preprint b: 3), notes that Chinese words that include the meaning of roundness almost always contain a rounded vowel. I add here Baxter's[9] reconstruction of Old Chinese to better illustrate the phenomenon:

圆 (圓) yuán	< hjwonX	< *wjan	'round',
圈 quān	< gjwen	< *gwrjen	'circle',
周 zhōu	< tsyun	< *tjiw	'circuit',
卷 juǎn	< kjwenX	< *krjon?	'roll',
环 (環) huán	< hwæn	< *wren	'ring',
围 (圍) wéi	< hjwɨj	< *wjɨj	'surround',
转 (轉) zhuàn	< trjwenX	< *trjon?	'rotate',
旋 xuán	< zjwen	< *ɦiswjen	'spin',
团 (團) tuán	< dawn	< *don	'ball',
弧 hú	< hu	< *gwa	'curve'.

Checking the pronunciation in Old Chinese, another piece of evidence supporting Chan's remark can be added: if a word does not contain a rounded vowel at the initial stage, the reconstructions in Old Chinese show that they often contained a labial velar which rounds the following element. It seems that these sound formations were iconically motivated.

It is evident that writing systems, especially the creation of Chinese characters on bones and shells, give us a clue to a cognitive mechanism which is not always attested in alphabetic languages. In the inscriptions on bones, some graphs already contained plurality information (Guo Pan 2004, Behr Wolfgang 2006, Xu Dan 2009b):

---

9 The reconstruction system is taken from Baxter (1992). The character is followed by the Pinyin transcription (a conventional alphabet system for Chinese), the Middle Chinese phonological system based on the *Qièyùn* which is the first rime dictionary dated from 601 AD, and finally by the reconstruction in Old Chinese, marked by an asterisk.

⽷ 丝 (絲) *sī*	'silk'	[two strands of silk],
燊 森 *sēn*	'forest'	[⽊ 木 *mù*, three trees],
焱 焱 *yàn*	'flame'	[⽕ 火 *huǒ*, three fires],
劦 协 (協) *xié*	'put force together'	[⼒ 力 *lì*, three forces],
𠬪 友 *yǒu*	'befriend'	[⼿ 手 *shǒu*, two hands],
乑 众 (眾) *zhòng*	'people'	[⼈ 人 *rén*, three men under the sun]

In this list, a contemporary standard character is printed after each graph found in the bone inscriptions to facilitate comparison. It is followed by a *Pinyin transcription* (a conventional alphabet system for Chinese) and a translation. An interpretation of the graph form is given in square brackets. From a cognitive point of view, these writing forms confirm that *"more of form is more of content"* (Lakoff and Johnson 1980: 127). It is clear that an added graph form means an added quantity. These examples are likely between imagic iconicity (by their image characteristics) and diagramatic iconicity (by their relationships reflecting those in the natural world) according to Haiman's definition (1980). On the one hand, these graphs resemble images reflecting realty, and on the other hand, the degree of abstraction of these graphs is already remarkable in mirroring the relationship between these referents.

Another example favoring the hypothesis that plurality marking and reduplication are both iconically motivated is sign languages. Here I only cite the cases of Chinese Sign Language (cf. the textbook *Zhongguo shouyu* [Chinese Sign Language] 2003) and German Sign Language (Pfau and Steinbach, 2005). The Chinese Sign Language textbook provides examples expressing plurality. To express one person, two index fingers form the character 人 *rén* 'man', and to express plurality, three fingers (index, middle and ring fingers) of two hands form the character 众 *zhòng* 'people' in a clockwise circle. This process is quite similar, as we have just seen, to that of bone inscriptions. No single example in which a small quantity needs a repetition of the gesture is attested. According to Pfau and Steinbach (2005: 580–581), to express "children" in German Sign Language, a sideward reduplication of the whole sign is imposed and to communicate "books", a tripling (at the same place as opposed to sideward reduplication) is required. Again, the added quantity is assumed by the added gesture but not the inverse.

As has been mentioned at the beginning of this section, reduplication can also express diminution in Agta (spoken in Philippines), Nez Perce (northwestern United States), Thompson (found in Canada), and attenuation in Quileute (spoken in the United States), Swahili, Thai, Mandarin and Tagalog (Moravcsik 1978: 322–323). How can we explain these counterexamples to iconicity if we confirm that reduplication is iconically motivated? Kiyomi (1995) distinguishes two kinds of reduplication: one is iconic and the other is non-iconic. She considers that the second one "can be compared to regular affixation" (Kiyomi 1995: 1149). I agree with her core idea proposing that reduplication in human languages can be identified at different stages of a continuum. In other words, most instances of reduplication indicating more content are iconic and some less iconic, i.e. the quantification concept is no longer prominent and in some others is non-iconic, having become a morphological means. In the last case, reduplicated words are reanalyzed: the reduplicated part has lost its original meaning, acquiring a new status: it has become a grammatical word. For example, reduplication was used for past tense (Swadesh 1971, cited by Kiyomi 1995) in old Indo-European languages. Section 1, *Table 1* shows, however, that today's European languages completely lack reduplication. A gradual process may exist, and these reduplications expressing diminution must diachronically originate from iconic ones (or from other constructions). Kiyomi also hints at this, suggesting that "iconic use of reduplication seems to be more widely observed than non-iconic use. One may well assumes that the initial use of reduplication was iconic and that later noniconic interpretations were developed" (1995: 1163)[10].

5 Conclusion

In this paper, I have showed that reduplication, widely found in human languages, is complementary with plural marking. They constitute different means of marking plurality. One language can have diverse types of marking to express quantity. Reduplication and plural marking represent the main types of marking attested on different continents. I have supposed that reduplication must initially be iconically motivated. The augmented quantity and the plus-degree constitute the core meaning of reduplication. Those instances of reduplication indicating a diminution or a smaller quantity should be derived from the iconic ones, and have become a morphological device parallel to other affixation functions. The creations of Chinese characters, as well as German and Chinese sign languages, illustrate well the primitive stage of reduplication's iconic function, demonstrating conceptual structures that reflect our perception of the relationship between material entities.

---

10 See also the analysis in the Introduction.

References

Ait-Hamou, Khaled. 1979. *Structure et typologie de la quantification dans les langues naturelles* (Document de linguistique quantitative N° 36). Paris : Jean-Favard.

Association of Chinese deaf persons. 2003. *Zhongguo shouyu* [Chinese Sign Language]. Beijing: Huaxia chubanshe.

Baxter, William H. 1992. *A Handbook of Old Chinese phonology*. (Trends in Linguistics Studies and Monographs 64). Berlin/New York: Mouton de Gruyter.

Behr, Wolfgang. 2006. "Homosomatic juxtaposition" and the problem of "syssemantic" (*huì yì*) characters. In *Ecriture chinoise. Données, usages et représentations* [Chinese writing. Data, use and representations], Françoise Bottéro and Redouane Djamouri (eds.), 75–114. Paris: EHESS/CRLAO.

Bisang, Walter. 2012. Numeral classifiers with plural marking. A challenge to Greenberg. *This volume*.

Bo, Wenze. 2003. *Studies of the Mulao*. Beijing: Minzu chubanshe.

Chang, Hong'en. 1986. *Outline of the Lahu Grammar*. Beijing: Minzu chubanshe.

Chen, Guoqing. 2002. *Studies of the Kemu*. Beijing: Minzu chubanshe.

Chen, Guoqing. 2005. *Studies of the Kemie*. Beijing: Minzu chubanshe.

Chen, Xiaoyun. 1988. Hasake yu zhong ci de chongdie [Reduplicated words in Kazakh]. *Minzu Yuwen* 3: 44–50.

Comrie, Bernard. 2008. The Areal Typology of Chinese: Between North and Southeast Asia. In *Chinese Linguistics in Leipzig CLE 2*, Redouane Djamouri, Barbara Meisterernst and Rint Sybesma (eds.), 1–21.

Croft, William. 1990. *Typological and Universals*. Cambridge: Cambridge University Press.

Dai, Qingxia. 2005. *Studies of the Langsu*. Beijing: Minzu chubanshe.

Dai, Qingxia and Jiang Ying. 2004. Mengya qi liangci de leixingxue tezheng-Jingpo yu liangci de ge'an yanjiu [Typological characteristics of classifiers at a primitive stage-the case of Jingpo], *Studies on Sino-Tibetan languages: Papers in honor of Professor Hwang-Cherng Gong on his seventieth Birthday*, 315–325. Taipei: Academia Sinica.

Downing, Pamela. 1996. *Numeral Classifier System: The Case of Japanese*. Amsterdam/Philadelphia: John Benjamins Publishing Company.

Dryer, Matthew S. 1992. The Greenbergian word order correlations. *Language*, Volume 68: 1, 81–138.

Feng, Shengli. 2009. *Hanyu de yunlü, cifa yu jufa* [Interactings between Morphology, Syntax and Prosody in Chinese] (revised edition). Beijing: Beijing Univeristy Press.

Gao, Yongqi. 2003. *Studies of the Mang*. Beijing: Minzu chubanshe.

Gao, Yongqi. 2004. *Studies of the Buxing*. Beijing: Minzu chubanshe.

Givón, Talmy. 1983. Iconicity, isomorphism, and non-arbitrary coding in syntax. In *Iconicity in Syntax*, John Haiman (ed.), 187–219. Amsterdam/Philadelphia: John Benjamins Publishing Company.

Greenberg, Joseph. 1972. Numeral classifiers and substantival number: problems in the genesis of a linguistic type. *Language Universals* 9: 1–39.

Guo, Pan. 2004. *Hanyu sheshu wenti yanjiu* [Studies on numbers in Chinese]. Beijing: Zhonghua shuju.

Hagège, Claude. 1985. Le chinois, l'ordre des mots et l'ordre du pensable [Chinese, word order and the order of the thinkable]. *T'oung Pao* LXXI: 263–274.

Hagège, Claude. 2005. Word classes in isolating languages. In *Lexicology*, D. Alan Cruse *et al.* (eds.), vol. 2: 976–980. Berlin: Walter de Gruyter.

Haiman, John. 1980. The Iconicity of grammar: Isomorphism and motivation. *Language* 56: 3, 515–540.

Haiman, John (ed.). 1985. *Iconicity in Syntax*. Amsterdam/Philadelphia: John Benjamins Publishing Company.

Haspelmath M., M. S. Dryer, D. Gil and B. Comrie (eds.). 2005. *The World Atlas of Language Structures*. Oxford: Oxford University Press.

The World Atlas of Language Structures Online (*WALS Online*).

He, Jiren and Jiang Zhuyi. 1985. *Outline of Naxi Grammar*. Beijing: Minzu chubanshe.

Hurch, Bernhard (ed.). 2005. *Grammar, Comparative and general-Reduplication*. Berlin/New York: Mouton de Gruyter.

Jin, Haiyue. 2005. Han-Chao yu shuliang duanyu de xingshi ji yuyi bijiao [Syntactic and semantic comparison of numeral classifiers in Chinese and Korean]. In *Han-Zang yuxi liangci yanjiu* [Studies of classifiers in Sino-Tibetan], Li Jinfang and Hu Suhua (eds.), 499–505. Beijing: Zhongyang minzu daxue chubanshe.

Kiyomi, Setsuko. 1995. A new approach to reduplication: a semantic study of noun and verb reduplication in the Malayo-Polynesian languages. *Linguistics* 33: 1145–1167.

Lakoff, George and Mark Johnson. 1980. *Metaphors We Live by*. Chicago: The University of Chicago Press.

Li, Daqin. 2002. *Studies of the Geman*. Beijing: Minzu chubanshe.

Li, Daqin. 2004. *Studies of the Sulong*. Beijing: Minzu chubanshe.

Li, Jinfang. 1999. *Studies of the Buyang*. Beijing: Zhongyang minzu daxue chubanshe.

Li, Xulian. 1999. *Studies of the Lai*. Beijing: Zhongyang minzu daxue chubanshe.

Li, Yongsui. 2002. *Studies of the Kongsang*. Beijing: Zhongyang minzu daxue chubanshe.

Li, Yongsui. 2002. *Studies of the Sangkong*. Beijing: Zhongyang minzu daxue chubanshe.

Li, Yunbing. 2000. *Studies of the Laji*. Beijing: Zhongyang minzu daxue chubanshe.

Li, Yunbing. 2005. *Studies of the Bugeng*. Beijing: Minzu chubanshe.

Liang, Min and Zhang Junru. 2002. *Studies of the Biaohua*. Beijing: Minzu chubanshe.

Lin, Lianyun. 1985. *Outline of the Salar Grammar*. Beijing: Minzu chubanshe.

Liu, Guangkun. 1998. *Studies of the Mawo Qiang*. Chengdu: Sichuan minzu chubanshe.

Liu, Danqing. 2003. *Yuxu Leixingxue yu Jieci Lilun* [Word Order Typology and a Theory of Adposition]. Beijing: Commercial Press.

Lu, Shaozun. 2001. *Studies on Pumi Dialects*. Beijing: Minzu chubanshe.

Lu, Shaozun. 2002. *Studies on Menba Dialects*. Beijing: Minzu chubanshe.

Mao, Zongwu. 2004. *Studies on the Mian of Yao*. Beijing: Minzu chubanshe.

Mao, Zongwu and Li, Yunbing. 2002. *Studies of the Jiongnai*. Beijing: Zhongyang minzu daxue chubanshe.

Mao, Zongwu, Meng Chaoji and Zheng Zhongze. 1982. *Outline of the Yao language Grammar*. Beijing: Minzu chubanshe.

Michaud, Alexis and Morgenstern Aliyah (eds.). 2007. *Faits de Langues N29: La Réduplication*. Paris: Ophrys.

Moravcsik, Edith A. 1978. Reduplicative constructions. In: Greenberb J. (ed.) *Universals of Human Languages* Vol. 3, 297–334. Stanford: Stanford University Press.

Mu, Shihua. 2003. *Studies on the Kazhuo*. Beijing: Minzu chubanshe.

Ortmann, Albert. 2000. Where plural refuses to agree: Feature unification and morphological economy. *Acta Linguistica Hungarica*, Vol. 47: 249–288.

Ouyang, Jueya, Cheng Wan and Yu Cuirong. 1984. *Outline of the Jing Grammar*. Beijing: Minzu chubanshe.

Paris, Marie-Claude. 2007. Un aperçu de la réduplication nominale et verbale en mandarin [Survey of nominal and verbal reduplications in Mandarin]. *Faits de Langues 29: La Réduplication*, 63–76. Paris: Ophrys.

Peyraube, Alain. 2000. Ordre des constituants en chinois archaïque [Order of constituents in Old Chinese]. In *Ordre des mots et typologie linguistique* [Word Order and linguistic typology], Anaïd Donabédian and Xu Dan (eds.), 99–110. (Cahiers de Linguistique de l'INALCO 3.)

Pfau, Roland and Markus Steinbach. 2005. Backward and sideward reduplication in German Sign Language. In *Grammar, Comparative and general-Reduplication*, Bernhard Hurch (ed.), 569–594. Berlin/New York: Mouton de Gruyter.

Rubino, Carl. 2005. Reduplication: Form, function and distribution. In *Grammar, Comparative and general-Reduplication*, Bernhard Hurch (ed.), 11–29. Berlin/New York: Mouton de Gruyter.

Sagart, Laurent. 1999. *The Roots of Old Chinese*. Amsterdam/Philadelphia: John Benjamins Publishing Company.

Sanches, Mary. 1973. Reprint. Numeral classifiers and plural marking: an implicational universal. *Language Universals* 11: 1–22, 1971.

Sapir, Edward. 1921. *Language: An Introduction to the Study of Speech*. New York: Harcourt, Brace, and World.

Sun, Hongkai, Huang Chenglong, Zhou Maocao. 2002. *Studies of the Rouruo*. Beijing: Zhongyang minzu daxue chubanshe.

Sun, Hongkai, Hu Zengyi and Huang Xing. 2007. *Zhongguo de yuyan* [The Languages in China]. Beijing: Commercial Press.

Sun, Hongkai and Liu Guangkun. 2005. *Studies of the Anong*. Beijing: Minzu chubanshe.

Swiggers, Pierre. 1993. Coup d'œil historiographique. *Faits de Langues : Motivation et iconicité* 1: 21–28.

Wang, Fushi. 1985. *Outline of the Miao Grammar*. Beijing: Minzu chubanshe.

Wang, Li. 1958. *Outline of the Chinese Language History*. Beijing: Kexue chubanshe.

Wang, Qingfeng. 2005. *Studies of the Manchu*. Beijing: Minzu chubanshe.

Xiang, Bolin. 2008. *Studies of the Jiarong*. Beijing: Minzu chubanshe.

Xu, Dan. 2006. *Typological Change in Chinese Syntax*. Oxford: Oxford University Press.

Xu, Dan. 2009a. *Xiayou Shixingyu de mouxie tedian* [Some syntactic features of Down-river Shixing]. *Minzu yuwen* 1: 25–42.

Xu, Dan. 2009b. Cong Zhanguo zonghengjia shu kan Xi Han chuqi fushu gainian de biaoda [Plurality in Chinese at early Han seen in the Zhanguo zonghengjia shu], *Lishi yuyanxue yanjiu* 2: 83–94. Beijing: Commercial Press.

Xu, Dan and Fu, Jingqi. 2011. Liangci jiqi leixingxue kaocha [Classifiers and some typological considerations], *Yuyan kexue* [Sciences in linguistics], 6: 1–14.

Xu, Lin and Zhao, Yansun. 1984. *Outline of the Bai Grammar*. Beijing: Minzu chubanshe.

Xuan, Dewu, Jin Xiangyuan, Zhao Xi. 1985. *Outline of the Korean Grammar*. Beijing: Minzu chubanshe.

Yang, Tongyin. 2000. *Studies of the Mo*. Beijing: Zhongyang minzu daxue chubanshe.

Zeitoun, Elizabeth. 2007. La réduplication en rukai mantauran. *Faits de Langues 29: La Réduplication*, 37–47. Paris: Ophrys.

Zhang, Jichuan. 1986. *Outline of the Cangluo Menba Grammar*. Beijing: Minzu chubanshe.

Zhang, Junru. 1999. *Studies on Zhuang Dialects*. Chengdu: Sichuan minzu chubanshe.

Zhang, Min. 1997. Cong leixingxue he renzhi yufa de jiaodu kan hanyu chongdie xianxiang [Reduplication in Chinese – A typological and cognitive grammar study], *Guowai Yuyanxue* 2: 37–45.

Zhang, Min. (preprint a). *From construction Grammar to construction morphology: an MSDT approach to Chinese symmetric constructions*.

Zhang, Min. (preprint b). *Ziran jufa lilun yu hanyu yufa xiansixing yanjiu* [About naturalist grammar and iconicity in Chinese grammar].

Zhou, Maocao. 2003. *Studies on Maqu Tibetan*. Beijing: Minzu chubanshe.

Zhou, Yaowen and Luo, Meizhen. 2001. *Studies on Dai Dialects*. Beijing: Minzu chubanshe.

II Numeral classifiers and their diachronic development

Shengli Feng

3 The Syntax and prosody of classifiers in Classical Chinese[1]

Abstract: Based on Borer's theory of nominal structure (2005: 95), this paper offers a syntactic analysis of countable nouns in Pre-Archaic Chinese (ca. 1000 BC and before) and the development of classifiers in Archaic Chinese (1000 B.C.– 200 A.D.). It is argued that the emergence of classifiers in Archaic Chinese, though syntactically licensed, was prosodically motivated and in turn, constructed a sub-case of a typological change from the synthetic property of Pre-Archaic Chinese (before 1000 BC) to the analytical characteristics of Post-Archaic Chinese, around the time of Eastern Han (25–220 AD).

Keywords: classifier, syntactic change, prosodic grammar, typological change of Classical Chinese

1 The Syntax of Countable Nouns and Classifiers

It is well known that nouns in Mandarin Chinese must co-occur with a classifier when counting. For example:

(1)   a.   唐僧有三個徒弟

         Táng Sēng yǒu sān gè túdì

         Tang Seng have three CL disciple

         'Tang Seng has three disciples.'

     b.   *唐僧有三徒弟

         Táng Sēng yǒu sān túdì

         Tang Seng have three disciple

         'Tang Seng has three disciples.'

---

1 I would like to express my sincere gratitude to Professor Cheng Zhang (張赬) not only for the inspiration of her insight on the grammatical nature of early classifiers in classical Chinese, but also for her generosity of providing access to her paper, on which some important statistics and conclusions of this current work are beneficially based. I would also like to thank Professor Hu Suhua (胡素華) for providing Modern Yi examples for the prosodic argument developed in this paper. All mistakes, of course, are mine.

Though classifiers like *gè* 個 are also called Measure Words (especially in pedagogically designed textbooks), there is a clear distinction between classifier and measurer in linguistic analysis, as shown in the following example:

(2) a. 三條魚
     sān   tiáo   yú
     three stripe fish
     'three fish'

   b. 三尾魚
     sān   wěi yú
     three tail fish

   c. 一 枚 / 頭 魚
     yì   méi / tóu   yú
     one stick / head fish
     'one fish'

(3) a. 三桶水
     sān   tǒng shuǐ
     three pail water
     'three pail of water'

   b. *三个水
     *sān   gè   shuǐ
      three CL water
     '*three water'

   c. 三桶魚
     sān   tǒng yú
     three pail fish
     'three pail of fish'

Though both *fish* and *water* in English do not have a plural form, one can say 'one fish' but not 'one water'. 'Water' cannot be counted without a container while 'fish' can be counted with different classifiers in Chinese, namely, *tiao* 'long-thing' in Mandarin (2a), *wei* 'tail' in southern Chinese dialect (2b), *mei* 'stick' and *tou* 'head' in Han Dynasty (206 BC–220 AD). Thus, a container for measuring things (like the 'water') is called a *measure–word* (容量詞 *rongliangci*) which functions like a noun, whereas a grammatical category that must be used when counting things is called a *classifier,* which is a functional category. Therefore, a measure–word cannot be substituted by a (general or universal) classifier as in (3b), whereas a (general or universal) classifier can be substituted by a measure–word (3c).

The grammatical property of classifiers can further be characterized in Y. R. Chao's terminology. In his textbook *Chinese Primer* (1948), the so-called classifiers today were named *Auxiliary Noun* (AN). As pointed out by Huang (2007),[2]

---

2 In our co-taught course "Historical Syntax of Chinese" at Harvard University, 2007.

the term 'AN' is compatible with the modern theory of lightverbs which function as auxiliary verbs that assist to classify different types of actions/events (cf. inchoative, causative, performative, eventive, experiential, existential, etc.). As a result, VPs that have a light-verb structure (VP-shell) will be paralleled by NPs that have a light-noun structure (classifiers):

(4) ... $[_{clP}$ *cl* $[_{NP}$ [N]]]

   ... $[_{vP}$ *v* $[_{VP}$ [V]]]

The parallelism between noun phrase syntax and verb phrase syntax is further developed and elaborated in Hagit Borer's book *In Name Only* (2005: 95), as shown in the following structure:

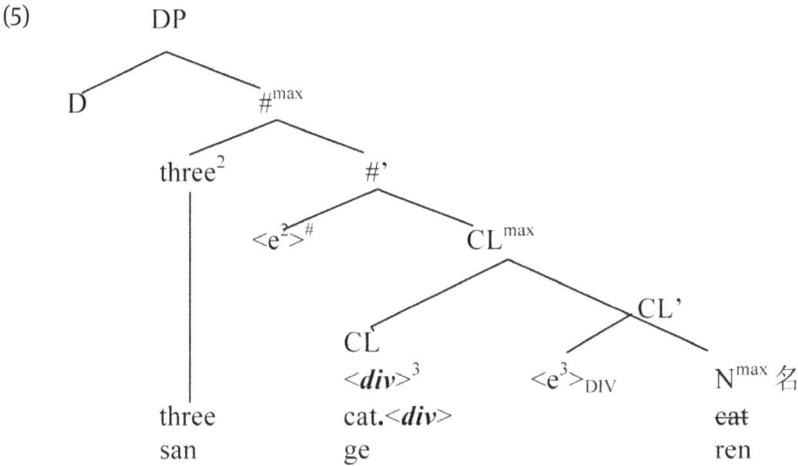

(5)

```
                    DP
           _____/_____
          D                  #^max
                        ____/\____
                   three^2        #'
                     |       ____/_____
                     |   <e^2>^#          CL^max
                     |              _____/_____
                     |            CL                  CL'
                     |          <div>^3          ____/_____
                     |                       <e^3>_DIV        N^max 名
                  three      cat.<div>                          eat
                   san          ge                              ren
```

In the above structure, it is claimed that the classifier head has an open value $<e>_{DIV}$, and the $_{DIV}$ stands for 'divider'. The assumption behind this is that the plural suffix (as -s in English) and the independent classifier (as *ge* in Chinese) can both assign range to $<e>_{DIV}$, and the distinction between them stems from the fact that the 'plural' marker is a spell-out of an abstract head feature *<div>* on a moved N-stem (i.e., 'cat-s' in [5]), whereas the 'classifier' is an independent f-morph (i.e., *ge* in [5]).

Within this system, plural morphology and independent classifier both have the grammatical function as a divider (*div*, henceforth) for nouns in human languages. The crucial fact on which Borer's theory is based is this: "plural morphology and classifier morphology never co-occur" (Borer 2005). That is to say, the plural maker and classifier are in complementary distribution, which is basically true. If this is so, it is not surprising that the plural morphology and the classifier are two sides of same coin: only the realization of **div** varies among different languages.[3]

Given the nominal structural theory developed by Borer, the **div** of noun phrases and the INFL of verb phrases may have a similar grammatical function in locating entities (for nouns) or actions (for verbs) in concrete spatiotemporal reality, respectively. Thus, the grammatical function of time-spatialization 時空 *shikonghua* (or, individualization 個體化 *getihua*[4]) will bring the two categorical structures together in pretty much the same fashion as shown in (6):

(6)   DP: $[_{DP}$ D $[_{\#P}$ # $[_{CL}$ [N]]]
       CP: $[_{CP}$ C $[_{IP}$ I $[_{VP}$ [V]]]

The DP that has a '#' (a numerical node) is similar to CP that has an I (an inflection node) in the sense that the numerical node is required by the realization of *div* for all entities to be individualized in reality, whereas the inflection node is requested by all actions/events to be spatialized in reality. The parallelism between DPs and CPs so designed has some significant consequences. One of the important predictions is this: it becomes possible to have a set of variations among different languages. That is, there can be languages without plural morphology such as Chinese, as well as languages without classifiers such as English. However, no languages have neither a plural morphology nor a classifier system, because the theory requires all languages to have a **div** which must be realized by one way or the other.[5] Unfortunately, as seen in next section, this prediction is challenged by the nominal structure in Pre-Archaic Chinese, where there was none of them, neither plurality nor classifier.

---

3 See Massam (2009) for an alternative analysis based on Borer's theory.

4 The notion of individualization is not new. Actually, Lyons has already discussed the notion for the function of classifier as presupposing an individuated object (1977: 464). 大河内康憲 Dahenei Kangxian (1993) later used this notion to analyze Chinese nouns by claiming that the classifiers have the function of individualizing an entity. Liu (2008), on the other hand, argued that classifiers do not give more content information but merely individualize the noun they modify. Liu Hui (2009) further distinguishes event classifier from entity classifier arguing that both of them are used for individualization.

5 Of course the **div** can also be realized by other means such as dividing marker (分界标记 *fenjie biaoji*) or referential marker (特指标记 *tezhi biaoji*). I would like to thank the anonymous reviewer for pointing out the distinction between referentiality, plurality and classifier. This will be discussed when dealing with the data from classical Chinese in next section.

2 The Challenge from Classical Chinese

A notable fact in Archaic Chinese is this: there were neither classifiers nor plural markers in the nominal structural system, as exemplified in (7).

(7) a. 人而無恥, 不知其可。 (*Odes*, ca. 1000–600 BC)

   rén   ér   wú chǐ,   bú zhī   qí kě.

   person but no sham, not know its accept

   'It is not acceptable that a man has no sham.'

   b. 三人行, 必有吾師。 (*Lunyu*, ca. 400 BC)

   Sān   rén   xíng, bì   yǒu   wú shī.

   three person walk, must have my teacher

   'Among three people, there must be a teacher for me.'

Given examples in (7), it follows that either Bore's theory must be modified, or something else was going on with respect to the nominal system of Archaic Chinese. For the latter, Sagart (1999: 107) has suggested:

> "It is tempting to regard the functions of *k- in verbs and nouns as being fundamentally one: *k- would serve for actions and objects that are well-delimited in time and space, and hence usually concrete and countable. If so, disappearance of *k- between the Old Chinese and Middle Chinese periods deprived Chinese of a means of distinguishing between count and mass nouns. This may have been a factor in the rise of numeral classifiers in Chinese during the same period."

Although it has been seriously criticized and disbelieved by Professor Mei Tzulin,[6] no insights and suggestions have been offered by him for why there is neither plural morphology nor classifiers in Archaic Chinese. On the other hand, Sagart's hypothesis does bring fresh air into the vexed problem and motivate new investigations on the Archaic Chinese NP structures. As we will see below, the idea that there may be special makers employed in nominal structures of Archaic Chinese has inspired scholars to look closely into some peculiar nominal expressions in the language. For example 有 *Gwɯʔ/yǒu*:

(8) a. 盤庚遷于殷, 民不適有居。 (*Shangshu*, ca. 1000 BC)

   Pán Gēng qiān yú Yīn, mín   bú shì   YOU-jū.

   Pan Geng move to Yin, people not suit YOU-place.

   'Pan Geng had moved to Yin (but) the people were not comfort with that place.'

---

6 At the Harvard Symposium on Chinese Historical Syntax; April, 2008.

b. 有王雖小，元子哉。 (*Shangshu*, ca. 1000 BC)

   YOU-wáng suī   xiǎo, yuán zǐ   zāi.
   YOU-Prince though little, first son prt.

   'The Prince, though little, is the first son'.

c. 摽有梅，其實七兮。 (*Odes*, ca. 1000–600 BC)

   piào YOU-méi,   qí   shí qī   xī.
   fall YOU-plum, their prt. Seven prt.

   'The plums are falling and only seven are left!'

It has long been recognized by traditional scholars (cf. Wang 1980) that *you* 有 (**Gwɯʔ*)[7] behaves like a noun-prefix, though no precise grammatical function (or meaning) has been proposed in the literature. Based on the nominal theory given by Borer, and the hypothesis given by Sagart, I would like to argue for the possibility that the **Gwɯʔ* may be indeed a realization of the ***div*** in Proto-Chinese, and it became a remnant in Archaic Chinese. Examples given in (8) actually support this hypothesis. Let's look at them again closely:

(9) a. *Pán Gēng qiān yú Yīn, mín bú shì YOU-jū.*

         'Pan Geng had moved to **Yin**, (but) the people were not comfortable with **that**-place.'

     b. *YOU-wáng suī xiǎo, yuán zǐ zāi.*

         '**The**-Prince, though little, is the **first son**'.

     c. *piào YOU-méi, qí shí qī xī.*

         '**The plums** are falling and only **seven** are left!'

Obviously, all of **Gwɯʔ* 有 used in the above environments have a referential property (i.e., referring to an entity in the sentence). It refers to *Yin* 'the Capital City' in (9a), *Yuanzi* 'prince' in (9b) and *qi shi* 'the seven nuts' in (9c), respectively.

There were also other prefix-like morphemes documented in Pre-Archaic Chinese, exhibiting a function akin to **Gwɯʔ*, like 唯/隹 (**G*ʷ*i/wéi*):

---

7 The phonological reconstruction used here is based on the system of *Phonology of Archaic Chinese* (上古音系 *Shanggu yinxi*).

(10) a. 公車折首百又十又五人，執訊三人。

      Gōng Jū zhé   shǒu bǎi   yòu shí yòu wǔ rén,
      Gong Ju break head hundred and ten and five person,

      zhí-xùn sān   rén.
      arrest   three person.

      'Gong Ju killed hundred and fifteen person and arrested three.'

      唯孚車不克以…唯馬歐盍。(多友鼎 *Duo You Ding*)

      WEI fú   jū   bù kè yǐ… WEI mǎ   qū   xì.
      WEI captured carriage not can use… Wei horse harness sad

      '**The** captured carriages are useless … and **the** horses are harnessed badly.'

  b. 白公父作簠, 擇之金，佳鐈佳鑪。(白公父簠 *Bai Gongfu Fu*)

      Báigōng Fǔ zuò   Fǔ, zé   zhī jīn,
      Baigong Mr. make Fu, choose it   copper,

      WEI jiáo   WEI lú
      WEI jiao (material) WEI lu (material)

      'Mr. Baigong made a Fu[8], chose nice metal for it: **the** elegant Jiao and **the** elegant Lu.'

Whether or not all *Gʷi-s 唯/隹 in Pre-Archaic Chinese functioned like *Gwɯʔ is another issue. Examples in (10) show quite clearly that *Gʷi does have a function of specifying an individual entity in the sentence.

Regarding facts in (9)–(10),[9] it is plausible that there may be a referentiality or specificity system in the nominal structure of proto-Chinese, even if only a few observable remnants are left in Archaic Chinese, due presumably to the typological change from syntheticity (before Archaic Chinese, 1000 BC) to analyticity (after Archaic Chinese, 200 AD).[10]

Given the possibility suggested above, I would like to argue that the morphosyntactic realization of **div** proposed by Borer must be further elaborated according to diachronic facts in Archaic Chinese. That is, **div** may also be realized

---

8 A kind of ritual vessel used for worship of god and ancestors in Archaic Chinese.

9 See also Redouane Djamouri 罗端 (2010) for further evidence about YOU as Divider marker in Archaic Chinese (even if he treats YOU as a plural marker which is technically different from the analysis given here.)

10 For more arguments on the typological change from Old Chinese to Middle Chinese see Zhang 1939, Xu 2006, Huang 2007 and Feng 2009.

by specificity and referentiality in terms of individualization of the entity in human languages through either independent morpheme or affixation in a language. That is to say, time and space can also be individualized as specific referential entities. Put differently: identifying an object and counting an object have the same effect of making the object an individual entity. Therefore, the two apparently different functions actually have the same effect structuralized as *div* seen in (5). If this is so, it will resolve the vexing problem raised by (Pre-)Archaic Chinese (a system with neither plural nor classifier) and encourage researchers to search for new discoveries about the old nominal systems from Pre-Archaic to Archaic Chinese, as well as to search for reasons for the newly developed classifiers, which will be explored in next section.

6 The Problems Involved in the Emergence of Classifiers

As seen in section one, the realization of *div* varies in different languages. In section two, we have argued that the *div* may be realized by specific and referential markers (特指／有指標記 *tezhi/youzhi biaoji*) in Proto- and Archaic Chinese. Given these facts, we are ready to see a parametric change from a referential-lexically realized *div*-system (Pre-Archaic Chinese) to a classifier-realized *div*-system (Post-Archaic Chinese). As pointed out in Wang (1980), Liu (1965), Peyraube (1998), Zhang C. (2009) and many others, the change of the nominal structure began roughly in the Shang dynasty (1600–1046 BC) and was basically established during the Wei-Jin Periods (ca. 400 AD).[11] For example:

(11) *Ca. 11th Century BC, Shang-Zhou Dynasties*
      [N Num N/CL]

   a. 馬三匹
       mǎ   sān   pǐ
       horse three mate/CL
       'three horses'

---

11 The term 'established change' used here refers to the grammar (i.e., the structure and its function) of classifiers, not individual changes (i.e., from *mei* to *tiao, tou* and *wei* for fish … etc.)

206 BC–220 AD, Han Dynasty
[N Num CL]

b. 竹竿萬个 (*Shi Ji, Huozhi Liezhuan*)

    zhú-gān   wàn   gè

    bamboo-pole ten-thousand CL

    'ten thousand bamboo poles'

[Num CL N]

c. 一个嫡男 (*Guoyu Wuyu*)

    yí   gè dí   nán

    one CL legitimate son

    'a son of first wife.'

200–500 AD, Wei-Jin Period
[Num CL N]

d. 三个石柱 (*Sou Shen Ji*)

    sān gè shí   zhù

    three CL stone pole

    'three stone poles.'

A striking phenomenon involved in the classifier development is the fact that generic classifiers were developed earlier than specific classifiers at the beginning of the emergence of classifiers. Zhang (2009) observed that in the Han dynasty documents, there were 55 nouns occurring with a general classifier (*mei*) whereas only 11 took either a specific classifier or a generic one among all the nouns that took classifiers. Up to the Wei-Jin Period, however, there were 75 nouns that co-occurred with a general classifier but 43 nouns that occurred with a specific classifier. That is:

(12) Statistics of Classifiers in Han Period and Wei-Jin Period.

	Ns with General classifiers	**Ns with specific classifiers**
Han Dynasty (206 BC–220 AD)	55	11
Wei-Jin Period (220–420 AD)	75	43

The statistics in (12) indicates that during the Han Dynasty, "generic classifiers were used for nouns that do no have a specific numerical classifier," (Zhang 2009) whereas the ones that take a generic classifier in the Han Dynasty developed to occur with specific classifiers during the Wei-Jin Period. For example (taken from Zhang, 2009):[12]

(13) List of Classifiers in Han Period and Six Dynasties

Nouns	Han Period (206 BC–220 AD)	Six Dynasties (222–589 AD)
杯 cup	枚 *méi* 'stick', 具 *jù* 'utensil'	口 *kŏu* 'mouth', 枚 *méi* 'stick'
筆 writing brush	枚 *méi* 'stick'	枚 *méi* 'stick', 枝 *zhī* 'branch', 管 *guăn* 'bamboo branch'
車 carriage	枚 *méi* 'stick', 乘 *shèng* 'a set of carriage horses', 兩 *liăng* 'pair of wheels'	乘 *shèng* 'a set of carriage horses', 兩 *liăng* 'pair of wheels'
刀 knife	枚 *méi* 'stick'	口 *kŏu* 'mouth', 枚 *méi* 'stick', 具 *jù* 'utensil'
豆 been	枚 *méi* 'stick'	粒 *lì* 'granule', 个 *gè* 'individual', 枚 *méi* 'stick', 顆 *kē* 'granule'
斧 axe	枚 *méi* 'stick'	口 *kŏu* 'mouth', 枚 *méi* 'stick'
弓 bow	枚 *méi* 'stick', 具 *jù* 'utensil', 張 *zhāng* 'opening'	張 *zhāng* 'to open a bow'
狗 dog	枚 *méi* 'stick'	个 *gè* 'individual', 頭 *tóu* 'head'
龜 turtle	枚 *méi* 'stick'	枚 *méi* 'stick', 頭 *tóu* 'head'

---

12 Zhang has exhaustively calculated the classifiers used in 17 texts from Han to Wei-Jing and Southern-Northern Dynasties.

Nouns	Han Period (206 BC–220 AD)	Six Dynasties (222–589 AD)
雞 chicken	枚 *méi* 'stick', 只 *zhī* 'single'	頭 *tóu* 'head', 只 *zhī* 'single'
蛋 egg	枚 *méi* 'stick'	枚 *méi* 'stick', 顆 *kē* 'granule'
箭 arrow	枚 *méi* 'stick'	只 *zhī* 'single'
鏡 mirror	枚 *méi* 'stick'	个 *gè* 'individual', 枚 *méi* 'stick'
鳥 bird	枚 *méi* 'stick'	口 *kǒu* 'mouth', 頭 *tóu* 'head'
牛 cow	枚 *méi* 'stick', 皮 *pí* 'skin', 頭 *tóu* 'head'	口 *kǒu* 'mouth', 頭 *tóu* 'head'
錢 currency	枚 *méi* 'stick'	个 *gè* 'individual', 枚 *méi* 'stick', 文 *wén* 'lines'
券 bamboo bond	枚 *méi* 'stick'	支 *zhī* 'branch'
繩 string, rope	枚 *méi* 'stick'	枚 *méi* 'stick', 條 *tiáo* 'strip'
石 stone	枚 *méi* 'stick'	枚 *méi* 'stick', 片 *piàn* 'piece', 段 *duàn* 'section'
矢 arrow	發 *fā* 'shoot', 个 *gè* 'individual', 枚 *méi* 'stick', 支 *zhī* 'branch'	發 *fā* 'shoot', 只 *zhī* 'single'
獸 animal	个 *gè* 'individual'	頭 *tóu* 'head'
樹木 threes	枚 *méi* 'stick', 樹 *shù* 'tree'	个 *gè* 'individual', 根 *gēn* 'root', 株 *zhū* 'stem'

Nouns	Han Period (206 BC–220 AD)	Six Dynasties (222–589 AD)
索 cable, rope	枚 *méi* 'stick'	張 *zhāng* 'opening'
席 mat	枚 *méi* 'stick', 具 *jù* 'utensil'	具 *jù* 'utensil', 領 *lǐng* 'collar'
印 stamp	枚 *méi* 'stick'	枚 *méi* 'stick', 紐 *niǔ* 'knob'
魚 fish	枚 *méi* 'stick', 頭 *tóu* 'head'	頭 *tóu* 'head', 首 *shǒu* 'head', 枚 *méi* 'stick'
珠 pearl	枚 *méi* 'stick'	孔 *kǒng* 'eyelet'
竹竿 bamboo pole	個 *gè* 'individual'	個 *gè* 'individual', 節 *jié* 'node'

While there is no doubt, as Zhang has observed, that *mei* and *ge* were used as generic classifiers as long as they emerged as numerical-classifiers in the Han dynasty, a distinction between the two seems not have been recognized in the literature. For example:

– 枚 *méi* in Han Period
(taken from Zhang Cheng 2009, Chen Lianjun 2003, Wei Desheng 2000, Huang Shengzhang 1961, Peyraube 1998, Zhang Junzhi 2004, etc.)

(14) a. 絮巾一枚，黃布禪衣一領 ... (EPT51·66)
   xù   jīn   yì   méi, huáng bù   chán   yī   yì   lǐng ...
   cotton towel one **mei**, yellow cloth Buddhist gown one collar...
   'one cotton towel and one yellow buddhistic cloth gown.'

   b. 繩十枚。(EPT59·124A)
   shéng shí méi
   robe   ten **mei**
   'ten robes.'

c. 木十五枚…車二枚,…軸一。(EPT57·60)

mù   shí-wǔ méi … chē   èr méi, … zhóu yī.

timber fifteen **mei** … carriage er **mei** … axle yi.

'fifteen trunks … two carriages … (and) one axle.'

d. 筆一枚。(M6D13, Zheng)

bǐ   yì   méi.

brush one **mei**

'one (writing) brush.'

e. 具樁六枚，鉤十枚，弓二枚，弩二枚。(Ju Jian: 383)

jùzhuāng liù méi, gòu   shí méi, gōng èr   méi,

juzhuang six **mei**, hook ten **mei**, bow two **mei**,

nǔ   èr méi.

cross-bow two **mei**,

'there are six Juzhuang-s, ten hooks, two bows and two cross-bows.'

f. 梁王曰:"若寡人國小也, 尚有 (徑寸之珠照車前後各十二) 乘者十枚 (奈何以萬乘之國而無寶乎?)"
(Shi Ji, Tianjing Zhongwan Shijia)

Liáng Wáng yuē: "ruò   guǎrén guó   xiǎo yě, (…)"

Liang King say: though my   country small prt. (…)

shàng yǒu (…) shèng   zhě shí méi (…)."

still   have (…) carriages Prt. ten **mei** (…)."

'The King of Liang said: "though my country is smaller, I still have ten (…) sets of carriages (…)."'

g. 鳥一枚。(Shuo Wen)

niǎo yì   méi.

bird one **mei**

'one bird.'

h. … 大柔十枚…。(Shang Han Lun)

…dà-róu   shí méi…

…Darou (herbs) ten **mei**

'ten Darou herbs.'

i. … 取四方石一枚, 六方石一枚。(Zhong Ben Qi Jing)

…qǔ   sì-fāng   shí yì méi, liù-fāng shí yì   méi.

…Take quadrilateral stone one **mei**, hexagon stone one **mei**

'…to take one quadrilateral stone and one hexagon stone.'

– 簡/个 *gè* in Han Dynasty

(taken from Zhang Cheng 2009, Hong Cheng 1963 and Da Zhengyu 2004)

(15)   a.   其禮 … 少牢則羊左肩七個 … (*Liji, Shaoyi*)

        qí lǐ…   Shàoláo zé   yáng zuǒ-jiān   qī   gè…

        Its ritual… Shaolao then sheep left-shoulder seven **ge**

        'By Ritual, seven sheep left-shoulders are used for Shaolao worship.'

    b.   譬如群獸然，一个負矢，群獸皆走。(*Guoyu, Wuyu*)

        pìrú qún   shòu rán, yī   gè fù shǐ,   qún   shòu jiē zǒu.

        For group animal like, one **ge** get arrow, group beast all run.

        'Like animals, if one got shot, the others all run away.'

    c.   一個嫡女 … ，一個嫡男 … 。(*Guoyu, Wuyu*)

        yí   gè dí-nǚ…,   yí   gè dí-nán…

        one **ge** legitimate daughter…, one **ge** legitimate-son.

        'one legitimate daughter…, one legitimate-son.'

    d.   竹竿萬个。(*Shi Ji, Huozhi liezhuan*)

        zhú-gān   wàn   gè.

        bamboo-pole ten-thousand **ge**

        'Ten thousand bamboo poles.'

    e.   鹿皮四个。(*Guoyu, Qiyu*)

        lù   pí   sì   gè.

        deer skin four **ge**

        'four deer skins.'

– 個 *gè* in Wei-Jin Period **(**taken from Liu Shiru: 1965)

(16)   a.   … 取其剔齒纖一个。

        (Lu Yun, *Yu Xiong Pingyuan Shu*)

        …qǔ   qí tī-chǐ-qiān   yí   gè

        …take his pick-clean-teeth-stick one **ge**

        '…take one toothpick.'

    b.   且寺內先有數个猛狗，但見一狼，狗無不競來吠齧。

        (Wang Zhao, *Sheli Ganying Jibielu*)

        qiě sì   nèi   xiān yǒu shù   gè měng   gǒu,

        Temple inside have   several CL violent dog,

dàn   jiàn yì   láng, gǒu wúbù jìng lái   fèi   niè.
sudden see one wolf, dog all   even come bark bite.

'The temple has several violent dogs and when they suddenly saw a wolf, all of them barked and came out to fight.'

c. 善法寺...有兩个樺樹...

(Wang Zhao, *Sheli Ganying Jibielu*)

Shànfǎ sì...   yǒu liǎng gè Huà shù...
Shanfa Temple... has two **gè** Hua tree

'There are two Hua trees in (...) Shang fasi.'

d. 堂屋西壁下...有三个石柱。 (*Sou Shen Ji*, Vol. 1)

táng-wū   xī   bì   xià...   yǒu sān   gè   shí   zhù.
central-room west wall under... have three **gè** stone pole

'there are three stone poles...under the west wall of the central room.'

e. 天生男女共一處，願得兩个成翁嫗。

(*Hengchuiquci, Zhuonuo Ge*)

tiān   shēng nán nǚ   gòng yí   chù,
Haven birth male female all   one place,

yuàn-dé   liǎng gè chéng   wēng   yù.
wish-have two **gè** become old-man old-woman

'The haven made male and females together, (I) wish (your) two love each other forever.'

f. 誰論洛水，一个河神。

(Yu Xin, *Liangdonggong xingyuming*)

shuí lùn Luò shuǐ, yí   gè Hé Shén
who say Luo river, one **gè** River God

'Who says of Luo, a God of the River.'

The *méi* 枚, though used for most nouns (and thus earning it the name of generic classifier), occurs overwhelmingly in the [N + Num + *mei*] structure in (and before) the Han Dynasty; whereas the *gè* 個/箇, though rarely used as a classifier before Han, as Zhang (2009) has pointed out, commonly occurs in the structure of [Num + *ge* + N] in the Vei-Jin Period. That is to say, even if *méi* 枚 and *gè* 箇 were both used as general classifiers occurring with a number and a noun, they were different chronologically and structurally:

(17)   Chronology and structure of calssifiers in Han Period and Wei-Jin Period

Chronology	Structure
Han Dynasty (and before)	[Noun Num CL (méi/gè)]
Wei-Jin Period (and after)	[Num CL (gè/méi) Noun]

This contrast, as we observe here, is extremely important for the development of classifiers in classical Chinese.

First, as argued in Wu Fuxiang, Feng Shengli and Huang Zhengde (2006), the structure of [N Num CL] (i.e., 人十個 *rén shí gè* 'people ten CL') and the structure of [Num CL N] (i.e., 十個人 *shí gè rén* 'ten CL people') are different. The former is a predicative structure while the latter is nominal, as evidenced in the following example (taken from Wu *et al.*, 2006)[13]:

(18)   賜米人五斛。(*Quan Jin Wen*, Vol. 30)

 cì   mǐ   rén   wǔ   Hú.
give   rice   person   five   Hu   (a measure of grain)

'give every person five Hu of rice.'

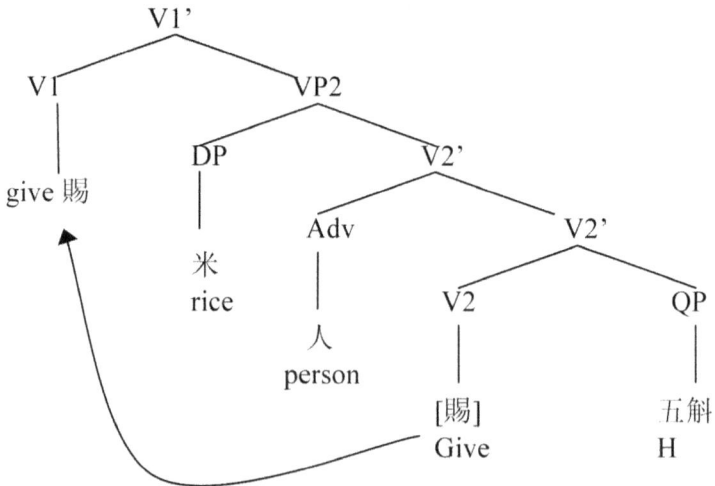

---

13 The analysis and the tree diagram presented here were developed by J. Huang in Wu Fuxiang, Feng Shengli and J. Huang (2006), see also Liu (1965: 48–52) for more examples of this type. The following example also supports the predicate analysis:

Though the [N + Num + (adverb) + CL] is a predicate structure shown by the example (18) before the Wei-Jin Period (220–420 AD), it does not logically mean that the same linear forms in (Pre-)Archaic Chinese should be analyzed the same as there are for the Wei-Jin Period, given the argument that Pre-Archaic Chinese may be a different type of language in terms of (1) its word order (i.e., an SOV language as Yu (1981), Feng (1995)... etc., have suggested), (2) its nominal system (i.e., a lexically-realized *div* type language as seen above) and (3) its typology (i.e., an synthetic language as SL. Zhang (1945), D. Xu (2000) and J. Huang (2010) have suggested). In addition to the above properties, Classifiers (or semi-classifiers) in Modern minority SOV languages (like the Yi language exemplified in [23]) also developed from the nominal structure of [N Num CL]. Taking all these considerations into account, it is plausible to consider the [N Num CL] structures in (Pre-)Archaic Chinese as remnants of the lexically-realized *div* system. In other words, it is possible that the [N Num CL] is analyzed as a nominal structure in the old SOV grammar in Pre-Archaic Chinese, and also as a predicate structure in the newly developed analytical language after the Eastern Han (Feng 2009). To illustrate this point, comparing the two syntactic analyses in (19):

(19)   Earlier Structure

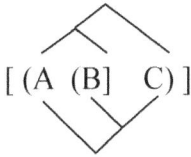

[(A (B]   C)]

Later Structure

(19) represents a structure of any phrases. The re-bracketing process is what 'reanalysis' is about and it happens all the time in the history of syntactic changes of human languages.[14] Under the hypothesis given above, the [N Num

---

(i)   腎有兩枚。 (*Shi Ji, Bianque Liezhuan*)
      shèn yǒu liǎng méi
      kidney has two   mei
      'there are two kidneys'

14 It is always possible that an early-structure, say A, can be reanalyzed as a late-structure B in two different asynchronous systems. For example, the SOV word order in Archaic Chinese (cf. 汝何知 *rǔ hé zhī* 'You what know') is a remnant structure from Proto-Chinese and it was reanalyzed within the SVO system of Archaic Chinese by movement of the *wh*-object to a preverbal position (Feng 1996).

mei] and [Num *ge* N] will be treated differently from previous analysis because if [N Num *mei*] is a nominal structure (of the old SOV system), it will be different from the nominal structure of [Num CL N] (of the new SVO grammar).[15] If, on the other hand, the [N Num *mei*] is a predicate structure (through a reanalysis on the old structure by new generations of the Late Han dynasty), it will also be different from the nominal structure of [Num CL N] as well. That is:

(20) [N Num *mei*]$_{NP}$ (Pre-Archaic) ≠ [Num *ge* N]$_{NP}$ — typological difference

  [N Num *mei*]$_{VP}$ (Post-Han) ≠ [Num *ge* N]$_{NP}$ — structural difference

The above hypothesis is strongly supported by a stunning fact given in (17): as far as chronology and the original property of generic classifiers are concerned, the generic classifier positions are almost in complementary distribution. Before Han, generic classifiers (overwhelmingly *mei*) occur in [N Num **CL**], while after Han, generic classifiers (mainly *ge*) occur in [Num **CL** N], in each of their early stages of classifier developments.

These facts raise some interesting and important questions with respect to previous analysis.

First, if *mei*, as a generic classifier, developed from a [N Num **CL**] predicate structure before (or during) Han according to Wu *et al.* (2006), but *ge*, as a generic classifier, originated from the [Num **CL** N] nominal structure during and after Han as seen before, how could the two different structures produce a same result of generic classifiers? This question is difficult to answer by treating the [N Num *mei*] as a predicate structure (Wu *et al.* 2006), because within that structure (i.e., the [Num *mei*] predicate), *mei* cannot be a classifier since there is no noun for which a classifier is needed. Put differently, there is no classifier position within the [Num *mei*] predicate, and this inevitably leaves us with a "predicate-classifier" contradiction. Obviously, the predicate-hypothesis cannot explain why generic classifiers like *mei* developed in a [N, [Num mei]$_{Predicate}$] structure. On the other hand, the plausible answer, as suggested above, may be this: the [N Num *mei*] may be indeed a nominal structure of the SOV system in Pre-Archaic Chinese before (and around) the 11th century BC, and accordingly, a generic classifier like *mei* could legitimately be developed in that position.

---

15 Actually, there is evidence showing that a head-initial nominal structure in archaic Chinese (cf. 瞻彼中林 *zhān bǐ zhōng lín* = look it middle wood 'look at the inside of woords') changed to a head-final structure such as *zhōng lín* 中林 'inside woods' > *lín zhōng* 林中 'woods inside'. Examples like this support the argument made here for the word order change of Classifiers-nominal structures from archaic Chinese to medieval Chinese. I would like to thank the anonymous reviewer for pointing this out for me.

Given this analysis, it becomes plausible why generic classifiers were first developed in the final position of the nominal structure and the predicate-classifier contradiction can be resolved as well. Of course, under this analysis the structure given in (18) will be taken as a result of reanalysis by later generations (SVO speakers) on the old SOV system.

While the predicate-classifier contradiction can be resolved as seen above, there is still an empirical question difficult to resolve by traditional analysis, namely, why generic, rather than specific classifiers were created in the beginning (but not later on) of classifier developments? The general view of classifier development is that specific classifier/s developed first and then more general classifiers, building upon the specific ones, developed later on. However, the actual fact is just the opposite: a generic one (like *mei*) appeared in the beginning and specific ones followed. Why is that so?

In fact, Zhang has clearly recognized the question and made an interesting suggestion: it was the requirement of grammar, not that of semantics as some scholars have believed, that gave rise to the category of numeral classifier which emerged and formed in the period of Late Archaic Chinese (200 AD). This syntactic explanation, as I would like to argue, has significantly advances our understanding of the development of classifiers in Chinese because it provides deeper insight of the grammatical requirements: the classifier is required by syntax, thus the generic one/s is/are favored to fill up the classifier position wherever and whenever there is one.

Though the syntactic approach has brought a significant insight into the study of Chinese classifier developments, it encounters a serious challenge when we scrutinize the data exemplified as follows ([21a] is repeated from [16b]).

(21) a. 且寺內先有數个猛狗，但見一狼，狗無不競來吠齧。
       (Wang Zhao, *Sheli Gangyin Jibielu*)

       qiě sì   nèi   xiān yǒu shù   gè měng   gǒu,
       Temple inside have   several CL violent dog,

       dàn   jiàn yì   láng, gǒu wúbù jìng lái   fèi   niè.
       sudden see one wolf, dog all   even come bark bite.

       'The temple has several violent dogs and when they suddenly saw a wolf, all of them barked and came out to fight.'

     b. 七枚熱鐵丸…十八鐵丸。 (*Fa yuan zhu lin*)

       qī   méi rè tiě   wán… shí-bā   tiě   wán
       seven CL hot iron ball… ten-eight iron ball…

       '(there are) seven hot iron balls… (and) eighteen iron ball…'

If, as one would expect, the general classifier is required by grammar, why does the grammar not equally require a/the general classifier in the same environment? This question cannot be adequately answered with a purely syntactic approach. The dilemma we are facing is this: there must be a grammatical requirement otherwise it is difficult to explain why a general classifier was developed in the early stages of classifier developments. Yet, there must not be such a requirement, otherwise it is difficult to explain why there are nouns that do not need a classifier in the same syntactic environment by the same writer. To put it differently, there is hardly a syntactic reason why *měng gǒu* 猛狗 'violent dog' needs *gè* 個, while *láng* 狼 'wolf' does not in (21a); and why *rè tiě wán* 熱鐵丸 'hot iron ball' needs *méi* 枚 when there are seven, while *tiě wán* 鐵丸 'iron ball' does not when there are eighteen in (21b). If there is no syntactic reason for why some nouns need a classifier *mei/ge* but some others do not, the emergence of general classifiers cannot be attributed to a requirement of grammar, because there is no grammar (categorical requirement) required in examples like (21).

Of course, the random emergences of some syntactic features (cf. the ***div*** in the present case) may reflect an unstable rate of grammatical change that varies in time and place as is sometimes observed in diachronic syntax in different languages. However, it is crucial to note that the rate-variation of a new grammar generally results from (or determined by) various linguistic factors, including (1) different syntactic environments, (2) different semantic fields, (3) different stylistic devises (文白之差 *wén-bái-zhī-chā*), (4) different genre (文體的區別 *wéntǐ de qūbié*), (5) different register (語體的不同 *yǔtǐ de bùtóng*), or even different grammars between two generations (cf. diglossia).[16] Unfortunately, there were no obvious examples that would be considered as factors that could give rise to the classifier variations in classical Chinese. What we actually found are free variations like the following.

(22) a.   夫人曰：我今與汝**百**枚金錢。其婢報曰：我不須。
      夫人複告：與汝二**百**！乃至千枚金錢。
      (*Zengyi'ahan Jing*)

      fū-rén   yuē: wǒ jīn   yǔ   rǔ   bǎi   méi
      Madam   say: I   now give you hundred **mei**

      jīn-qián.   Qí   bì   bào   yuē:
      gold-money. Her slave-girl reply say:

---

16 See Feng (2010a) for relevant discussions on stylistics, genre and diglossia of a Register Grammar (语体语法 *Yuti Yufa*).

wǒ bù xū.   Fū-rén fù   gào: yǔ   rǔ   èr   bǎi!
I   not need. Madam again tell: give you two hundred!

Nǎi zhì   qiān   méi jīn-qián.
Even upto thousand ***mei*** gold-money.

'The madam said: "now I give you one hundred (pieces of gold) money." Her slave-girl replied: "I don't need it". Madam tell her again: "give you two hundred!" (The number of money) even (goes) up to one thousand.'

b. (菩薩)探囊中五百銀錢，盡用與之。瞿夷念: 華極直數錢，
    乃雇五百。貪其銀寶，與五莖華，自留二枚。
    (*Taizi Ruiying benqi Jing Shang*)

    (*Púsà) tàn   náng zhōng wǔ bǎi   yín-qián,*
    Buddha search bag inside five hundred silver-money,

    jìn yòng yǔ   zhī. Qú Yí niàn: huā   jí
    all use   give her. Qu Yi think: flower outmost

    zhí   shù qián, nǎi gù   wǔ bǎi.:   tān
    worth few money, even spend five hundred crave

    qí yín-bǎo,   yǔ wǔ jīng huā, zì   liú. èr   méi
    its silver-gem, give five stem flower, self keep two ***mei***

    'Buddha searched out five hundreds of silver-money from his bag and gave them all to Ju Yi. Ju Yi thought that the flowers cost outmost a few pieces of silver, he even spent five hundred for it. But she is greedy for the money, so she gave five flowers to Buddha and kept two for herself.'

As seen in (22a) and (22b), *mei* appears randomly with the same noun: *jīn-qián* 金錢 'gold-money' or *yín-qián* 銀錢 'silver-money'. It shows clearly that the alternative usages of the generic classifier have nothing to do with the different types of nouns, and hardly any genre or styles are responsible for the variations as well. This, once again, causes a problem for the syntactic account.

Now we are facing a syntactic dilemma again: on the one hand, the appearance of general classifiers indicates a change of grammatical system of the numerical structure NP; on the other hand, the non-categorical (or random) usages of the general classifiers give no condition for the syntactic approach to be held. The problem then is: why there are general classifiers randomly appearing in the same syntactic environments in the beginning of their development?

Based on the facts given before and regarding the syntactic problems outlined above, I would like to propose that the emergence of the general classifiers is motivated by the grammar of prosody. That is to say, a classifier is required or at least preferred in environments where prosody is defective and thus a classifier is used to overcome the prosodic defect. This implies that in environments where prosody is satisfied, no metrical help is necessary and thus a classifier is optional. This hypothesis explains, as seen in next section, why there are variations between [N [Num]$_\sigma$ [CL]$_\sigma$] and [N [Num]$_{\sigma\sigma}$ __ in the (Pre-)Han times, and between [[Num]$_\sigma$ [CL]$_\sigma$ N] and [[Num]$_{\sigma\sigma}$ __N] during and after Han dynasties (ca. 206 BC–220 AD), during the process of the change. In other words, whether or not the nominal structure in early stages of their developments is formed with a classifier, is a reflection of the prosodic requirement, a topic that will be explored in details in next section.

7 Prosodically Motivated Classifiers in Archaic Chinese

How could prosody affect the emergence of classifiers in a nominal structure? Before we answer this question, it is worthwhile to look at the prosodic behavior of the classifiers in Modern Yi, a minority language spoken in southern China (tested by Hu).

(23) *Mandarin*   *Modern Yi*

 a. *wǔ gè rén*   a'. *co   nga yuo*   a''. *co   *nga*
     five CL people   people five CL   people five
     'five people'

 b. *wǔshí gè rén*   b'. *co   nge-ci yuo*   b''. *co   nge-ci*
     fifty CL people   people fifty   CL   people fifty
     'fifty people'   'fifty people'   'fifty people'

 c. *wǔ gè rén*   c'. *co   -ma *nge*   c''. *co   -ma nge ci*
     five CL people   people CL   five   people CL fity
     'five people'   'five people'   'fifty people'

What we can see from the above examples is clearly a prosodic effect on the numerical forms in its nominal structure:[17]

---

17 In Yi, the Cl for 'people' varies depending on the number and phonological environment, but they will not affect the argument presented here.

(24) (i) In the structure of [N + monosyllabic numerical form], if the
           NF (numerical form/number) is monosyllabic, then the NF is
           not acceptable (23a″);

     (ii) In the [N + monosyllabic numerical form +CL], if the NF + CL
           form is a disyllabic unit, then the result is acceptable (23a′).

     (iii) If the NF is disyllabic itself, the result is also acceptable
           (i.e., [N + disyllabic numerical form + __])
           even if there is no CL (23b″/c″).

The striking fact about the classifier structure in Modern Yi is that in the
final position of the numerical expressions, whether or not there is a classifier
depends on the prosodic qualities of the numerical form. If it is monosyllabic,
a CL is needed for otherwise the [N + Num] form is prosodically ineffable. If,
on the other hand, the numerical form is disyllabic, then the result of [N + Num]
is grammatical without the CL. Doubtlessly, prosody affects the use of the
classifier.

Given the prosodically constrained classifier in Yi, I would like to suggest
that the emergence of classifiers in classical Chinese may also be affected by
the same force of prosody. This hypothesis is supported by the following facts.
First, like the examples in Yi, when the numeric word is monosyllabic, it hardly
occurs at the end of the NP. For example, there are hardly any cases like the
following in our data:[18]

(25) a. *左肩七 (cf. [15a])

          * zuǒ-jiān   qī
          left-shoulder seven'

     b. *竹竿萬 (cf. [15d])

          * zhú-gān   wàn
          bamboo-pole ten-thousand'

---

18 We are well aware that there are a few counterexamples like the following found in classical
documents *Zuozhuan* (左传, 定公年):

(ii) 公子地有白马四。
      Gōngzi Dì yǒu bái-mǎ   sì
      Gongzi Di has white-horse four
      'Gongzi Di has four white-horses.'

However, it is undeniable that monosyllabic numbers often occur with a classifier in a nominal
structure as seen above and the exceptions are sporadically few. Nevertheless, more work is
needed to account for the exceptions in future research.

c. *絮巾一 (cf. [14a])

    * *xù-jīn*   *yī*
    cotton-twale one'

Secondly, monosyllabic numeric words seem also to be excluded from the [[Num]$_\sigma$ __ [NN]$_{\sigma\sigma}$] structure, hence there are almost no examples like (26).

(26) a. *一負矢 (cf. [15b])

      * *yī* *fù* *shǐ*
      one got shoot'

  b. *一嫡男 (cf. [15c])

      * *yì* *dí-nán*
      one legitimate-son'

  c. *數猛狗 (cf. [16b])

      **shù* *měng-gǒu*
      few violent-dog'

  d. *三石柱 (cf. [16d])

      **sān* *shí-zhù*
      three stone-pole'

  e. *千金錢 (cf. [22a])

      **qiān* *jīn-qián*
      thousand gold-money

Given the "non-existent" evidence and the proso-syntactic hypothesis above, it is expected that monosyllabic numerical words should commonly occur with a classifier in [N Num CL] before (and during) Han and in [Num CL N] during (and after) Han. This prediction is born out as shown in examples seen above and given below.

(27) – [N Num + CL]

  a. 斧二枚。(*Dunhuang Hanjian*: 690)

      fǔ *èr* *méi*
      axe two *mei*

      'two axes'

b. = (14e) 具椿六枚，鈎十枚，弓二枚，弩二枚。(*Jujian*: 383)

   jùzhuāng liù méi, gōu shí méi, gōng èr méi, nǔ èr méi.
   juzhuang six **mei**, hook ten mei, bow two **mei**, cross-bow two **mei**,
   'there are six Juzhuang-s, ten hooks, two bows and two cross-bows.'

c. 買狗四枚。(*Jujian*: 343)

   mǎi gǒu sì méi
   buy dog four **mei**
   'To buy four dogs.'

d. 痱樹一枚。(*Jujian*: 516)

   fēi-shù yí méi
   fei-tree one **mei**
   'one Fei tree.'

– [Num + CL NN]

e. = (15c) 一個嫡女...，一個嫡男...。(*Guoyu, Wuyu*)

   yí gè dí-nǚ...,   yí gè dí-nán...
   one **ge** legitimate daughter..., one **ge** legitimate-son.
   'one legitimate daughter..., one legitimate-son.'

f. = (16c) 善法寺...有兩个樺樹...。
   (王劭 Wang Zhao, 舍利感應記別錄 *Sheli Ganying Jibielu*)

   Shànfǎ sì...   yǒu liǎng gè Huà shù...
   Shanfa Temple... has two **ge** Hua tree
   'There are two Hua trees in (...) Shang fasi.'

g. = (16d) 堂屋西壁下...有三个石柱。(*Sou Shen Ji*, Vol. 1)

   táng-wū xī bì xià... yǒu sān gè shí zhù.
   central-room west wall under... have three **ge** stone pole
   'there are three stone poles...under the west wall of the central room.'

The commonly observed classifiers almost all occur after a monosyllabic numerical word, indicating strongly that it is prosody that motivates the use of classifier in the very beginning of their developments.

Although we don't have native speakers to provide grammatical judgments on the prosodic structures (as we have for the Modern Yi examples), the examples given in (25) and (27) are quite self-evidenced: a classifier emerges when the number is monosyllabic (such as *er* 'two', *qī* 'seven', *bǎi* 'hundred', *qiān* 'thousand'), while it can be omitted if the number is disyllabic (such as *èr-bǎi* 'two hundred', *wǔ-bǎi* 'five hundred', *shí-bǎ* 'eighteen'), in both the [N Num CL] and the [Num CL N] structures as summarized in (28).

(28)　a.

$$f$$

[NN　$[\#]_\sigma$　$[\ ]_\sigma$]$_{DP}$
絮巾　一　**CL** (枚)

　　b.

$$f$$

$[[\#]_\sigma$　$[\ ]_\sigma$　NN]$_{DP}$
三　**CL** (个)　石柱

Obviously, the proso-syntactic pattern of [N+ $[[\#]_\sigma + [CL]_\sigma]$] in Chinese parallels the proso-syntactic pattern in Modern Yi (23). The correlation between the two languages should not be considered a coincidence, instead it may reflect a mechanism of more general process in classifier developments, as Dai Qingxia and Jiang Yin (2005) have observed:[19]

> "In Tibetan-Burman languages, if the numerical words are monosyllabic, then individual classifiers are relatively well-developed; if, on the other hand, the numerical words are polysyllabic, individual classifiers are generally underdeveloped or extremely rare [藏緬語中，凡是數詞是單音節的，個體量詞就比較發達；數詞是多音節的，個體量詞就不夠發達或者極少]."

> "The numerical words in Jingpo language are mostly polysyllabic, as a result, individual classifiers are not able to be developed; On the other hand, the numerical words in Ha'ni language are all monosyllabic ... individual classifiers are thus flourished there [景頗語的數詞以多音節爲主，所以個體量詞得不到發展；而哈尼語的數詞都是單音節的 ... 個體量詞就很豐富]."

Given the cross-linguistics tendency summarized by Dai and Jiang, it becomes quite plausible that prosody may indeed be the trigger for the birth of classifier syntax not only in Chinese but also in Burman-Tibetan languages as well.

This hypothesis receives further support from a parallel development of the light-verb syntax. It has been observed (Xu 2003; Hu 2005, Feng 2008) that there were more and more phonetically realized lightverbs after Eastern Han Dynasty (ca. 25 BC–220 AD). For example, do/make 作 *zuò*:

---

19 I would like to thank Professor Hu Suhua for confirming with the principle author of the paper the statements given here.

(29) – *zuò mèng* 作夢 (*Fayuanzhulin*, Vol. 76)

a. 其夜**作夢**，見有人來。

　　qí　yè　　zuò　　mèng,　jiàn　yǒu　rén　lái

　　that　night　make　dream,　see　have　men　come

　　'(He) had a dream that night, (in the dream) he saw a man coming.'

a′. (顆)夜**夢**之曰...(*Zuozhuan*)

　　(kē) yè　　mèng　zhī　yuē...

　　(Ke)　night　dream　him　say...

　　'One night, Ke dreamed about him saying...'

　 – *zuò-hūn* 作婚 (*Fobenxing Jijing*, Vol. 18)

b. 仁者何用工巧之人共**作婚**為？

　　rén zhě　　　　hé　yòng　gōng-qiǎo　zhī

　　benevolent man　why　need　artistry　　's

　　rén　gong　　zuò-hūn　　　wéi

　　man　together　make-marriage　Question-Particle

　　'Why a benevolent man need to marry a artistry's daughter?'

b′. (相如)與卓氏**婚**，饒於財。
　　(*Shi Ji, Sima Xiangru Liezhuan*).

　　(xiàngrú) yǔ　Zhuó Shì hūn,　　ráo yū cái.

　　(Xiangru)　with　Zhuo Ms. marriage,　rich on fortune

　　'Xiangru got married with Ms. Zhuo (who made him) a great fortune.'

　 – *zuò yǒu* 作友 (*Fobenxing Jijing*, Vol. 25)

c. 我不用汝與我**作友**

　　wǒ bú yòng rǔ　yǔ　wǒ zuò　yǒu.

　　I　not need you with me make friend

　　'I don't need to make a friend with you.'

c′. 無**友**不如己者。(*Lunyu, Xue Er*)

　　wú yǒu　　bù rú jǐ　zhě.

　　not friend no as self one.

　　'(One) should not make a friend with one who is not as good as you.'

　　Why does the covert (zero) lightverbs in Archaic Chinese become overt (i.e., phonetically realized) during (and after) Eastern Han? Other than external (social or cultural) reasons, Feng (2008) argues that the phonetically realized lightverb syntax in late Archaic Chinese is motivated by prosody. Consider the following examples:

(30)   a.   不鼓而鳴。(*Fobenxing Jijing*)

bù gǔ   ér   míng.
Not drum but sound

'The drum sounded without drumming it.'

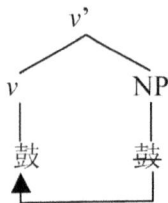

b.   時彼大眾...或復騰鈴，或復打鼓。 (*Fobenxing Jijing*, Vol. 8)

shí bǐ   dà-zhòng... huò fù   téng líng, huò
time these people...   some again toss bell, some

fù   dǎ   gǔ.
again beat drum

'At that time, those people...some tossed bells and some drummed drums again'

c.   復教打鼓振鈴，遍告城內人。 (*Fobenxing Jijing*, Vol. 14)

fù   jiào dǎ gǔ   zhèn líng, biàn   gào chéng-nèi rén.
again let beat drum shake bill, everywhere tell city-inside people

'Let them beat the drum and shake the bills again, telling the city people everywhere.'

d.   天魔軍眾忽然集，處處打鼓震地噪。 (*Fobenxing Jijing*, Vol. 29)

Tiān   mó jūn   zhòng hū-rán jí,   chù-chù
Heaven evil army many sudden gather, everywhere

dǎ gǔ   zhèn dì   zào.
beat drum shack earth noisy

'The army of the heaven-evil suddenly gathered. They drummed everywhere and shaken the earth so noisy.'

f. 不久打鼓，明星欲出。 (*Fobenxing Jijing*, Vol. 36)

bù jiǔ　dǎ　gǔ,　míng xīng yù　chū.

not-long beat drum, bright star almost out

'After while, (they) beat drums and then the bright stars come out.'

In (Pre-)Archaic Chinese, nouns like 鼓 *gǔ* 'drum' can easily be verbalized (i.e., denominative) through a head-movement to the empty position '*v*' shown in (30a); In Late Archaic Chinese, however, the empty *v* must be filled up with a phonetically realized (light-) verb in order to meet the prosodic grammar of the language. The prosodic requirement for phonetically realized lightverb is evidenced by the fact that there was hardly any covert lightverb-operation used as an independent foot in the environments where overt lightverbs were used ('( )' represents footing group):[20]

(31)　a.　*(或复) (鼓 _)

huò　fù　　gǔ

some again drum

'some drummed drums again'

b.　*(复教) (鼓 _) (振铃)

fù　　jiào gǔ　zhèn　líng

Again let　drum shake bell

'Let them beat the drum and shake the bills again.'

c.　*(處處) (鼓 _) (震地) (噪)

Chù-chù　gǔ　zhèn　dì　zào.

everywhere drum shack earth noisy

'They drummed everywhere and shaken the earth so noisy.'

d.　*(不久) (鼓 _), (明星) (欲出)

bù jiǔ　gǔ,　míng xīng yù　　chū.

Not long drum, bright stars almost come.

'After while, (they) beat drums and then the bright stars almost come out.'

---

20 Note that the *gu* in (30a) is not used as an independent foot, instead, it forms a foot with *bu* which licenses its denominative process prosodically.

The "non-existent" examples in (31) can be systematically accounted for by their defective prosody, that is, *gǔ* 'drum,' as a monosyllable word, cannot stand along under the disyllabic foot requirement of the language at that time. As a result, (31) confirms the hypothesis that it is prosody that motivates the covert lightverbs to become overt in environments where prosody is defective, which parallels to examples (23) and (28).

Given all the arguments above, it becomes quite convincing that prosody may not only trigger the overt light nouns to appear, but also the covert light verbs to become overt. If this is so, the syntactic operations of the phonetically realized *v* (i.e., lightverbs) and the morphologically realized ***div*** (i.e., lightnouns or classifiers) receive a unified explanation: both of them are activated by a prosodic factor in the Late Archaic Chinese grammar.

8 Final Remarks and Conclusion

Regarding the prosodic analysis of the newly developed lightverbs and light-nouns in classical Chinese given above, one may ask why there are parallel proso-syntactic changes between the two functional categories during and after Late Archaic Chinese. The answer, as I would like to suggest, lies in the theory of diachronic syntax. First, according to recent studies on diachronic syntax (Kroch 2000, Ian 2008), internal syntactic changes are subject to a parametric setting (or choice) similar to synchronic variations among different languages. This theoretical assumption entails that there should be no impossible variation allowed by UG (Universal Grammar). Informally speaking, new grammars in the course of syntactic change are hidden operations of the computational system of the language and potentially ready for activation by a next generation of native speakers through relevant (internal or external) factors in the language. Under this scenario and given the fact that independent classifiers and overt lightverbs were newly developed in Late Archaic Chinese, a legitimate question then is: What is/are the factor/s that activates the syntactic operation of the overt light-verbs and lightnouns? More specifically, what is/are the factor/s that activates the ***div*** system for the new classifier operation, and, by the same token, motivates the phonological system to spell out the empty lightverbs as well? As I have suggested above, it is prosody that triggers the change of the grammar not only for the syntax of light verbs and nouns, but also other prosodic grammars such as the newly developed disyllabic VV compounds, the [*bei* VV] structures, the VR structures, and the *ba*-construction … etc., which are all motivated under the same force of prosody. As a result, the newly developed classifiers in the present study are merely a sub-case of a global change activated by prosody, and thus provide additional evidence for the hypothesis that prosody has changed the Old Chinese from a synthetic language (with a system of segmental-phonological morphology) to an analytical language (with a system of suprasegmental-phonological morphology), around the time of Eastern Han (Feng 2009).

If the theory presented here is correct and acceptable, it will explain not only some diachronic syntax in terms of a prosodic parameterization, but also some changes of literary forms in terms of their poetic prosody (cf., the four-syllable-per-line poem changed into five- and seven-syllable-per-line poems after Han; Feng 2010b), an interesting and interdisciplinary area for future research.

References

Bei, Luobei (貝羅貝). 1998. 上古、中古漢語量詞的歷史發展 *Shanggu, Zhonggu Hanyu liangci de lishi fazhan* [The Developement of Classifiers in Archaic and Medieval Chinese], 語言學論叢 *Yuyanxue Luncong*, Vol. 21: 99–122.

Borer, Hagit. 2005. *In Name Only*. Oxford: Oxford University Press.

Campbell, Rod. 2004. Focus, classifiers and quantification typology: A brief account of cardinal expression in Early Inscriptional Chinese. In *Meaning and form: Essays in Pre-modern Chinese grammar,* Ken-ichi Takashima and Jiang Shaoyu (eds.), 19–41. Munich: Lincom Europa.

Dai, Qingxia and Jiang Ying (戴慶夏, 蔣穎). 2005. 論藏緬語的反響型名量詞 *Lun Zangmian yu de fanxiang xing mingliangci* [The echo noun-classifiers in Tibeto-Burman Language]. 中央民族大學學報 *Zhongyang Minzu Daxue Xuebao* 32: 124–129.

Dai, Qingxia and Jiang Ying (戴慶夏, 蔣穎). 2004. 萌芽期量词的类型学特征景颇语量词的个案研究 *Mengya qi liangci de leixingxue tezheng-Jingpo yu liangci de ge'an yanjiu* [Typological characteristics of classifiers at a primitive stage – the case of Jingpo], *Studies on Sino-Tibetan languages: Papers in honor of Professor Hwang-Cherng Gong on his seventieth Birthday*. Taipei: Academia Sinica, 315–325.

Djamouri, Redouane. 2010. 甲骨文中和上古汉语文献中名词前"有"表复数的形式 *Jiaguwen zhong he shanggu Hanyu wenxian zhong mingci qian "you" biao fushu de xingshi* [Plurality expression '*you*' before Noun Phrases in documents of Oracle and Bone Inscriptions and in Old Chinese. In 量与复数的研究 *Liang yu fushu de yanjiu* [Quantification and Plurality], Dan Xu (ed.), 123–139. Bejing: Shangwu Yinshuguan.

Dobson, W. A. C. H. 1962. *Early Archaic Chinese*. Toronto: Toronto University Press.

Feng, Shengli. 1996. Prosodically Constrained Syntactic Changes in Early Archaic Chinese. *Journal of East Asian Linguistics*, 4: 323–371.

Feng, Shengli. 2008. 轻动词移位与古今汉语的动宾关系 *Qingdongci yiwei yu gujin hanyu de dongbin guanxi* [Light verb Movement in Modern and Classical Chinese]. 语言科学 *Yuyan Kexue* 1: 3–16.

Feng, Shengli. 2009. 论汉语韵律的形态功能与句法演变的历史分期 *Lun hanyu yunlü de xingtai yu jufa yanbian de lishi fenqi* [On the morphological function of prosody and the chronology of syntactic changes in Chinese. 历史语言学研究, 第二辑. *Lishi Yuyanxue Yanjiu* 2: 11–31.

Feng, Shengli. 2010a. 论语体的机制及其语法属性 *Lun yuti de jizhi jiqi yufa shuxing* [On Mechanisms of Register System and its grammatical property]. *Zhongguo Yuwen* 5: 400–412.

Feng, Shengli. 2010b. A Prosodic Explanation for Chinese Poetic Evolution. *Tsing Hua Journal of Chinese Studies* 2: 223–257.

Hong, Cheng (洪誠). 2000. 關於漢語史材料運用的問題 *Guanyu hanyu shi cailiao yunyong de wenti*. [Issues about historical textual resources]. In *Hong Cheng Wenji*, Hong Cheng (ed.). Nanjing: Jiangsu Guji Chubanshe.

Hong, Yifang (洪藝芳). 2000. 敦煌吐魯番文書中之量詞研究 *Dunhuang Tulufan wenshu zhong zhi liangci Yanjiu* [Studies on Classifiers of Dunhuang Tulufan Wenshu]. Taipei: Wenjing Press.

Huang, Shengzhang (黃盛璋). 1961. 兩漢時代的量詞 *Liang Han shidai de liangci* [Classifiers in two Han dynasties]. *Zhongguo Yuwen* 8: 21–29.

Huang, C.-T. James. 1987. Existential sentences in Chinese and (in)definiteness. In *The Representation of (In)definiteness*, E. Reuland and A. ter Meulen (eds.), 226–253. Cambridge MA: MIT Press.

Huang, Zaijun (黃載君). 1964. 從甲文、金文量詞的應用，考察漢語量詞的起源和發展 *Cong jiawen, jinwen liangci de yingyong kaocha hanyu liangci de qiyuan he fazhan* [Investigation of the origin and development of classifiers based on the usages of classifiers in Aoracle-bone and Brangze incriptures]. *Zhongguo Yuwen* 6: 432–441.

Hu, Chirui (胡敕瑞). 2005. 从隐含到呈现 (上) — 试论中古词汇的一个本质变化 *Cong yinhan dao chengxian (shang) – Shilun zhonggu cihui de yige benzhi Bianhua* [From Implying to Presenting (Part I): An Essential Change of Chinese Vocabulary in the Middle Times]. 语言学论丛, *Yuyanxue Luncong*, Vol. 31: 1–21.

Kroch, Tony. 2000. Syntactic Change. *The Handbook of Contemporary Syntactic Theory*, Mark Baltin and Chris Collins (eds.), 699–729. Oxford: Blackwell.

Larson, Richard. 1988. On the double object construction, *Linguistic Inquiry* 19: 339–391.

Li, Yuming (李宇明). 2000. 拷貝型量詞及其在漢藏語系量詞發展中的地位 *Kaobeixing liangci jiqi zai hanzang yuxi liangci fazhan zhong de diwei* [Classifers of the copy-type and their status in the devopment of classifiers in Sino-Tibetan Chinese]. *Zhongguo Yuwen* 1: 27–34.

Liu, Danqing (刘丹青). 2008. 漢語名詞性短語的句法類型特征 *Hanyu mingci xing duanyu de jufa leixing tezheng* [Syntactic types and characteristics of noun phrases in Chinese]. *Zhongguo Yuwen* 1: 5–21.

Liu, Hui (刘辉). 2009. *The Syntax and Semantics of Event Classifiers in modern Chinese*. Ph.D. diss. Shanghai Normal University.

Liu, Shiru (劉世儒). 1965. 魏晋南北朝量詞研究 *Weijin Nanbeichao liangci yanjiu* [*Studies on Classifiers in Weijin North-South dynasties*]. Beijing: Zhonghua Shuju.

Lü, Shuxiang (呂叔湘). 1982. 中國文法要略 *Zhongguo Wenfa Yaolüe* [An Outline of Chinese Grammar]. Beijing: Shangwu Yinshuguan.

Lyons, John. 1977. *Semantics*: Volume 2. Cambridge: Cambridge University Press.

Massam, Diane. 2009. On the separation and relatedness of classifiers, number and individuation in Niuean. *Language and Linguistics* 10 (4): 669–699.

Peyraube, Alain. 1991. Some Remarks on the History of Chinese Classifiers. *Santa Barbara Papers in Linguistics* 3: 106–126.

Peyraube, Alain. 1998. On the History of Classifiers in Archaic and Medieval Chinese. In *Studia Linguistica Serica* 漢語研究 *Hanyu Yanjiu,* Benjamin K. T'sou (ed.), 131–145. City University of Hong Kong.

Roberts, Ian and Anna Roussou. 2003. *Syntactic Change – A Minimalist Approach to Grammaticalization*. Cambridge: Cambridge University Press.

Sagart, Laurent. 2000. *The Root of Old Chinese*. Amsterdam/Philadelphia: John Benjamins Publishing Company.

Shen, Pei (沈培). 1994. 殷墟甲骨卜辭語序研究 *Yinxu jiagu buci yuxu yanjiu* [Studies on Word Order in Yinxu's Oracle bone scriptures]. Taipei: Wenjin Press.

Tang, C.-C. Jane (湯志真). 1996. *Ta mai-le bi shi zhi* and Chinese phrase structure. 中央研究院 歷史語言研究所集刊 *Zhonyang yanjiuyuan lishi yuyan yanjiusuo jikan* [Bulletin of the Institute of History and Philology] 67: 445–502.

Wang, Li (王力). 1989. 漢語史稿 *Hanyu Shigao* [The History of Chinese]. Beijing: Shangwu Yinshuguan.

Wu, Fuxiang (吳福祥). 2005. 魏晉南北朝時期漢語名量詞範疇的語法化程度 *Weijin Nanbeichao shiqi hanyu mingliangci fanchou de yufahua chengdu* [Degree of Grammaticalization of noun-classifiers in Weijin South-North Dyansties], 第三屆漢語語法化問題 國際學術討論會論文, Disanjie Hanyu Yufahua wenti Guoji Xueshu Taolun Hui Lunwen [Paper presented at the Third International Conference on Issues of Grammaticalization in Chinese.

Wu, Fuxiang (吳福祥). 2007. 魏晉南北朝時期漢語名量詞範疇的語法化程度 *Weijin Nanbeichao shiqi hanyu mingliangci fanchou de yufahua chengdu* [Degree of Grammaticalization of noun-classifiers in Weijin South-North Dyansties]. In 語法化與語 法研究 (三) *Yufahua yu yufa yanjiu (san)* [Grammaticalization and Studies on Grammar, III], Shen Jiaxuan, Wu Fuxiang and Li Zongjiang (eds.), 246–268. Beijing: Commercial Press.

Wu, Fuxiang, Feng Shengli and Huang Zhengde (吳福祥、冯胜利、黄正德). 2006. 汉语 "数量名" 格式的来源 *Hanyu 'shu liang ming' geshi de laiyuan* [The origin of the construction of 'numeral + classifier + noun' in Chinese]. *Zhongguo Yuwen* 5: 387–400.

Xu, Dan (徐丹). 2003. 趋向动词 '来／去' 与语法化. *Quxiang dongci 'lai/qu' yu yufahu*a. [Gramamticalization and the directional verbs *lai* and *qu*]. Paper presented at the Research Center of Chinese Linguistics at Peking University, 25 December 2003.

Xu, Dan (徐丹). 2006. *Typological Change in Chinese Syntax*. Oxford: Oxford Press.

Yang-Drocourt, Z. 1993. *Evolution syntaxique des classificateurs chinois du 14ème siècle av. J. C. au 17ème siècle*. Paris, Thèse de Doctorat de 1'EHESS.

Zhang, Cheng (張頔). 2012. 漢語通用量詞的發展與漢語量詞範疇的確立 *Hanyu tongyong liangci de fazhan yu hanyu liangci fanchou de queli* [The relation between the development of general classifiers and the establishment of the category of numeral classifiers in Chinese]. *Journal of Chinese Linguistics* 40: 2, 307–321.

Zhang, Shilu (张世禄). 1939. 因文法的问题谈到文白分界 *Yin wenfa wenti tandao wen-bai de fenjie* [From Grammar to the distinction between literate-ness and classical-ness]. 语文周刊 *Yuwen Zhoukan*, 30–32.

Zhang, Yanjun (張延俊). 2002. 也論漢語 "數量名" 形式的產生 *Ye lun hanyu 'shu-liang-ming' xingshi de chansheng* [On the birth of the form 'Number, Classifier, Noun' in Chinese]. 古漢語研究 *Guhanyu Yanjiu* 2: 26–29.

Zhengzhang, Shangfang (鄭張尚方). 2009. 上古音系 *Shanggu Yinxi*. Shanghai: Shanghai Educational Press.

Lin Jang-Ling and Alain Peyraube

4 Individuating classifiers in Early Southern Min (14th–19th centuries)

Abstract: The paper analyses the evolution of the nature and function of the individuating classifiers in Southern Min from the 14th c. to the 19th c. A brief historical sketch of the classifiers (CLs) is first provided and the main hypotheses previously forwarded are discussed. The conclusions of the study are:

(i) The first stage of the cyclic process involving a broad diversification of the classifiers and increase in their number, as well as the strong tendency to acquire a function of classification, are also obvious in Southern Min.

(ii) There is nevertheless no evidence to confirm the tendencies of the second stage of the cyclic change, i.e. change from specific classifiers to general classifiers and change from the classifying functions of the CLs to the quantifying functions.

If the second stage of the cyclic evolution is not seen, it might be either because the process started only later, in the second half of the 20th century, or because this second stage is only a process involved in the Northern Chinese dialects and not in the Southern ones.

Keywords: classifiers, Southern Min dialect, historical syntax, typological syntax, diachronic change

1 Introduction

This paper will analyse the evolution of the nature and function of the individuating classifiers (CLs) in Southern Min from the 14th c. to the 19th c.[1] A CL is a word which theoretically must occur before a noun (N) and after a number (Num) and/or a demonstrative (+Num) or another quantifier, like *jǐ* 幾 'several', *měi* 每 'every', etc. Such a standard definition (see Chao 1968, Li and Thompson

---

1 This research has been supported by funding from an ANR (Agence Nationale de la Recherche, France) grant on 'Diachronic change in Southern Min' (DIAMIN, ANR-08-BLAN-0174). We express our gratitude to the ANR. We would also like to thank the anonymous reviewer of our paper and Prof. Chin-fa Lien for their comments and criticisms that we were able to take into account in the final version. We believed that this has substantially improved our analysis, adopting the usual caveat that we take responsibility for all the interpretations and errors.

1981, Zhu 1982, Peyraube 1998a, 1998b) does not allow us to make the desirable distinction between CLs and measure words (MWs). MWs can indicate (i) standards for length, weight, volume and area; (ii) aggregates; (iii) containers; (iv) portions of entities.[2] MWs are probably language universals, while the CLs are not. If they are quite common in East-Asian languages, they have no equivalents in Indo-European languages. Our paper will only deal with individuating CLs (*gètǐ liàngcí* 個體量詞). Since Greenberg (1974), it is commonly assumed that languages with numeral classifiers (our individuating classifiers) do not have obligatory plural marking. For a thorough discussion of Greenberg's universal claim, see Bisang in this volume.

The seven documents of the corpus of this study are operas in the Southern Min language that were performed in Fujian, Taiwan and North-eastern Guangdong from the 14th century to the 19th century. The main texts used are:

(i) The *LI JING JI* 荔鏡記 and its different versions later called *LI ZHI JI* 荔枝記:

  - *Li Jing Ji* (abbreviated hereafter as LJJ–1566) 荔鏡記 [Romance of the Litchis and the Mirror], 1566 edition. Supposedly written in both Chaozhou and Quanzhou dialects (Wu Shou-Li, 2001a). 7335 Chinese characters.
  - *Li Zhi Ji* (abbreviated hereafter as LZJ–1581) 荔枝記 [Romance of the Litchis] 1581 edition. Written in the Chaozhou dialect (Wu Shou-Li, 2001b). 4361 Chinese characters.
  - *Li Zhi Ji* (LZJ–1651) 荔枝記 [Romance of the Litchis] 1651 edition. Written in both Chaozhou and Quanzhou dialects (Wu Shou-Li, 2001c). 8208 Chinese characters.
  - *Li Zhi Ji* (LZJ–1884) 荔枝記 (*Romance of the Litchis*) 1884 edition. Written in both Chaozhou and Quanzhou dialects (Wu, Shou-Li, 2001d). 9147 Chinese characters.

(ii) Other operas that have never been the object of any linguistic study but have been analyzed from a literary and historical point of view by van der Loon (1992) and Wu Shou-Li (2002a, 2002b, 2003):

  - *Jin Hua nü* (JHN) 金花女 *Lady Jinhua* (1573–1620 edition). Written in the Chaozhou dialect (Wu Shou-Li, 2002a). 1469 Chinese characters.
  - *Su Liuniang* (SLN) 蘇六娘 *Dame Su Liuniang* (1573–1620 edition). Written in the Chaozhou dialect (Wu Shou-Li, 2002b). 783 Chinese characters.
  - *Tongchuang Qin Shu Ji* (TCQSJ) 同窗琴書記 *The Romance of the classmates with lute and books*, 1782 edition. Written in the Quanzhou dialect (Wu Shou-Li, 2003). 2007 Chinese characters.

---

2 These MWs are called CLs by most of the Chinese linguists, who nevertheless distinguish *dùliànghéng liàngcí* 度量衡量詞 [measure CLs], *jítǐ liàngcí* 集體量詞 [collective CLs], *róngliàng liàngcí* 容量量詞 [CLs of content], *bùfèn liàngcí* 部分量詞 [partitive CLs], and *gètǐ liàngcí* 個體量詞 [individuating CLs].

It is important to note that the two versions of LJJ–1566 and LZJ–1651 already available both indicate in the first pages that these are re-editions of a former version that has been modified. It is then difficult to determine which one has to be considered as the earlier version (van der Loon 1992, Wu 2001a, Wu 2001b).

The following main hypotheses concerning the evolution of the system of CLs in Chinese (see Peyraube and Wiebusch 1993, Peyraube 1998a, 1998b) will be tested in this study, i.e.:

1. Is there any tendency for the CLs, starting in the Late Medieval period (7th– 13th c.) and ending up to the Modern period (18th–19th c.) to be more and more diversified and to acquire, besides their former role of quantification, an important function of qualification/classification?

2. Is there any tendency for the CLs, starting in the 19th century, to have their number decreased and to begin to lose the function of qualification, keeping only their main function of quantification?

Our paper will start with a brief historical sketch of the CLs, from the Pre-Medieval to the Late Medieval period, and from the Late Medieval to the Modern period, with a description of the situation in Northern Chinese for the same time-span period (14th–19th centuries) based on research already done on the different versions of the *Lao Qida* 'The Old Sinologist' (see Peyraube and Lin: 2010). We will then give the details of the situation in Early Southern Min (ESM), before interpreting the outcomes of the descriptive study in the conclusion.

2 Brief Historical Sketch

There are MWs in Archaic Chinese (11th–3rd c. BC) but no individuating classifiers. The Chinese CLs appeared during the Pre-Medieval period (2nd c. BC–3rd c. AD), always in the post-nominal position, as in:

(1) 羊萬頭

    yáng wàn ***tóu***

    sheep ten/thousand CL

    'ten thousand sheep'

(2) a. 雞子五枚   b. 狗一枚

      jīzǐ wǔ ***méi***   *gǒu yī* ***méi***

      egg five CL   dog one CL

      'five eggs',   'one dog'.

Most of the examples found are contained in inscriptions on bamboo or wooden tablets excavated from ruins at a border garrison in North-western China. The appearance of these CLs might have been due to the loss of an infix 'r', possibly a plurality marker in Archaic Chinese (Peyraube 1988b). See also Feng on *the syntax and prosody of classifiers in Classical Chinese*, this volume). When they appeared, the CLs had only a syntactic role in quantified noun phrases (NPs). They did not have any semantic role in classifying nouns. From the Pre-Medieval to the Late Medieval period (7th–13th c. AD), the CLs quantify and do not classify, i.e. they do not code-or very little-any semantic characterization of the nouns they modify. Moreover, they are not very diversified. Many nouns, which will be used later with different more specific classifiers, are used at that time with one general classifier, typically *méi* 枚.

Starting in the Late Medieval period, CLs become more and more widespread. Almost 70% of quantified NPs involve classifiers in the *biànwén* 變文 'transformational texts' dated from 850 to 1025, and this proportion increases as time goes on. Moreover, the CLs are now found in a pre-nominal position. There has been a word order change: N + Num + CL > Num + CL + N.

Méi 枚 is no longer a general CL. It has been replaced by *ge* 個 which takes on a very extended use with every kind of noun, including abstract nouns, as in:

(3)   臣有一個問頭。

    *chén yǒu   yī **ge** wèntóu*
    I   have a   CL question
    'I have a question'.

But the most important change that occurred during this time is the following: The CLs, whose main function was to quantify and individualize the nouns they modify, have acquired too an important function of qualification / classification by Late Medieval. The use of specific CLs with certain nouns appears to be more systematic during this period, especially in literary texts where specific CLs are numerous, also probably for rhetorical and stylistic reasons (see Feng, this volume, Zhang to appear).

From the Late Medieval period to the Modern period (19th c.), the CLs are still diversifying and, besides their former role of quantification, they also increasingly take on this new function of qualification / classification. What is important to note is that around the end of the Modern period they start to lose this function of qualification, and their number begins to decrease, as there is a tendency of lexical unification of all the specific CLs into one CL: *ge* 個, at least in Northern Mandarin and Northern dialects. A hypothesis of cyclic change has therefore been put forward by Peyraube (1998b), which can be formalized as follows:

(4) Hypothesis of Cyclic change:

CL		CL		CL
[+ Quantification]		[+ Quantification]		[+ Quantification]
[– Diversification]	>	[+ Diversification]	>	[– Diversification]
[– Classification]		[+ Classification]		[– Classification]

This hypothesis has been partially confirmed for Northern Chinese in the study of Peyraube and Lin (2010) on the five different versions of the *Lao Qida* 老乞大 'The Old Sinologist' (LQD) dated from the 14th c. to the 18th c.:
- *Gǔběn Lǎo Qǐdà* 古本老乞大 representing the language of 14th c. Northern Chinese (19,138 Chinese characters in the document);
- *Lǎo Qǐdà yànjiě* 老乞大諺解 1745 edition but representing the language of the beginning of the Ming dynasty (15th c., 19,207 Chinese characters in the document);
- *Fānyì Lǎo Qǐdà* 飜譯老乞大 (before 1517);
- *Lǎo Qǐdà xīn shì* 老乞大新釋 and
- *Chóngkān Lǎo Qǐdà* 重刊老乞大 (18th c. language).

In the first version, Peyraube and Lin have counted 25 CLs for 303 occurrences, with 217 occurrences of *ge* 箇. There are more different CLs in the later versions, with fewer occurrences of *ge*. Their conclusion, however, is that the process of diversification of CLs and the function of classification / qualification did not start in Northern Chinese before the 15th century. In the next section, we consider the development of classifiers in Southern Min.

3 The Early Southern Min Situation

We have found 43 CLs in the seven documents of our corpus. See *Table 1* below with the number of occurrences in every document.

An analysis of the statistics in *Table 1* allows us to make the following claims: There are many more CLs used in the Southern Min documents than in the different versions of *The Old Sinologist*, for instance 0.37% of classifiers in the whole LJJ (27 classifiers in a document of 7,335 characters) against only 0.13% in the first edition of the LQD (25 CLs in a document of 19,138 characters), dated

Table 1: The 43 Individual Classifiers in Southern Min opera documents from 14th to 19th centuries.[3]

Opera	CLs/Opera	Total characters	Year/language	phit4 疋	be2 尾	tiao5 條	tsiah4 隻	ki1 枝	bing5 名	ui1 位	e5 個	e5 个
Lì Jìng Jì	27	7335	14th–15th c.	0	1	1	4	13	7	15	0	35
Lì Zhī Jì	20	4361	1581	2	0	0	3	5	0	7	6	118
Jīnhuānǔ	9	1469	1573–1620	0	0	1	0	0	0	3	34	0
Sū Liùniáng	11	783	1573–1620	0	0	1	1	0	0	0	5	0
Lì Zhī Jì	29	8208	1651	2	8	5	3	19	1	9	2	0
TCQSJ	14	2007	1782	0	0	2	0	8	1	8	11	0
Lì Zhī Jì	31	9147	1884	0	5	5	5	13	2	11	17	0
Total 14th–19th c.	43			4	14	15	16	58	11	53	75	153

Opera	CLs/Opera	Total characters	Year/language	tng3 頓	siu2 首	tiuN1 張	nia2 領	kiaN7 件	te3 塊	piN2 片	tuaN7 段	tiuN5 場	hong1 封	
Lì Jìng Jì	27	7335	14th–15th c.	2	3	1	2	2	5	0	2	6	19	
Lì Zhī Jì	20	4361	1581	0	0	2	0	7	5	0	1	13	12	
Jīnhuānǔ	9	1469	1573–1620	0	0	0	0	1	0	0	0	5	0	
Sū Liùniáng	11	783	1573–1620	0	0	0	1	1	0	2	0	0	1	
Lì Zhī Jì	29	8208	1651	3	3	3	5	6	10	0	3	5	12	1
TCQSJ	14	2007	1782	0	2	0	0	2	1	0	1	2	1	
Lì Zhī Jì	31	9147	1884	0	1	4	6	5	3	1	7	8	11	2
Total 14th–19th c.	43			5	9	10	14	24	24	3	14	39	56	

3 As we do not know what the pronunciation was from the 14th–19th centuries, we have used here, as is usually the custom, a transliteration based on the online edition of *Tái rì dà cídiǎn* 台日大辭典, published by the Institute of Linguistics of Academia Sinica, Taiwan, which has kept some pronunciations of the 19th century, as attested in the dictionary of Douglas (1873), This system is called the Taiwanese Church Romanization.

Opera	CLs/ Opera	Total char- acters	Year/lan- guage	tshu2 處	piN2 扁	ke3 架	iun5 輪	khau2 口	tsuaN2 盞	piN3 柄	pak4 幅	pun2 本	keng1 間	tso7 座
Lì Jìng Jì	27	7335	14th– 15th c.	3	0	0	3	3	7	1	0	0	1	1
Lì Zhī Jì	20	4361	1581	0	0	1	2	2	0	0	1	1	0	1
Jīnhuā nǚ	9	1469	1573– 1620	0	0	0	0	0	1	1	0	1	0	0
Sū Liùniáng	11	783	1573– 1620	0	1	0	0	0	1	1	0	0	0	0
Lì Zhī Jì	29	8208	1651	0	0	0	3	6	6	13	0	0	0	2
TCQSJ	14	2007	1782	0	0	0	1	0	0	0	0	0	0	0
Lì Zhī Jì	31	9147	1884	0	0	0	3	3	7	10	0	0	0	2
Total 14th–19th c.	43			3	1	1	12	14	22	26	2	1	1	6

Opera	CLs/ Opera	Total char- acters	Year/lan- guage	kah 甲	tshut4 出	tsang5 欉	kai3 介	kak4 角	khi2 起	khu3 坵	ting2 頂	lui2 蕊	kha1 腳	tsi2 只
Lì Jìng Jì	27	7335	14th– 15th c.	0	0	0	0	0	0	0	0	0	0	1
Lì Zhī Jì	20	4361	1581	0	0	0	0	0	0	0	0	0	0	
Jīnhuā nǚ	9	1469	1573– 1620	0	0	0	2	0	0	0	0	0	0	
Sū Liùniáng	11	783	1573– 1620	0	0	0	0	0	0	0	0	0	0	
Lì Zhī Jì	29	8208	1651	0	0	0	0	1	2	1	2	3	2	0
TCQSJ	14	2007	1782	0	1	0	0	0	0	0	0	1	0	0
Lì Zhī Jì	31	9147	1884	1	0	1	0	1	1	1	1	2	2	0
Total 14th–19th c.	43			1	1	1	2	2	3	2	3	6	4	1

approximately to the same period. The number of occurrences of these CLs is also higher in the LJJ, although the number of *ge* is particularly large in the LQD.

The number of CLs increases from the 14th c. to the 17th c. but seems to decrease again from the 17th c. on, especially in the later versions of the LZJ: 0.37% in the LJJ, 0.46% in the LZJ–1581, 0.61% in the JHN (16th c.), 0.14% in the SLN (16th c.), but 0.35% in the LZJ–1651 and 0.34% in the LZJ–1884, while the percentage in TCQSJ–1782 remains quite high (0.7%).

We also notice that CLs used after demonstratives are quite rare, figures for which, are not given in *Table 1*. We counted only 4 CLs used in 24 occurrences. Most of the time, the structure 'Demonstrative + N' is found used without any classifiers.

Let us now analyse the details of our findings.

3.1 The classifier *e5* (*GE* 個) and its evolution through the five centuries

There are three classifiers *e5*: 箇, 个, 個. Examples:

(5)　十箇九箇不踏五娘仔一倍。 (*LJJ*, chapter 8, 1566 edition)

　　tsap8 ***e5*** *kau2* ***e5*** *m7*　*tah8*　*goo7-niu5-a tsit8 puei7*
　　Ten　CL nine　CL NEG COMP Wuniangzi　one　time
　　'Nine or ten (girls) could not compete with a single Wuniangzi.'

(6)　拾一个卵到來。 (*LJJ*, 22, 1566 edition)

　　khioh4　*tsit8*　***e5***　*nng7*　*to3-lai5*
　　Pick-up　one　CL　egg　return-come
　　'Pick up one egg back (to me).'

(7)　好一個白老鼠。 (*LZJ*, 39, 1581 edition)

　　ho2　*tsit8*　***e5***　*peh8*　*niau2-tshu2*
　　Good　one　CL　white　mouse
　　'one good white mouse'

Are these three CLs real variants of one another? In other words, is it the same morpheme used across all situations, and thus the different characters are a simple matter of writing preferences, as today for both simplified and complex forms of the same word? The answer is probably no.

First of all, we can notice that the first character listed for *e5* 箇 is marginal. This situation is different from the one found in *The Old Sinologist* where the character 箇 is by far the most frequent CL (a general one) in all the versions, from the 14th c. up to the 18th c. Moreover, for the remaining two, important changes have occurred around the end of 16th century or at the beginning of 17th century in the Southern Min texts. One of them, *e5* 個, has imposed itself over the two others, as shown in the Table 1 above.

(8) 我只一個腳正是得桃腳。 (*LZJ*, 17, 1651 edition)

    gua2 tsi2 tsit8 **e5** *tsiaN3 shi7 tit4-tho5 kha1*
    1SG this one CL exactly is   play   foot

    'This foot of mine is precisely for playing.'

These three *e5* 箇, 个 and 個 are not only used as classifiers. They are also employed as determinative particles (genitive use or relative pronouns) (see examples 9 and 10, 11 and 12 respectively), or as adjectival particles, as in (13). In such cases, it is only the third *e5* 個 which is used. We have found only two exceptions in the entire database: one example of the first one (*e5* 箇) and one example of the second one (*e5* 个). Examples:

(9) 只正是月內个宮殿。 (*LJJ*, 6, 1566 edition)

    *tsi2 tsiaN3   shi7 geh8 lai7   **e5**   kiong1-tian7*
    This precisely is   moon inner PRT palace

    'This is precisely the palace inside the moon.'

(10) 你個阿爹呾話好笑。 (*JHN*, 147, 1573–1620 edition)[4]

    *li2 **e5** a-tia1 taN3-ue7 ho2-tshio7*
    2SG PRT father speak   funny

    'What your father says is funny (ridiculous).'

(11) 掠我呾個話你都不聽。 (*JHN*, 540, 1573–1620 edition)

    liah8 gua5 taN3 **e5** *ue7 li2 dioh m7   thiaN1*
    Even I   say   PRT word you all   NEG listen

    'You do not even listen to all the words I say.'

---

4 *TaN3* 呾 'say' is a typical word of the Chaozhou dialect (Shi and Wu 1997), which does not exist in Taiwanese of today. The transliteration here is the one used in the contemporary Chaozhou dialect.

(12)   未出嫁個查某仔。 (*LZJ*, 18, 1884 edition)

    bue7 tshut4-ke3 **e5**   *tsa-boo2-a2*
    NEG out-marry PRT girl

    'The girl who is not yet married.'

(13)   庭前花開 紅個紅 (…); (*JHN*, 147, 1573–1620 edition)

    tiaN5 tsing5 hue1   khui1 ang5 **e5**   *ang5*
    Yard front flower bloom red   PRT red

    'Flowers are blooming in front of the yard, red and (…)'

(14)   (…) 白個白 即是爽利。 (*JHN*, 147, 1573–1620 edition)

    peh8 **e5**   *peh8 tsiah4 shi7 song2-li7*
    white PRT white truly is   beautiful

    '(…) white, (they) are truly beautiful.'

Notice that the caracter 个, when used as a particle, is not pronounced *e5* but *ko3*, as has been noticed by Shi and Wu (1997).

Finally, other uses of *e5* in adverbial phrases such as *tsin1-ko3* 真箇, 真个 and 真個 meaning 'really' are:

(15)   三三哥，尔真箇好笑。 (*LJJ*, 26, 1566 edition)

    saN1-saN1-ko1 li2   **tsin1-ko3** *ho2-tshio7*
    saN1-saN1-ko1 2SG really   funny

    'Sansange, you are really funny!'

(16)   真个悶殺 人心。 (*LJJ*, 8, 1566 edition)

    tsin1-ko3 *bun7-sat4 lang5   sim1*
    really   stuffy-kill person heart

    '(It is) really annoying!'

(17)   真個快活是無比。 (*TCQSJ*, 1, 1728 edition)

    tsin1-ko3 *khuaN3-uah8 shi7 bu5-bi2*
    really   pleased   is   incomparable

    '(It is) really happiness, without any doubt!'

3.2 Different semantic categories

3.2.1 Classifiers used for persons

The three *e5* (簡, 个, 個) are commonly and widely used for persons, but also *ui1* 位 – curiously not attested in the *LQD* – and *bing5* 名, the last one used most of the time when referring to officials, except in example (19) below. Examples:

(18) 今即一位娘仔... (*LJJ*, 6, 1566 edition)

    *taN tsiah4 tsit8 **ui1** niu5-a2*
    now this   one CL lady
    'This lady, now...'

(19) 犯人一名陳三。 (*LJJ*, 45, 1566 edition)

    *huan-lang tsit8 **bing5** Tan5-SaN1*
    Criminal one CL   Tan5-SaN1
    'One criminal, Chen San.'

3.2.2 Classifiers used for animals and plants

Within the animate category of animals as opposed to persons, we find the following CLs very commonly used, especially the first one which has replaced the *e5* 個 of Early Southern Min: *tsiah4* 隻 (20), *be2* 尾 (21) and *phit4* 疋 (22). *Tsiah4* 隻 is used for horses, donkeys, pigs and dogs (two cases are also attested with the noun 'boat'), *be2* 尾 for snakes and birds (orioles),[5] *phit* 疋 for horses, but also for textiles, as in the Northern Chinese *LQD*. We also find *tiau5* 條 for sheep in the *JHN* (one example), but *tiau5* 條 is more used for roads or hand-kerchiefs, and also for shoelaces (only three examples).

(20) 將只一隻馬送乞你做相謝錢。 (*LZJ*, 16, 1581 edition)

    *tsiong1 tsi2 tsit8 **tsiah4** be2   sang3 khit4 li2   tsue3 siong1-sia7 tsiN5*
    PTM   this one CL   horse give PREP 2SG make thank   money
    '(I) am giving you this horse to thank (you).'

---

5 On the CL *be2*, see Tai (1999).

(21)　二尾蛇相交。 (*LZJ*, 4, 1651 edition)

　　ji7 **be2** *tsua5 saN-kau1*

　　two CL snake tie-together

　　'Two snakes tied together.'

(22)　天有一疋長長緞。 (*LZJ*, 25, 1581 edition)

　　iau2 u7　　tsit8 **phit4** *tng5-tng5 tuan7*

　　still there-is one CL　　long-long satin

　　'There is still one very long bolt of satin.'

Within the inanimate category of plants and flowers, we have very few examples in our corpus. Two CLs are found used for plants: *ki1* 枝 (see eg. 23) and *tsang5* 欉. *Ki1* 枝 is also used for artefacts, as in (24) and (25):

(23)　一枝牡丹乞伊摘去。 (*TCQSJ*, 4, 1728 edition)

　　tsit8 **ki1** *boo2-tan1 khit4 i3　　tiah1-khi3*

　　One CL peony　　PREP 3SG pick-go

　　'Pick one peony flower for her.'

(24)　一枝燭火暗又光。 (*LJJ*, 48, 1566 edition)

　　tsit8 **ki1** *tsik4-hue2 am3 iu7　kng1*

　　One CL candle　　dark and bright

　　'One candle, (sometimes) dark and (sometimes) bright.'

(25)　一枝掃帚 ... 都不成樣。 (*LZJ*, 1884)

　　tsit8 **ki1** *sau3-tshiu2 ... to　　m7　tsiaN5　iuN7*

　　One CL broom ...　　even NEG look-like shape

　　'(That) one broom ... does not look like anything.'

3.2.3 Abstracts nouns and emotions

For words and sentences, we have *ku3* and for emotions of all kinds, we have *tiuN5* 場, *tuaN7* 段, *piN2* 片:

(26)　恁兄有一句話要共你呾。 (*LZJ*, 27, 1581 edition)

　　lin1 hiaN　u7　　tsit8 **ku3** *ue7　beh4 ka7 li2　taN3*

　　2PL brother have one CL　word want to　2SG tell

　　'Your brother wants to tell you a word.'

(27) 枉你一場空歡喜。 (*LZJ*, 1581)

ong2　li2　tsit8　**tiuN5**　khang1　huaN1-hi2
In-vain 2SG one CL false joy

'(I let) you have a false joy in vain.'

(28) 一段好恩愛。 (*LZJ*, 14, 1651 edition)

tsit8　**tuaN7**　ho2　un1-ai3
one CL nice love

'one nice love'

(29) 一片傷心無解拆命隨燈影 ... (*SLN*, 7, 1573–1620 edition)

tsit8　**piN2**　siong1-sim1　bo5　kai3-thiah4　mia7　sui5　ting1　iaN2
one CL break-heart NEG relieve life follow lantern shadow

'One broken heart is never relieved, (my) life goes along by the shadow of the lantern...'

3.2.4 Shape and length of objects

There is no clear differentiation related to the shape of the objects, their length, cylindrical nature, flatness, roundness, etc. as is the case in Southern Min of today.[6] One exception, however, is *hong1* 封 systematically used for letters (49 occurrences), like in contemporary Mandarin, but not in Taiwan Southern Min (TSM) of today, where the CL for letters is *tiuN1* 張.

(30) 持紙筆來我寫一封書去。 (*SLN*, 4, 1573–1620 edition)

tshi5　tsua2　pit4　lai5　gua2　sia2　tsit8　**hong1**　su1　khi2
Take paper pen come 1SG write one CL letter go

'Bring me a pen and paper to write a letter.'

There is another instance of a so-called CL regularly used for small and round objects: *liap8* 粒 for which we have three examples but only with the noun 'rice', as in:

---

6 See however Lien and Chiu (forthcoming)'s study of the shape classifiers in Earlier Southern Min texts, which distinguishes between one-dimensional shape classifiers, two-dimensional classifiers, and three-dimensional shape classifiers.

(31) 我算有十四五粒米。 (*LZJ*, 9, 1651 edition)

    gua2 sng3   u7   tsap8-si3-goo7 **liap8** *bi2*

    1SG   calculate there-is ten-four-five   *grain* rice

    'By my calculation, there are fourteen or fifteen grains of rice.'

We nevertheless consider that in the documents of our corpus this *liap8*, as it is only used with the noun 'rice', is not a CL but a MW, as in English or French 'a grain of rice' 'un grain de riz'. It is only later that this *liap8* has been used in Taiwanese for nouns like:

'pearl':   一粒珠仔 *tsit8 liap8 tsu1-a2* 'a pearl';

'seal':   一粒印仔 *tsit8 liap8 in3-a2* 'one seal';

And even for big and round objects like:

'eggs', 'balls', and 'mountains':

一粒卵 *tsit8 liap8 nng7*   'an egg',

一粒球 *tsit8 liap8 kiu5*   'a ball',

一粒山 *tsit8 liap8 suaN1* 'a mountain'.[7]

The difference with Mandarin is evident here as in Mandarin the word is only used for small and round objects (see Yang 1991).

3.3 Classifiers that disappeared after the 16th–17th century or were very rarely used.

We also noticed that the following CLs have progressively disappeared: *ke3* 架, which is no longer in use in contemporary TSM, *keng1* 間 that disappeared in the 16th c., but surprisingly came back into use today, *tng3* 頓, *tso7* 座, *pun2* 本, *pak4* 幅, and *piN2* 扁, but that are very rarely used in our documents. Examples:

(32) 阿娘許前頭一架鞦韆在許。 (*LZJ*, 6, 1581 edition)

    A-niu5 hit4   tsing5-thau5 tsit8 **ke3** *tshian7-tshiu1 sai7 hia1*

    lady   there front   one CL swing   be-at there

    'Lady, there is one swing over there, in the front.'

---

7 In the *Arte de la lengua Chio Chiu* (Mechior de Mançano, 1620), however, *liap8* is used for grains, and also for beads, precious stones and stars.

(33) 繡床頭邊一扁箱。 (*SLN*, 7, 1573–1620 edition)

    siu3   *tshng5 thau5 piN1 tsit8* **piN2** *siuN1...*

    embroidered bed   front   side   one   CL   travel-case

    '(There is) a travel case in the front, at the bed-head.'

Another interesting case is the CL *khau2* 口 that disappeared in the 20th century. It is only used in the operas of *Li Jing Ji* (1566) and *Li Zhi Ji* (1581, 1651, 1884), often used with the noun 'betel-nuts' *pin7-nng5* 檳榔.

(34) 請亞娘食一口檳榔。 (*LJJ*, 14, 1566 edition; *LZJ*, 5, 1651, and *LZJ*, 8, 1884)

    tshiaN2 a-niu5 tsiah8 tsit8 **khau2** *pin7-nng5*

    invite   Lady   eat   one   CL   betel-nut

    'Please, Lady, have a betel-nut.'

3.4 New classifiers appearing after the 17th c.: *kha1* 腳, *lui2* 蕊, *ting2* 頂, *khu3* 坵, *khi2* 起, *kak* 角

Examples:

(35) 一腳籠仔縛有四耳。 (*LZJ*, 9, 1651)

    tsit8 **kha1** *lang2-a2 pak8 u7*   *si3*   *hiN7*

    one   CL   basket   tie   have four ear

    'The four handles of the basket are tied.'

(36) 一坵菜仔在許后溝。 (*LZJ*, 20, 1651 edition)

    tsit8 **khu3** *tshai3-a2 ti3 hi2*   *au7*   *kau1*

    one   CL   vegetable at there back hollow

    'There is a vegetable field in the back hollow.'

The case of the CL 角 *kak4* which emerged in the 17th c. is particularly interesting since it already existed in the 'transformational texts' (*biànwén* 變文) of the Tang dynasty:

(37) 泉州陳都爺差人下一角文書。 (*LZJ*, 43, 1884)

    tsuan5-tsiu1 Tan5 too3-ia5 tshe3 lang5   *he7*   *tsit8* **kak4** *bun5-su1*

    Quánzhōu   Chén Minister send person give one   CL   document

    'The Minister Chén of Quánzhōu sent somebody to give (you) a document.'

The following ones appeared in the 19th c.: *tsang5* 欉, *tshut4* 出, *kah* 甲:

(38) 再繡一欉好綠竹。 (*LZJ*, 23, 1884 edition)

tsai3 siu3 tsit8 **tsang5** ho2 lik8 tik4
again embroider one CL good green bamboo

'Embroider another good green bamboo.'

(39) 待小七做一出張飛思奔個曲。 (*LZJ*, 18, 1884 edition)

thai7 sio2-tshit4 tso3 tsit8 **tshut4** TiuN-Hui1 su3 phun1 **e5** khik4
wait Xiǎoqī do one CL Zhāng-Fēi think run PRT melody

'Waiting for Xiǎoqī to compose a melody named Zhāng-Fēi thinking of running away.'

Only in the edition of 1884, do we find this case of *tshut4* 出 used to classify a following noun. In the previous editions (those of the *Li Jing Ji* (1566) and the *Li Zhi Ji* (1581, 1651), *tshut4* 出 appears many times without any following noun, just for numbering the scenes of the play. Nowadays *tshut4* 出 is no longer used as the classifier for melodies, but it is still used for operas and movies.

4 Conclusion

Our detailed study of the evolution of the CLs in Southern Min between the 14th and the 19th centuries leads us to the following conclusions:

We did not find any strong evidence to confirm the main tendencies of the second stage of the cyclic change that were mentioned in the introduction, i.e. change from specific classifiers to general classifiers and change from the classifying function of the CLs to the quantifying function.

However, the first stage of this cyclic process involving a broad diversification of the classifiers and increase in their number is obvious.

If we did not see the second stage of the cyclic evolution, it might be either because the process started only later, in the second half of the 20th century and is outside the scope of our study, or because this second stage is only a process in the Northern Chinese dialects and not in the Southern ones, which is also a likely scenario. To be confident in putting forward this second scenario, we would need, however, a good picture of the evolution of the classifier system in other Southern Chinese dialects.

Appendix – List of abbreviations

CL	Classifier
COMP	Comparative morpheme
ESM	Early Southern Min
JHN	*Jin Hua nü* 金花女 (*Lady Jinhua*)
LQD	*Lao Qida* 老乞大 (*The Old Sinologist*)
LJJ	*Li Jing Ji* 荔鏡記 (*Romance of the Litchis and the Mirror*)
LZJ	*Li Zhi Ji* 荔枝記 (*Romance of the Litchis*)
MW	Measure Word
N	Noun
NP	Noun Phrase
NEG	Negation
Num	Number
PREP	Preposition
PRT	Particle
PTM	Pre-transitive marker
SLN	*Sū Liùniáng* 蘇六娘 (*Dame Su Liuniang*)
TCQSJ	*Tóngchuāng Qín Shū Jì* 同窗琴書記
	(*Romance of the classmates with lute and books*)
TSM	Taiwanese Southern Min
1SG	First single person
2SG	Second single person
2PL	Second plural person
3SG	Third single person

References

Bisang, Walter. 2012. Numeral classifiers with plural marking. A challenge to Greenberg. *This volume.*

Chao, Yuen Ren. 1968. *A Grammar of Spoken Chinese*. Berkeley/Los Angeles: California University Press.

Douglas, Carstairs. 1873. *Chinese-English Dictionary of the Vernacular or Spoken Language of Amoy with the Principal Variations of the Changchew and Chinchew Dialects*. Supplement by Thomas Barclay. London: Trübner and Co. 1873; Taipei: SMC publishing Inc., 1990.

Feng, Shengli. 2012. The Syntax and Prosody of Classifiers in Classical Chinese. *This volume.*

Greenberg, Joseph. 1974. Numeral classifiers and substantival number: Problems in the genesis of a linguistic type. *Proceedings of the 11th International Congress of Linguistics*, 17–37. Bologna.

Li, Charles N. and Sandra A. Thompson. 1981. *Mandarin Chinese: A Functional Reference Grammar*. Berkeley/Los Angeles: California University Press.

Lien, Chin-fa and Chiu Liching Livy. *Forthcoming*. Shape Classifiers in Earlier Southern Min Texts.

Melchior de Mançano. 1620. *Arte de la lengua Chiõ Chiu*. Ms: University of Barcelona.

Peyraube, Alain. 1998a. On the History of Classifiers in Archaic and Medieval Chinese. In *Studia Linguistica Serica*, T'sou, Benjamin K (ed.), 39–68. City University of Hong Kong.

Peyraube, Alain. 1998b. Shanggu, zhonggu hanyu liangci de lishi fazhan [Historical Evolution of Classifiers in Ancient and Medieval Chinese]. Beijing: *Yuyanxue luncong* 21: 99–122.

Peyraube, Alain and Thekla Wiebusch. 1993. Le rôle des classificateurs nominaux en chinois et leur évolution historique : un cas de changement cyclique. *Faits de langue* 2: 51–61.

Peyraube, Alain and Lin Jang-Ling. 2010. *Laoqida* de geti liangci he yuyan xunhuan xianxiang zhi guanxi [Individuating Classifiers in Lao Qida and the language cyclic change]. *Hanyushi xuebao* 10: 1–9.

Shi, Bing-Hua and Wu Shou-Li. 1997. *Nanguan xiwen: Chen San and Wuniang*. [Chinese Southern Min operas: Chen San and Wuniang]. Volume I and II. Taiwan: Tainan wenhua zhongxin.

Tai, James H-Y. 1999. A note on the classifier bue[53] in Southern Min. In *Contemporary Studies on the Min Dialects*, Ting Pang-hsin (ed.). Journal of Chinese Linguistics Monographs 14.

van der Loon, Piet. 1992. *The Classical Theatre and art Song of South Fukien*. Taipei: Nan-Tian publications.

Wu, Shou-Li. 2001a. *Min jiajing kan Li-jing-ji xi wen jiao li* [Annotated Texts of the Romance of Li Jing Ji of Ming Jiajing Edition]. Taipei: Cong-Yi publications.

Wu, Shou-Li. 2001b. *Min Wanli kan Lizhi-ji xi wen jiao li* [Annotated Texts of the Romance of Li Zhi Ji of Ming Wanli Edition]. Taipei: Cong-Yi publications.

Wu, Shou-Li. 2001c. *Qing Shunzhi kan Lizhi-ji xi wen jiao li* [Annotated Texts of the Romance of Li Zhi Ji of Ming Shunzhi Edition]. Taipei: Cong-Yi publications.

Wu, Shou-Li. 2001d. *Qing Guangxu kan Lizhi-ji xi wen jiao li* [Annotated Texts of the Romance of Li Zhi Ji of Ming Guangxu Edition]. Taipei: Cong-Yi publications.

Wu, Shou-Li. 2002a. *Min Wanli kan Jin Huanü xiwen jiao li* [Annotated Texts of Jin Huanü of Min Wanli Edition]. Taipei: Cong-Yi publications.

Wu, Shou-Li. 2002b. *Min Wanli kan Su Liuniang xiwen jiaoli* [Annotated Texts of Su Liuniang of Min Wanli Edition], 182. Taipei: Cong-Yi publications.

Wu, Shou-Li. 2003. *Qing Qianlong kan Tongchuang-Qin-Shu-Ji xiwen jiao li* [Annotated texts of the Romance of Tongchuang-Qin-Shu-Ji of Qing Qianlong Edition]. Taipei: Cong-Yi publications.

Yang, Hsiu-Fang. 1991. *Taiwan Minnanyu yufa gao* [Taiwanese Southern Min Grammar]. Taipei: Da-An publications.

Zhang, Cheng. 2012. *Hanyu tongyong liangci de fazhan yu hanyu liangci fanchou de queli* [The relation between the development of general classifiers and the establishment of the category of numeral classifiers in Chinese]. *Journal of Chinese Linguistics* 40: 2, 307–321.

Zhu, Dexi. 1982. *Yufa jiangyi* [Lectures in Grammar]. Beijing: Commercial Press.

III The expression of plurality

Christoph Harbsmeier

5 Plurality and the subclassification of Nouns in Classical Chinese

Abstract: This paper provides a survey of the role of the semantic categories 'plural' and 'singular' in an uninflected language like classical Chinese, which does not generally use explicit markers for the plural.

Keywords: syntax, plural, pronoun, noun, word class

1 Introduction

The history of the plural in the Chinese language has been the subject of extensive research in the last century.[1] Most of this research is concerned with the history of plural suffixes such as *chái* 儕, *bèi* 輩, *měi* 每, *-men* 們 as they evolved slowly from the Late Warring States period onwards.

The definition of the plural is by no means trivial: for example *mín* 民 'people' refers to more than one person, but whether or not the word has to be read as plural remains a highly sensitive question which fortunately need not concern us in this paper.

To start out with, a few terminological points are important for the methodology in what follows:

1. By the term 'collective' I refer to the kind of plural noun that refers to an enumerable closed set of items, as usually does the term *zhū hóu* 諸侯 'the feudal lords'. For example, when we call *shèng wáng* 聖王 'the sage kings' it is considered mostly collective: this is because it tends to refer to a closed enumerable set. If, on the other hand I call *xián shèng* 賢聖 'the worthy and the sages' plural and not collective, this is because these *xián shèng* 賢聖 are not considered to constitute a closed enumerable set of any kind.
2. The term 'non-referential' is evidenced in a noun like *jūn zǐ* 君子 'the gentleman', the non-specifiable reference of which does not allow (and even less invites) the question to which item in this world is being referring.

---

1 Klaus Kaden (1964) remains the most detailed monograph on the subject. Like most of the rest of the literature it mainly concentrates on the explicit marking of plural nouns with plural markers in the history of the language. But see also in particular Iljic (2001).

The present paper does not deal with the history of plural suffixes but with the existence in pre-Buddhist classical Chinese of a wide range of nouns with plural meanings that are not recognisable by any plural suffixes. These un-marked semantically plural nouns must be seen in the context of a range of sub-classifications that are essential for a proper description of the classical Chinese language. It is in the nature of things that this paper must remain largely descriptive: there seems to me to be ample reason to emphasise the need to be sure of the philological evidence we are talking about before it makes good methodological sense to launch into abstract theoretical linguistic discussion.

A great deal of attention has been paid to the distinction between plural morphology on the one hand, and the problems around the semantics of plurality on the other.[2]

The sub-classification of classical Chinese nouns[3] must begin with the establishment of at least the following nominal subcategories:

Table 4: Nominal subcategories of classical Chinese nouns

Nominal subcategories	Definition	Abbreviation	Exemple
1. 數/可數	'count noun'	*nc*	樹 'tree'
2. 質/質物	'mass noun'	*nm*	水 'water'
3. 質/數	'primarily mass'	*nm?*	毛 'hair/hairs'
4. 關	'relational noun'	*n[post-N]*	身 'one's (own) body'
5. 數/質	'primarily count'	*nc?*	木 'tree/timber'
6. 抽/抽象	'abstract noun'	*nab*	義 'rectitude'
7. 單/單數	'*singulare tantum*'	*npro@sing*	予 'I'
8. 單/複	'primarily singular'	*NP@sing?*	先君 'deceased ruler'
9. 複/複數	'*plurale tantum*'	*NP@plur*	子女 'children'
10. 複/單	'primarily plural'	*NP@plur?*	先王 'former kings'
11. 群/群體	'collective'	*NP@coll*	先聖 'the former sages'
12. 群/單	'primarily collective'	*NP@coll?*	諸侯 'feudal lords'
13. 泛/泛指	'non-referential'	*NP@nonref*	君子 'the gentleman'

---

2 See Wiese (1995) and Wiese (1996). There is also a rich literature on the formal semantics of mass nouns and the plural that can provide helpful parameters of analysis, such as Chierchia, Gennaro (1998) and Eschenbach (1993).

3 The most detailed magisterial traditional treatment of classical Chinese grammar remains Zhou Fagao (1993). For a representative treatment of nouns in Chinese grammars see He Leshi and Yang Bojun (1992: 80–93). Yi Mengchun (1992: 106–113) and Li Zuofeng (1993: 172–213) and Yang Bojun (1998: 14–24) are more detailed. None of these books touch upon the problems of the non-referential nouns and the unmarked plural that are at issue in this paper.

In what follows I shall concentrate mainly on the sub-classification of nouns with respect to number, of which I shall discuss a fair number of example expressions.[4]

I shall begin with some preliminary considerations on the distinction between mass nouns and count nouns, well aware that the plural of mass nouns (three kinds of wine) is quite different from that of count nouns (three bottles).

One of the first things an ancient Chinese child must grasp when learning classical Chinese words to refer to 'trees' is that *shù* 樹 and *mù* 木, though both referring to trees, differ radically in that *shù* 樹 always refers to one or more trees, whereas *mù* 木 very often is a mass noun and refers to the material trees are made of: 'wood; timber'.

Thus the learner must learn that there are *mù jī* 木屐 'clogs' but not *shù jī 樹屐 just as there are only *mù jī* 木雞 'wooden cocks' and not *shù jī 樹雞. Again, this is not a matter of some arbitrary idiom a child has to learn by heart. The child is not as insensitive as all our dictionaries continue to be. The child learns that *shù* 樹 is a count noun *nc* while *mù* 木 very often functions as a mass noun *nm*.

Again, if one assumes, for a moment, that *jūn zǐ* 君子, when it means 'gentleman' non-referential and does not normally allow the question 'who exactly do you mean' (i.e. is technically *NP@nonref*), then the discussion to whom the word refers in the current phrase:

(1) 君子曰 (*Zuǒ zhuàn* 左傳)

    jūn zǐ yuē

    'the gentleman will say'

It is not so difficult to answer but grammatically inappropriate in the context. In the philosophical meaning 'person of superior character, superior person' the word *jūn zǐ* 君子 is hardly ever a singular referring expression in pre-Han literature, whereas in the meaning 'person of superior social status' the reference can occasionally be singular.

The contrast of *jūn zǐ* 君子 'person of superior character' with *gōng zǐ* 公子 'prince' and also with the rarer *wáng zǐ* 王子 'prince' is so striking because *jūn zǐ* 君子 'person of superior character; the gentleman' is usually non-referential, and *gōngzǐ* 公子 as well as *wáng zǐ* 王子 are hardly ever used non-referentially.

---

4 Textual examples are tagged in the online version of *Thesaurus Linguae Sericae* (url:tls.uni-hd.de).

In other words, one can usually ask to whom the word *gōngzǐ* 公子 refers to, and one can very rarely ask to whom *jūn zǐ* 君子 concretely refers.

A learner of classical Chinese will have to learn that *shèng zhě* 聖者 'the sage' or *rén zhě* 仁者 'the benevolent person' are not so much plural as non-referential, and these words always tend to be non-referential: 'the sage', 'the humane person' does not invite the question to which individual was specifically identified by such an expression.

It is only in Han times, for example in the work of the poet and lexicographer Yang Xiong 楊雄 (53 BC–AD 18), that the phrase *shèngrén* 聖人 came to have the standardised singular reference to Confucius which has remained current since then.

Similarly, when it comes to the verb *yuē* 曰 'say', after a non-referential noun of this sort, as in *jūn zǐ yuē* 君子曰 'the gentleman will comment' a competent child reading classical Chinese knew that it is not a good idea to ask such questions as 'exactly when' the saying occurred. The reading of verbs with nonreferential subjects tends to be tenseless.

The objection that there is no tense in classical Chinese is irrelevant to this particular point: the question 'when' is as inappropriate in ancient Chinese as it is in a language with tense. The case in hand demonstrates that the conceptual category TENSE can be present even when it cannot be morphologically marked. The inadmissibility of the question *hé shí* 何時 'at what time' clinches the point just as much as the inadmissibility of a tense marker would.

2 Subcategorisation of nouns with respect to number: Singulars

2.1 Singulare tantum

I turn now more specifically to the subcategorisation of nouns with respect to number. The feature of being a *singulare tantum*, i.e. usable only with singular reference, establishes another important category of nouns, like that of the non-referential nouns. This feature does not attach to words as such, but to words under a given meaning: The second person pseudo-pronoun *jūn* 君 'you', when used alone, is *singulare tantum*, but the noun *jūn* 君 'ruler; rulers' is not. 'You-plur' has to be *zhū jūn* 諸君 in classical Chinese whereas in Ming dynasty colloquial Chinese *nǐ* 你 is often plural, as in *nǐ liǎngge* 你兩個 which would have to be *nǐmen liǎngge* 你們兩個 in modern Standard Chinese.

The quality of being *singulare tantum*, like that of being non-referential, as attached to one word in one meaning, can obviously change. Thus, in OBI inscriptions *wáng* 王 'His Majesty' is omnipresent. The cases where *wáng* 王 is plural are marginal and are so few that they can be counted on one hand. Moreover, it is quite possible to claim the word *wáng* 王 in fact has a different extended meaning on those few occasions where non-Shang kings are referred to by the term *wáng* 王.

In later times, *wáng* 王, as in *xiān wáng* 先王 'the former kings' was used in the plural. By contrast, *wáng zhě* 王者 'a true king' has neither singular nor plural reference. It remained non-referential. The question to which actual individual *wáng zhě* 王者 is used to refer is grammatically inappropriate, and logically not to the point, one might even say.

3 Subcategorisation of nouns with respect to number: Plurals

3.1 Non-referential and typically plural nominal expressions

I now turn to a brief survey of nominal expressions that typically exclude singular interpretation either because they are typically non-referential or because they are typically plural.

3.1.1 Non-referentiality marked by *rén-* 人-

Prefixed *rén* 人 creates non-referential rather than merely indefinite nominals in a wide range of common cases like the following:

– n *chén* 臣	'minister'	NP@nonref	*rén chén* 人臣	'a minister'
– n *jūn* 君	'ruler'	NP@nonref	*rén jūn* 人君	'a ruler of men'
– n *zhǔ* 主	'ruler'	NP@nonref	*rén zhǔ* 人主	'a ruler of men'
– n *fù* 婦	'wife'	NP@nonref	*rén fù* 人婦	'a wife'
– n *zǐ* 子	'child'	NP@nonref	*rén zǐ* 人子	'a child'
– n *nú* 奴	'slave'	NP@nonref	*rén nú* 人奴	'a slave'
– n *lì* 吏	'employee'	NP@nonref	1. *rén lì* 人吏	'an employee'
			2. *guān lì* 官吏	'official'
– n *yì* 役	'corvee'	NP@nonref	*rén yì* 人役	'a corvee labourer, labourer'
– n *shī* 師	'teacher'	NP@nonref	*rén shī* 人師	'a teacher'

3.1.2 Plurality suggested by preposed guó 國

Prefixed *guó* 國 has a similar but not identical effect as *rén* 人 above in a number of instances:

– *n chén* 臣	'minister'	*guó chén* 國臣	NP@nonref
		'the ministers of the state'	
– *n rén* 人	'person'	*guó rén* 國人	NP@nonref
		'the (senior) citizens of the state'	
– *n shì* 士	'gentleman'	*guó shì* 國士	NP@nonref
		'a state hero; the state heroes; be a state hero; as a state hero'	
– *n gōng* 工	'artisan'	versus NP@coll	*guó gōng* 國工
		'skilled artisans of the state'	
– *n zǐ* 子	'son'	versus NP@coll	*guó zǐ* 國子
		in the meaning of 'relatives of senior ministers etc in the state'	
– *n lìng* 令	'ordinance'	versus NP@plur	*guó lìng* 國令
		'ordinances of the state'	
– *n jūn* 君	'ruler'	versus NP@nonref	*guó jūn* 國君
		'a ruler of a state'	
– *n lǎo* 老	'the old'	NP@coll	*guó lǎo* 國老
		'the distinguished people of great age in the state'	
– *n sōu* 叟	'old man'	NP@coll	*guó sōu* 國叟
		'distinguished people of great age in the state'	

It remains important to remember that there are neat exceptions to this pattern. *Guó wáng* 國王 is in fact found at least once in *Lùnhéng* 論衡 in the plural referring to kings of barbarian states, and this expression became the standard word in Buddhist texts to refer in the singular to the king of a state in the singular. Thus one must note the significant changes in Buddhist literary Chinese to the pre-Buddhist regularities discussed in the present paper.

3.1.3 Plurality marked by preposed yǒu 有?

Some constructions with preposed *yǒu* 有 invite a plural default interpretation, while sometimes apparently not excluding a contextually enforced singular interpretation:

– *NP@plur*   *yǒu tǔ* 有土   'owners of land' NOT: 'an owner of land'
– *NP@plur*   *yǒu sī* 有司   'holders of office'
– *NP@plur*   *yǒu gōng* 有功   'havers of merit'
– *NP@plur*   *yǒu bāng* 有邦   1. 'rulers';
                                    2. 'countries'

– *NP@plur*   *yǒu zuì* 有罪   'havers of guilt'
– *NP@plur*   *yǒu dào* 有道   'havers of the Way'
– *NP@plur*   *wú dào* 無道   'lackers of the Way'
– *NP@plur*   *yǒu dé* 有德   'havers of virtue in general'

3.1.4 Plurality marked by preposed negation

– *Non-referential nouns in wú* 無:
   – *NP@plur*   *wú yì* 無義   'those without a just cause'
   – *NP@plur*   *wú chǐ* 無恥   'those without shame'
   – *NP@plur*   *wú dào* 無道   'those without the Way' as in 伐無道 *fá wú dào*
                                    'attack those without the Way'
   – *NP@plur*   *wú gū* 無辜   'those without guilt' as in 殺無辜 *shā wú gū*
                                    'kill those without guilt'
   – *NP@plur*   *wú zuì* 無罪   'those without crimes' as in
                                    不殺無罪 *bù shā wú zuì*
                                    'not kill people who have no crimes'

– *Non-referential nouns in bù* 不:
   Non-referential nominals in *bù* 不 are typically non-referential. Standard examples include the following:

– *NP@nonref*   *bù gū* 不辜   'the innocent; an innocent person'
– *NP@nonref*   *bù xiào* 不肖   'the incompetent; an incompetent person'
– *NP@nonref*   *bù rén* 不仁   'the cruel; the heartless; a heartless person'

3.2 Unmarked predictably plural subject and agent nominalisation

All the following monosyllabic deverbal nouns must properly be interpreted as exocentric constructions along the lines of *n[post-N]@nonref* because they involve a lexically retrievable nominal head.

– n@plur	*rén* 仁	'the good persons; good persons'	
– n@nonref	*rūn* 惇	'the earnest'	
– n@nonref	*què* 愨	'the sincere'	
– n@nonref	*chūn* 純	'the pure'	
– n@nonref	*xìn* 信	'the trusty'	
– n@nonref	*nìng* 佞	'skilful talkers'	
– n@nonref	*chí* 侈	'the extravagant'	
– n@nonref	*gōng* 公	'the public-spirited'	
– n@nonref	*sī* 私	'the selfish'	
– n@nonref	*sú* 俗	'the vulgar'	
– n@nonref	*xián* 賢	'the worthy'	
– n@nonref	*xiōng* 凶	'the wicked'	
– n@nonref	*è* 惡	1.'the bad' 2. 'bad deeds'	
– n@nonref	*Zuì* 罪	'the guilty; convicted culprits'	
– n@nonref	*Fá* 罰	'those who have been fined/punished'	
– n@nonref	*Lì* 力	'the powerful'	
– n@nonref	*Zhòng* 重	'political heavyweights'	
– n@nonref	*Jiǎn* 儉	'the thrifty; the frugal'	
– n@nonref	*Yǒng* 勇	'the courageous'	
– n@nonref	*Bèi* (sic!) 北	'those who flee, the fugitives'	
– n@nonref	*Fú* 服	'the submissive'; 'those who have surrendered'	
– n@nonref	*dù* 妒	'the jealous'	
– n@nonref	*zhì* 知 / 智	'the wise'	
– n@nonref	*jiàn* 健	'the vigorous/energetic'	
– n@nonref	*pí* (sic!) 罷	'the exhausted'	
– n@nonref	*xīn* 新	'newcomers'	
– n@nonref	*jiù* 舊	'old ones (tools)' also: 'old acquaintances'	
– n@nonref	*shēng* 生	'the living'	
– n@nonref	*sǐ* 死	'the dead'	
– n@nonref	*huǐ* 毀	'slanderers'	
– n@nonref	*yù* 譽	'panderers'	

– *n@nonref*   *sì* 駟   'quartet of horses'
– *n@nonref*   *jīn* 金   'metal musical instruments'
– *n@nonref*   *shí* 石   'stone musical instruments'
– *n@nonref*   *sī* 絲   'string musical instruments'
– *n@nonref*   *zhú* 竹   'bamboo musical instruments'

4 Plurality and compound words

Another explicit way of excluding singular reference readings for nouns is the use of compounds. I shall give a sample range of this below.

– *n@plur*   *cān fēi* 驂騑   'side horses in a quartet of horses'
– *n@plur*   *fú mǎ* 服馬   'the two central horses of a quartet of horses'
– *n@plur*   *zhōng gǔ* 鐘鼓   'bells and drums'

4.1 Spirits: some *pluralia tantum*

First, consider that the monosyllabic words for ghosts and spirits are open to singular and plural interpretation:

guǐ 鬼   *n* 1. 'ghost';   2. 'ghosts'
shén 神   *n* 1. 'spirit';   2. 'spirits'

Contrarily, the following are collective or non-referentially abstract nouns which can never be used to refer to single spirits, they are *pluralia tantum*:

– *NP@nonref*   *guǐ shén* 鬼神   'ghosts and spirits'
                               cannot refer to a single sprite of which one is
                               not sure whether it is ghost or spirit.
– *NP@nonref*   *shén míng* 神明   'the spirits and the luminous'
– *NP@nonref*   *míng shén* 明神   'the bright/higher spirits'
– *NP@nonref*   *shén qí* 神祇   'the spirits'
– *NP@nonref*   *shén guǐ* 神鬼   'the spirits and ghosts'

4.2 Documents

The case of documents is interesting because it brings out a pervasive analytic problem: How one is to decide whether a compound is additive or merely epexegetic, in technical terms, is whether it constitutes a *hendiadys* or not:

jīng 經   nc   'classic(s)'

diǎn 典   nc   'revered text(s)'

shū 書   nc   'document(s)'

jí 籍   n   'document(s)'

– *NP@plur*   *jīng diǎn* 經典   'classics'

– *NP@plur*   *jīng shū* 經書   'classics'

– *NP@plur*   *jīng jí* 經籍   'classics'

– *NP@plur*   *diǎn jí* 典籍   'classical documents'

– *NP@plur*   *shū qì* 書契   'written documents' 書契以來 *shūqì yǐ lái* 'from the invention of documents, since there are documents'

There are cases where such distinctions between plural and singular reference of complex nouns simply have to be learned by heart. The following all regularly have plural reference:

– *NP@coll*   *xiān shèng* 先聖   'the former sages' and

– *NP@coll*   *xiān shèng wáng* 先聖王   'the former sage kings'

These are special because they are normally used to refer to a closed set. They are thus not ordinary *pluralia tantum*:

– *NP@coll xiān wáng* 先王 'the former kings':
is extremely common and also nearly always plural, referring to a closed set of traditionally listed individuals.

The list may vary, but the ability to list the 'former kings' does not. Thus the term must count as a *plurale tantum*, with very few exceptions where the context forces a singular reading.

In contrast:

– *NP@plur xiān jūn* 先君 'our deceased ruler':
which looks very much the same, and is also very common, but which in an overwhelming majority of cases invites an interpretation in the singular.

It remains important that a very definite context will occasionally impose or enforce reference to a contextually determinate set of rulers.

4.3 Friends: exclusion of singular reference interpretation

In the case of the ancient Chinese terminology for friendship, the facts are particularly interesting. The near-synonym compounds all exclude singular reference interpretation:

– *yǒu* 友 and *péng* 朋 can refer to a single friend or colleague.
– *qīn* 親 *n@plur* 'friends, close allies' I have so far not found with such singular reference. All references in TLS are in the plural as are the references for *n@plur qīn* 親 'relatives', which seems to be as plural as *NP@plur qīn qī* 親戚 'relatives'.
– *péng yǒu* 朋友 can occasionally be used with indefinite singular reference, but is never definite, mostly plural or non-referential.
– *zhī yīn* 知音, *gù rén* 故人 are often singular and indefinite in reference.

But not so for the following coordinate compounds which tend to refer to closed sets:

– *NP@coll*	*xí gù* 習故	'confidants'
– *NP@coll*	*jìn xí* 近習	'confidants'
– *NP@coll*	*dǎng rén* 黨人	'members of the faction',
– *NP@coll*	*zhī yǒu* 知友	'friends'
– *NP@coll*	*péng dǎng* 朋黨	'associates'
– *NP@coll*	*jìn qīn* 近親	'those close to one'
– *NP@coll*	*zuǒ yòu* 左右	'senior officials, senior aides'
– *NP@coll*	*gǔ gōng* 股肱	'helpers' may have some singular uses although I am unable to trace them for the moment.

4.4 Concubines

bì 婢   'maid'
qiè 妾   'concubine'
– *NP@coll*   *bì qiè* 婢妾   'maids and concubines'

4.5 Sages and Men of Talent

– *NP@plur*   *xián cái* 賢才   'the worthy and talented'
– *NP@plur*   *xián shèng* 賢聖   'the worthy and the sage'
– *NP@plur*   *shén shèng* 神聖   'the divine sages'
– *NP@coll*   *shèng wáng* 聖王   'the sage kings' is mostly collective, but
                                      sometimes predicative.

4.6 Guests

Guests and merchants are referred to as groups only by the standard compounds:

bīn 賓   'honoured guest'
kè 客   'foreigner; guest'
– *NP@plur*   *bīn kè* 賓客   '(the various) guests, visitors of various kinds'

4.7 Merchants

shāng 商   '(itinerant) trader'
gǔ 賈   '(sedentary) merchant'
– *NP@plur*   *shāng gǔ* 商賈   'traders of all kinds'

4.8 Thieves

tōu 偷   'petty thief'
zéi 賊   'thief'
– *NP@plur tōu zéi* 偷賊 'thieves of all kinds'

4.9 Troubles

jiān 艱 'trouble'

nàn 難 'difficulty'

– *NP@plur jiān nàn* 艱難 'difficulties of all kinds'

4.10 Shamans

The monosyllables are singular and the binominal is plural, but in this case for the manifest reason that both sexes are included:

wū 巫 'female shaman > shaman'

xí 覡 'male shaman, sorcerer'

– *NP@plur wū xí* 巫覡 'shamans (male or female)'

4.11 Teeth

Even the case of words for teeth and bones follows the expected pattern:

chǐ 齒 'tooth; teeth'

yá 牙 'fang; fangs; teeth'

– *NP@plur chǐ yá* 齒牙 'the teeth (of all kinds)'

4.12 Bones

One is not so sure of the salience in the semantic contrast between the following words for bones to decide for sure whether that distinction is neutralised in the following:

hái 骸 'skeleton; bones'

gǔ 骨 'bone; bones'

– *NP@plur hái gǔ* 骸骨 'the bones'

4.13 Boxes

Boxes and coffers raise a similar problem because the semantic difference between the two is not neat enough to ensure that thee two terms are not taken in this context as synonyms the basic distinction between which is neutralised in this collocation:

Qiè 篋   'basket; bamboo box'

Kuì 匱   'box'

– *NP@plur   Qiè kuì* 篋匱   'boxes and coffers'

4.14 Garments

yī 衣 'garment'

fú 服 'formal garment'

– *NP@plur*   *yī fú* 衣服   'garments'

– *NP@plur*   *yī shàn* 衣衫   'garments'

– *NP@plur*   *yī qiū* 衣裘   'garments and cloaks'

– *NP@plur*   *yīhè* 衣褐   'coarse garments'

– *NP@plur*   *yīcháng* 衣裳   'garments, upper and lower'

A host of questions arise in connection with clothes particularly. We need to investigate whether one may go out and buy one *rú yī* 儒衣 'Confucian garb', or one *bù yī* 布衣 'coarse garment', and whether one can buy three of such, in classical Chinese. I think one probably can. But our present concern is that you cannot *tuō yī fú* 脫衣服 'take off your garment' in pre-Buddhist Chinese.

4.15 Buildings and Institutions

gōng 宮   'building(s)'

shì 室   'house(s)'

diàn 殿   'palace(s)'

lú 廬   'home(s)'

shè 舍   'simple dwelling(s)'

wū 屋   'dwelling(s)'

cāng 倉   'large granary of rectangular shape'

qūn 囷   'small round granary'

lín 廩   'large square granary'

kù 庫   'storehouse designed for weapons and the like'

fǔ 府   'building housing archives as well as other government supplies and precious objects'

One must ask oneself how one decides whether the following are additive or epexegetic with neutralised semantic contrast:

– *NP@plur*   *gōng shì* 宮室   'buildings'
– *NP@plur*   *gōng diàn* 宮殿   'palaces'
– *NP@plur*   *lú shè* 盧舍   'cottages'
– *NP@plur*   *shì wū* 室屋   'homes'
– *NP@plur*   *diàn wū* 殿屋   'palatial buildings'
– *NP@plur*   *jiā shì* 家室   'families/homes'
– *NP@plur*   *xiáng xù* 庠序   'schools of all kinds'
– *NP@plur*   *cāng qūn* 倉囷   'the granaries of various kinds'
– *NP@plur*   *cāng lín* 倉廩   'the granaries of various kinds'
– *NP@plur*   *qūn cāng* 囷倉   'the granaries of various kinds'
– *NP@plur*   *fǔ kù* 府庫   'the storehouses of various kinds, civil and military'
– *NP@plur*   *cāng kù* 倉庫   'the storehouses of various kinds, for food and weapons'

4.16 Laws and Regulations

Even for abstract concepts the pattern is maintained:

fǎ 法   'law; the law'
hào 號   'legal order'
lìng 令   'order, legal command'
lǜ 律   'ordinance'
dù 度   'regulation'

The compounds are all plural in reference, but it is not always clear in which cases we have epexegetic synonym compounds and where we have additive compounds:

– *NP@plur*   *fǎ lìng* 法令   'legal orders of all kinds'
– *NP@plur*   *fǎ dù* 法度   'laws and regulations'
– *NP@plur*   *fǎ lǜ* 法律   'laws of all kinds'
– *NP@plur*   *hào lìng* 號令   'legal commands of all sorts'

In all such cases there may remain some doubt whether they are to be construed as synonym compounds *hendiadys* or as additive compounds.

The above examples could be multiplied. But they suffice to establish and exemplify a fairly regular pattern of number-related distinctions in classical Chinese that deserve detailed study, and that so far have received little attention in the grammatical literature.

5 A special case of singular nouns: Proper names

5.1 The notion of *singulare tantum* in proper names

The problems surrounding the notion of *singulare tantum* in proper names are special and sometimes complex. For example, the proper name *Yáo* 堯 is surely a singular referring expression, and yet *shí Yáo* 十堯 'even ten Yáo's' is common enough in the literature. The addition of the number changes the meaning of the word and makes the term general 'a person like Yáo'. The non-referential term is different from the plain singular-reference proper name.

One might be inclined to think that *dì* 帝 'thearch' is also *singulare tantum* but the term clearly develops an extended meaning in such current contexts as *wǔ dì* 五帝 'the Five Thearchs' which in turn never takes an indefinite meaning 'five of the thearch category'. And indeed, at no point does *dì* 帝 seem to mean any such thing as the indefinite 'a thearch'.

6 Pronouns and the categorical distinction between singular and plural

The case of first person pronouns, by contrast with the other cases I have presented so far, has been noticed by many a long time ago. Consider a scribe's or diviner's child in oracle bone times, learning his first-person pronouns:

- *yú* 余, he will have to learn, is always strictly singular and contrasts with another person in the singular.
- *wǒ* 我, he will quickly come to understand, is practically never singular and refers collectively to 'our party, we' as opposed to the 'others' in the plural.

In order to use these two words correctly, the child needs the categorical distinction between singular and plural.

In the following contexts, the child will know that *wǒ* 我 would be un-acceptable:

(2) 祖辛害余。(*HEJI 174*)

zu Xīn hài yú

'Ancestor Xin is harming me.'

(3) 羌甲祟余。(*HEJI 1803*)

jiāngjiǎ suì yú

'Jiangjia is sending me misfortune.'

(4) 己亥卜王。(*HEJI 2*)

jǐhài bǔ wáng

On jihai (day 36) cracks were made and (divined:)

(5) 余曰婦鼠毋祝 。(*HM*)

yú yuē fù shǔ wú zhù

'I should declare: Lady Rat should not offer incantations.'

In Warring States times, a child would know that *wǒ* 我 often does make assertive or contrastive self-reference, but that at the same time, the word *wǒ* 我 (like the new and unassertive 'light' first person pronoun *wú* 吾, and unlike the experiential old *yú* 余) currently has plural reference. In order to learn one's way with pronouns, as a learner of classical Chinese one has to handle the categories of singular versus plural proficiently.

6.1 Second person pronouns

– *qīng* 卿 and *nǎi* 乃/迺 are always *npro@sing* singular.
– *n@pro.sing jūn* 君 'my lord' on its own, and *n@pro.sing wáng* 王 'your majesty' are not pronouns, but nouns that function pronominally. Used with-out modifiers they have singular reference.

Now, by Han times, the construction *zhū jūn* 諸君 has become perfectly current and thus creates a situation where *jūn* 君 'you' is unambiguously singular and *zhū jūn* 諸君 'you gentlemen' is unambiguously plural.

While 二三子 *èr-sān-zǐ* 'you young people' is explicitly non-singular, i.e. *plurale tantum*, in reference, and often, though not always, functions like a pronoun.

6.2 Deictic pronouns

When *qí rén* 其人 does not have its pregnant idiomatic meaning 'the right (kind of) person', it appears to be regularly *singulare tantum* and seems never translatable as 'these people'.

Consider:

– *NP@sing cǐ rén* 此人 'this person': the person identified is hardly ever plural.
– *NP@sing sī rén* 斯人 'such a person' is not plural in pre-Buddhist literature

Preposing the deictic *ruò* 若 'this' has regular singular reference, one can obtain *ruò rén* 若人 'this man'.

Contrastingly:

– *NP@plur bǐ rén* 彼人 'these people' only very occasionally refers to a single person in pre-Buddhist texts, and it thus differs significantly from *cǐ rén* 此人 in a way that one would not predict. (In Buddhist texts, on the other hand, the reference is indifferently singular or plural.)

7 The problem of individualised mass nouns

Count nouns must be distinguished from collective nouns. Thus we have:

– *nc rén* 人 as in:

(6) 三人行必有我師焉。(*LY*)

  sān rén xíng bì yǒu wǒ shī yān

  'When three persons walk along there is bound to a teacher for me among them'

– *nm@coll mín* 民 as in *wú mín* 五民 'five kinds of people', namely *shì* 士 'scholars', *nóng* 農 peasants, *shāng* 商 'merchants', *gōng* 工 'craftsmen', *gù* 賈 'traders'.

Physically, *rén* 人 and *mín* 民 are one and the same thing, and they certainly are increasingly many. The *mín* 民 have always been especially many, but they are not generally counted by individuals but by kind. (*Wàn mín* 萬民 'myriad people' are many more than 10 000, whereas *wàn rén* 萬人 'ten thousand people' would typically have to be something like that number.)

Should we analyse *mín* 民 as a collective plural, *les gens du peuple* or collective singular *le peuple?* One might well want to argue that Chinese is underdetermined with respect to this distinction.

7.1 Some cases of suspected *singularia tantum*

Consider next the case of *guó* 國: the phrase *zhì* (or perhaps better: *chí*) *guó* 治國 does not translate into 'govern states' but 'govern one's state'.

This is because just as *shēn* 身 in *xiū shēn* 修身 is understood along the lines of *qí shēn* 其身 'his person' or *jǐ shēn* 己身 'his own person', so the word *guó* 國 in *zhì guó* 治國 'govern the state' is understood along the lines of *qí guó* 其國 'the relevant state; one's state'. The default interpretation of words like *guó* 國 and *shēn* 身 is in the singular, although there is nothing to prevent one, by explicit use of words, to impose a plural reading, as in *zhū guó* 諸國 'the various states'.

Considering:

- *n@sing shēn* 身 'person' itself is *singulare tantum:* this word normally refers to the person of a single human.
- *NP@sing rén wù* 人物 'personality' may seem puzzling, because there clearly could be many such personalities. But in classical Chinese the tendency is for this phrase to have singular reference.

8 Conclusion

Pluralia tantum, singularia tantum, non-referential nouns, and mass nouns are well known and well described in many languages. The present paper has shown that these categories are entirely relevant for the description of classical Chinese even at a stage of the language when the marking of the plural was extremely marginal in the written language as we know it.

An important part of this investigation is the discovery that the plural interpretation of classical Chinese, though not marked by suffixes, is nonetheless predictable and regular in many instances. The coherent sets presented in this brief survey could and should surely be expanded to include later evidence than that focussed on in this paper.

As a non-explicit hidden category, plurality plays an important cognitive part in in the acquisition of classical Chinese grammar even before learners of Chinese had to learn to handle their own 'plural suffixes' which were superimposed upon the evolving system described in this paper rather than replacing it.

Abbreviations and conventions[5]

nab	'abstract noun'
nc	'count noun'
nc?	'count noun occasionally used as mass noun'
nm	'mass noun'
nm?	'mass noun occasionally used as a count noun'
@	'marker between syntactic category and semantic feature'
n@nonref	'non-referential noun'
n@plur	'plural noun'
npro@sing	'singular pronoun'
n@pro.sing	'noun with pronominal function, singular'
p[post-N]	'particle modified by a preceding nominal expression that is omitted/understood'
NP@coll	'collective complex nominal expression'
NP@coll?	'collective complex nominal expression, occasionally used non-collectively'
NP@nonref	'non-referential complex nominal expression'
NP@plur	'plural complex nominal expression'
NP@plur?	'plural complex nominal expression, occasionally used in the singular'
NP@sing	'singular complex nominal expression'
NP@sing?	'singular complex nominal expression, occasionally used in the plural'

References

Chierchia, Gennaro. 1998. Plurality of mass nouns and the notion of 'semantic parameter'. In *Events and Grammar*, S. Rothstein (ed.), 53–103. Dordrecht: Kluwer.

---

5 For a systematic presentation of the notation system of which this is a small part see Harbsmeier (2010).

Corbett, Greville. 2000. *Number*. Cambridge Textbooks in Linguistics. Cambridge: Cambridge University Press.

Eschenbach, Carola. 1993. Semantics of Number. *Journal of Semantics* 10: 1–31.

Kaden, Klaus. 1964. *Der Ausdruck von Mehrzahlverhältnissen in der modernen chinesischen Sprache*. Berlin.

Gupta, Anil. 1980. *The Logic of Common Nouns: An Investigation in Quantified Model Logic*. New Haven: Yale University Press.

Harbsmeier, Christoph. 2010. Clavis Syntactica. A Key to Some Basic Syntactic Categories in Classical Chinese (I). *Hanyushi xuebao* 漢語史學報. 10: 35–56.

He, Leshi (何樂士) and Yang Bojun (楊伯峻). 1992. *Gu Hanyu yufa ji qi fazhan* 古漢語語法及其發展. [Evolution and Grammar of Classical Chinese] Beijing: Yuwenchubanshe.

Iljic, Robert. 2001. The Origin of the Suffix -men 們 in Chinese. *Bulletin of the School of Oriental and African Studies, University of London* 64 (1): 74–97.

Jespersen, Otto. [1909] 1940. *A Modern English Grammar on Historical Principles*, London: Allen and Unwin.

Li, Zuofeng (李佐豐). 1993. *Wenyan shici* 文言實詞. [Content words in Classical Chinese] Beijing: Yuwen Chubanshe.

Link, Godehard. 1983. The Logical Analysis of Plurals and Mass Terms: A Lattice-theoretical Approach. In *Meaning, Use, and Interpretation of Language*, In: R. Bäuerle (eds.), 302–323. Berlin/New York.

Ritter, Elizabeth. 1992. Cross-Linguistic Evidence for Number Phrase. *Canadian Journal of Linguistics* 37 (2): 197–218.

Wiese, Heike. 1995. Semantische und konzeptuelle Strukturen von Numeralkonstruktionen. *Zeitschrift für Sprachwissenschaft* 14 (2): 181–235.

Wiese, Heike. 1996. *Zahl und Numerale. Eine Untersuchung zur Korrelation konzeptueller und sprachlicher Konstruktionen*. Ph.D. Diss., Humboldt-University Berlin.

Yang, Bojun (楊伯峻). 1998. *Gu jin Hanyu cilei tongjie* 古今漢語詞類通解 [Lexical categories of Ancient and Contemporary Chinese], Beijing: Beijing Chubanshe.

Yi, Mengchun (易孟醇). 1992. *Xian Qin yufa* 先秦語法 [Pre-Qin Grammar], Changsha: Hunan Daxue Chubanshe.

Zhou, Fagao (周法高). 1993. *Zhongguo gudai yufa* 中國古代語法 [Ancient Chinese Gammar], Taipei: Academia Sinica.

Barbara Meisterernst

6 Number in Chinese: a diachronic study of *zhū* 諸 from Han to Wei Jin Nanbeichao Chinese

Abstract: In this paper the syntactic and semantic constraints of the plural word *zhū* 諸 are at issue. It will be hypothesized that semantically the basic function of *zhū* 諸 is to refer to a well defined plural set of items, that the *zhū*-NP is definite and referential, and that syntactically, *zhū* 諸 rather has to be analysed as an adjective than as a determiner (definite article). The analysis of the diachronic development of *zhū* 諸 is presented within the framework of the Animacy Hierarchy and it shows a considerable extension of the employment of *zhū* 諸 from [+ANIMATE] [+HUMAN] to [−ANIMATE] nouns, whereas nouns at the top of the Animacy Hierarchy, i.e. personal pronouns, are excluded from a selection by *zhū* 諸. In a separate section on the syntactic constraints of *zhū* 諸 it will be shown that, although the basic syntax within the *zhū*-NP remains the same, a number of changes and extensions can be observed in its syntactic constraints, too. In a last section the semantic constraints of *zhū* 諸 in a Buddhist text, the *Gaoseng Faxian zhuan*, from the beginning of the 5th century, will be at issue with particular regard to its referentiality and its relation to other plural constructions in this text.

Keyword: number words, plural, referentiality, definiteness, Animacy Hierarchy, Han period Chinese, Wei Jin Nanbeichao Chinese

1 Introduction

Number marking is one of the most widespread – and at the same time underestimated – inflectional categories of the noun; it is "most commonly represented by a morpheme indicating plural number, but occasionally in addition by morphemes indicating either singular number or dual number" (Dryer 1989: 865), or even higher number such as trial etc. However, there are also languages which do not have any obligatory or regular marking of number as e.g. Classical Chinese where the category number is neither marked for the noun nor for the verb: "the meaning of a noun can be expressed without reference to number", it is "outside the number system" and nouns express a "general number" (see Corbett 2000: 10). There are even some languages that lack the category number for personal pronouns, the lexical items most likely to be marked by it (Corbett 2000: 50). For instance, Kawi (Old Japanese) is reported to be lacking plural nouns or pronouns, although there are certain quantifiers to indicate plural meanings such as 'many' and 'all' (Corbett 2000). Since languages of this kind are not widespread, linguists have claimed that all languages have number despite the evident counterexamples. Usually languages lacking number are characterized by a *general number* to the effect that a distinction between singular and plural can be made "when it matters" (Corbett 2000: 14); this usually implies a distinction between singular/general and plural. Several syntacto-semantic characteristics may induce an explicit distinction of the plural in languages with *general number*. They can be of different kinds, e.g. topic versus non-topic, referential versus non-referential, human versus non-human, definite versus indefinite (Corbett 2000: 14f). The marking of number under particular constraints can lead to a quasi-obligatory employment of number marking for particular kinds of nouns, frequently for [+HUMAN] nouns. Within these constraints, the 'Animacy Hierarchy' is one of the most important criteria for the employment of plural marking.[1] According to this theory, personal pronouns are the most likely nominal items to show a distinction between singular and plural, followed by kinship terms, which are followed by nouns which have the semantic characteristics [+HUMAN], [+ANIMATE], and with [−ANIMATE] nouns at the lowest point of this hierarchy. This hierarchy also proves to be relevant in the employment of plural markers in Classical and pre-Tang Chinese and accordingly it will be one of the criteria applied in the following discussion.

1.1 Number in Classical and pre-Medieval Chinese

According to Norman (1988: 120) Classical Chinese belongs to those languages which are characterised by the "lack of a number distinction" for personal pronouns, i.e. the nominal items most likely to be marked in this respect (Corbett 2000: 56).[2] However, according to Pulleyblank (1995: 76) and many others,[3]

---

1 Corbett (2000: 56f) presents tables on the 'Animacy Hierarchy' where he discusses different possibilities of plural marking on the following line: "speaker > addressee > 3rd person > kin > human > animate > inanimate".

2 However, Norman notes that during and after the Han period different markers of plurality appear in combination with pronouns, but they are very likely not yet obligatory during these periods. Norman supports this hypothesis with the fact that Modern Chinese dialects display a variety of different plural forms which according to him argues for a late occurrence of an obligatory number distinction with pronouns. This can also be supported by the fact that apparently, dialects show different stages of grammaticalisation in marking the plural (Yue 2003: 85f).

3 See also for instance Wang (1980, 2004), Zhou (1980), Tang (2001), Zhang (2001).

there was a lexical distinction between singular and plural personal pronouns in Pre-Classical Chinese. In the earliest extant literature, the oracle bone inscriptions, two morphologically distinct groups of pronouns for the first person are attested: a singular form characterized by the approximant initial *j*- in Middle Chinese, referring almost exclusively to the king:[4] *yú* 余 (EMC *jiǎ*), *yǔ* 予 (EMC *jiǎ'*) and Pre-Classical *yí* 台 (EMC *ji*), together with *zhèn* 朕 (EMC *drim'*),[5] and a plural form represented by pronouns with the nasal initial *ŋ*- in Middle Chinese, referring to the Shang collectively, including *wú* 吾 (EMC *ŋɔ*), *wǒ* 我 (EMC *ŋa'*), and Pre-Classical *áng* 卬 (EMC *ŋaŋ*).[6] In Classical Chinese, this clear distinction vanishes: while pronouns with the approximant (or dental) initial do not change their number, the pronouns with a nasal initial start to be employed as general pronouns, indifferent of number. Accordingly, in Classical Chinese there is a distinction between general (singular and plural) number and the singular in the first person pronoun (Unger 1987, I: 14, see also Harbsmeier, this volume), i.e. the singular and not the plural is particularly marked. A similar, although less obvious distinction can also be assumed for the second person pronoun: *ěr* 爾 (EMC *ɲi'*) and *ruò* 若 (EMC *ɲiak*) indicate general number (singular and plural) in Classical Chinese, and *rǔ* 汝, 女 (EMC *ɲiə'*) seems to be confined to the singular (Unger 1987, III: 150f, Zhang 2001: 26f).[7] Apart from the personal pronouns of the first and the second person, no morphological or lexical distinction of number can be assumed for Pre-Classical and Classical Chinese.

However different kinds of plural in Classical Chinese can be marked by different lexical items, i.e. the category number can be marked if pragmatically required, i.e. "when it matters". These lexical items are adverbial quantifiers marking plural number, i.e. completeness of a set of items with regard to the subject or the object, such as *jiē* 皆 'all', usually a subject quantifier, but not confined to it (Harbsmeier 1981: 78f), *jìn* 盡 'all, exclusively' predominantly quantifying the object (Harbsmeier 1981: 67f),[8] and a few others.[9] Additionally, already in Classical Chinese there exist the adjectival, definite quantifiers *zhū* 諸,

---

4 The reconstructions of Middle Chinese are taken from Pulleyblank (1991).

5 In Wang (1980, 2004: 302) all first person pronouns of this category are reconstructed with the voiced dental initial *d*-.

6 For a comprehensive discussion on personal pronouns see also Zhou (1959) among many others.

7 This paper does not intend to join the comprehensive discussion on personal pronouns in Chinese; the hypotheses represented above concerning the system of personal pronouns are merely intended to show that the morphological situation of Chinese is more complicated than Norman's remark suggests.

8 For a comprehensive discussion of Harbsmeier's analyses see Wei (2004: 291f).

9 For the purpose of this paper these quantifiers are all regarded as adverbial quantifiers, although they are obviously subject to different syntacto-semantic constraints the exact nature of which still has to be established.

qún 群, and *zhòng* 眾, expressing the plural of the noun they modify. Furthermore, after the Classical period some plural markers which attach to nouns and pronouns appear more regularly (see also Norman 1988: 120); these are mainly *děng* 等, *cáo* 曹, and *bèi* 輩, or a combination of two of them, e.g. *děng bèi* 等輩.[10] Their employment is not obligatory yet during the periods between Han and Tang, and when they first appear they do not express a simple, but rather an associative plural, i.e. *wǒ děng* 我等 does not mean 'we', but 'me and others'.[11] This can be evidenced by the fact that they often attach to names, and they actually have to be analyzed as nouns which form a coordinative construction with the first noun.[12] These markers are not at issue in the following discussion which focuses on a diachronic analysis of the number word *zhū* 諸. *Zhū* 諸 is confined to the modifier position, i.e. it precedes a head noun, and thus differs syntactically from the above mentioned plural words, which all follow the noun they pluralize. The main part of the discussion consists of three sections: in section three the diachronic development of *zhū* 諸 with respect to the 'Animacy Hierarchy' is of particular interest; in section four the syntactic constraints of *zhū* 諸 and their changes are analyzed; and in section five the semantic constraints of *zhū* 諸 in a text from the beginning of the 5th century, the *Gaoseng Faxian zhuan* (*Faxian*), are at issue. This text is a genuine Chinese text, a travel report, and not a translation text, although it certainly contains elements that ultimately derive from or are patterned on original Buddhist texts in a Middle Indian language. The data for the diachronic study is mainly taken from the *Shiji* 史記 (around 100 BC) as representative for the Classical and Han period literature and from the *Sanguo zhi* 三國志 compiled in the 3rd century CE as an example of a non-Buddhist text from the Wei Jin Nanbeichao period, but regular reference will be made to earlier instances of *zhū* 諸 e.g. in the Pre-Classical and Classical texts collected in the *Shisanjing*, and in the Classical philosophical literature. Occasionally, particularly in the section on the syntax of *zhū* 諸, data from other texts from the same period as the *Fǎxiǎn*, in particular the *Mioofa lianhua jing*, translated by Kumarajiva into Chinese, will also be taken into account.

---

10 This combination is attested e.g. in the *Miaofa lianhua jing* (Taisho 262; 33c) as a plural marker of the 1st person pronoun *wǒ* 我.

11 See Corbett (2000: 101) "Many languages have what have been called 'associative plurals', or 'group plurals' … These forms consist of a nominal plus a marker, and denote a set comprised of the referent of the nominal (the main member) plus one or more associated members."

12 A number of articles have been devoted to these plural words, since they structurally resemble the plural marker *mén* 們 in Modern Chinese and as its predeccessors have probably paved the way for *mén* 們.

In languages such as Classical Chinese in which general number is expressed by a bare NP, the analysis of the bare NP as referring to a kind or to a specimen, an individual item, has to be supported by additional syntactic evidence.[13] A number of syntactic tests have been proposed in Harbsmeier (1991) to distinguish between different kinds of nouns, i.e. mass nouns on the one hand, and generic and count nouns on the other (see also Harbsmeier, this volume). Nevertheless, the exact constraints which favour an analysis of a bare NP as being specific and plural and not generic in Classical Chinese still deserve some more investigation. Additionally, the question arises under which circumstances a specification of number is pragmatically required, i.e. "when it matter(s)". An unmarked NP with a plural meaning can refer to an indefinite, but also to a definite set of items as will be shown in section five. However, it can be expected that, if the marking of the plural of a particular set of specimens is required pragmatically, the plural marker must be definite. In generic uses as e.g. *The lion is a noble beast*, referring to a kind and not to a specimen, the distinction between singular and plural is not relevant, the same proposition in the plural *Lions are noble beasts* does not differ semantically, the plural noun still refers to a kind. In Classical Chinese many bare NPs can refer to a kind (the number is irrelevant), but also to a singular item or a set, a plurality of items. Unless the NP is particularly marked for plural, apparently only contextual devices or additional syntactic evidence can induce an interpretation of the NP as generic, i.e. as referring to a kind, or as specific, referring to individual items in the real world.[14]

2 The number word *zhū* 諸

In the following discussion the diachronic development of the number word *zhū* 諸, its syntactic constraints, and its semantic function in a Buddhist text from the early 5th century will be at issue. According to Corbett (2000: 133) languages can have special 'number words', just for the purpose of indicating

---

13 See Krifka (1995: 399) "It seems that every language which allows for bare NPs at all uses them as expressions referring to kinds. Furthermore, kinds seem to be ontologically prior to specimens..." If a real object is to be named, this object has to be related to a kind, whereas talking about a kind does not necessitate having a real object in mind. According to Krifka (1995: 406) nouns in Chinese (Modern Chinese) are on a par with mass nouns and mass noun constructions in English. This analogy is based on the fact that mass nouns require classifier and measure phrases to become countable (see also Chierchia 1998: 55). Nevertheless, the situation of nouns in Classical Chinese differs considerably from that in Modern Chinese.
14 However, in Harbsmeier (this volume) a number of nouns is listed which have a predictable generic, singular, or plural reading.

number. He quotes Tagalog as an example in which almost any constituent can be pluralized by the clitic word *mga*. But according to the examples he presents, the plural NPs are not definite; this would distinguish *mga* from the always definite plural marker at issue in this paper. Dryer (1989) discusses different kinds of number or plural words, e.g. plural words as numerals, as articles etc. As the following discussion reveals, it is difficult to assign one of the more general categories established by Dryer to the plural word *zhū* 諸. Possibly adjectival plural words in Pre-Tang Chinese establish a category of their own according to what Dryer labels "Plural words as a multiword minor category of their own" (Dryer 1989: 877) and for which he quotes Vietnamese as one example.

In Classical and Pre-Classical Chinese the character *zhū* 諸 mainly writes two (or three) different words: 1, the adjectival plural marker 'all, members of the class of" (Pulleyblank 1995), and 2, a fusion of the object pronoun *zhī* 之 and either the final particles *hū* 乎 or *yú* 與, or the preposition *yú* 於 (when followed by another noun) (e.g. Pulleyblank 1995: 9, Kennedy 1964: 63). The latter function is not at issue in this paper. However, it has to be conceded that, corresponding to the decrease of *zhū* 諸 as a fusion word referring to *zhī* 之 + preposition in Han period and Pre-Medieval Chinese, an increase of the number of object NPs marked for plural by *zhū* 諸 can be observed, although the object position was always available for the *zhū*-NP.

According to Pulleyblank (1995: 126) the number word *zhū* 諸 "is a derivative of the same pronominal root as *zhī* 之 and *zhě* 者" expressing "membership of a class rather than a numerical totality".[15] The syntactic and the semantic constraints of *zhū* 諸 are more comprehensively discussed in Harbsmeier (1981: 166f).[16] According to him *zhū* 諸 "refers to the members of a welldefined set" (Harbsmeier 1981: 167) which is often subclassified (Harbsmeier 1981: 168), and it never serves to simply "quantify what it precedes" (Harbsmeier 1981: 169). Although *zhū* 諸 predominantly modifies animate nouns (ibidem), it is neither restricted to them nor to "nobles, feudal lords and the like", contradicting Dobson's claim (Dobson 1959: 32).[17] Harbsmeier implicitly claims that *zhū* 諸 is

---

15 See also Harbsmeier (1981: 166): "... *zhu* which even etymologically contains an element *zhi* 之 that can mean 'this'."

16 A list of examples (34 entries) is presented in the Thesaurus Linguae Sericae (TLS), where as a plural word it is glossed by 'all', 'many', and by 'plural prefix'. (http://tls.uni-hd.de/procSearch/procSearchLex.lasso, 04.02.2010).

17 In his study on 'Late Han Chinese', Dobson does not discuss *zhū* 諸 as a plural word; he only refers to *zhū* 諸 in its function as a fusion word (allegro word in his terminology) stating that in Late Han Chinese these were often not correctly understood anymore (Dobson 1964: 61f).

referential in contrast to *wàn* 萬 which can refer "to an infinite, unclassified 'open' set of things". Most of what Harbsmeier claims for *zhū* 諸 will be confirmed in the following discussion for the Classical period and also partly for later periods (see also Wei 2004: 297). In the Chinese linguistic literature pluralic *zhū* 諸 is either labeled as a pronoun, *dàicí* 代詞 (*Gudai hanyu xuci cidian* 2000: 858), or as an adjective (*Wenyan wen xuci da cidian*).[18] According to a commentary of the *Shuowen jiezi* (*Gudai hanyu xuci cidian* 2000: 858) *zhū* 諸 indicates plural in a sense of 'more than one'.

In the linguistic literature on the development of plural markers, *zhū* 諸 is usually just mentioned and discussed in passing in analyses of the development of plural markers, particularly the plural marker *mén* 們 and the syntactically closely related other post-nominal plural words such as *děng* 等 etc.[19] This is due to the fact that *zhū* 諸 differs syntactically from the latter and thus does not follow the same path of grammaticalisation. Plural words such as *děng* 等 start as independent nouns in coordinative constructions, usually expressing associative plurals, and they develop into plural markers which can attach to personal pronouns, interrogative pronouns and different kinds of nouns losing their associative meaning according to their degree of grammaticalisation.

3 The diachronic development of *zhū* 諸 according to the Animacy Hierarchy

In the following discussion on the diachronic development of *zhū* 諸 particular focus will be on the semantic features of the modified noun according to the Animacy Hierarchy. It will be hypothesized that in Classical times *zhū* 諸 mostly modifies [+ANIMATE], and in particular [+HUMAN] nouns, despite the occasional occurrence of [−ANIMATE] nouns, and that these constraints are less strictly applied in later periods, although [+HUMAN] nouns remain predominant also in the Buddhist literature. Additional emphasis will be on the semantic function of *zhū* 諸 and it will be shown that NPs modified by *zhū* 諸 are always definite and evidently referential; in most cases they do not merely refer to objects in the real world, but they exhibit an explicit reference to a set of items previously mentioned in the narrative, i.e. they serve to create textual or discourse reference.

---

18 In both reference works it is glossed by several syntactically and semantically quite diverse quantifiers.

19 See, for instance, Yang (2001). A short paragraph is devoted to *zhū* 諸 in Wei (2004: 297).

The distance between the object of reference and the referential NP with *zhū* 諸 can be considerable. Although in Classical Chinese it is not always easy to draw a formal line between count nouns and mass nouns,[20] the nouns selected by *zhū* 諸 usually seem to be equivalent to count nouns, including plural count nouns referring to groups.[21] This has already been stated briefly in Harbsmeier (1991: 55) who classifies *zhū* 諸 as a modifier selecting count (and generic) nouns, but not mass nouns. This hypothesis is supported by the later development of the *zhū*-NP. However, the semantics of *zhū* 諸 do not provide unambiguous evidence for a distinction between count and mass: according to an analysis of *zhū* 諸 as a quantifier 'all', proposed in the linguistic literature, the determination of the selected nouns as mass nouns would not be excluded theoretically (according to Chierchia's (1998: 56) definition): the quantifier 'all' can refer to both plurals and mass nouns. Contrastingly, according to an analysis of *zhū* 諸 as a definite, referential plural marker, the modification of mass nouns would be excluded: mass nouns cannot take plural morphology, because they are already plural (Chierchia 1998: 70).[22]

3.1 The number word *zhū* 諸 with [+ANIMATE] nouns

In this section, representative occurrences of nouns which have the feature [+ANIMATE] will be discussed. *Zhū* 諸 predominantly modifies [+HUMAN] nouns; however, it apparently does not pluralize personal pronouns and accordingly it does not serve to pluralize nouns at the top of the Animacy Hierarchy. Although during its development it extends its function considerably to the pluralisation

---

20 The employment of classifiers and measures phrases which according to many linguistic studies argues for an analysis of Modern Chinese nouns as mass nouns is not obligatory yet in Classical Chinese (for a very interesting analysis of the system of classifiers in Classical Chinese see Feng, in this volume). However, measure phrases appear already in Classical Chinese and belong to the diagnostics introduced by Harbsmeier to distinguish between mass and count nouns in Classical Chinese (1991: 52f). In his analysis, Harbsmeier clearly shows that there are syntactic tests to determine if a noun is a count noun and he thus refutes Graham's arguments in favour of the mass noun hypothesis for Classical Chinese (Graham 1986: 196f). (See also Harbsmeier this volume.)

21 Groups are equated to singular count nouns in Chierchia (1998: 67).

22 According to Chierchia's definition (1998: 91f), the definite article applies to a set and returns its greatest element, which does not exclude a definition of *zhū* 諸 as a definite article semantically, but as will be demonstrated below, its syntactic constraints argue against an analysis as a definite article.

of [–ANIMATE] nouns, i.e. down the Animacy Hierarchy, the modification of personal pronouns remains excluded from its functions.[23]

In Pre-Classical and in Classical Chinese *zhū* 諸 is most frequently attested in combination with the noun *hóu* 侯 'marquis': *zhūhóu* 諸侯 'the feudal lords'. This composition is regularly attested in the texts collected in the *Shisanjing* and from quite early on it can be regarded as a term, a compound with the meaning "members of that class of people, not necessarily every single one of them" (Pulleyblank 1995: 126), also occasionally employed in the singular. A few examples of its singular reference are presented in Harbsmeier (1981: 170). As a fixed expression, the term *zhūhóu* 諸侯 will be left out of the following discussion. Besides this title, other titles appear modified by *zhū* 諸 on a regular basis, some of which will be presented below. In all examples the *zhū*-NP is definite and referential.

3.1.1 *Zhū* 諸 modifies kinship terms, [+HUMAN] [+KIN] nouns

Although in most instances *zhū* 諸 modifies titles and denominations, it also regularly, if only occasionally, selects kinship terms such as *fù* 父 'father', *xiōng* 兄 'older brother' and *dì* 弟 'younger brother' etc., which in the Animacy Hierarchy follow personal pronouns; these are already attested in the *Shisanjing* collection, i.e. in the Pre-Classical and Classical literature. The frequency of kinship terms does not increase considerably in the Han period text *Shiji*: additionally, in the following two examples the terms rather serve as a general reference to older people than to a concrete kinship relation.

In all of the following examples (1) to (5) the *zhū*-NP refers evidently to the preceding narrative, but not always – e.g. in examples (1) and (5) – a concrete point of reference. In example (2) the first *zhū*-NP is followed by the adverbial all-operator *jiē* 皆 'all'. Existential and all-operators frequently combine with *zhū*-NPs and they usually refer to all or a sub-set of individual items of a well-defined set. In examples (2) and (3) the *zhū*-NP has an overt point of reference: in (2) to 'elders' mentioned earlier in the narrative; the NP selected by *zhū* 諸 usually refers to a plurality of objects, even if unmarked for number.[24] In example (3)

---

23 According to an anonymous reviewer this might be due to the fact that *zhū* 諸 seems to be anaphoric. However, as some of the examples demonstrate *zhū* 諸 can appear in the scope of a demonstrative pronoun which itself is anaphoric.
24 In the speech part of example (2) a second *zhū*-NP is attested which has the semantic characteristic [–ANIMATE].

the referential character of the *zhū*-NP is even more obvious; the overt point of reference *jī* 姬 'lady' appears in the first clause of example (3) immediately preceding the clause in which the *zhū*-NP surfaces. Although not always occurring as a kinship term, *jī* 姬 as a term respectfully referring to a 'wife', is discussed in this section. In example (5), the noun is doubly modified for plural by *qún* 羣 'flock' and *zhū* 諸, i.e. *zhū* 諸 selects an NP which is already marked for plural. Additionally the NP is preceded by a verbal modifier which functions as an adjective; the set of items determined by *zhū* 諸 is – due to the presence of an adjectival modifier – well defined.

(1) 沛父兄諸母故人日樂飲極驩 (*Shiji*: 8,389)

    Pèi fù   xiōng   zhū mǔ   gù rén rì   lè
    Pei father older.brother PL   mother old man day happy

    yǐn   jí   huān,...
    drink utmost joy

    'Fathers and older brother and (all) the mothers of Pei, the old acquaintances, daily drank happily wine and enjoyed themselves extremely...'

(2) 諸父老皆曰:「平生所聞劉季諸珍怪, 當貴,...」 (*Shiji*: 8,350)

    zhū fù lǎo jiē yuē: píngshēng suǒ wén Liú Jì zhū
    PL   elder all say: always   REL hear Liu Ji PL

    zhēn   guài,   dāng guì,...
    valuable extraordinary, should honour,...

    All the elders said: 'According to what we always have heard about the marvellous and extraordinary things of Liu Ji he should be honoured,...'

(3) 厲公多外嬖姬, 歸, 欲盡去群大夫而立諸姬兄弟。 (*Shiji*: 39,1680)

    Lì gōng   duō   wài   bì   jī,   guī,
    Li marquis many outside favourite lady, return,

    yù   jìn   qù   qún dàifū
    wish completely remove flock dignitary

    ér   lì   zhū jī   xiōng   dì
    CON establish PL lady older.brother younger.brother

    'Marquis Li had many favourites abroad, and when he returned he wanted to remove all the dignitaries and establish the brothers of (all) the ladies.'

(4) 「孤欲令諸兒各據一州也。」 (*Sanguo zhi*: 6,194)

    gū yù   líng zhū ér gè   jù   yī   zhōu   yě

    I   wish order PL   son each occupy one province FIN

    'I want each of the sons to occupy one of the provinces.'

(5) 諸羣從子弟，其未有侯者皆封亭侯 (*Sanguo zhi*: 4,147)

    zhū qún cóng   zǐ   dì,   qí   wèi

    PL   PL   follow son younger.brother, those NEG_{Asp}

    yǒu hóu   zhě jiē fēng   tínghóu

    have marquis ZHE all enfeoff neighbourhood.marquis

    'Of all the sons and younger brothers who followed [him] those who did
    not have a marquisate yet were enfeoffed as 'neighbourhood marquis'.'

3.1.2 *Zhū* 諸 modifies [+HUMAN] [+TITLE], nouns which refer to positions, titles etc.

In the Classical and Han period literature titles are the most frequently attested
nouns in a *zhū*-NP. In the following examples (6) and (7) no concrete point of
reference is provided in the immediately preceding narrative. In example (6)
zhū 諸 precedes the title *chén* 'subject, minister', a combination which is already
attested in the *Shisanjing*.[25] Although they are not mentioned explicitly, *zhū chén*
諸臣 evidently refers to the defined group of personal ministers of duke Huai.
The denomination *gōngzǐ* 公子 in example (7) is not infrequently attested in
the *Shiji*.[26] A point of reference is implied by the comparison 'like the set of
noble scions who live as commoners'.

(6) 諸臣圍懷公，懷公自殺。 (*Shiji*: 6,287)

    zhū chén   wéi   Huái gōng, Huái gōng zì   shā

    PL   vassal enclose Huai duke, Huai duke self kill

    '(All) the ministers surrounded duke Huai and he killed himself'.

---

25 This combination is listed in the TLS as referring to a speaker's group 'WE'. (http://tls.uni-hd.de/procSearch/procSearchLex.lasso, 04.02.2010) which would be the counterpart to *zhū jūn* 諸君 in example (12) which refers to a plural addressee. But this does not seem to be the case in the Classical literature yet. In *Shiji* it is one of two instances, both referring to the ministers as a group and not serving as substitutes for a first person pronoun. In the *Hanshu* it is not attested at all.

26 There is only one instance in the *Shisanjing*.

(7) 「願與妻子為黔首，比諸公子。」 (*Shiji*: 6,274)

yuàn yǔ qī zǐ wéi qiánshǒu, bǐ zhū gōngzǐ
wish with wife child be commoner, like PL noble.scion

'I wish to be a commoner with my wife and children like all the noble scions.'

Quite frequently *zhū* 諸 modifies the title *jiàng* 將 'general' and variants of it. This combination is not attested in the *Shisanjing* yet, but occurs frequently in the *Sanguo zhi*. As in example (2), in example (8) the *zhū*-NP is followed by the all-operator *jiē* 皆; contrastingly, in example (10) it is followed by the existential operator *huò* 或 'one, some'. In example (8) the *zhū*-NP refers to a definite group of generals partly referred to in the preceding narrative; in example (9) the reference is contextually determined, and in example (10) only one of the well-defined set of generals is denoted.

(8) 諸別將皆屬宋義，號為卿子冠軍。 (*Shiji*: 7,304)

zhū biéjiàng jiē shǔ Sòng Yì, hào wéi
PL general all be.attached.to Song Yi, call make

qīngzǐ guān jūn
Honourable Scion cap army

'All the generals were attached completely to Song Yi, and he (the king) called him "Honourable Scion, Head of the Army."'

(9) 將北征三郡烏丸，諸將皆曰： (*Sanguo zhi*: 1,29)

jiāng běi zhēng sān jùn Wūwán,
FUT north make.expedition.against three prefecture Wuwan,

zhū jiàng jiē yuē:
PL general all say

'When he was going to launch an expedition against the Wuwan of the Three Prefectures, the generals all said: ...'

(10) 諸將或問： (*Sanguo zhi*: 1,29)

zhū jiàng huò wèn
PL general someone ask:

'One of the generals asked:'

In the following examples, titles are employed to refer to the addressee in a speech part. In cases like this, the *zhū*-NP is evidently referential and definite, whether there is direct reference back to the preceding narrative or not. However, this *zhū*-NP has an overt point of reference, *zhū jiàng* 諸將, in the introduction to the speech part.

(11)　諸卿觀之，自今已後不復敗矣。(*Sanguo zhi*: 1,16)

　　　zhū qīng　　guàn　　zhī, zì　　jīn　yǐ　hòu bù　fù　　bài　　yǐ
　　　PL　minister　consider　OBJ, from　now　CON later NEG again defeat FIN

　　　'If [you] the ministers consider this, then from now on we will not be defeated again.'

Example (12) is one of a series of instances of *zhū jūn* 諸君 'gentlemen' occurring as a term of address. This term is already occasionally attested in the *Zuozhuan* and appears quite regularly from the *Shiji* on. Since *jūn* 君 is regularly attested as a polite substitute for a 2nd person pronoun, *zhū* 諸 serves to pluralize a quasi-pronoun; however, it never extends to the pluralization of genuine personal pronouns. The function referring to a plurality of addressees increases considerably in the Buddhist literature, where e.g. the term *bǐqiū* 比丘 'monk' regularly appears in a *zhū*-NP.

(12)　弟為諸君所困，故來救之。(*Sanguo zhi*: 7,222)

　　　dì　　　　　　wéi　zhū jūn　　　suǒ　kùn,
　　　younger.brother PASS PL　gentleman PASS distress,

　　　gù　　lái　jiù　zhī
　　　therefore come rescue OBJ

　　　'My younger brother has been distressed by you, gentlemen, therefore I came to rescue him.'

In example (13) the head noun *kè* 客 'retainer' is modified by *zhū* 諸 referring to a point of reference in the preceding narrative, quoted here in example (14); in example (14) even the number and one member of the group are defined explicitly, and to this group the *zhū*-NP in example (13) refers back.[27] The NP in example (14) is followed by *děng* 等 evidently expressing an associative plural. Although *kè* 客 is not a genuine title, it is employed as the denomination of an officially acknowledged function at court, and is accordingly listed in this section.

---

27 The structural differences between the complex NP in (13) and that in (3) where *zhū* 諸 refers to the modifier *jī* 姬 'honourable wife' will be discussed in section 4.

(13) 於是上賢張王諸客，以鉗奴從張王入關 (*Shiji*: 89,2585)

 yúshì   *shàng*   *xián*   *Zhāng wáng zhū kè,*   *yǐ*
 thereupon emperor value Zhang king PL retainer, with

 qián   *nú*   *cóng*   *Zhāng wáng rù*   *guān*
 collar slave follow Zhang king enter gate

 'Thereupon the emperor valued those retainers of king Zhang who with
 slaves' collars followed him to enter the gate...'

(14) 客孟舒等十餘人。(*Shiji*: 89,2584)

 kè   *Mèng Shū děng*   *shí yú*   *rén*
 retainer Meng Shu PL$_{ASSOC}$ ten more man

 'the retainer Meng Shu and his associates, more than ten men'.

3.1.3 *Zhū* 諸 modifies names, [+HUMAN] [+NAME] nouns

From very early on *zhū* 諸 is attested in combination with the collective or group
name *xià* 夏 as in *zhū Xià* 諸夏, which – as a term – can also refer to 'China' or
the 'Chinese' in general (see TLS: http://tls.uni-hd.de/procSearch/procSearchLex.
lasso, 04.02.2010). But, particularly from the Han period on, it can also select
proper names referring to individuals. These proper names are confined to family
and clan names, i.e. names which can be pluralized; individual proper names
referring to ONE particular individual are excluded from it, since they usually
cannot refer to a plurality. This is an obvious extension of the employment of
zhū 諸 in comparison to the Classical period. Since proper names are by definition referential, the NP selected by *zhū* 諸 is evidently referential, too, referring
to a set of individuals sharing this proper name at a particular time and place,
i.e. in a contextually defined world, but not to all possible members of this
family at all times and places.[28] A comparison between *zhū* 諸 and *děng* 等 in
combination with proper names reveals the basic difference between both plural
markers. In example (14) the proper name is followed by the noun *děng* 等
meaning 'Meng Shu and the others', which does not imply that the 'others'
belong to the set of people identified by a common proper name,[29] whereas in

---

28 See a similar analysis for *zhūhóu* 諸侯 in Harbsmeier (1981: 169) who claims that it can
never mean "all feudal lords, past, present and future."
29 The same employment of *děng* 等 is still attested in the *Faxian*, where it often attaches to
names, meaning 'X and the others'.

examples (15) to (17) the *zhū*-NP refers to a well-defined set of people identified by their common proper name.

(15)   太后稱制，議欲立諸呂為王，問右丞相王陵。(*Shiji*: 9,400)

    Tàihòu chēng zhì,   *yì*   *yù*   *lì*   *zhū Lǚ wéi*
    Taihou call   decree, discuss wish establish PL   Lü be

    wáng, wèn yòu   *chéngxiàng Wáng Líng*
    king,   ask   right   chancellor   Wang Ling

    'The Taihou had [her orders] all called decrees, she discussed whether she wanted to enthrone the Lüs as kings and asked the Chancellor of the Right Wang Ling.'

(16)   田單者，齊諸田疏屬也。(*Shiji*: 82,2453)

    Tián Dān zhě,   *Qí zhū Tián shū*   *shǔ*   *yě*
    Tian Dan ZHE, Qi PL   Tian distant relative FIN

    'Tian Dan was a distant relative of the Tians of Qi.'

(17)   「諸袁事漢，四世五公，可謂受恩。」(*Sanguo zhi*: 7,236)

    zhū Yuán shì   *Hàn, sì*   *shì*   *wǔ gōng, kě*
    PL   Yuan serve Han, four generations five duke, can

    wèi shòu   *ēn*
    call receive benevolence

    'The Yuans served Han for four generations and five dukes, one can say that they received benevolence.'

3.1.4 *Zhū* 諸 modifies nouns referring to superhuman beings, [+SUPERHUMAN] nouns

Zhū-NPs with nouns referring to superhuman beings as in the following example with the noun *shén* 神 'spirit, god' are already attested in the *Shiji*, but become more frequent in the Buddhist texts at issue here. The noun *shén* 神 is not yet attested in the texts collected in the *Shisanjing*, and there is only one instance in *Mozi*.[30]

---

30 In all three instances of the combination *zhū guǐ shén* 諸鬼神 in the *Shisanjing* (Li, *SSJZS*: 1301 上; 1634 上), *zhū* 諸 is not a number word.

(18) 朕親郊祀上帝諸神。(*Shiji*: 10,430)

zhèn	*qīn*	*jiāo*	*sì*	*shàng*	*dì*	*zhū*	*shén*
we	personally	suburban	sacrifice	Supreme	Deity	PL	spirit

'We will personally perform the suburban sacrifice to the Shangdi and the spirits.'

3.1.5 *Zhū* 諸 modifies nouns which have the characteristic [+HUMAN]

In contrast to all the nouns listed above which have the characteristic [+HUMAN][31], but which refer to human beings in particular relationships, i.e., their relations in kin or state and which all have a positive notion, in the following example *zhū* 諸 modifies a [+HUMAN] noun which refers to a human being in rather unpleasant circumstances.

(19) 諸囚皆叩頭，願自效 (*Sanguo zhi*: 26,727)

zhǔ	*qiú*	*jiē*	*kòu*	*tóu,*	*yuàn*	*zì*	*xiào*
PL	prisoner	all	bow	head,	wish	self	hand.over

'The prisoners all bowed their heads to the ground and wished to hand themselves over, ...'

The frequency of a *zhū*-NP with the prototypical [+HUMAN] noun *rén* 人 'man, human being', without any additional relations implied, increases only in the Buddhist literature.[32] In the following quite singular example from the *Shiji* the noun is additionally marked for plural by the plural word *zhòng* 眾; the entire NP is followed by the all-operator *jiē* 皆. In the Buddhist literature *zhòng* 眾 regularly appears e.g. in a *zhū*-NP with the noun *shēng* 生: *zhòngshēng* 眾生 'the living beings, humans'. The point of reference of the *zhū*-NP is defined by the *zhě*-phrase preceding it.

(20) 市行者諸眾人皆曰：(*Shiji*: 86,2525)

Shì	*xíng*	*zhě*	*zhū*	*zhòng*	*rén*	*jiē*	*yuē*
Marketplace	walk	ZHE	PL	crowd	man	all	say:

'Those walking in the marketplace, the many people, all said:'

---

31 With the exception of the category d) [+SUPERHUMAN].

32 No instances are attested in the *Faxian*, but it appears regularly in the *Miaofa lianhua jing*.

3.1.6 *Zhū* 諸 modifies a complex nominalised VP

Not infrequently *zhū* 諸 is attested modifying a complex nominalized VP, a headless relative clause marked by the determiner *zhě* 者.[33] In a relative clause *zhě* 者 functions as a relative operator which binds the head position inside the clause (Aldridge 2009: 243). As a relative operator, *zhě* 者 "does not add any semantic or pragmatic import like definiteness" (Aldridge 2009: 243); the definiteness of the NP in the examples presented is induced by the plural word *zhū* 諸. Examples like these are already occasionally attested in the Classical literature, e.g. in the *Zuozhuan*. These NPs refer to a set of specific items defined by the relative clause. In general, different kinds of modifiers including relative clauses can occur between the plural word *zhū* 諸 and the head of the NP, here represented by the relative operator *zhě* 者. Accordingly, relative clauses can be considered an extension of a complex *zhū*-NP with an additional modifier besides the plural word *zhū* 諸: [$_{zhu\text{-}NP}$ *zhu* [$_{NP}$ MOD N]]; as any *zhū*-NP they can be followed by the all-operator *jiē* 皆 (see exemples [22] and [23]). Usually, but not exclusively, the head which is not overtly present has the characteristic feature [+HUMAN].

(21) 諸喪邑者 (*Zuo, Xiang* 27)

    zhū sàng yì zhě

    PL loose city ZHE

    'Those who lost their cities' (cf. Unger 1987: 182)

(22) 當是時，詔捕諸時在旁者，皆殺之。(*Shiji*: 6,257)

    dāng shì shí, zhào bǔ zhū shí zài páng zhě, jiē shā zhī

    at this time, edict arrest PL time be.at side ZHE, all kill OBJ

    'At this time, he issued an edict to arrest those who had been near him at the time, and kill them all.'

---

33 A new analysis of *zhě* 者 has been proposed in Aldridge (2009: 240): "*Zhe* is a functional category *n* positioned between D and NP. It functions as a determiner in the sense that it semantically binds the variable introduced by the predicate NP and projects a phrase which can appear in argument position." In the above presented examples *zhě* 者 always takes a clause (a TP) as its complement. The constituent as a whole expresses given information (Aldridge 2009: 242).

(23) 長安士庶咸相慶賀，諸阿附卓者皆下獄死。 (*Sanguo zhi*: 6,179)

Cháng'ān shì   shù   xián xiāng qìng hè,
Chang'an noble normal.people all   each   luck congratulate,

zhū ē   fù   Zhuō zhě jiē xià   yù   sǐ
PL   show.partiality attach Zhuo ZHE all submit trial die

'The nobility and the normal people of Chang'an congratulated each
other, and those who had been attached to Zhuo were all convicted
and died.'

The relative operator *zhě* 者 of the nominalized VP can also be deleted,
resulting in an unmarked relative clause; the non-overt head is pluralized by
zhū 諸 as in the following example from the *Shiji*.

(24) 秦王之邯鄲，諸嘗與王生趙時母家有仇怨，皆阬之。 (*Shiji*: 6,233)

Qín wáng zhī Hándān, zhū cháng yǔ   wáng shēng Zhào
Qin king   go Handan, PL once   with king   live   Zhao

shí   mǔ   jiā   yǒu   qiú   yuàn,   jiē kēng zhī
time mother family have grudge resentment, all trap OBJ

'The king of Qin went to Handan, and all those who bore a grudge and
resentment against his mother's family when the king was born in Zhao,
he trapped (and buried them alive).'

3.1.7 *Zhū* 諸 modifies [+ANIMATE] [–HUMAN] nouns

Occasionally, *zhū* 諸 also modifies non-human animate nouns, animals, or the
noun *wù* 物 'creature, thing', mostly referring to living beings. The extension of
zhū-NPs to [–HUMAN] nouns seems to start with the Han period.[34] In example
(25) two different analyses seem to be possible: first, the *zhū*-NP is the last of
several generic NPs thus providing some evidence for Harbsmeier's assumption
that *zhū* 諸 selects generic nouns (Harbsmeier 1991: 55) besides count nouns.[35]

---

34 These *zhū*-NPs are very rare before the Han period; there is only one instance in the
Zhuangzi of *zhū wù* 諸物.
35 Harbsmeier (1991: 57) suspects that the noun *wù* 物 is rather a generic than a count noun
and that *wàn wù* 萬物 refers to 'the ten thousand kinds of things' rather than to 'the ten
thousand individual things', but he concedes that more evidence is needed to support either
of the two possibilities. This analysis is also supported by the translation by Nienhauser *et al.*
(2002: 244).

The second analysis would be: the *zhū*-NP is the head of a complex modifier structure: 'the living beings from distant quarters such as'. According to this analysis, the *zhū*-NP is referential and definite in contrast to the modifying NPs, which all refer to kinds. This analysis also seems to account for example (26) where the *zhū*-NP evidently refers to a predefined set of objects, although no point of reference can be traced in the preceding narrative.[36] The compound *niǎoshòu* 鳥獸 always seems to be employed in the plural, whether marked by *zhū* 諸 or not, similar to e.g. the NP *fùlǎo* 父老 'elders' in example (2).

(25) 縱遠方奇獸蜚禽及白雉諸物，頗以加祠。(*Shiji*: 12,475)

    zòng   *yuǎn fāng*   *qí*   *shòu*   *fēi qín jí*   *bó*   *zhì*
    release far   region strange animal fly bird and white pheasant

    zhū wù   *pō* *yǐ* *jiā* *sí*
    PL   creature, quite take add sacrifice

    'One released strange quadrupeds, flying birds, and white pheasants, all these living beings from distant quarters to take them to add to the sacrifices.'

(26) 「諸鳥獸無用之物」(*Sanguo zhi*: 13,417)

    zhū niǎo shòu   *wú*   *yòng zhī* *wù*
    PL   bird quadruped not.have use   SUB thing

    '(All the various) animals and useless things, . . .'

3.2 The number word *zhū* 諸 with [−ANIMATE] nouns

The number of instances of *zhū* 諸 selecting [−ANIMATE] nouns increases during the Han, and considerably during the Wei Jin Nanbeichao period. However, most of the nouns still retain the feature [+ANIMATE] and even [+HUMAN].[37] The [−ANMINATE] nouns in this section include locative nouns, abstract nouns, and nouns referring to concrete [−ANIMATE] items. Additionally they contain collective nouns such as *jūn* 軍 'army', referring to an abstract group in which [+HUMAN] members are included. Since group nouns can be equated to singular

---

36 The fact that *niǎoshòu* 鳥獸 can be modified by the quantifying adjective *duō* 多, even if only one instance in the *Shanhai jing* (*Shanhaijing* 4 東山經) is attested, argues according to Harbsmeier (1991: 52) for a count noun reading.

37 In the Classical literature NPs with a [−ANIMATE] noun are extremely infrequent; one example with the abstract noun *hài* 害 from *Han Fei* is quoted in Harbsmeier (1981: 168).

count nouns, a noun such as *jūn* 軍 'army' can be listed as an abstract term for an institution, thus referring to a concrete singularity, a [+ABSTRACT] singular noun.[38]

3.2.1 *Zhū* 諸 modifies collective, group nouns referring to institutions [+COLLECTIVE] [+INSTITUTION]

In the first *zhū*-NP in this section the group noun *jūn* 軍 'army' is additionally modified by the adjective *bài* 敗 'defeated'. Instances of *zhū jūn* 軍 without an additional modifier are attested in the *Hanshu*, and, frequently, in the *Sanguo zhi*.[39] In example (28), the *zhū*-NP is followed by the existential operator *huò* 或 'some, someone'.

(27)   至滎陽，諸敗軍皆會。(*Shiji*: 7,324)

    zhì   *Xíngyáng, zhū bài*   *jūn*   *jiē huì*

    arrive Xingyang, PL defeat army all meet

    'When they arrived in Xingyang, their defeated armies had all met again.'

(28)   諸軍或從斜谷道，或從武威入。(*Sanguo zhi*: 9,281)

    zhū jūn   *huò*   *cóng* *Xiégǔ dào,* *huò*   *cóng Wǔwēi rù*

    PL   army some follow Xiegu road, some from Wuwei enter

    'Some of the armies followed the Xiegu road, some entered from Wuwei.'

3.2.2 *Zhū* 諸 modifies [+LOCAL] nouns, nouns referring to places

Similarly to the number of nouns referring to institutions, the frequency of locative nouns only starts to increase during the Wei Jin Nanbeichao period. In example (30) the locative NP is additionally modified by the adjective *pàn* 叛 'rebellious' which defines the range of commanderies and districts

---

[38] See note 21. These nouns evidently differ from nouns usually referring to a plurality such as *fùlǎo* 父老 'elders' and *niǎoshòu* 鳥獸 'quadrupeds and birds = animals' which also seem to be collective terms.

[39] There are no instances either in the *Shisanjing* or in the collections of Classical philosophical texts in the Academia Sinica database.

(29) 諸廟及章臺、上林皆在渭南。(*Shiji*: 6,239)

> *zhū miào   jí   Zhāng tái,   Shànglín jiē zài   Wèi nán*
> PL   royal.temple and Zhang-Terrace, Shanglin all be.at Wei south
>
> 'The royal temples and the Zhang-Terrace and Shanglin, they all were
> situated to the south of the Wei.'

(30) 紹歸，復收散卒，攻定諸叛郡縣。(*Sanguo zhi*: 1,22)

> *Shào guī,   fù   shōu   sàn   zú,   gōng   ding*
> Shao return, again collect scatter soldier, attack settle
>
> *zhū pàn   jùn   xiàn*
> PL rebel commandary district
>
> 'Shao returned and collected the scattered soldiers, and he attacked and
> pacified (all) the rebellious commandaries and districts.'

(31) 淵到，諸縣皆已降。(*Sanguo zhi*: 9,271)

> *Yuān dào,   zhū xiàn   jiē yǐ   xiáng*
> Yuan arrive, PL   district all already surrender
>
> 'When Yuan arrived, the districts had all already surrendered.'

3.2.3 *Zhū* 諸 modifies abstract, [–ANIMATE] [+ABSTRACT] nouns

Abstract nouns are already very occasionally attested in the Classical literature.
In example (32) the plural word *zhū* 諸 indicates that the 'canon (of laws)' at
issue belongs to a well-defined definite set, the modified noun *lyùlíng* 律令
apparently has to be analysed as a group noun. In example (33), the *zhū*-NP is
additionally modified by the short-distance demonstrative pronoun *cǐ* 此 'this'
which reinforces the definite reading of the *zhū*-NP. The frequency of a combination of *zhū* 諸 with a demonstrative pronoun only increases during the Wei Jin
Nanbeichao period.

(32) 與趙禹共定諸律令，務在深文。(*Shiji*: 122,3138)

> *yǔ   Zhào Yǔ gòng   dìng   zhū lyùlíng,   wù*
> with Zhao Yu together establish PL   statutes, work.on
>
> *zài   shēnwén*
> be.at strict.application.of.law
>
> 'Together with Zhao Yu he established the canons and he worked on
> being very strict in the application of the law.'

(33) 凡此諸事，皆法之所不取。(*Sanguo zhi*: 14,442)

     fán   *cǐ* *zhū shì,*   *jiē fǎ* *zhī* *suǒ bù*   *qǔ*

     altogether this PL   affair, all law SUB REL NEG take

     'Altogether these affairs are all [of a kind] which the law does not grasp, ...'

3.2.4 *Zhū* 諸 modifies concrete, [−ANIMATE] [+CONCRETE] nouns

In examples (34) to (36) the *zhū*-NP refers to a well-defined set of concrete items respectively; in example (35) the set of 'commentaries' is defined by several modifying NPs preceding it, *zhū* 諸 immediately precedes the head of the complex NP.

(34) 豐等欲因御臨軒，諸門有陛兵，誅大將軍，以玄代之。
     (*Sanguo zhi*: 9,299)

     Fēng děng yù *yīn*   *yù*   *lín*   *xuān,*   *zhū mén yǒu*

     Feng other wish rely.on driver approach carriage, PL   gate have

     bìbīng   *zhū*   *dà jiàngjūn,*   *yǐ* *Xuán dài*   *zhī*

     imperial.guard, execute great general, with *Xuan* replace OBJ

     'Feng and the others wanted to approach the high carriage with the help of the driver, but (all) the gates had imperial guards, and they executed the great general and replaced him with Xuan.'

(35) 及作周易、春秋例，毛詩、禮記、春秋三傳、國語、爾雅諸注，
     又注書十餘篇。(*Sanguo zhi*: 13,420)

     jí   *zuò*   *Zhōuyì, Chūnqiū lì,*   *Máo shī, Lǐjì, Chūnqiū*

     and make *Zhouyi, Chunqiu* example, *Mao shi, Liji, Chunqiu*

     sān   *zhuàn,*   *Guóyǔ, Ěryǎ zhū zhù,*   *yòu*

     three tradition, *Guoyu Erya* PL annotation, and

     zhù   *shū* *shí yú*   *piān*

     annotate book ten more section

     'and he made (all) the annotations of the *Zhouyi*, of the examples of the *Chunqiu*, The Songs of Mao, the *Liji*, the three traditions of the *Chunqiu*, the *Guoyu*, and the *Erya*, and he also annotated more than ten books.'

(36) 值天大風，諸船綆紲斷絕，漂沒著岸。(*Sanguo zhi*: 57,1339)

zhì   tiān   dà   fēng,   zhū chuán gěng xiè   duàn   jué,
meet heaven great wind, PL boat   rope cord cut.off break,

piāo mò   zhù   àn
float disappear arrive shore

'They met with a bad wind, and the ropes of the boats were cut off and broke, they floated and disappeared from the shore.'

With regard to the Animacy Hierarchy, an obvious extension from [+ANIMATE] to [−ANIMATE] nouns selected by *zhū* 諸 can be observed. In the Classical literature, *zhū* 諸 most frequently appears in the compound *zhūhóu* 諸侯. Additionally, a considerable range of other titles and occupational denominations appears in a *zhū*-NP, these are the most common nouns attested in the Classical period.[40] New titles and denominations are added during the Han and the Wei Jin Nanbeichao periods. Kinship terms are already early attested in *zhū*-NPs, but are in general not very frequent, and are additionally often employed metaphorically. Genuine personal pronouns are never selected by *zhū* 諸, and since kinship terms are only infrequently selected, *zhū* 諸 predominantly selects nouns on the lower levels of the Animacy Hierarchy. During the Han and the Wei Jin Nanbeichao periods the employment of *zhū* 諸 is obviously less confined, and it regularly selects [−ANIMATE] nouns, such as e.g. group nouns referring to institutions, abstract and concrete nouns, and locative nouns. It usually selects singular count nouns which are pluralised by *zhū* 諸, but also some nouns which already refer to a plurality. It cannot be entirely excluded that it also very occasionally selects generic nouns, referring to a plurality of kinds rather than of individual items in the real world. The *zhū*-NP is always definite and referential independently from an overt point of reference in the preceding narrative.

Table 5: Plurals with *zhū* 諸 and the Animacy Hierarchy

Grade of Animacy	Pronouns (1,2,3)	Kinship terms	Human	Animate, non-human	Non-Animate
Classical period	No	Yes	Yes	Almost non-existent	Almost non-existent
Han period	No	Yes	Yes	Yes	Yes
Post-Han periods	No	Yes	Yes	Yes	Yes

---

40 In the *Shisanjing* collections titles such as *gōng* 公 'duke', *dàfū* 大夫 'dignitary', *chén* 臣 'minister', *bó* 伯 'count' etc. are not infrequently attested.

4 The syntax of *zhū* 諸

As with regard to the Animacy Hierarchy, extensions of employment can also be observed in the syntax of the *zhū*-NP, although its basic structure remains unaltered. One of the syntactic characteristics prevailing from Classical to Wei Jin Nanbeichao Chinese is the combination of a *zhū*-NP with an adverbial quantifier following it. The quantifiers attested are: the all-operator *jiē* 皆 'all' in examples (2), (8), (9), (19), (20), (22)–(24), (27), (29), (31), (33), and more; the existential operator *huò* 或 'some, one' in examples (10) and (28), the distributive all-operator *gè* 各 'each' in examples (4), and (45), and the negative operator *mò* 莫 'none'.[41] Of these quantifiers the all-operator *jiē* 皆 'all' is most frequently attested.[42] A *zhū*-NP quantified by one of these operators can be of varying complexity; it can be:

a) a simple *zhū*-NP [諸 N];
b) an NP explicitly marked for plural, e.g. by the plural word *zhòng* 眾, see example (20);
c) a relative clause modified by *zhū* 諸;
d) a *zhū*-NP in combination with a demonstrative pronoun (e.g. example [33]); or
e) several coordinated NPs including a *zhū*-NP (e.g. example [29]).

The all-operator includes the totality of items of the well-defined set referred to by the *zhū*-NP in the predication, whereas the existential operator selects one or several items of this well-defined set. This structure increases in number during the Wei Jin Nanbeichao period.

Within the *zhū*-NP, the plural word *zhū* 諸 behaves like a regular modifier such as a demonstrative pronoun, an adjectival, nominal or verbal modifier. In

---

41 Corbett (2000: 111) "Distributive and collective meaning may be specified by independent words in analytic constructions, particularly determiners (equivalents of 'each', 'every') and adverbials (distributive 'here and there', 'one at a time'; collective 'together', 'jointly')." In Classical Chinese these distributive and collective quantifiers frequently combine with the plural word *zhū* 諸 which accords well with Corbett's claim (Corbett 2000: 114) that "distributives should not be considered additional values comparable with the basic number values like singular, dual, and plural, nor as subdivisions of these."
42 According to Chierchia (1998: 56) determiners – which correspond semantically to the above summarised quantifiers – interact with the mass/count distinction. The above mentioned quantifiers in Chinese occur either only with count nouns (*gè* 各 'each'), with plurals and mass nouns (*jiē* 皆 'all'), or are unrestricted (*huò* 或 'some'). Since the system of quantifiers in Classical and Pre-Tang Chinese still requires further analysis, the equation of the Chinese quantifiers with the determiners according to Chierchia must remain tentative at present, and is not at issue in this paper.

complex NPs consisting of two independent nouns [NP [NP_{mod} NP_{head}]] there seems to be a fixed word order with regard to *zhū* 諸 and other nominal modifiers: i.e. *zhū* 諸 always modifies the noun it immediately precedes (see also Harbsmeier 1981: 166) as in the contrasting examples (3) = (37) and (13) = (38) and (64) and (65). Example (37) has the structure [NP [zhu-NP *zhū* N [NP N]]], and example (38) has the structure [zhu-NP [NP N [zhu-NP *zhū* N]]]. NPs of this kind are attested from the Classical literature on. In example (39) the pluralised head noun is preceded by a complex NP with a pronoun pluralised by *děng* 等 which in these instances is already fully grammaticalised as a plural marker.[43] The modifier *zhǒngzhǒng* 種種 qualifies the *zhū*-NP as generic.

(37)   (= 3) 屬公多外嬖姬，歸，欲盡去群大夫而立諸姬兄弟。(*Shiji*: 39,1680)

Lì gōng   duō   wài   bì   jī,   guī,   yù
Li marquis many outside favourite lady, return, wish

jìn   qù   qún   dàifū
completely remove flock dignitary

ér   lì   zhū jī   xiōng   dì
CON   establish PL lady older.brother younger.brother

'Marquis Li had many favourites abroad, and when he returned he wanted to remove all the dignitaries and establish the brothers of (all) the ladies.'

(38)   (= 13) 於是上賢張王諸客，以鉗奴從張王入關。(*Shiji*: 89,2585)

yúshì   shàng   xián   Zhāng wáng zhū kè,   yǐ
thereupon emperor value Zhang king PL retainer, with

qián nú   cóng   Zhāng wáng rù   guān
collar slave follow Zhang king enter gate

'Thereupon the emperor valued those retainers of king Zhang who with slaves' collars followed him to enter the gate...'

(39)   如是等種種諸苦。(*T09n0262_p0013a23*)

rú   shì   děng zhǒng zhǒng zhū kǔ
like this PL   kind kind   PL bitterness

'all kinds of bitterness like these'

---

43 Many examples of demonstrative, personal, and interrogative pronouns pluralized by *děng* 等 are attested in the *Miaofa lianhua jing* and in other Buddhist texts.

If the nominal head is modified by an adjective, one of the plural words *qún* 羣 and *zhòng* 眾, a verb employed as an adjectival modifier, or a relative clause, these modifiers always follow *zhū* 諸 and precede the head noun (example [5] = [40]), or the relative operator *zhě* 者 which binds the overt or non-overt head of the relative clause as in examples (22) to (24). In example (40) the NP is additionally modified by the verbal modifier *cóng* 從 'following, those who follow'.[44]

(40) (5 =) 諸羣從子弟，其未有侯者皆封亭侯 (*Sanguo zhi*: 4,147)

zhū qún cóng zǐ dì,   qí   wèi
PL   PL   follow son younger.brother, those NEG$_{Asp}$

yǒu hóu   zhě jiē fēng   tínghóu
have marquis ZHE all enfeoff neighbourhood.marquis

'Of all the sons and younger brothers who followed [him] those who did not have a marquisate yet were enfeoffed as 'neighbourhood marquis'.'

The position of a demonstrative pronoun in relation to *zhū* 諸 seems to be less regular: both orders DEM *zhū* / *zhū* DEM occur. In the *Shiji* and the *Hanshu* the order *zhū* DEM is attested (example 41); this word order corresponds to the general syntactic constraints of *zhū* 諸 with regard to additional (non-nominal) modifiers of the NP.[45] However, in the only genuine example in the Pre-Han literature from the *Shijing*,[46] the (long-distance) demonstrative pronoun *bǐ* 彼 precedes *zhū* 諸 (DEM *zhū*), similar to *cǐ* 此 'this' in example (33) and (43) below.[47] According to the frequency of instances with the order DEM *zhū* 諸 in the post Han literature, a change of word order can be assumed for the later periods. This is particularly evident in the frequent examples in the *Miaofa lianhua jing*.[48]

---

44 For *zhòng* 眾 see example (20).

45 Two more examples with this structure are attested in the *Shiji* (27,1337 and 28,1377). The same examples as in *Shiji* also appear in the *Hanshu* (25A, 11209; 26,1297; 95,3838).

46 In the *Shijing* there are also a few instances of the *zhū*-NP preceded by the personal pronoun *wǒ* 我, always in the order [personal pronoun *zhū*-NP].

47 There are more examples in the *Sanguo zhi* which exhibit this word order. In the Classical literature, there are additionally several instances of a demonstrative pronoun preceding the compound *zhūhóu* 諸侯, excluded from this discussion.

48 This text has been chosen in particular for the syntactic discussion, since it shows a much greater variety of *zhū*-NPs than the *Faxian* text. This is due to the fact that it is much longer, but also to the fact that it is a translation text where plural marking certainly frequently simply mirrors a plural ending in the original text.

(41) 諸此國頗置吏焉。(*Shiji*: 116; 2993)

zhū cǐ guó pǒ zhì lì yén
PL this country MOD establish official FIN

'And all these countries established officials there.'

(42) 孌彼諸姬。(*Mao Shi, Guo feng SSJZS*: 309 上)

luán bǐ zhū jī
beautiful that PL lady

'beautiful are those Ji(-family) ladies (my relatives)'[49]

(43) = (33) 凡此諸事，皆法之所不取。(*Sanguo zhi*: 14,442)

fán cǐ zhū shì, jiē fǎ zhī suǒ bù qǔ
altogether this PL affair, all law SUB REL NEG take

'Altogether these affairs are all [of a kind] which the law does not grasp,...'

(44) 為此諸佛子，說是大乘經。(*T09n0262_p0008a10*)

wèi cǐ fó zǐ, shuō shì dàshèng jīng
for this Buddha child, tell this Mahayana sutra

'For (all) these sons of the Buddha I preach this sutra of the Mahayana'

Besides the innovative employment of demonstrative pronouns in combination with a *zhū*-NP, another innovation from the same period, i.e. the combination of a *zhū*-NP with a numeral, can be observed. The occurrence with numeral determiners argues for the analysis of the *zhū*-NP as indicating genuine plurality of individual count nouns; mass nouns always require an additional measure word or classifier.[50] In the following example, *zhū* 諸 is followed by a complex number, and the *zhū*-NP is quantified by the distributive quantifier *gè* 各 'each', one of the syntactic diagnostics presented in Harbsmeier (1991: 52) for count nouns. In example (46) *zhū* 諸 is additionally preceded by the demonstrative pronoun *shì* 是, in example (47) the number is indefinite. In example (48), the *zhū*-NP is additionally marked by the plural marker *děng* 等.

---

49 The translation which is based on Karlgren's translation is quoted from the TLS (http://tls.uni-hd.de/procSearch/procSearchTxt.lasso, 08.02.2010).
50 See Chierchia (1998: 55, 83f), who resumes and explains the basic facts on count and mass nouns. See also Harbsmeier (1991: 57).

(45) 諸二十四長亦各自置千長、百長、什長。 (*Shiji*: 110,2891)

Zhū èr shí sì zhǎng yì gè zì zhì qiān
PL two ten four chief also each self establish thousand

zhǎng, bó zhǎng, shí zhǎng,
chief, hundred chief, ten chief

'Each of the twenty-four chiefs respectively establishes himself the 'chiefs of thousands', 'chiefs of hundreds', 'chiefs of ten', ...'

(46) 是諸八王子，妙光所開化。 (*T09n0262_p0005a27*)

shì zhū bā wángzǐ, miào guāng suǒ kāi huà
this PL eight prince, Wonderfully Bright REL open change

'These eight princes whom Wonderfully Bright converted...'

(47) 是諸無量千萬億大德聲聞，皆已成就。 (*T09n0262_p0025a22*)

shì zhū wú liàng qiān wàn yì
this PL not.have measure thousand ten.thousand hundred.thousand

dà dé shēngwèn, jiē yǐ chéng jiù
great virtue voice.hearer, all already complete perfection

'These immeasurable thousand, ten thousand, a hundred thousand virtuous voice-hearers have all already completed perfection.'

(48) 汝諸人等，皆是吾子，我則是父。 (*T09n0262_p0015a16*)

rǔ zhū rén děng, jiē shì wú zǐ, wǒ zé shì fù
you all people PL, all be I son, I then be father

'You and (all) the people, you are all my children, and I am the father, ...'

Syntactically, the *zhū* 諸 NP is more versatile during and after the Han than during the Classical period, although the basic word order remains unaltered. In complex NPs [NP$_{mod}$ NP$_{head}$] *zhū* 諸 always directly attaches to the noun it modifies. In all other cases, with the exception of demonstrative pronouns, the modifier appears between *zhū* 諸 and the head noun, and *zhū* 諸 thus has scope over the entire complex NP. With regard to demonstrative pronouns, a change of word order from *zhū* DEM to DEM *zhū* can be observed from the Han period on to the effect that the post Han literature displays the same word order as the only Pre-Han literature example from the *Shijing*. Numerals hardly ever attach to the *zhū*-NP in the Classical literature; however, they appear on a regular basis in the position following *zhū* 諸 from the *Shiji* on, arguing for the fact that the modified noun is a count noun. According to the evidence presented no syntactic tendency for a grammaticalisation of *zhū* 諸 as a plural prefix can be observed during the time at issue in this paper:[51] It never attaches directly to the modified head, but remains an independent plural word separable from the head noun by a considerable number of syntactic elements. For the Classical literature an analysis of *zhū* 諸 as a determiner, i.e. as a definite article, seems in most instances syntactically possible. However, since the number of determiners within an NP is confined to one, the few instances with additional pronouns (demonstrative or personal) preceding *zhū* 諸 in the Pre-Classical and Classical literature, together with the later development of the *zhū*-NP, argue against this analysis; a combination of *zhū* 諸 with a demonstrative or personal pronoun would violate this constraint. Accordingly, the adjectival analysis of *zhū* 諸 seems syntactically more appropriate, since the number of modifying adjectives within one NP is not limited.[52]

5 The plural word *zhū* 諸 in the *Gaoseng Faxian zhuan*

In the present section the syntactic and semantic constraints of the plural word *zhū* 諸 in one particular text, the *Gaoseng Faxian zhuan* (short *Faxian*), will be at issue. This text can – at least for the most part – be considered a genuine narrative and is accordingly structurally closer to a text such as the *Shiji* than many parts of the *Miaofa lianhua jing*.[53] In the following discussion NPs marked by *zhū* 諸 will be contrasted to NPs with identical nouns in different plural constructions, e.g. in unmarked plurals, explicitly marked plurals, reduplications, etc. in order to reveal the semantic differences between the different realisations of the plural in this text. For this purpose, a selection of representative nouns has been chosen. In contrast to the majority of examples discussed in section 3, where a *zhū* 諸-NP refers back to an overt point of reference in the preceding narrative, this is not necessarily the case in the *Faxian*; however, the *zhū*-NP

---

51 See Haspelmath (1995: 363), who summarises the syntactic effects of grammaticalisation as follows: "syntactically it means a loss of freedom of position and often eventually cliticization and affixation".

52 See Radford (1997: 39).

53 The *Miaofa lianhua jing* also contains narrative parts, but these are always translated and were not originally written in Chinese.

almost always seems to be definite and referential. The examples are again listed according to their animacy features.

5.1 *Zhū* 諸 modifies [+ANIMATE] nouns in the *Faxian*

In this section, nouns referring to human and superhuman beings will be discussed. The latter are particularly frequent in Buddhist literature. In example (49), the noun *wáng* 王 and in (50) the NP *guówáng* 國王 is modified by the plural word *zhū* 諸. In (49) the NP refers to the well-defined set of 'the kings at the time of the Buddha'. The NP *guówáng* 國王 in (50) is analysed as a compound due to the fact that it is frequently attested in the *Faxian* in the singular and in marked and unmarked plurals, and accordingly *zhū* 諸 modifies the entire NP.

(49) 佛在世時諸王供養法式相傳至今。(*T51n2085_859a29*)

fó zài shì shí zhū wáng gōngyǎng fǎshì
Buddha be.at world time PL king offer.sacrifice method

xiāng chuán zhì jīn
each transmit arrive today

'The rule during the time when the Buddha was still alive that the kings made their offerings has been transmitted up to now.'

(50) 諸國王長者居士為眾僧起精舍。(*T51n2085*_p0859b12)

zhū guówáng zhǎng zhě jūshì wèi zhòng sēng qǐ qīngshè
PL king eldest ZHE layman for PL monk erect vihāra

'The kings and the chiefs and layman erected vihāras for the monks.'

In example (51) the noun *wáng* 王 is pluralised by reduplication referring to the kings as separate objects in space and time and not as a set of items in its entirety. Contrary to simple pluralisation, reduplication is distributive; it expresses "rather the occurrence of an object here and there, or of different kinds of a particular, than plurality" (Boas 1911b: 444, quoted after Corbett 2000: 112). In example (52) the compound *tiānwáng* 天王 is preceded by a numeral and marked for plural by the obviously fully grammaticalised *děng* 等.[54]

---

54 The combination of an NP with a numeral in combination with the plural word *děng* 等 is already attested in the *Shiji* (e.g. *SJ*: 5,181), but there *děng* 等 evidently expresses an associative plural.

(51) 後王王相傳無敢廢者。(*T51n2085*_p0859b13)

    hòu   *wáng wáng xiāng chuán*   *wú gǎn fèi*   *zhě*
    afterwards king   king   each   pass.on NEG dare abolish ZHE

    'Afterwards the kings have passed it on from one to the other and have
    not dared to abolish it.'

(52) 佛為諸天說法四天王等守四門父王不得入處。(*T51n2085*_p0861b02)

    fó   *wèi zhū tiān shuō*   *fǎ*   *sì*   *tiānwáng*
    Buddha for PL   *deva* explain dharma four *devarāja*

    děng shòu sì   *mén fù*   *wáng bù* *dé* *rù*   *chǔ*
    PL   guard four gate father king NEG can enter place

    'the place where the Buddha explained the law to the devas and where
    the four *devarājas* guarded the four gates and where the fatherly king
    could not enter'

The plural can also be unmarked in nouns such as *wáng* 王, although in
most of the instances in *Faxian* an unmarked noun *wáng* 王 is singular. This
tendency is apparently not valid for all NPs, e.g. not for the noun *shāngrén*
商人 'merchant' in example (58). In example (54) – in the narrative preceding
example (50) – the NP *guówáng* 國王 is bare, but it is marked as well-defined
by the quantifier *jiē* 皆 which selects all items from a well-defined set.[55] The NP
preceding *jiē* 皆 predominantly seems to refer to a set of individual items which
induces an analysis of the NP as definite 'the Ns, all'.

(53) 凡沙河已西天竺諸國。國王皆篤信佛法供養眾僧。
    (*T51n2085*_p0859a26)

    fán   *shāhé yǐ*   *xī*   *Tiānzhú zhū guó,*   *guówáng*
    altogether desert and west India   PL country, king

    jiē dǔ xìn   *fó*   *fǎ*   *gòngyǎng zhòng sēng*
    all firm believe Buddha dharma offer   PL   monk

    'Altogether in the countries west of the desert and in India, the kings all
    firmly believe in the Buddha's dharma, and when they make offerings to
    the monks...'

---

55 According to Harbsmeier (1981: 80) *jiē* 皆 does not quantify mass nouns, but regularly
"quantifies over individual items".

In example (54) the personal pronoun *wǒ* 我 'I, we', marked for plural by *děng* 等, appears in the modifier position of a *zhū* 諸 NP; *zhū* 諸 seems to have scope over both the nouns *shī* 師 'teacher' and *héshàng* 和上 (for *héshàng* 和尚) 'monk'.[56] A *zhū*-NP additionally marked by a pronoun already expresses definiteness and referentiality, and the function of *zhū* 諸 is thus reduced to the marking of plurality, its function of expressing definiteness and referentiality being redundant.[57]

(54) 我等諸師和上相承以來未見漢道人來到此也。(*T51n2085*_p0860c08)

wǒ	*děng*	*zhū*	*shī*	*héshàng*	*xiāng*	*chéng*	*yǐ*	*lái*
I	PL	PL	teacher	monk	mutually	receive	CON	come

wèi	*jiàn*	*Hàn*	*dào*	*rén*	*lái*	*dào*	*cǐ*	*yě*
NEG$_{Asp}$	see	Han	religious	man	come	arrive	here	FIN

'According to what (all) our teachers and monks transmitted from one to the other until now they have never seen a religious man from the Han coming here.'

In example (55) the noun *shāngrén* 商人 'merchant' is pluralised by *zhū* 諸. The overt point of reference is represented here in example (56); in this example the noun refers to an unmarked plural. Although the NP is (56) is bare, it is not indefinite. An unmarked plural can be quantified by the all-operator *jiē* 皆 'all' as in example (57).

(55) 諸商人躊躇不敢便下。(*T51n2085*_p0866a26)

zhū	*shāngrén*	*chóuchú*	*bù*	*gǎn*	*biàn*	*xià*
PL	merchant	hesitate	NEG	dare	easy	let.down

'The merchants hesitated and did not dare to leave [him] behind.'

---

56 This analysis contradicts Deeg's rather free translation (2005: 538) according to which the *zhū*-NP seems to be indefinite.

57 Redundancy in quantification seems to be quite common if one assumes that *zhū* 諸 predominantly functions as a quantifier, expressing all-quantification. Only a comprehensive study of the different quantifiers and their combination can reveal their exact syntactic and semantic constraints respectively. However, it can be assumed that quantifiers such as *jiē* 皆 quantify over the predicate whereas the quantificational force of *zhū* 諸 is confined to the *zhū*-NP. Additionally, quantification is apparently not the only function of *zhū* 諸.

(56) 商人荒懅不知那向。(*T51n2085*_p0866a11)

shāngrén huāng   jù   bù zhī ná   xiàng
Merchant frightened terrified NEG know which direction

'The merchants were frightened and did not know in which direction they went.'

(57) 商人賈客皆悉惶怖。(*T51n2085*_p0866a18)

shāngrén gǔkè   jiē xī   huángpù
merchant merchant all completely scared

'The merchants were all scared.'

   In example (58) two different *zhū*-NPs appear, one referring to a complex [−ANIMATE] noun phrase, and the second to a [+ANIMATE] NP which is already marked for plurality by the plural word *qún* 群. Double plural marking is in general quite infrequent and particularly rare with *qún chén* 群臣. The noun *chén* 臣 is also attested in the unmarked plural and marked by *děng* 等; both cases are exemplified in (59). Apparently identical to a *zhū*-NP, the NP + *děng* 等 in example (59) is definite and referential.

(58) 并諸白氎種種珍寶沙門所須之物。共諸群臣發願布施眾僧。
    (*T51n2085*_p0857c15)

bìng zhū dié   zhǒngzhǒng zhēn   bǎo
take PL white.cotton.cloth all.kinds.of precious jewel

shāmén   suǒ xū   zhī wù,   gōng   zhū qún
Shramana REL need SUB thing, together PL flock

chén   fāyuàn   bùshī   zhòng sēng
minister Buddhist.vow distribute PL   monk

'He (the king) takes white cotton cloth and all kinds of precious things the monks could need and together with (all) his ministers he distributes them among the monks professing the Buddhist vows.'

(59) 即問臣等誰能為我作地獄主治罪人者。臣答言。
    (*T51n2085*_p0863c02)

jí   wèn chén   děng shuí néng wèi wǒ zuò   dìyù
then ask minister PL   who can for I make hell

zhǔ   zhì   zuì rén zhě. Chén   dá   yán
master govern guilt man ZHE. Minister answer say

'Then he asked the ministers: "Who can be master of the hell for me and govern the guilty people?" The ministers said: . . .'

Identical to the texts already discussed in section 3, in the *Faxian* the *zhū*-NP can include other modifiers; in example (60) the adjectival modifier consists of a complex NP.

(60) 國內大德沙門諸大乘比丘皆宗仰焉。(*T51n2085*_p0862b12)

    guó nèi   dà   dé   shāmén   zhū dàshèng   bǐqiū
    state within great virtue Shramana PL Mahayana bhiksu

    jiē zōngyǎng yán
    all esteem   FIN

    'The Shramanas of great virtue and the bhiksus of the Mahayana in this state all show him their esteem.'

In the following example an indefinite numeral follows the *zhū*-NP as an appositional measure phrase. The *zhū*-NP is assumed to be definite,[58] referring to a closed set of items consisting of numberless individual members. The noun *tiān* 天 'deva' usually appears in the marked plural, unmarked plurals are not attested, and it only rarely has a singular reading. The noun *fó* 佛 'Buddha' in example (62) has, at least in the *Faxian*, to be marked for plurality, either by *zhū* 諸 or by a numeral; all unmarked instances of *fó* 佛 in this text refer to the Buddha in the singular.

(61) 諸天無數從佛來下。(*T51n2085*_p0859c19)

    zhū tiān wú   shù   cóng fó   lái   xià
    PL deva not.have number follow Buddha come down

    'The numberless Devas followed the Buddha down [to the earth].'

(62) 凡諸佛有四處常定。(*T51n2085*_p0861b10)

    fán   zhū fó   yǒu sì   chǔ   cháng   dìng
    altogether PL Buddha have four place regularly established

    'Altogether the Buddhas have four places which are established for them all.'

5.2 *Zhū* 諸 modifies [–ANIMATE] nouns in the *Faxian*

Not infrequently *zhū* 諸 modifies [–ANIMATE] noun phrases, in particular locative nouns. In example (63) a compound of the modifier head structure similar to *guówáng* 國王, but with an [–ANIMATE] head, is modified by *zhū* 諸, the NP is

---

58 Against Deeg's (2005: 532) translation according to which it is analysed as indefinite.

followed by the postposition *zhōng* 中 'middle'. The analysis of *sēngshì* 僧室 as a compound is supported by the distributive adverbial *chǔ chǔ* 處處 'place by place' following the NP, which clearly quantifies a plurality of locative nouns. Additionally, it accounts for the fact that the noun *sēng* 僧 is usually pluralised by *zhòng* 眾 and not by *zhū* 諸; there is no instance of *zhū sēng* 諸僧 in the entire *Faxian*. Contrastingly, in example (64) *zhū* 諸 has scope only over the [–ANIMATE] modifyer *guó* 國 of a complex NP with the [+ANIMATE] head *shāngrén* 商人. The same *zhū*-NP *zhū guó* 諸國 appears as the head of a complex NP in example (65). In example (66) the locative *zhū*-NP is preceded by a demonstrative pronoun.

(63)　諸僧室中處處穿石作窗牖通明。(*T51n2085*_p0864b04)

zhū　*sēngshì*　　*zhōng*　*chǔ*　*chǔ*　*chuān*　　　*shí*
PL　monk.house　middle　place　place　bore.through　stone

zuò　*chuāngyǔ*　*tōng*　　*míng*
make　window　　penetrate　light

'Everywhere in the monks' houses one drilled the stone to make windows and let the light come in.'

(64)　其國本無人民。正有鬼神及龍居之。諸國商人共市易。
(*T51n2085*_p0864c16)

qí　*guó*　*běn*　　*wú*　　*rén*　*mín,*　*zhèng yǒu*
that　country　originally　not.have　man　people,　just　have

guǐ　*shén*　*jí*　*lóng*　　*jū*　*zhī,*　*zhū guó*　　*shāngrén*
ghost　spirit　and　dragon　live　OBJ,　PL　country　merchant

gōng　　*shì*　*yì*
together　trade　exchange

'Originally that country did not have any people, there were only ghosts and spirits and dragons living there, and the merchants from all the countries together exchanged trade there.'

(65)　法顯本求戒律。而北天竺諸國。皆師師口傳無本可寫。
(*T51n2085*_p0864b17)

Fǎxiǎn běn　　*qiú*　*jièlyù,*　*ér*　*běi*　*Tiānzhú zhū guó,*
Faxian　originally　search　vinaya,　but　north　India　　PL　country,

jiē shī　*shī*　*kǒu*　*chuán*　*wú*　　*běn*　　*kě*　*xiě*
all　teacher　teacher　mouth　transmit　not.have　originally　can　write

'Originally, Faxian was looking for the vinaya scriptures, but in all the countries of Northern India, the teachers transmitted [them] orally from one to the other, and there were no originals which could be copied.'

(66) 自上苦行六年處。及此諸處。(*T51n2085*_p0863b12)

zì   shàng kǔ   xíng liù nián chǔ, jí   cǐ   zhū guó
from high suffering do   six year place, arrive this PL place

'From the place where he executed ascetism for six years up to these places...'

Identically to [+ANIMATE] nouns, [−ANIMATE] (here: locative) nouns can be pluralised by reduplication with the same effect as in example (51) with the [+ANIMATE] *wáng* 王. The completeness of the set of items expressed by reduplication is indicated by the all-operator *jiē* 皆 and not, as could be expected, by the distributive all-operator *gè* 各.

(67) 眾僧住止房舍。床蓐飲食衣服都無闕乏。處處皆爾。
(*T51n2085*_p0859b14)

zhòng sēng zhù zhǐ fángshè, chuáng rù   yǐn   shí
PL   monk live stop house, bed   mat drink eat

yīfú   dōu wú quē   fá, chǔ chǔ   jiē ěr
clothes all NEG defect lack, place place all be.like

'In the houses where the monks lived, beds and beddings, food and drink, and clothes, all were never lacking, and all places were like this.'

According to the examples presented, the basic semantic constraints of *zhū* 諸 remain the same as they were during the Classical and Han periods. However, its employment has extended considerably with regard to the Animacy Hierarchy; this development starts during the Han period and is more or less fully advanced in the 3rd century AD. The syntactic development of the *zhū*-NP in the *Faxian* is less advanced than in the *Miaofa lianhua jing*. This is certainly due to the fact that the *Faxian* is a comparatively short text and that it is for the most part a genuine Chinese text and not a translation from a language with morphological plural marking. Most, but not all of the nouns selected by *zhū* 諸 can also appear in other plural constructions, including the unmarked plural. Some of the nouns discussed have to be analysed as singular, unless they are explicitly marked for plural by *zhū* 諸 or other plural markers. The latter fact might reveal a tendency for an obligatory marking of the plural, at least for some nouns in Buddhist literature. This tendency is not unique in languages, since number marking can become "as good as obligatory" for certain nouns whereas general number still exists elsewhere in the system (Corbett 2000: 15). The most remarkable tendency in the *Faxian* seems to be a decrease of textual or discourse referentiality of the *zhū*-NP. Whereas in the earlier non-Buddhist texts in most of the instances the *zhū*-NP refers back to an overt point of reference in the preceding narrative and evidently serves to create textual reference, this is much less the case in the *Faxian*. Additionally, this decrease of referentiality seems to lead to the impression that the *zhū*-NP is not always definite.[59] However, the overwhelming majority of examples of the *zhū*-NP refer to well-defined items in the real world. If the *zhū*-NP has to be analysed as generic, it refers to a set of different kinds and accordingly differs semantically from a bare NP referring to a kind. Additionally, according to the more grammaticalised employment of plural words such as *děng* 等, the differences between a NP marked for plural by *zhū* 諸 and one marked by *děng* 等 seem to diminish.

6 Conclusion

According to the data presented above the following analysis of *zhū* 諸 will be proposed. Since the overwhelming number of nouns selected by *zhū* 諸 are count nouns, both analyses of *zhū* 諸, i.e. as a quantifier 'all', and as a definite referential plural marker, are possible. However, an occasional employment of *zhū* 諸 in combination with generic nouns cannot be excluded, although in most of the examples presented, the generic does not seem to be the only possible analysis. The plural word *zhū* 諸 cannot only select singular count nouns, but also unmarked plural NPs, NPs which are already marked for plural, or NPs which usually have a plural reading such as *niǎoshòu* 鳥獸 'animals', or *fùlǎo* 父老 'elders'. Very occasionally some of the latter NPs, but not all of them, seem to induce a generic reading referring to a plurality, a set of kinds 'all the (different) kinds of', thus contrasting to a bare NP referring merely to ONE particular kind: 'all kinds of animals' versus e.g. 'bear (as a kind)'. These nouns behave differently from group nouns which are pluralised identically to singular count nouns: *zhū jūn* 諸軍 has the meaning 'all the armies', the plural is identical to a plural of a count noun as in 'all the generals', it does not mean 'all the members of the army'. Whereas a *zhū*-NP with a group noun refers to a plurality of the respective group in the same way as to the plurality of singular items (atoms), which "have sets of atoms as their extension",[60] the *zhū*-NP with one of the above mentioned plural NPs refers to the individual members (or

---

59 Maybe this assumption exaggerates the fact that Deeg occasionally translates *zhū*-NPs as indefinite plurals. It certainly has to be checked against more data from e.g. Buddhist translation texts where pluralisation with *zhū* 諸 seems to be ubiquitous.

60 See Chiercha (1998: 67, 62), who distinguishes between two different sets of atoms, i.e. "collectives and ordinary individuals".

possibly various kinds) within this plural set: i.e. *zhū fùlǎo* 諸父老 refers to 'all the members of the union of 'elders''.[61] When selected by *zhū* 諸 all the items of the plural set, whether individuals or kinds, are identified as singular items (or kinds) within a plural set; the function of *zhū* 諸 to include the different members of the set (or union) remains the same, whether it selects a singular count noun and pluralises it or an already pluralised noun; they only differ in perspective.

Syntactically, *zhū* 諸 has to be analysed as an adjectival modifier, not a determiner, i.e. a definite article, since it can combine with determiners such as demonstrative and personal pronouns. The word order within the *zhū*-NP is subject to strict constraints which – with one exception – do not change during the time at issue here, although a considerable development in the syntax of the *zhū*-NP can be observed. Since *zhū* 諸 can always be separated from the head noun it selects by additional modifiers, no tendency to grammaticalise into a plural prefix can be observed in the texts at issue.

The basic semantics of *zhū* 諸 are: It is **definite**, **referential**, and **quantifying**. Its quantifying notion, i.e. the notion of inclusion, is stronger than that of a definite article, but *zhū* 諸 is not confined to this notion; as Harbsmeier already assumed, *zhū* 諸 "can *never* simply quantify what it precedes" (Harbsmeier 1981: 169). As a quantifier it does not entirely correspond either to the adjectival quantifier 'all' in English – sometimes translations by 'all' seem odd –, or to the quantifier *jiē* 皆 'all' in Classical and pre-Medieval Chinese. However, similar to the all-operator *jiē* 皆 it almost always quantifies over a well-defined set, a plurality, including all members of the set, but contrary to *jiē* 皆 it does not focus on the inclusion. Although the *zhū*-NP is always plural, the function of *zhū* 諸 cannot be reduced to pluralisation; this is made most evident by the fact that the noun selected by *zhū* 諸 can already refer to a plurality. Historically, and as some of the examples from the *Faxian*, particularly with the noun *shāngrén* 商人, have demonstrated, neither definiteness nor plurality depend on the presence of *zhū* 諸, it is employed pragmatically, i.e. 'when it matters'. However, besides the marking of the plural 'when it matters' the presence of *zhū* 諸 obviously adds some semantic content to the selected NP, which according to the data presented can be designated as referentiality. The predominant function of the *zhū*-NP in the Han period literature, but also in the *Sanguo zhi*, is to refer back to a set of objects already defined in the preceding narrative by – frequently – bare NPs which can already be definite and plural; i.e. its basic function is to create textual or discourse reference. This basic function of

---

61 A plural noun such as 'elders' has the *U*-closure (the *union*) of its singular counterparts as extension (minus the atoms) (see Chiechia 1998: 67).

zhū 諸 seems to become less predominant during its history, although the *zhū*-NP remains definite and referential in the texts at issue in this paper. The extension of the syntactic and semantic constraints in the employment of *zhū* 諸 pave the way for its development into a more generally employed plural marker in the Buddhist literature. Although *zhū* 諸 can certainly be labelled as a plural word, pluralisation most obviously is not its only function, at least not in Han period and genuine Chinese Wei Jin Nanbeichao period literature.

References

Aldridge, Edith. 2009. Old Chinese Determiner *Zhe*. In *Historical Syntax and Linguistic Theory*, Paola Crisma and Giuseppe Longobardi (eds.), 233–248. Oxford: Oxford University Press.

Bach, Emmon, Jelinek, Eloise, Kratzer, Angelika, and Partee, Barbara H. 1995. *Quantification in Natural Languages, Volume I*. Dordrecht: Kluwer Academic Publishers.

Chierchia, Gennaro. 1998. Plurality of Mass Nouns and the Notion of "Semantic Parameter". In *Events and Grammar*, In: Susan Rothstein (ed.), 53–104. Dordrecht/Boston/London: Kluwer Publishers.

Chu, Yongan (楚永安). 1986. *Wenyan fushi xuci* 文言復式虛詞 [Complex function words in the Literary Language]. Beijing: Zhongguo Renmin daxue chubanshe.

Corbett, Greville G. 2000. *Number*. Cambridge Textbooks in Linguistics. Cambridge: Cambridge University Press.

Deeg, Max. 2005. *Das Gaoseng Faxian-Zhuan als religionsgeschichtliche Quelle*. Wiesbaden: Harrassowitz.

Dobson, W.A.C.H. 1959. *Late Archaic Chinese*. Toronto: University of Toronto Press.

Dobson, W.A.C.H. 1964. *Late Han Chinese*. Toronto: University of Toronto Press.

Dryer, Matthew. 1989. Plural words. *Linguistics* 27: 865–895.

Dryer, Matthew. 1992. The Greenbergian Word Order Correlations. *Language* 68 (1): 81–138.

Graham, Angus. C. 1986. *Studies in Chinese Philosophy and Philosophical Literature*. Singapore: Institute of East Asian Philosophers.

Gudai hanyu xuci cidian 古代漢語虛詞詞典, [Dictionary of function words of Ancient Chinese]. 2000. Beijing: Shangwu yinshuguan.

Haspelmath, Martin. 1995. Diachronic Sources of 'All' and 'Every'. In *Quantification in Natural Languages, Volume I*, Emmon Bach *et al.*, 363–382. Dordrecht: Kluwer Academic Publishers.

Harbsmeier, Christoph. 1981. *Aspects of Classical Chinese Syntax*. London and Malmö: Curzon Press.

Harbsmeier, Christoph. 1991. The Mass Noun Hypothesis and the Part-Whole Analysis of the White Horse Dialogue. In *Chinese Texts and Philosophical Contexts*, *Essays dedicated to Angus C. Graham*. In: Henry Rosement, Jr. (ed.). LaSalle: Open Court.

Huang, James C.-T-, Li, Audrey Y.-H., Li Yafei. 2009. *The Syntax of Chinese*. Cambridge Syntax Guides. Cambridge: Cambridge University Press.

Kennedy, George. 1964. A. *Selected Works of George A. Kennedy*. In: Li Tien-yi (ed.). Yale: Yale University, Far Eastern Publications.

Krifka, Manfred. 1995. Common nouns: A contrastive analysis of Chinese and English. In *The Generic book* In: Gregory, N. Carlson and Francis J. Pelletier (eds.), 398–411. Chicago: University of Chicago Press.

Nienhauser, William H., Jr *et al.* 2002. *The Grand Scribe's Records, Volume II.* Bloomington and Indianapolis: Indiana University Press.

Norman, Jerry. 1988. *Chinese. Cambridge Language Surveys.* Cambridge: Cambridge University Press.

Pulleyblank, Edwin G. 1991. *Lexicon of Reconstructed Pronunciation in Early Middly Chinese, Late Middle Chinese, and Early Mandarin.* Vancouver: UBC Press.

Pulleyblank, Edwin G. 1995. *Outline of Classical Chinese Grammar.* Vancouver: UBC Press.

Radford, Andrew. 1997. *Syntax. A minimalist introduction.* Cambridge: Cambridge University Press.

Tang, Lizhen (唐丽珍). 2001. *Shilun Hanyu rencheng daici fushu xingshi de fazhan yanbian* 試論漢語人稱代詞復數形式的發展演變 [Discussion on the development of the plural forms of personal pronouns on Chinese]. *Nanjing shifan daxue wenxue yuan xuebao* 2: 70–73.

Unger, Ulrich. 1987. *Grammatik des Klassischen Chinesisch*, vol. I, III. Münster (unpublished).

Wang, Li (王力). 2004. Reprint. *Hanyu shigao* 漢語史稿 [Sketch of the history of Chinese]. Beijing: Zhonghua shuju, 1980.

Wei, Pei-chüan (魏培泉). 2004. *Han Wei Liuchao cheng daici yanjiu* 漢魏六朝稱代詞研究. Taibei: Academia Sinica.

Wenyan wen xuci da cidian 文言文虛詞大詞典 [Dictionary of the form words of the Literary Language], 1988. Taibei: Dongxin wenhua tushu gongsi.

Yue, Ann O. 2003. Chinese Dialects: Grammar. In *The Sino-Tibetan Languages*, Randy LaPolla and Graham Thurgood (eds.), 84–125. London: Routledge.

Yang, Xiuying (杨秀英). 2001. *Cong yuan wen fushu biaoshi fa kan fushu ciwei "men" de chansheng* 從愿文复数表示法看复数词尾"们"产生 [The emergence of the plural suffix "men" following the rules of plural marking in original texts]. *Yindu xuekan* 2: 99–102.

Zhang, Yujin (張玉金). 2001. *Jiaguwen yufa xue* 甲骨文語法學 [The grammar of the Oracle Bone inscriptions]. Shanghai: Xuelin chubanshe.

Zhou, Fagao. 1959. *Zhongguo gudai hanyu* 中國古代漢語 [The Ancient Chinese language]. Taibei: Academia Sinica.

Zhou, Shengya. 1980. *Lun shanggu Hanyu rencheng daici fanfu de yuanyin* 論上古漢語人稱代詞繁複的原因 [Discussion on the cause for the complexity of personal pronouns in ancient Chinese]. *Zhongguo yuwen* 2.

Online resources: www.cbeta.org. Accessed: 15.12.2009.

Hanji dianzi wenxian 漢籍電子文獻. Academia Sinica. http:// hanji.sinica. edu.tw/index.html? Accessed: Januray, February 2010.

Thesaurus Linguae Sericae (TLS). http://tls.uni-hd.de/procSearch /procSearch Lex.lasso. Accessed: 04. February 2010, 08. February 2010.

Marie-Claude Paris

7 *Bu-tong* 'different' and nominal plurality in Mandarin Chinese

Abstract: This paper studies the distribution and the semantic values of the two lexemes *bu-tong* and *bu yiyang* in Mandarin. Even though both items seem to be synonymous when predicated of plural subjects, it is shown that, in other contexts, *bu-tong* and *bu yiyang* behave very differently, both in syntax and in semantics. Only *bu-tong* can indicate nominal plurality, just like English *different* or French *différents*.

Keywords: open scale predicates, closed scale predicates, non-identity, non-similarity, plural noun modifier, French *différents*

Introduction*

In this paper I study two Mandarin lexemes *bu-tong* 'different' and *bu yiyang* 'different'[1], which appear to be synonymous. I will show that, under closer scrutiny, both items behave, in fact, (very) differently both in syntax and semantics. *Bu yiyang* can only appear in predicate position: it is construed as an open scale scalar predicate. *Bu-tong*, on the contrary, can function both as a closed scale scalar predicate *and* as a noun modifier. The noun modifier *bu-tong* 'different' indicates plurality: it behaves in the same fashion as the invariable noun modifier *different* in English or as French *différents*, which is only attested as a plural form. (See Carlson 1987, Moltmann 1992, Beck 2000 and Alrenga 2009) for

---

* I would like to thank Xu Dan for inviting me to present a paper at the international conference 'Quantification and plurality. Number and person in the languages of Asia', ANR06-Blan0259, held in Paris on July 5th, 2009. I have presented different versions of this paper on different occasions. I am grateful to the audiences at the 4th Conference of the European Association of Chinese Linguistics, Budapest, the 22th Journées de Linguistique d'Asie Orientale, Paris, the 20th North American Conference on Chinese Linguistics, Ohio State University, the Department of English and Linguistics, National Taiwan Normal University and the Department of Chinese Language and Literature, Sun Yatsen University, Kaohsiung. I am also grateful to Tsai Mei-chi, Shyu Shu-Ying and Marie-Thérèse Vinet for their friendly help and to an anonymous reviewer for his/her comments. Last, but not least, I address my warm thanks to the Taiwanese Ministry of Education whose 2009 grant has allowed me to finally write my ideas down. The usual disclaimers apply.
1 I will justify below why I write *bu-tong* as one word (*lianxie*) and *bu yiyang* as two words.

English *different*. See Laca and Tasmowski (2001, 2003, 2004), and Tovena and van Peteghem (2001, 2003) for French *différent(s)*.

This paper is organized as follows. Firstly, I will present contexts in which *bu-tong* and *bu yiyang* alternate, and, secondly, contexts in which they cannot. Then I will try to pinpoint the syntactic and semantic differences between these two items. In conclusion, I will stress the differences between *bu-tong* and *bu yiyang*, especially insofar as plurality is concerned.

1 The similar distributions of *bu-tong* and *bu yiyang*

In this section, I will list a few syntactic contexts in which *bu-tong* 'different' and *bu yiyang* 'different' alternate. Firstly, I will study the noun modifier position and secondly, the predicative position.

1.1 In nominal modifying position

In (1a), (1b) and (2a), (2b) below, *bu-tong* 'different' and *bu yiyang* 'different' not only substitute for each other, they also alternate, i.e. they are synonymous.

(1) a. 學生們買了不同的書。

        Xuesheng-men mai-le   **bu-tong de** *shu*.
        student-Pl   buy-Sfx different *de* book

        'The students bought different books.'

    b. 學生們買了不一樣的書。

        Xuesheng-men mai-le   **bu yiyang de** *shu*.
        student-Pl.   buy-Sfx different *de* book

        'The students bought different books.'

(2) a. 每個蘋果各貼了三個不同的標籤。

        Mei ge pingguo ge   *tie-le*   *san*   *ge*
        each Cl apple   individually stick-Sfx three Cl

        bu-tong de *biaoqian*.
        different *de* label

        'Three different labels were stuck on each apple.'

b. 每個蘋果各貼了三個不一樣的標籤。

Mei ge pingguo ge   tie-le   san   ge
each Cl apple   individually stick-Sfx three Cl

bu yiyang de *biaoqian.*
different   *de* label

'Three different labels were stuck on each apple.'

The same applies to *bu-tong* and *bu yiyang* 'different' in predicative position.

1.2 In predicative position

In (3)–(6) below, *bu-tong* and *bu yiyang* 'different' are predicated of plural subjects, which can be either collective or distributive or ambiguous between the two interpretations. In all cases, both lexemes are synonymous.

(3) a. 學生談的問題都不同。

*Xuesheng tan de wenti   dou **bu-tong**.*
student   talk *de* question all   different

'All the questions that the students talked about were/are different.'

b. 學生談的問題都不一樣。

*Xuesheng tan de wenti   dou **bu yiyang**.*
student   talk *de* question all   different

'All the questions that the students talked about were/are different.'

(4) a. 他們個個都不同。

*Tamen gege dou **bu-tong**.*
Pl3   Cl.Cl. all   different

'They are all different.'

b. 他們個個都不一樣。

*Tamen gege dou **bu yiyang**.*
Pl3   Cl.Cl. all   different

'They are all different.'

(5) a. 所有的孩子性格都不同。

*Suoyoude haizi xingge   dou **bu-tong**.*
all   child personality all   different

'All the children have different temperaments.'

b. 所有的孩子性格都不一樣。

*Suoyoude haizi xingge dou **bu yiyang**.*
all child personality all different
'All the children have different temperaments.'

(6) a. 張三跟李四不同。

*Zhangsan gen Lisi **bu-tong**.*
Zhangsan and Lisi different

'Zhangsan and Lisi are different.'

b. 張三跟李四不一樣。

*Zhangsan gen Lisi **bu yiyang**.*
Zhangsan and Lisi different

'Zhangsan and Lisi are different.'

In (7) and (8) below, *bu-tong* and *bu yiyang* 'different' are predicates in a comparative construction. What is compared here is a (unmentioned) property which holds of *zhei ge banfa* 'this method' and which varies at different moments in time.

(7) 這個辦法跟以前不同。

*Zhei ge banfa gen yiqian **bu-tong**.*
this Cl. method and before different

'This method is different from before.'

(8) 這個辦法跟以前不一樣。

*Zhei ge banfa gen yiqian **bu yiyang**.*
this Cl. method and before different

'This method is different from before.'

Moreover, the following degree adverbials *you yi dian* 'a bit', *feichang* 'very', *wanquan* 'completely' can all modify *bu-tong* and *bu yiyang*, as illustrated in (9)–(14). Thus, in predicative position, both *bu–tong* and *bu yiyang* are scalar adjectives.

(9) ... 有一點不同   (10) ... 有一點不一樣

... ***you** **yi** **dian** bu-tong*   ... ***you** **yi** **dian** bu yiyang*
have a bit different   have a bit different
... 'are somewhat different'   ... 'are somewhat different'

(11) ... 非常不同

... ***feichang*** *bu-tong*
　　very　　different

... 'very different'

(12) ... 非常不一樣

... ***feichang*** *bu yiyang*
　　very　　different

... 'very different'

(13) ... 完全不同

... ***wanquan*** *bu-tong*
　　completely different

... 'are totally different'

(14) ... 完全不一樣

... ***wanquan*** *bu yiyang*
　　completely different

... 'are totally different'

Other degree modifiers, such as *chabuduo* 'almost', which set an end point on a vertical scale or a distance close to a maximal point, can appear neither with *bu-tong* nor with *bu yiyang*, as shown in (15) and (16).

(15) *差不多不同

　****chabuduo*** *bu-tong*
　　almost　　different

(16) *差不多不一樣

　****chabuduo*** *bu yiyang*
　　almost　　different

In sum, in all the examples provided above — (1)–(16) — *bu-tong* and *bu yiyang* share the same distributions (and meanings). In the following, I will study contexts in which *bu-tong* and *bu yiyang* can be opposed.

2 The non similar distributions of *bu-tong* and *bu yiyang*

In this section, I will oppose *bu-tong* and *bu yiyang* when they occupy two different types of syntactic environments: first, the noun phrase position, and, second, the verb phrase position.

2.1 *Bu-tong* and *bu yiyang* within the Noun Phrase

Bu-tong 'difference' can function as the *nominal* head of a Noun Phrase, cf. (17), but *bu yiyang* is rarely accepted in such a context, cf. (18).

(17) 他們的不同

[[*tamen de*] ***bu-tong***]]$_{NP}$
Pl3　　*de*　difference

'their difference'

(18) ??他們的不一樣

??[[*tamen de*] ***bu yiyang***]]$_{NP}$
　Pl3　　*de*　difference

2.2 *Bu-tong* and *bu yiyang* in the Verb Phrase

Bu-tong and *bu yiyang* 'different' can appear in two different types of predicative positions. In (19)–(30) they are main predicates, whereas in (31)–(33) they are predicate modifiers.

2.2.1 *Bu-tong* and *bu yiyang* as main predicates

In the four pairs (19)–(26) below, *bu-tong* and *bu yiyang* 'different' stand in contrast. While *bu-tong* is not acceptable, *bu yiyang* is. The differences in acceptability between (19)–(22) can be interpreted as follows: *Bu-tong* is not acceptable in (19) and (21) because it is predicated of a Subject noun which refers to a group, i.e. to a collective noun. Moreover, *hen* 'very' cannot modify *bu-tong* as illustrated in (21). *Bu yiyang*, on the contrary, is compatible with collective nouns, as in (20) and (22); moreover it allows degree modification by means of *hen* 'very'. In (25), *bu-tong* is not acceptable in the (scalar) *degree* complement construction, marked by *de* 得, contrary to *bu yiyang* in (26), because both these (scalar) predicates are construed on different scales. *Bu-tong* is built on a closed scale, *bu yiyang* on an open scale.[2] This is corroborated by the fact that the

---

2 I will oppose both these scalar predicates in terms of the relative/absolute dichotomy, as used by Kennedy and McNally (2005: 370–372) in their description of *very* in English. *Bu yiyang* is an open scale predicate whose Standard of comparison is relative, i.e. context dependent, while *bu-tong* is a closed scale predicate whose Standard is not context dependent. A referee has pointed out that Mandarin *hen* might not be a good test to oppose *bu-tong* and *bu yiyang*. In my view it is, because both lexemes behave differently in the adverbial and complement positions (*zhuangyu* 狀語 vs *buyu* 補語, in the pairs [31]–[32] and [25]–[26]); moreover they allow different degree modifiers. See also examples (34)–(35) below and (50).

Here are some more distributional differences between *bu-tong* and *bu yiyang*. *Xiangdang* 'relatively' is acceptable with *bu-tong*, but not with *bu yiyang*. *Shi ... de* is acceptable with *bu yiyang*, but much less so with *bu-tong*.

(i) *xiangdang bu-tong de kanfa*
    relatively different *de* viewpoint
    'relatively different viewpoints'

(ii) **xiangdang bu yiyang de kanfa*
    relatively different *de* viewpoint

(iii) ??*A gen B shi bu-tong de*
    A and B be different *de*

(iv) *A gen B shi bu yiyang de*
    A and B be different *de*
    'A and B are different.'

degree modifier *hen* 'very' is not accepted with predicative *bu-tong*, cf. (21). In the same fashion, *bu-tong* cannot be reinforced by the emphatic coordinator *bing* 'moreover'. On the contrary, the scalar open scale adjective *bu yiyang* is fully grammatical both in degree predicative constructions — whether *bu yiyang* occupies the predicative construction (*weiyu* 謂語, in [22]) or the degree comple-ment construction (*chengdu buyu* 程度補語, in [26]). *Bu yiyang* can be emphati-cally marked by the coordinator *bing* 'moreover', as illustrated in (24).

(19)　＊大家都不同

　　　*Dajia　　　dou **bu-tong**
　　　everybody　all　different

(20)　大家都不一樣。

　　　*Dajia　　　dou **bu yiyang**.
　　　everybody　all　different
　　　'Everybody is different.'

(21)　＊這個委員會很不同

　　　*Zhei　ge　weiyuanhui　**hen　bu-tong**
　　　this　Cl.　assembly　　very　different

(22)　這個委員會很不一樣。

　　　*Zhei　ge　weiyuanhui　**hen　bu yiyang**.
　　　this　Cl.　assembly　　very　different
　　　'This assembly is different.'

(23)　＊這兩個瓶子並不同

　　　*Zhei　liang　ge　pingz　**bing　　　bu-tong**
　　　this　two　　Cl.　bottle　moreover　different

(24)　這兩個瓶子並不一樣。

　　　*Zhei　liang　ge　pingz　**bing　　　bu yiyang**.
　　　this　two　　Cl　bottle　moreover　different
　　　'These two bottles are really different.'

(25)　＊他們長得不同

　　　*Tamen　zhang　　de　**bu-tong**
　　　Pl3　　　grow up　*de*　different

(26)　他們長得不一樣。

    Tamen zhang　　de (hen) bu yiyang.
    Pl3　　grow up *de* (very) different
    'They look different.'

In (27)–(33) below, I will oppose two types of constructions indicating (in) equality. In the first type, the property which serves as a basis for comparison is left undefined and *bu-tong/bu yiyang* are main predicates. In the second case, the property which serves as a basis for comparison is asserted and *bu-tong/bu yiyang* are modifiers of the main predicate.

2.2.2 *Bu-tong* and *bu yiyang* as main predicates in (in)equality constructions

In the first two pairs – (27)–(28) and (29)–(30) – the relevant property, which allows for the comparison between Zhangsan and Lisi is left unsaid. ([6a] and [6b] above are repeated below in [27]–[28]] for ease of exposition).

(27)　張三跟李四不同。

= 　*Zhangsan* gen Lisi **bu-tong**.

(6a)　Zhangsan and Lisi different
    'Zhangsan and Lisi are different.'

(28)　張三跟李四不一樣。

= 　*Zhangsan gen Lisi* **bu** *yiyang*.

(6b)　Zhangsan and Lisi Neg identical
    'Zhangsan and Lisi are different.'

While the pair (27)–(28) is acceptable, notice that the negation *bu* plays a different role in the two members of the pair. From (27), (29) cannot be generated, while from (28), (30) can. The negative counterpart of *bu-tong*, i.e. (the positive form) *tong* 'same' cannot stand in predicative position, as seen in (29).[3] On the

---

3 The affirmative form *tong* cannot be a free form: it is a bound form, which cannot stand alone as a predicate.

    Only compound forms such as *xiangtong* 'similar' or *tonghang* 'same occupation' = 'colleague' ... are allowed. Compare (i) with (ii) and (iii).

(i)　**tamen tong*　　(ii) *tamen xiangtong*　　(iii) *tamen tonghang*
    Pl3　　same　　　　Pl3　　similar　　　　Pl3　　same-occupation
    　　　　　　　　　'They are similar.'　　　'They are colleagues.'

contrary, the negative counterpart of *bu yiyang*, i.e. (the positive form) *yiyang* 'identical', can stand in predicative position, cf. (30). This is why the negation *bu* is written as part of the word *bu-tong* in (27), but it is external to *yiyang* 'identical' in (28).

(29) *張三不跟李四同

     *Zhangsan **bu**   gen Lisi **tong**

     Zhangsan Neg and Lisi same

(30) 張三不跟李四不一樣。

     *Zhangsan **bu**   gen Lisi **yiyang**.

     Zhangsan Neg and Lisi identical

     'Zhangsan and Lisi are not alike.'

     'Zhangsan and Lisi are different.'

From the grammaticality contrast in the pair (29)–(30), one can conclude that the role played by the negation *bu* in *bu-tong* is different from the role it plays in *bu yiyang*. *Bu-tong* is one word; it is an X°, in which *bu-* functions as a lexical negation: *bu-* is a bound form, a prefix. Contrary to *bu-tong*, *bu yiyang* is not an X°: it is an XP, a phrase, where *bu* functions as a syntactic negation. Being a free form, as is expected, *bu* can occupy different positions, as illustrated in (28) and (30).[4]

Now that we have opposed *bu-tong* and *bu yiyang* as main predicates, we are in a position to study their behaviors as predicate modifiers.

---

4 According to an anonymous reviewer, whom I thank, the ungrammaticality of (23) is due to the morpho-syntax of *tong*. Because *bing bu* cannot be followed by a bound form, the sequence **bing bu-tong* is ill-formed. The contrast between the pair (i) and (ii) illustrates this constraint: *zu* 'enough' is a bound form and (i) is ungrammatical, whereas *chongzu* is a free form and (ii) is grammatical.

(i) **bing*   *bu* *zu*   (ii) *bing*   *bu* *chongzu*

    moreover Neg enough   moreover Neg enough

                              'really not sufficient'

See Teng (1975) for a distinction between syntactic and lexical negation. Some speakers of Taiwan Mandarin do not accept (30), because of the position of the negative marker *bu*, but speakers of Mainland China accept it; see also Tiee (1986: 165).

2.2.3 *Bu-tong* and *bu yiyang* as predicate modifiers in comparative constructions

Like the pair (27)–(28) above, the pair (31)–(32) below also involves a comparative of (in)equality construction. But, in (31)–(32) the dimension along which the two individuals Zhangsan and Lisi are compared, i.e. their height, is stated.

(31)　*張三跟李四不同高

　　　*Zhangsan gen Lisi **bu-tong** gao
　　　Zhangsan and Lisi different tall

(32)　張三跟李四不一樣高。

　　　*Zhangsan gen Lisi **bu yiyang** gao.*
　　　Zhangsan and Lisi different　tall

　　　'Zhangsan is not as tall as Lisi.'

Notice that *bu-tong* cannot modify the scalar property *gao* 'be tall' in (31), while *bu yiyang* in (32) can. Hence, we can conclude that *bu-tong* is not a degree modifier, while *bu yiyang* is. As expected from (30) above, where the negation *bu* precedes the standard of comparison, (32) has a counterpart where the (syntactic) negation *bu* precedes the whole (big) predicative phrase $_{VP}$[*bu gen Lisi yiyang gao*]$_{VP}$, cf. (33). The scope of *bu* is wider in (33) than in (32).

(33)　張三不跟李四一樣高。

　　　*Zhangsan **bu**　gen Lisi **yiyang** gao.*
　　　Zhangsan Neg and Lisi alike　tall

　　　'Zhangsan is not as tall as Lisi.'

In summary, in this section I have shown that, contrary to *yiyang*, *bu-tong*:
1) can function as a noun meaning 'difference', cf. (17),
2) cannot be predicated of a collective noun, cf. (21),
3) is a lexeme in which the negative marker *bu-* is a bound form, a prefix, cf. (29),
4) cannot function as a degree modifier in a comparative construction, cf. (31).

Thus, the distribution of *bu-tong* is much more varied than that of *bu yiyang*. While *bu yiyang* functions both as a predicate *and* as a (predicate) modifier, *bu-tong* can be a predicate, cf. (9)–(13), but cannot be a predicate modifier, cf. (31). The (regular) distribution of *yiyang* shows that it is always scalar, while *bu-tong* is not always scalar. This distributional and semantic contrast between *bu-tong* and *bu yiyang* allows us to predict that the degree modifiers with which *bu yiyang* cooccur are more numerous than those which *bu-tong* accepts. *Bu yiyang* can easily be modified by *hen* 'very', cf. (22), and by *bu tai* 'not much' in (35), contrary to *bu-tong*, cf. (21), (34). (See also note 2).

(34) *不太不同   (35) 不太不一樣

　　　 ***bu tai** *bu-tong*   **bu tai** *bu* yiyang
　　　　 Neg too different   Neg too Neg identical

　　　　　　　　　　　　　　　　 'not much different'

In sum, *bu* in *bu yiyang* is a free form, which can occupy different positions. Besides, *yi yang* can be decomposed into the numeral *yi* 'one' and the classifier *yang* 'sort': it means 'one'/ 'a single sort'.[5]

In the next section I will dwell more on the semantic opposition between *bu-tong* and *bu yiyang*.

3 The meaning difference between *bu-tong* and *bu yiyang*

In this section, I will study the meaning differences between *bu-tong* and *bu yiyang* in simple sentences, with a SV and a SV(O) word order, respectively. (S stands for Subject and O for Object). The subjects are always plural NPs. In the first paragraph *bu-tong* and *bu yiyang* appear in predicate position; in the second paragraph, they appear in prenominal Object position. There I will investigate the semantic dependency between S and O.

3.1 Plurals NPs in Subject position

Both (36) and (37) below are grammatical, but they are not really synonymous in a given context.

(36) 這些問題不同。

　　　 *Zhei xie   wenti   **bu-tong**.*
　　　 this a few question different

　　　 'These questions are different.'

---

5 For a study of *yiyang* 'same' and its synonyms, see Tsai (2008).

(37) 這些問題不一樣。

> *Zhei xie   wenti   **bu yiyang**.*
> this a few question different
>
> 'These questions are different.'

(36) can be discourse initial, but (37) cannot. (37) needs a preceding discourse to be interpreted. What *bu-tong* 'different' asserts about *zhei xie wenti* ('these questions') in (36) is that they are different, in the sense that they are different from each other: they are *distinct*. Each *individual* question constituting the set of questions *zhei xie wenti* 'these questions' can be opposed to another question, which is a member of the set. Hence *bu-tong* asserts a *non-identity* relation between *individuals*. In contrast, *bu yiyang* 'different' in (37) presupposes that a preceding set of questions holding a certain *property* was mentioned. It asserts that the specific set mentioned (*zhei xie wenti* 'these questions') presents a different property or different properties from the aforementioned set. In (37), the questions themselves are not different from each other, but rather they are different from another set of questions mentioned before: different properties are attributed to these two sets. Hence *bu yiyang* asserts a *non-similar* relation in terms of *properties*. The interpretation of *bu yiyang* is sentence external: it is deitic or anaphoric. In other words, *bu yiyang* is D(iscourse)-linked and has an *external* reading, while *bu-tong* is not D-linked and has an *internal*[6] reading.

In sum, it could be said that *bu-tong* has a *quantitative* reading in (36), whereas *bu yiyang* has a *qualitative* reading in (37). *Bu-tong* indicates *distinctness* and *bu yiyang dissimilarity*. The domain of quantification of *bu-tong* is (individual) objects, i.e. tokens; that of *bu yiyang* is properties, i.e. types. Hence, one can predict that *bu-tong* can function as a marker of plurality.

In the next section, I will try to justify what I have just said about *bu-tong* and *bu yiyang* by using a different type of syntactic environment. I will study *bu-tong* and *bu yiyang* as nominal modifiers contained in plural NPs which occupy the postverbal position.

3.2 Plural NPs in Object position

In the same way as the pair (36)–(37) is not synonymous, I will show that the pair (38)–(39) is also not synonymous.

---

6 See Carlson (1987).

(38) 張三和李四想住不同的城市。

    *Zhangsan he   Lisi xiang zhu **bu-tong de** chengshi.*
    Zhangsan and Lisi want live different de city

    'Zhangsan and Lisi want to live in different cities.'

(39) 張三和李四想住不一樣的城市。

    *Zhangsan he   Lisi xiang zhu **bu yiyang de** chengshi.*
    Zhangsan and Lisi want live different   de city

    'Zhangsan and Lisi want to live in different cities.'

In (38) *bu-tong* can only be interpreted sentence internally: it has a "dependent" reading. *Bu-tong* takes its reference from each member of the conjoined NP subject – i.e. Zhangsan and Lisi – and pairs one individual with an object, a city in this case. It pairs Zhangsan with New York and Lisi with San Francisco in (40). Hence *he* 'and' is interpreted distributively and *bu-tong* is also distributive.[7]

Thus (38) could be naturally followed by (40). The antonym reading of *bu-tong* in (38), is *tong yi* + classifier 'the same', as can be seen in (41). *Tong yi* 'the same' indicates individual identity.

(40) 張三想住在紐約，李四想住在舊金山。

    Zhangsan xiang zhu zai Niuyue,   Lisi xiang zhu
    Zhangsan want live at New York Lisi want live

    zai Jiujinshan.
    at San Francisco

    'Zhangsan wants to live in New York, Lisi wants to live in San Francisco.'

(41) 張三和李四想住同一個城市。

    *Zhangsan he   Lisi xiang zhu **tong yi   ge** chengshi.*
    Zhangsan and Lisi want live same one Cl city

    'Zhangsan and Lisi want to live in the *same* city.'

The fact that *tong yi* 'the same' necessitates the presence of a nominal classifier *ge*, i.e. an individuator, before the noun *chengshi* 'city', corroborates

---

7 A reviewer has suggested characterizing *bu-tong* as distributive. If *bu-tong* is seen as a distributor, then its lack of occurrence with a collective noun, as in (21) and (55), immediately follows.

what I have said above in Section 3.1. *Tong yi* 'the same' and its antonym *bu-tong* 'different' belong to the domain of quantification of (countable) nouns.

Now that I have described the role played by *bu-tong* in (38) above, what remains to be explained is the role played by *bu yiyang* in (39). Just like (37) above, (39) needs a preceding context to be interpreted. *Bu yiyang* indicates that a certain type of city was mentioned before and that Zhangsan and Lisi, each or both, want(s) to live in a city different from the type precedingly mentioned. Hence (39) could be followed, for example, by (42) or (43). In (42) the conjunction *he* 'and' in (41) is interpreted as distributive, whereas in (43) *he* 'and' is interpreted as collective.[8] In (42), a pairing is established between one individual and one type of city; in (43), a pairing is established between the group formed by Zhangsan and Lisi and (only) one type of cities. If the preceding context stated that Peter and Mary want to live in a small city, (43) would be an adequate discourse continuation, stating that, contrarily to Peter and Mary, Zhangsan and Lisi want to live in a big city.

(42)　張三想住文化城市，李四想住農業城市。

　　　*Zhangsan xiang zhu **wenhua** chengshi, Lisi xiang zhu **nongye** chengshi.*
　　　Zhangsan want live culture　city　　　Lisi want live rural　　city

　　　'Zhangsan wants to live in a *cultural* city, Lisi in a *rural* city.'

(43)　張三和李四想住很大的城市。

　　　*Zhangsan he　Lisi xiang zhu **hen da de** chengshi.*
　　　Zhangsan and Lisi want live very big *de* city

　　　'Zhangsan and Lisi want to live in a *big* city.'

Yiyang 'same'/'identical' in (44) stands as the antonym of *bu yiyang* in (39). (41) and (44) are not synonymous at all.

(44)　張三和李四想住一樣的城市。

　　　*Zhangsan he　Lisi xiang zhu **yiyang de** chengshi.*
　　　Zhangsan and Lisi want live alike　*de* city

　　　'Zhangsan and Lisi want to live in the same type of /in *similar* cities.'

---

8 Huang (2002) treats *he* 和 'and' as a collective conjunction. In my opinion, *he* 和 'and' as well as *gen* 跟 'and' allow both a collective and a distributive reading, cf. Paris (2010).

In sum, in this section I have tried to show that, in certain contexts, pre-nominal *bu-tong* and *bu yiyang* have different meanings. *Bu-tong* stresses the (internal) difference between individual *objects*. *Bu yiyang* asserts that the *properties* of the objects it applies to are dissimilar. *Bu-tong* says that the members of *a plurality of objects* are *not the same*; *bu yiyang* says that *the properties* which hold of an object or of a plurality of objects are not of one sort: they are *not alike*, they are not similar.

In the following, I will provide other contexts where I oppose prenominal *bu-tong* and *bu yiyang*. I will try to characterize *bu-tong* as a marker of plural count nouns.

4 *Bu-tong* as a marker of noun plurality: properties

In a context where a list of objects is mentioned, *bu-tong* serves as a "redundant marker of plurality"[9], as shown in (46), which is a follow up of (45). In such a context, *bu yiyang* cannot be used, cf. (47). A, B, C and D stand for the names of four different poems in (45). In (46) *bu-tong* is licensed by the indefinite plural marker *(yi) xie* 'a few'. The meaning of *bu-tong* 'different' is not completely redundant with that of *(yi) xie* 'a few'. Because it is distributive, *bu-tong* stresses that the plurality described by *(yi) xie* does not constitute a group. On the contrary, it is composed of atomic elements.

(45)　A、B、C、D 跟 E，這幾首詩有個共同點。

　　　A, B, C, D gen E, zhei ji　shou shi　you　ge gongtong dian.
　　　A B C D　　and E　this 1–9 Cl.　poem have Cl. common point

　　　'A, B, C , D and E ... these poems present a common point.'

---

9 I borrow this term from Leeman (2004). It is analogous to what Carlson (1987) labels as a « seemingly otiose adjective ». As noted by an anonymous reviewer, this label might be too strong. I use it just to stress the parallelism between the use of Mandarin *bu-tong* and French *différents* in *prenominal* position (*différents* must be plural here). Just like *bu-tong*, *différent* cannot cooccur with a singular noun, cf. (ia) and (iia). With a singular noun, another noun modifier translated as *another* must be used: *ling* in Mandarin and *autre* in French. Both are D-linked.

(i)　　*yi ben bu-tong de shu　　vs. (ib)　ling yi ben shu.

(iia)　*un différent livre　　　vs. (iib)　un autre livre

See Laca and Tasmowski (2004) for a thorough analysis of French *différents* as a noun modifier and Tovena and van Peteghem (2001, 2003) for *autre*.

(46) 這些不同的詩 ...

　　zhei xie **bu-tong** *de shi*
　　this a few different *de* poem
　　'these different poems' ...

(47) *這些不一樣的詩 ...

　　zhei xie **bu yiyang** *de shi*
　　this a few different *de* poem

In sentences where the subject is indefinite, that is where a new topic of discourse is introduced, by definition only *bu-tong* can appear. *Bu-tong* emphasizes the cardinality of the subject NP in (48). The prevalent reading of (48) then is that of an event reading, such as, for instance: 'On three different occasions, a customer called you'. *Bu yiyang* cannot be substituted for *bu-tong*, because it never is discourse new: it needs a preceding context to be interpreted: it is deictic or anaphoric. Compare (48) and (49). As is expected when *bu-tong* functions as a noun modifier, it is not scalar. (50) is ill-formed, because the degree adverbials *wanquan* 'completely' or *hen* 'very' modify *bu-tong*.

(48) 有三個不同的客戶打電話來找你。

　　You san ge **bu-tong** *de kehu　da dianhua lai zhao　ni.*
　　have three Cl. different *de* customer to telephone to look for you
　　'Three different customers called up and looked for you.'

(49) *有三個不一樣的客戶打電話來找你

　　You san ge* **bu yiyang *de kehu　da dianhua lai zhao　ni.*
　　have three Cl. different *de* customer to telephone to look for you

(50) *有三個完全/很不同的客戶打電話來找你

　　You san ge* **wanquan/hen *bu-tong de kehu*
　　have three Cl. completely/very different *de* customer
　　da dianhua lai zhao　ni
　　to telephone to look for you

If indeed *bu-tong* is a marker of nominal distributive plurality, one expects that it should cooccur with count nouns whose cardinality is superior to one, but not with mass nouns, nor with collective nouns. Such a prediction is carried out. The mass nouns *shui* 'water' or *qian* 'money' cannot be modified by *bu-tong*, cf. (51)–(52), but the count nouns *paiz* 'brand' and *huobi* 'currency' can, cf. (53)–(54). As is expected, the collective noun *xuesheng-men* '(a group of) students' also cannot be modified by *bu-tong*, cf. (55); but mass nouns which are rendered countable by means of the classifier *zhong* 'sort' can, cf. (56)–(57).[10]

---

10 This fact has been called to my attention by a referee.

(51) *不同的水

    *bu-tong de shui
    different *de* water

(52) *不同的錢

    *bu-tong de qian
    different *de* money

(53) 不同牌子的水

    bu-tong paizi de shui
    different brand *de* water
    'different brands of water'

(54) 不同的貨幣

    shui bu-tong de huobi
    water different *de* currency
    'different currencies'

(55) *不同的學生們

    *bu-tong de xuesheng-men
    different *de* student-Pl

(56) 三種不同的水

    san zhong bu-tong de shui
    three Cl/sort different *de* water
    'three kinds of water'

(57) 好幾種不同的錢

    hao ji zhong bu-tong de qian
    good 1–9 Cl/sort different *de* money
    'many sorts of currencies'

Conclusion

In this paper I have tried to determine in which contexts *bu-tong* and *bu yiyang* can substitute and in which contexts they cannot. Here are my main results: *bu-tong* is not always scalar, but *bu yiyang* is; *bu-tong* cannot be a degree modifier in comparative constructions, but *bu yiyang* can; *bu-tong* can function as a noun, but *bu yiyang* cannot. In the noun modifying position, *bu-tong* either indicates plurality (cf. [38]) or emphasizes it (cf. [48]), but *bu yiyang* does not. Nominal *bu-tong* indicates that the members of *a plurality of objects* are *not the same*. Hence *bu-tong* cannot cooccur with the numeral *yi* 'one', but it can cooccur with (countable) nouns unmarked for quantity.

    The fact that a sequence Numeral Phrase expression [Numeral + Classifier] + *bu-tong* in the NP is well-formed, as in (46) or (48), indicates that:

(i) plurality and number marking in Mandarin are not in complementary distribution: they are two different phenomena. This would entail reconsidering analyses which posit only one projection for Pl(urality) and for Number, as in Li (1999) or Borer (2005) and would favour approaches which distinguish them, cf. Fassi-Fehri and Vinet (2008),

(ii) contrary to Greenberg's (1974) generalization, the presence of *both* plurality marking *and* nominal classifiers is attested not only in Mandarin, but also in other Northern Kam languages, as shown by W. Bisang (2012 in this volume).

List of abbreviations

Cl	Classifier
Neg	Negation
Pl	Plural
Sfx	Suffix

References

Alrenga, Peter. 2009. Tokens, Types and Identity. In *Proceedings of the 38th Annual Meeting of the North East Linguistic Society*, Anisa Schardl, In: Martin Walkow and Muhammad Abdurrahman (eds.), Vol. 1, 53–65. Amherst: GLSA.

Beck, Sigrid. 2000. The Semantics of *different*: Comparison Operator and Relational Adjective. *Linguistics and philosophy* 23 (2): 101–139.

Bisang, Walter. 2012. Numeral Classifiers with Plural Marking – a Challenge to Greenberg. In *this volume*.

Borer, Hagit. 2005. *In Name Only. Structuring Sense, Volume I*. Oxford: Oxford University Press.

Carlson, Greg. 1987. *Same* and *different*: some Consequences for Syntax and Semantics. *Linguistics and Philosophy* 10: 531–566.

Fassi Fehri, Abdelkader and Marie-Thérèse Vinet. 2008. Nominal and Verbal Classes in Arabic and Chinese. In *Recherches linguistiques de Vincennes*, In: Lucia Tovena (ed.), 37: 55–83.

Greenberg, Joseph. 1974. Numeral Classifiers and Substantival Number: Problems in the Genesis of a Linguistic Type. In *Proceedings of the 11th International Congress of Linguistics*, Bologna – Florence, Aug. 28–Sept. 2, 1972, 17–37. Bologna: Il Mulino. Reprinted in: Greenberg (1990: 16–93).

Greenberg, Joseph. 1990. *On Language. Selected Writings of Joseph H. Greenberg*, In: Keith Denning and Suzanne Kemmer (eds.). Stanford: Stanford University Press.

Huang, C.-T. James. 2002. Distributivity and Reflexivity. In *On the Formal Way to Chinese Languages*, In: Sze-Wing Tang and Chen-Sheng Luther Liu (eds.), 21–45. Stanford: CSLI Publications.

Kennedy, Christopher and Louise McNally. 2005. Scale Structure, Degree Modification and the Semantics of Gradable Predicates. *Language* 81: 345–381.

Laca, Brenda and Liliane Tasmowski. 2001. Distributivité et Interprétations Dépendantes des Expressions d'Identité. In *Typologie des groupes nominaux*, In: Georges Kleiber, Brenda Laca & Liliane Tasmowski (eds.), 143–165. Rennes: Presses Universitaires de Rennes.

Laca, Brenda and Liliane Tasmowski. 2003. From Non-identity to Plurality: French *différent* as an Adjective and as a Determiner. In *Romance Languages & Linguistic Theory 2001*, In: Josep Quer, Jan Schroten, Mauro Scorretti, Petra Sleeman and Els Verheugd (eds.), 155–176. (Current Issues in Linguistic Theory). Amsterdam: John Benjamins.

Laca, Brenda and Liliane Tasmowski. 2004. *Différents*. In *Handbook of French semantics*, In: Francis Corblin and Henriette de Swart (eds), 109–118. Stanford: CSLI Publications.

Leeman, Danièle. 2004. Les Déterminants *divers* et *différents*: deux Manières de Présenter la Comparaison. In *Intensité, comparaison, degré* 1, In: Florence Lefeuvre and Michèle Noailly (eds), 243–255. (Travaux Linguistiques du Cerlico 17.) Rennes: Presses Universitaires de Rennes.

Li, Yen-Huei Audrey. 1999. Plurality in a Classifier Language. *Journal of East Asian Linguistics* 8 (1): 75–99.

Moltmann, Friederike. 1992. Reciprocals and *same/different*: towards a Semantic Analysis. *Linguistics and philosophy* 15 (4): 411–462.

Paris, Marie-Claude. 2010. Mandarin *gen* and French *et/avec*. Another Look at Distributivity and Collectivity. In *Contrasting Meaning in Languages of the East and West*, In: Dingfang Shu and Ken Turner (eds.), 512–530. (Contemporary Studies in Descriptive Linguistics 14). Berne: Peter Lang.

Tovena, Lucia and Marleen van Peteghem. 2001. *Différent* vs *autre* et l'Opposition Réciproque vs Comparatif. *Linguisticae Investigationes* 25 (1): 149–170.

Tovena, Lucia and Marleen van Peteghem. 2003. Facets of *different* in French: *différent* et *autre*. In *Empirical Issues in Formal Syntax and Semantics* 4, In: Claire Beyssade, Olivier Bonami, Patricia Cabredo Hoffer and Francis Corblin (eds.), 63–80. Paris: Presses de l'Université de Paris-Sorbonne.

Teng, Shou-hisn. 1975. Negation in Chinese. *Journal of Chinese Linguistics* 2 (2): 125–140.

Tiee, Henry Hung-Yeh. 1986. *A Reference Grammar of Chinese Sentences*. Tucson: The University of Arizona Press.

Tsai, Mei-chih. 2008. Tong zhong qiu yi. Hanyu Cidian Jinyici Yiyi yu Yongfa Fanlie Tantao [A Study of the Definitions and Examples in Chinese Dictionaries: the Case of 'same']. Word meaning and computing. *Proceedings of the 9th Chinese Lexical Semantics Workshop*, 436–448. Singapore: COLIPS.

Jingqi Fu

8 Plurality in the pronominal paradigms of Bai dialects[1]

Abstract: The Bai pronouns inflect for plurality, possessive and sometimes objective cases. Examining the pronominal paradigms of several Bai dialects, we argue, contrary to the analysis in which the plural is independently derived via vowel inflection, that the inflected plural is derived from 'pronoun + plural morpheme,' thus accounting for the different forms of the plural pronouns in Bai dialects on the basis of the plural ending. The same approach can be applied to Bai's pronominal cases, making Bai similar to other Tibeto-Burman languages in terms of how and when the plural marking and the cases in the pronominal system have developed.

Key words: plural pronouns, possessive case, objective case, Bai

1 Introduction

1.1 The Bai 白 language and dialects

The Bai language is an isolating language. However its pronouns inflect for plurality and case. We will investigate how plurality and case inflection arise in Bai, to account for this particularity of the language and to understand Bai in relationship to other Tibeto-Burman languages.

There are 1.8 million Bai according to the 2000 Census. The Bai people live mostly in Dali Autonomous Prefecture, in China's Southwestern Yunnan Province. Many Bai also speak Chinese and/or another ethnic minority language: Naxi, Yi, Lisu or Tibetan.

Since publication of the standard description of Bai (Xu and Zhao 1964, 1984), scholars have divided the Bai language into three major groups: the Central dialect group as represented by Jianchuan 剑川, the Southern dialect group as represented by Dali 大理, and the Northern dialect group represented by the former Bijiang 碧江 speech. Based on this three-way division, we will study the following dialects, with their sources listed:

---

1 This paper was supported by the grant Quantification et Pluralité ANR-06-BLAN0259 awarded by the Research Department of the French Government. We are grateful for the comments received at the Workshop on Quantification and Plurality held in Paris in 2009 and for Craig Baker's help with editing.

Jianchuan 剑川, Central Dialect Group:	
Jinxing 金星, Dashi 大石	Wang (2006)
Jinshan 金山	Lijiang Region Annals (2000)
	Fieldwork by Lin Xu and Jingqi Fu (2000)
Jinhua 金华	Xu and Zhao (1984)

Dali 大理, Southern Dialect Group:	
Zhoucheng 周城	Wang (2006)
Zhaozhuang 赵庄	Zhao (2009)

Northern Dialect Group:	
Lama 拉玛:	Li (2008),
Tuoluo 妥洛	Wang (2006)
Enqi 恩棋	
Gongxing 共兴	
Lemo 勒墨:	
Jinman 金满	Wang (2006)
Ega 俄嘎	Wang (2006), Fieldwork by
	Xu and Fu (2003)
Luobenzhuo 洛本卓	Fieldwork by Xu (1957)
	Fieldwork by Xu and Fu (2003)

Two isolates:	
Xishan 西山	Wang (2001)
Mazhelong 马者龙, 邱北县	Wang (2006)

Figure 1: The Bai dialects studied and their sources

1.2 Pronouns in Bai dialects

Table 1: Pronouns in Jinxing 金星 (Wang 2006: 86)

	Singular		Plural
	Subjective/Objective	Genitive	All cases
1st	ŋo³¹	ŋɯ⁵⁵	ŋɑ⁵⁵ (Ex.) jã⁵⁵ (In.)
2nd	no³¹ jĩ⁵⁵ (Res.)	nɯ⁵⁵	nɑ⁵⁵
3rd	mo³¹	mɯ⁵⁵	mɑ⁵⁵

Table 2: Pronouns in Dashi 大石 (Wang 2006: 86)

	Singular		Plural
	Subjective/Objective	Genitive	All cases
1st	ŋõ³¹	ŋɯ⁵⁵	ŋɑ⁵⁵ (Ex.) jã⁵⁵ (In.)
2nd	nõ³¹	nɯ⁵⁵	nɑ⁵⁵
3rd	pu³¹	pɯ⁵⁵	pɑ⁵⁵

Table 3: Pronouns in Jinhua 金华 (Xu and Zhao 1984: 10)

	Singular		Plural
	Subjective/Objective	Genitive	All cases
1st	ŋo³¹	ŋɯ⁵⁵	ŋɑ⁵⁵ (Ex.) jã⁵⁵ (In.)
2nd	no³¹ jĩ⁵⁵ (Res.)	nɯ⁵⁵	nɑ⁵⁵
3rd	mo³¹	mɯ⁵⁵	mɑ⁵⁵

Table 4: Pronouns in Jinshan 金山 (Lijiang Region Annals, 2000)

	Singular		Plural		
	Subjective	Objective	Genitive	Subj/obj	Genitive
1st	ŋõ³¹	ŋõ⁵⁵ nə³³	ŋɯ⁵⁵ vɯ²¹	ŋɑ⁵⁵ (Ex.)	ŋɑ⁵⁵ vɯ²¹
				ȵã⁵⁵ (In.)	ȵã⁵⁵ vɯ²¹
2nd	nõ³¹	nõ⁵⁵ nə³³	nɯ⁵⁵ vɯ²¹	nɑ⁵⁵	nɑ⁵⁵ vɯ²¹
	ȵi⁵⁵ (Res.)	ȵi⁵⁵ nə³³ (Res.)	ȵi⁵⁵ vɯ²¹		
3rd	u³¹ u⁵⁵ (Res.)	u³¹ nə³³	u⁵⁵ vɯ²¹	uɑ⁵⁵	uɑ⁵⁵ vɯ²¹

Table 5: Pronouns in Zhoucheng 周城 (Wang 2006: 86)

	Singular		Plural
	Subjective/Objective	Genitive	All cases
1st	ŋo³¹	ŋɯ⁵⁵	ŋa⁵⁵ (Ex.) ȵa⁵⁵ (In.)
2nd	no³¹	nɯ⁵⁵	na⁵⁵
3rd	bo³¹	pɯ⁵⁵	pa⁵⁵

Table 6: Pronouns in Zhaozhuang 赵庄 (Zhao 2009: 51)

	Singular		Plural	
	Subjective/Objective	Genitive	Objective	All cases
1st	ŋo³³	ŋɯ⁵⁵		ŋa⁵⁵ (Ex.) ȵa⁵⁵ (In.)
2nd	no³³	nɯ⁵⁵		na⁵⁵
3rd	po³³	pɯ⁵⁵	ɔ⁴⁴	pa⁵⁵

Table 7: Pronouns in Tuoluo 妥洛 (Wang 2006: 84)

	Singular		Plural
	Subjective/Objective	Genitive	All cases
1st	ŋɯ⁵⁵/ŋɔ²¹	ŋɯ⁵⁵	ue⁵⁵ (Ex.) a⁵⁵ ŋɔ²¹ (In.)
2nd	nɯ⁵⁵/nɔ²¹	nɯ⁵⁵	ni⁵⁵
3rd	bɯ⁵⁵/bɔ²¹	bɯ⁵⁵	bi⁵⁵

Table 8: Pronouns in Enqi 恩棋 (Wang 2006: 85)

	Singular		Plural	
	Subjective	Genitive	Objective	All cases
1st	ŋo^{43}/(ŋɯ^{43}/^{55})	ŋɯ^{43}/^{55}	ŋo^{43}	wi^{24} tsɿ^{21} (Ex.) a^{55} ʁo^{21} (In.)
2nd	no^{43} (nɯ^{43}/^{55})	nɯ^{43}/^{55}	no^{43}	ni^{24} tsɿ^{21}
	ni^{55} (Res.)			
3rd	vo^{43} (vɯ^{43}/^{55})	vɯ^{43}/^{55}	vo^{43}	vi^{24} tsɿ^{21}

Table 9: Pronouns in Gongxing 共兴 (Wang 2006: 84)

	Singular		Plural
	Subjective	Genitive	All cases
1st	ŋa^{42}	ŋa^{42}	ŋa^{55} xõ^{22} (Ex.) ʁaŋ^{24} (In.)
2nd	na^{42}	ni^{55}	ni^{42} xõ^{22}
3rd	ba^{42}	ba^{42}	ba^{42} xõ^{22}

Table 10: Pronouns in Jinman 金满 (Wang 2006: 85)

	Singular		Plural
	Subjective	Genitive/Objective	All cases
1st	õ^{42}/^{55}	õ^{55}	mi^{55} (Ex.) n̠a^{21} tʂɚ^{22} (In.)
2nd	no^{42}/^{55}	no^{55}	ni^{55} tʂɚ^{22}
3rd	bo^{42}/^{55}	bo^{55}	bi^{55} tʂɚ^{22}

Table 11: Pronouns in Ega 俄嘎 (Wang 2006: 85; Xu and Fu 2003)[2]

	Singular		Plural
	Subjective	Genitive/Objective	All cases
1st	ŋo^{42}/^{55}	ŋo^{55}	ŋui^{55} (Ex.) ŋui^{55} dze^{31}
			n̠o^{21} ɣo^{22} (In.)
2nd	no^{42}/^{55}	no^{55}	ni^{55} (dze^{31})
3rd	bo^{42}/^{55}	bo^{55}	bi^{55} (dze^{31})/bo^{55} xo^{31}

---

2 Table on Ega pronouns is based on Wang (2006) and our own fieldwork in 2003, data was provided by the same informant Mr. Sibo Hua. We noted and added the variants of plurals from the same speaker.

Table 12: Pronouns in Luobenzhuo 洛本卓 (Xu 1957; Xu and Fu 2003)[3]

	Singular		Plural
	Subjective	**Genitive/Objective**	**All cases**
1st	ŋo⁴²/⁵⁵	ŋo⁵⁵ (ŋɯ⁵⁵)	mi⁵⁵ (dʑɚ³¹)
2nd	no⁴²/⁵⁵	na⁵⁵ (ŋɯ⁵⁵)	ni⁵⁵ (dʑɚ³¹)
3rd	bo⁴²/⁵⁵	bo⁵⁵ (ŋɯ⁵⁵)	bi⁵⁵ (dʑɚ³¹), bo⁵⁵ xo³¹

Table 13: Pronouns in Xishan 西山 (Wang 2001)

	Singular		Plural
	Subjective/Objective	**Genitive**	**All cases**
1st	ŋɯ³¹	ŋɯ⁵⁵	ŋa⁵⁵ xõ²² (Ex.) ʁaŋ²⁴ (In.)
2nd	nɯ³¹	nɯ⁵⁵	na⁵⁵
3rd	pɯ³¹	pɯ⁵⁵	pa⁵⁵

Table 14: Pronouns in Mazhelong 马者龙 (Wang 2006: 87)

	Singular			Plural
	Subjective	**Genitive**	**Objective**	**All cases**
1st	ŋo³¹	ŋa⁵⁵ mɯ⁵⁵	ŋɚ⁵⁵ (nõ³³)	ŋa⁵⁵ xo³³
2nd	nən³¹	nɚ⁵⁵ mɯ⁵⁵	nɚ⁵⁵ (nõ³³)	na⁵⁵ xo³³
3rd	khi⁵⁵	khi⁵⁵ mɯ⁵⁵	khi⁵⁵ (nõ³³)	khi⁵⁵ xo³³

The *Table 15* summarizes the plural forms in the above dialects.

Table 15: Plural pronouns in Bai dialects

		Dialects	**Dialect Groups**
_ɑ⁵⁵/_a⁵⁵	Single form	ZC, ZZ	South
		JX, DS, JS	Central
		XS	
	Complex form	MZL _ a⁵⁵ + xo³³	Isolate
		(exc. 3rd)	North (*Lama*)
		GX _a⁵⁵ xõ²²	
		(exc. 2nd)	
_i⁵⁵	Single form	TL (exc.1st)	North (*Lama*)
		EG	North (*Lemo*)
	Complex form	EQ _i²⁴ + tsʅ²¹	North (*Lama*)
		JM _i⁵⁵ + tʂə²²	North (*Lemo*)
		EG _i⁵⁵ + tʂə²²	North (*Lemo*)
-o⁵⁵	Complex form	EG subj.pron + xɔ³¹	North (*Lemo*)

---

3 Table on Luobenzhuo is based on Xu (1957) and Xu and Fu (2003) fieldwork. The two informants, Mr. Alupa and Mr. Yinan Hu, are uncle and nephew, originally from the Village 2 of District 4 of former Bijiang County.

2 Deriving the plural pronouns

2.1 Origin of the Plural Suffix

The plural pronouns in various dialects have two forms: either inflected single syllable pronouns or complex form consisting of a singular pronoun and another morpheme. The rhyme of the plural pronouns, in either single or plural forms is either /a/ or /i/. There are two possible explanations to consider in order to account for the evolution of the plural pronouns in Bai. One is that the simple form is derived from the complex form, an analysis proposed in Chen (1987) for Yi and Bai languages; the other is that the simple form is derived independently, as in Wang (2006). We will argue for the complex form approach. Let us now explore the possibility that the simple form comes from the complex form and that the morpheme at the end of complex form is responsible for the vowel alteration in the plural pronouns. To do this we need to answer the question: what is this suffixal morpheme? From the charts above, we can see two forms of the plural suffix among dialects, listed in *Figure 2*.

Type I:	xo^{33} (MZL), xo^{44} (JH), xõ^{22} (GX), ɣo^{22} (EG, 1st Inc), xɔ^{33} (EG)
Type II:	tsʅ^{21} (EQ), tʂə^{22} (JM), tɕə^{44} (EG), dze^{33} (EG), tɕə^{44} (JS)

Figure 2: Two kinds of plural suffixes in Bai dialects.

The forms in each type can be considered cognates. Not only do they share the lexical meaning of human plural (see below), but they also have similar phonetic shape. In type I, all but EG have the same initial consonant, e.g. a fricative velar, and the vowel is a mid-back vowel (o/ɔ). The only difference is in tones. We will represent this group by /xo^{44}/. In type II, the initial consonant consists of a dental affricate varying in voicing and place of articulation between alveolar and palatal. The vowel is schwa-like. The dialects with forms of Type I are wide-spread, while the forms of Type II are limited to northern dialects, plus Jinshan of the Central dialect group, which is geographically closer to northern dialects. We will represent this group by EG's /dze^{31}/.

Let us examine the usage and distribution of these two morphemes in different dialect groups, starting with /xo^{44}/. This morpheme, to the extent we can find its use in the dialect, is a morpheme referring to human plural, used as a noun ending or a classifier. In Jinhua (Jianchuan) dialect, as shown below, this morpheme is attached to a noun or demonstrative and refers to a human group.

(1) a. *kṽ⁵⁵ xo⁴⁴* b. *tɕi³³ jṽ³³ thi³³ xo⁴⁴* c. *lɯ³¹ xo⁴⁴* (*Jinhua*)
         soldier Pl   sister   Pl   this Pl
         'soldiers'   'sisters'   'these people'
(Xu and Zhao 1984: 30)

When combined with a demonstrative or a question word, as shown in (2) and (3), this morpheme contrasts with its singular counterpart in (b) and with its non-human plural counterpart in (c):

(2) a. *lɯ³¹ xo⁴⁴*   b. *lɯ³¹ jĩ²¹*   c. *lɯ³¹ ja⁴²*
         this   people   this   person   this   things
         'these people'   'this person'   'these things'

(3) a. *a⁵⁵ na⁴⁴ xo⁴⁴*   b. *a⁵⁵ na⁴⁴ jĩ²¹*   c. *a⁵⁵ na⁴⁴ ja⁴²*
         which   person   which   person   which   things
         'which ones'   'which one?'   'What (things)?'
(Xu and Zhao 1984)

The morpheme /xo⁴⁴/ is treated as a classifier in Xu and Zhao (1984: 30). However it is more than a classifier, in (4), it is used as a nominal head of a compound or phrase.

(4) a. *Lo²¹ xo⁵⁵ ɕi⁴⁴ xo⁴⁴*   b. *pe⁴⁴ thu³³ xo⁴⁴*
         Proper Name person   walking   person
         Loxoɕi people   passers-by

This morpheme is widely distributed, even in dialects where it does not show up in the pronominal system. In Jinhua dialect, which we just discussed, it is not part of the pronominal system (cf. *Table 3*), despite its productive use in opposition to the non-human and the singular. Other dialects may also have this morpheme, whether or not it is in the dialect's pronominal system. The examples in (5)–(8) show the use of /xo⁴⁴/ in different dialects.

(5) a. *lɯ³¹ ɲi²¹*   b. *lɯ³¹ xuo³³*   *Dali*
         this person   this persons
         'this person'   'these people'

(6) a. *ni⁴⁴ sua⁴⁴ se³¹ xuo³³*   b. *sua⁴⁴ xa⁴⁴   xuo³³   Dali*
         young   person   speak Chinese person
         'young people'   'Han Chinese'

(7) a. *xã⁴²*   *xɔ³³*   b. *su⁴² nɔ³³ bu³³*   *xɔ³³*   *Lanping*
         Chinese person   mountain-that-side person
         'Han Chinese'   'mountain dweller' (Li, 2008)

(8) a. *pa⁵³ n̠ĩ³¹ xɔ³³*   b. *khv⁴⁴ tse⁴⁴ xɔ³³*   c. *bo⁵⁵ xɔ³³* *Ega*
         Bai   person   sister   person   that person
         'Bai people'   'sisters'   'those (people)'

As can be seen above, the use of /xo⁴⁴/ is widespread, found in all dialect groups, even in dialects where it is not used as pronominal plural (Jinhua, Jinshan, Dali). Its human plural meaning is constant, but its distribution within a dialect differs. In the Lemo dialect group it is found attached to nouns marking the human plural, and it is also used as a classifier with the same meaning. In Lama dialects (Lanping), for example, /xo⁴⁴/ is limited to the noun ending usage. In Dali and Jianchuan dialects, /xo⁴⁴/ functions as a plural ending on both nouns and NPs and as a classifier, with the meaning of a human plural.

Compared to /xo⁴⁴/, the use of /dze³¹/in (b) is more limited, both in its dialectal distribution and in its usage within a dialect. In the Northern dialect group, it is only found in the Lemo group. In the Central group, it is only found in Jinshan dialect. Taking the Ega dialect as representative of the Lemo Group, we can see that in (9), /dze³¹/ functions as classifier in conjunction with a demonstrative. In this position it can alternate with the more common *xɔ³³*, which as we have mentioned, serves as a plural suffix on nouns.

(9) a. *no⁴²*   *xɔ³³*   b. *no⁴²*   *dze³¹*
         this   Pl   this   Pl
         'these people'   'these people'

Unlike Ega, only the noun-ending usage of /dze³¹/ is found in Jinshan.

(10) a. *kv⁵⁵*   *tɕa⁴⁴*   b. *dʑi³¹ tɕa⁴⁴*
          soldier Pl   field Pl
          'soldiers'   'fields'
          Lijiang Region Annals (2000: 485)

While /xo⁴⁴/ is found across many dialects, with a constant meaning of a human plural, /dze³¹/ is limited to certain dialects, and its use restricted to either plural classifier or noun suffix in a given dialect. It is evident that /xo⁴⁴/ originated as a morpheme referring to human plural and extended its usage to mark the plural in the pronominal system. The origin of /dze³¹/, however, is less certain. It probably developed later than /xo⁴⁴/ because it is not part of compounds. In Lemo, a word meaning 'a group of people' is a likely source for the /dze³¹/: a⁵⁵ tṣeɹ²² (Yang, Zhao and Xu 2008: 1517). Its equivalents are also found in some of other dialects: Lanping (Miluoling): a²¹ tṣʌ²¹ and Lanping (Xinhua): a²¹ tɕø⁴², without them being used as plural suffix in the dialect. One possibility points to the Chinese loan word tɕa 家. And indeed the Lemo dialect has a word da⁴⁴ dze³³ to mean 'everyone' just like its Chinese counterpart. However another recent phonetic transliteration of the Chinese word tɕa 家 gives rise to a different word: guojia → kui²¹ tɕa³³. So this would at least be an older loan word.[4]

In summary, both /xɔ³³/ and /dze³¹/ are bound morphemes that refer to the human plural, either as a suffix on nouns or a head of a nominal expression and a classifier. While /dze³¹/ may be an older loan from Chinese, /xo⁴⁴/ is a widely spread morpheme referring to a human plural. It is reasonable to assume that their use in the pronominal system derives from their other use, the lexical meaning of a human plural.

2.2 The derivation of the plural pronouns

Assuming that the Bai plural starts out with a complex form 'Singular Pronoun + Plural Morpheme', we propose the following two derivations based on the two plural morphemes.

Table 16: Derivation of plural in northern dialects

Underlying form	Stage I	Stage 2
Singular pron + plural morpheme	o → i/ ___#front mid vowel	Deletion of plural suffix
–o + /dze³¹/	–i + /dze³¹/	–i
	EQ, JM	EG, TL

Table 17: Derivation of plural in Central and Southern dialects.

Underlying form	Stage I	Stage 2
Singular pron + plural morpheme	o → a/ ___#o	Deletion of plural suffix
–o + /xo⁴⁴/	–a + /xo⁴⁴/	–a
	MZL, GX,	Others

---

4 It is worth pointing out though that the local mandarin has a respective form for the second person that may be related to /tṣə²²/, as shown in (i):

(i) ni tɕie kə hao? (*Yunnan Mandarin*)
 you respectful Q good
 'How are you (resp.)?'

In the above derivations, all dialects start out with a complex form consisting of a singular pronoun and a plural suffix. They differ in terms of plural suffix and subsequent phonological rules. While northern dialects have /dze³¹/ as a plural suffix, others have /xo⁴⁴/ as a plural suffix. Consequently, the rhyme of the singular pronoun changes, triggered by the vowel in the suffix. In Northern dialects, the rhyme of the pronoun base /o/ fronts and raises to /i/ before /ə/ (or /e/) as a result of an assimilation rule. In Central and Southern dialects, the /o/ becomes /a/ when the plural morpheme has a /o/, a dissimilation rule.

The plural in Bai is very similar to Yi. Chen Kang (1987) has proposed a similar derivation for Yi. He argues that Bai follows the same pattern. More specifically, he considers the plural morpheme in some of the Yi dialects to be a morpheme indicating a human plural, which no longer has independent usage in the language, and that this suffixing morpheme has triggered a vowel change and a tone change in the pronominal root, via assimilation and dissimilation respectively.

(11) The derivation of the plural in Yi

Regressive assimilation of the root rhyme of the first person

$\eta a^{33} + yo^{34} \rightarrow \eta o^{21} + yo^{34} \rightarrow \eta o^{34}$ Lolo (Xide)

Chen proposes the same for Bai:

(12) Regressive dissimilation of the root rhyme and regressive assimilation of the tone of the first person

$\eta o^{31} + yo^{55} \rightarrow \eta a^{55} + yo^{55}$ Lemo

(13) Regressive dissimilation of the root rhyme and regressive assimilation of the tone of the first person

$\eta o^{31} + yo^{55} \rightarrow \eta a^{55} + yo^{55} \rightarrow \eta a^{55}$ Jianchuan

Our analysis is similar to Chen's in deriving the plural from a complex form of "pronoun base + plural morpheme"; but we differ from his account by assigning two distinct plural morphemes to Bai dialects. Chen's plural suffix in Bai was based on Xu and Zhao's (1964) description of Lemo Bai, which in turn was collected in the 1950's. Nowadays, only the voiceless /xo⁴⁴/ is found, with a different tone, and /dze³¹/. Therefore we have used /dze³¹/ as the plural morpheme for Lemo.

Deriving the two types of plural based on singular pronoun + plural puts Bai on a similar path as Yi languages. The current proposal differs from Wang's

(2006: 92) analysis, which derives the two types of Bai plural based on the reconstructed proto forms. In his system, Proto-Bai's pronominal system is an inflected paradigm and the endings observed in complex forms play an insignificant role. Specifically the plural in Proto-Bai has two patterns -*a* vs. -*i*, which in turn derive from the first and second persons, via leveling.[5] This distinction among dialects carries over to the present day Bai. Wang does say that plural often originates from the general or genitive pronominal form plus a plural suffix, but rules this possibility out for Bai. Our proposal has singled out the plural suffixes, and is able to capture the correlation of the plural forms with the suffix form (a-*o* vs. *i/e*). That is, in all the dialects with the -*i* type of plural pronouns, the suffix is a mid-vowel *I/e/ə*. In all the dialects with the -*a* type of plural pronouns, the plural suffix has a back rounded vowel, *o/ɔ*. More telling is the situation where various plural suffix forms exist in one dialect. In Ega for example, the same speaker could have either [xɔ³³] or [dze³¹] as plural suffix. However their combination with the pronoun base is not free. One finds (14) but not (15):

(14) *wĩ⁵⁵ dze³³, ni⁵⁵ dze³³, bi⁵⁵ dze³³, tɕi⁴⁴ dze³³, bo⁵⁵ xɔ³³*

(acceptable plural pronouns in Lemo)

(15) **wĩ⁵⁵ xɔ³³, *ni⁵⁵ xɔ³³*

(unacceptable plural pronouns in Lemo)

Under an account that links the vowel inflection of the pronoun rhyme with the suffix, this incompatibility is readily explained. Namely, the -*i* of the pronoun base is triggered by a mid-vowel in the plural suffix, while (-*o* →) -*a* is the result of dissimilation rule based on the -*o* in the suffix. This correlation would remain unexplained in Wang's account attributing the -*i*/-*a* of the plural pronouns to the vowels of proto-forms.

Moreover, Bai is not an inflected language. The only inflected forms are pronouns in their plural/singular distinction and in their case distinction and some forms of negative verbs (Xu and Zhao 1984). This begs the question how to explain these rare inflections in an otherwise isolating language. Bisang (cf. this volume) discusses classifiers in Weining Ahmao, a Miao language, that inflects for number (singular vs. plural), just like the Northern Kam languages; but also for definiteness and size. Weining Ahmao and the Northern Kam languages are otherwise isolating languages. These inflected classifiers are exceptions not only in terms of inflection, but also in terms of typological considerations.

---

5 Leveling is a process by which forms of similar grammatical functions become phonetically similar (Wang 2006: 80).

The explanation lies in how the classifier has evolved by fusing phonetically with other adjacent forms such as the number 'one'. The same is true for Bai plural pronouns. They are not inflected to start with, but rather are altered in their phonetic shape by being in close proximity with the following plural ending. Thus deriving Bai plural pronouns from complex forms is consistent with the general characteristic of the language, one that says Bai is not an inflected language.

3 Case

3.1 Possessive

While the plural pronouns in Bai do not have a distinct case form, the singular pronouns exhibit a regular vs. possessive case distinction, and sometimes a three-way distinction between subjective, objective and possessive case. Just like the plural pronouns, the possessive (and objective) cases present exceptions to the isolating character of the language. In addition, the lack of interaction between plural and cases raises the question of how plurality and case have derived with respect to each other. We now devote this section to examine the possessive and objective cases in Bai dialects, in connection with plurality.

A chart of possessive cases exhibited in Bai dialects is shown in *Table 18*.

Table 18: (Singular) Possessive Case in Bai Dialects

Possessive	Relationship with other Cases	Dialects	Dialect Groups
_ɯ⁵⁵	distinct from subject and stand-alone object	JX, JS DS, ZC, XS	Central South
_ɯ⁵⁵	same as subject	TL	North (Lama)
_ɯ⁴³	same as a variant of subject	EQ	North (Lama)
_o⁵⁵	same as object, same as a variant of subject	EG, JM	North (Lemo)
-a⁴²	same as subject	GX	North (Lama)
-i⁵⁵	same as plural subjective in rhyme		
-a⁴²	same as subject		
-a⁵⁵ mɯ⁵⁵	same as plural genitive	MZL	Isolate
-ə⁵⁵ mɯ⁵⁵	same as objective		
-i⁵⁵ mɯ⁵⁵	same as third person in all cases		

Just like the plural, the possessive case is remarkably uniform across dialects. Most dialects exhibit an -ɯ⁵⁵, differing from the base form (-o³¹) in vowel and tone. Some have a different tone (EQ) and some (Lemo) have a different rhyme. MZL exhibits distinct rhymes for each person, while GX has an unusual second person possessive. If a possessive form deviates from the standard -w^{55}, then it will be identical in form with either the subjective or objective form of the dialect.

To derive the possessive form, one can either treat it as vowel inflection, or as a vowel alteration due to context. Wang (2006) adopts the first approach, assigning a different rhyme to Proto-Bai's possessive. Just like in the case of plural pronouns, we will argue for the second approach: that the possessive in Bai is derived from a complex form, specifically from 'pronoun base + possessive ending'.

The possessive pronouns often show up in the complex forms. The reason that the pronominal charts in the grammar descriptions rarely display the complex form is that they focus on adjective possessives (e.g. *my* book). In the pronominal chart shown in *Tables 1* to *14,* only two dialects exhibit complex forms: Jinshan and MZL. The apparent difference between the single and complex forms may be due to the authors' preference. One needs to distinguish two situations: adjective possessive vs. the stand-alone possessive (my vs. mine).

In Jinshan dialect for example, the possessive is given in its stand-alone form: $\eta\mathrm{w}^{55}$ $\nu\mathrm{w}^{21}$, $n\mathrm{w}^{55}$ $\nu\mathrm{w}^{21}$, u^{55} $\nu\mathrm{w}^{21}$ (cf. *Table 4*). However, as an adjective, the possessive can appear without the ending:

(16) u^{55} ne^{44} εi^{33} a^{35}
      3rd grandma die Prt

      'His grandma has passed away.'
      Lijiang Region Annals (2000: 483)

Likewise, if a chart does not show the complex form, the complex form is nevertheless in use. The Ega pronominal chart (cf. Table 11), for example, shows the simple form, but in reality the complex form does exist both as an adjective and as a stand-alone possessive:

(17) ηo^{55} $m\mathrm{w}^{55}$ sv^{55} hu^{33}
      1stSP Poss. book good

      'My book is good.'

(18) $d\mathrm{w}^{55}$ bo^{55} ba^{31} $dz\mathrm{w}^{55}$ ηo^{55} $m\mathrm{w}^{55}$
      bean this Cl be   mine

      'These beans are mine.'

Since all possessive pronouns have a complex form, in their stand-alone use, we will consider the complex form as a candidate for deriving the possessive pronouns. In *Table 19*, we show the complex form of stand-alone possessives along with their adjective possessive counterparts.

Table 19: Complex form of Possessives

Dialect	Dialect group	The rhyme of adjective possessive pronoun	Stand-alone Possessive
Jianchuan	Central	-ɯ^{55}	ŋɯ^{55} va^{53}
Jinshan	Central	-ɯ^{55}	ŋɯ^{55} vɯ^{21}
Dali	Southern	-ɯ^{55}	ŋɯ^{55} nɔ^{55}
Lanping	Northern (Lama)	-ɯ^{55}	ŋɯ^{55} ʐɿ^{21}
Enqi	Northern (Lama)	-ɯ$^{43/55}$	*
Gongxing	Northern (Lama)	-a^{42}, -i^{55}, -a^{42}	*
Ega	Northern (Lemo)	-o^{55}	ŋo^{55} mɯ^{55}, no^{55} ŋɯ^{55}
Xishan	Isolated	-ɯ^{55}	ŋɯ^{55} no^{33}
MZL	Isolated	-a^{55}, ə^{55}, i^{55}	ŋa^{55} mɯ^{55}

* No data is available for these entries.

From this table we can see that, first of all, while its possessive ending may be different, the rhyme of the possessive pronoun remains the same, whether or not it is followed by an ending. It is -o^{55} in Ega and -ɯ^{55} in the remaining dialects (except for EQ with a different tone and MZL and GX with distinct forms). This implies that the ending does not currently trigger a vowel change in the base.

Second, possessive endings can be divided into two types. One group includes some kind of labial nasal velar combination: ŋv^{55}, mu^{55}, mɯ^{55}, va^{53}, vɯ^{21}, ŋɯ^{55}; and the other no^{33}, nɔ^{55}, and ʐɿ^{21}. In spite of their apparent differences, both groups are unified by their function and/or by sounds. The items in the first group not only share the nasal, velar, and labial combination, but they also serve as locative and indirect object markers. The possessive endings in the second group are unified by their function. Namely, no^{33}, nɔ^{55}, and ʐɿ^{21} are used as locative and objective markers in their respective dialects. As argued in (2008), the two locative particles ŋv^{55} and no^{33} of the Jianchuan dialect with the meaning of 'around' and 'on' are the sources of the direct and indirect object makers. The possessive endings are very likely the intermediate steps for the grammaticalization of locative to object markers. ('I have something on me' = 'I possess something.') Therefore the first group comes from a locative marker that means 'around' and the second group derives from a locative marker with the meaning of 'on'.

Given that the first group has a wider distribution, we will consider it to be the underlying possessive suffix. We can speculate that at some point the back vowel or velar consonant of the possessive marker triggered the rhyme change in the pronoun base.

(19) a. Pronoun + Possessive (locative) = Possessive Pronouns

  b. $o^{31} \rightarrow w^{55}/$ __# w^{55}

In most of the dialects with a $-w^{55}$, rule (19) has applied. This is the case for dialects in the Central and Southern groups. For Dali, Lanping and Xishan, which have possessive endings in the second group (no^{55}, z_1^{21}, and no^{33}), the rule must have applied prior to their current combination.

For Jinshan, we can see the process at work: the possessive particle is attached to a singular subjective or a plural subjective to make a singular possessive or a plural possessive, respectively. In the singular possessive, the stem vowel has undergone assimilation (cf. [19b]).

In the Lemo dialects (EG and JM), the rhyme of the possessive remains the same as that of the base form, in the adjective and stand-alone possessive forms. This implies the lack of rule (19b). It happens that in Lemo, possessive and objective have the same form, and they are also identical to a variant of the subjective form.[6] It is very likely that case distinction has started to disappear in these dialects, due to the lack of the possessive rule.

In MZL, the possessive form is not regular. The rhyme in the stem for each person is different. In the first person the rhyme is identical to that of the plural, while in the second person it is identical to that of the objective. The third person possessive is the same as in all other cases. Wang (2006) treats MZL as representing Proto-Bai forms, and proposes that the complex forms found in MZL are responsible for deriving the $-w^{55}$ of the possessive in other dialects via 'contraction'.

For possessive case, we have also proposed deriving it from the complex form "pronoun base + possessive ending". We have thus explained the $-w^{55}$ found in the possessive pronouns of most dialects through an assimilation rule triggered by the rhyme and the tone of the possessive ending, which itself derives from the locative marker.

---

6 Wang (2006: 96) points out some interesting syntactic restrictions on Possessive used as subject, indicating that the case distinction still exists.

3.2 Objective case

Compared to possessive case, the objective case is much more limited in Bai dialects. Most dialects have no distinct stand-alone objective, except when followed by an object marker. This is the case for the Jianchuan dialect group and Dali dialect group (and MZL). An example is given in (20), of Jianchuan.

(20) a. *no³¹ sẽ³³ mo³¹*
          2ndS know 3rdS
          'You know him.'

      b. *no³¹ mɯ⁵⁵   no³³ sẽ³³*
          2ndS 3rdSPoss OM   know
          'You know him.'

Notice that when the pronoun is followed by the objective marker, it takes on a form identical to that of the possessive pronoun. We will discuss the significance of possessive affiliation below.

There are three manifestations of the objective case in dialects: 1. When followed by an object marker, both tone and rhyme change (Jianchuan, cf. 20b) or the tone alone changes (Jinshan). For the majority of dialects (Southern and Central), the complex form of the objective case is shown in (21), with the -ɯ⁵⁵ of the pronoun identical to that of the dialect's possessive pronouns.

(21) *ŋo³¹ → ŋɯ⁵⁵/ ___no³³*

The stand-alone objective pronouns are identical in form to the possessives. Northern dialects Jinman, Ega, and Enqi exhibit stand-alone objective case (Wang 2006). They are either identical in form with possessive pronouns (Jinman, Ega) or partially identical with subjective pronouns (EQ, EG, JM). 3. The pronoun in the complex form takes on a different form (not identical to possessive or to subject): Zhaozhuang's third person singular and Mazhelong's three persons.

In these three manifestations of objective case, one must observe several notable properties: first, the objective case is usually complex, consisting of a pronoun and an object marker. Where it is not complex it shares some form with possessive/subjective pronouns (EG, JM, and EQ). Having a complex form contrasts objective case with genitive case and plural formation discussed above, in that the latter two are by and large single, stand-alone morphemes. This shows that the objective case is a later development, and has not developed long enough for the ending to drop or for the pronoun to undergo vowel alteration. The second notable property is the objective's affinity with the possessive form. Why is it that the pronoun takes on a possessive form when followed by an object marker? There are two possibilities to consider: one is to use the possessive as a basis for the formation of objective case. Namely, the objective case consists of possessive + object-marker. This derivation explains the complex forms of Jianchuan dialect group (and Dali group), and also the stand-alone forms of Jinman and Ega; but not Jinshan or those dialects whose objective pronouns are distinct from possessive pronouns (EQ, MZL).

The second possibility to explain the affinity between objective and possessive is to treat the affinity as accidental. The derivation in (21) illustrates this process. That is, the pronouns undergo tone sandhi and/or vowel alteration when suffixed with an object marker. This is a case of regressive dissimilation of both tones and vowels. Under this account, the stand-alone forms which are identical to possessive forms are more problematic, as there is no trigger to explain their form. However, in all of these stand-alone cases, there is a blending of objective and subjective case, so they could well be subjective forms. This phonological account has the added advantage of not having to deal with forms that are distinct from possessive (EQ and MZL), since the connection is accidental in the first place. Likewise, if a dialect has the unchanged pronoun form when followed by the object marker, as in Jinshan, it would simply be because the phonological rule does not apply. But if the possessive form is the basis for the objective case, it would create a contradiction.

Just like with plural formation, we derive possessive case and objective case from "subjective (singular) pronoun + suffix". Depending on the phonetic shape of the suffix, the rhyme and tone of the pronoun base will change (or not), which explains the shape of the resulting pronoun base. This account is different from Wang (2006), who posits a distinct vowel (and tone) in Proto-Bai. In his system, Proto-Bai's pronominal system is an inflected paradigm, and the endings observed in complex forms play an insignificant role.

Table 20: Nominative, Objective and Genitive 1st and 2nd Singular Personal Pronouns in Proto Bai. (Wang 2006: 90)

	Singular		
	Nominative	**Objective**	**Genitive**
1st	*ŋo3	*ŋæ1	*ŋa1
2nd	*nen3	*næ1	*ni1

Wang assigns a distinct form to objective case in Proto-Bai: -*æl*. The *ə* of MZL is thus derived via *æ* → *ə*. The other forms of objectives are derived via "leveling", where objective cases are replaced by nominative cases.

The cross-dialect distribution of objective case indicates that objective case is not a well-developed notion in Bai. It developed later than possessive case, due to lack of an independent form. It is tied to the object marker, which Dai (1990) independently argued to be a later development in Tibeto-Burman. While one cannot rule out that Proto-Bai may have had an objective case independent of nominative and genitive, very little trace is left. Our account of treating objective case as derived from the complex form "pronoun + object marker" readily explains the rhyme and tone alteration of the pronoun base, and makes the object case a later development, consistent with what Dai argued for the Tibeto-Burman languages in general.

Having derived plurality, possessive case and objective case from a complex form, how do the three interact with each other? One noticeable feature in Bai is that plural pronouns remain the same in various cases. Neither their rhyme nor tone change; in both possessive and objective, it is always /-a^{55}/. The possessive or objective derivation must apply to singular pronouns only, in order to trigger the vowel and tone change while leaving plural pronouns intact. In other words, the singular of subjective pronouns serves as the base for plural, possessive and objective endings.

To conclude, we have examined how plurality and case are expressed in the pronominal paradigms of Bai dialects. We propose deriving the plural, possessive and objective pronouns by a complex form of pronoun base followed by an ending (plural morpheme, or possessive/locative marker). By doing so, we account for the different forms of plural pronouns by means of the differences in the plural ending. This account is consistent with the general characteristic of Bai of being a non-inflected language, and shows Bai to be very much like other Tibeto-Burman languages in developing objective case later in its history.

References

Bisang, Walter. 2012. Numeral classifiers with plural marking. A challenge to Greenberg. *This Volume*

Chen, Kang (陈康). 1987. Yiyu daici li de 'shu' [The 'number' in the Loloish personal pronouns], Minzu Yuwen, 3: 128–26.

Dai, Qingxia (戴庆厦). 1990. Yimianyu de jiegou zhuci [The Grammatical Markers in Tibeto-Burman Languages]. *Zangmian yuzu yuyan yanjiu* [Research on Tibeto-Burman Languages]: 83–97. Beijing: Minzu.

Fu, Jingqi (傅京起) and Lin Xu (徐琳). 2008. From locative to object markers: the parallel development of two postpositions in Bai. In *Space in Languages of China Cross-linguistic, Synchronic and Diachronic Perspectives*, Xu Dan (ed.), 119–141. New York: Springer.

Li, Shaoni (李绍尼). 2008. Lanping Lama Baiyu gaikuang [Outline of Lanping Lama]. In *Dali congshu. Baiyupian* [Dali Series: Bai Language Volumes] Yang, Zhao and Xu (eds.). Yunnan: Minzu.

Lijiang Diquzhi. 2000. 丽江地区志 [Lijiang Region Annals] Yunan: Minzu.

Sun, Hongkai (孙宏开). 1996. Case markers of personal pronouns in Tibeto-Burman languages. *Linguistics of Tibeto-Burman Area*, 19 (3): 1–15.

Wang, Feng (王锋). 2001. Xishan baiyu gaikuang [The outline of Xishan Bai]. *Minzu yuwen* 5: 70–80.

Wang, Feng (汪锋). 2006. *Comparison of Languages in Contact: the Distillation Method and the Case of Bai*. Language and Linguistics Monograph Series B Taiwan: Academia Sinica.

Xu, Lin (徐琳) and Zhao Yansun (赵衍荪). 1964. Baiyu gaikuang [The outline of the Bai Language]. *Zhongguo Yuwen* 4: 321–335.

Xu, Lin (徐琳) and Zhao Yansun (赵衍荪). 1984. *Baiyu Jianzhi* [Survey grammar of the Bai language]. Beijing: Minzu.

Yang, Shiyu (杨世钰), Zhao Yinsong (赵寅松) and Xu Lin (徐琳) (eds.). 2008. *Dali Congshu. Baiyupian* [Dali Series: Bai Language Volumes]. Yunnan: Minzu.

Zhao, Yanzhen (赵雁珍). 2009. *Zhaozhuang baiyu cankao yufa* [The Reference Grammar of Zhaozhuang Bai], Ph.D. diss., Central University of Nationalities.

Hongyong Liu and Yang Gu

9 Frequentative aspect and pluractionality in Nuosu Yi[1]

Abstract: Nuosu Yi, a Tibeto-Burman language, employs three different ways to express frequentative events: (1) the first way is to use a preverbal temporal adverb, like the English *often* or *continuously*; (2) the second way is to use a postverbal frequentative aspect marker, like the West Greenlandic frequentative suffix *-tar*; (3) the third way is to let the temporal adverb and the frequentative aspect marker co-occur in the same sentence. This paper proposes a unified account for these three different ways of expressing frequentative events in Nuosu Yi. We argue that there exists a temporal pluractional operator in charge of the frequentative aspect reading. The pluractional operator is able to create unbounded pluralities of event times, hence giving rise to the repetitive/ frequentative reading. Among the three different ways mentioned above, in (1), the pluractional operator is implicit but trigged into effect by the temporal adverb, due to the strong semantic association between the pluractional operator and the temporal adverb. In (2) and (3), the pluractional operator is phonetically realized as the frequentative aspect marker.

Keywords: frequentative aspect, pluractional operator, temporal adverbs, Nuosu Yi

1 Introduction

The term "aspect" refers to different ways of viewing the internal composition of a situation.[2] Speakers of a language can employ the aspectual system of the language to encode the mental representations associated with different types of events or situations (*Aktionsart*), which are commonly categorized into bounded or unbounded in terms of telicity. Vendler (1967) proposes that atelicity arises mainly from the inherent lexical meaning of certain verbs like *walk, run, sing,*

---

1 We wish to thank Li Xiao, Lee Seunghun, Huang Zanhui and the anonymous reviewers for their useful comments and suggestions on several aspects of this paper. We also want to express our gratitude to our Nuosu Yi consultants: Hxi Lyrgursse and Axxi Axhuo. Our special thanks go to two linguists, Professors Wu Da and Hu Suhua, who are Nuosu Yi native speakers themselves, for their generous advice on the data and analysis presented in this paper.
2 Here the notion 'aspect' refers to *Aktionsart* or *situation aspect* in the sense of Smith (1997).

which indicate no inherent endpoints of the activity, while Verkuyl (1972) and Krifka (1989) propose that atelicity also arises from plural nominal complements like *build bridges*, *fix cars*, etc. Recently, Van Geenhoven (2005) proposes that atelicity also arises with predicates that express a nonstop continuity or a non-ending repetition, regardless of whether the verbs involved are telic (accomplishments and achievements) or atelic (states and activities). In this respect, the corresponding verbs may be inflected for what is called quantificational aspect.[3] According to Lieber (2010: 96), there are different quantificational aspects, and the distinctions concern things like the number of times an action is done or an event happens—once or repeatedly—or how frequently an action takes place. Among the quantificational aspects are semelfactive, iterative, and habitual aspects.[4] West Greenlandic has habitual or frequentative aspect, which is morphologically realized as a suffix on the verb stem. Van Geenhoven (2004) argues that this habitual or frequentative aspect marker should be analyzed as a pluractional operator, and contends that it is this operator that pluralizes achievement and accomplishment verbs so that in sentences containing durative adverbials such as *for an hour*, such pluralized verbs can occur as unbounded, atelic predicates.

Similar to West Greenlandic, Nuosu Yi also possesses an overt frequentative aspect marker.[5] However, different from the case in West Greenlandic, the Nuosu Yi frequentative aspect is not obligatorily overt. When the frequentative aspect marker is absent, Nuosu Yi will make use of temporal adverbs to express the frequentative reading of a sentence. The goal of this paper is to describe the different ways in which Nuosu Yi expresses the frequentative aspect, and to offer a unified analysis of these different ways of expressing pluralities of events.

---

3 Gerner (2003) examines the habitual aspect marker in a number of Yi dialects and proposes that two macro-distinctions in the aspect family be established. The first aspect category may be called temporal aspect comprising the *perfective* and *progressive* aspects. The second category should be labeled occurrence or quantificational aspect consisting of the *experiential*, *periodical*, and *habitual* aspects. This dichotomy is also echoed in Lieber (2010). Gerner (2003) regards the particle *ko³³ ʂɯ³⁴* as the habitual aspect marker in Nuosu Yi. In our opinion, this particle should be better referred to as a frequentative aspect marker, since in many cases it gives rise to a frequency reading rather than a habitual reading.
4 Some linguists may regard semelfactive as a kind of lexical aspect, determined by the inherent lexical meaning of the verb. Lieber (2010: 96) categorizes it as a kind of quantificational aspect, because in some languages, such as the Athapaskan language, Koyukon, there is a special verb stem for actions that are done just once. For example, the verb form *yeeltleł* means 'she chopped it once; she gave it a chop.'
5 Van Geenhoven (2004) mentions that many languages are found to have overt frequentative aspect marking. West Greenlandic, a polysynthetic language spoken in Greenland, is such a language. Other such languages include Aleut (see Golovko 1997), Nivkh (see Gruzdeva 1997), Squamish Salish (see Bar-el 2001), and Seneca (see Dahl 1985).

The paper is organized as follows: Section 2 illustrates the three different strategies employed by Nuosu Yi to express the frequentative or repetitive events. Section 3 offers a semantic account for the data in Section 2 based on the notion of unbounded pluractionality. Section 4 discusses how the frequentative aspect marker could be understood as a pluractional operator, and explores the broader typological implications. Section 5 concludes the paper.

2 Nuosu Yi frequentative aspect marking

Yi, which was also called Lolo in the past in China, is mainly spoken in the southwestern provinces of Sichuan, Yunnan, and Guizhou in China. It is a member of the Lolo-Burmese sub-branch of the Tibeto-Burman (TB) branch of the Sino-Tibetan language family. Yi includes a large number of varieties across the three provinces. The variety studied in this work is Nuosu Yi, which is a sub-dialect of the northern dialect of Yi. It is also referred to as Nosu, Northern Yi, Sichuan Yi, or Liangshan Yi in the literature. This variety is mainly spoken in Liangshan Yi Autonomous Prefecture, Sichuan Province, China. The basic word order of Nuosu Yi is SOV, which means a verb always follows all its arguments, but not necessarily in the sentence final position. Sentence final positions are normally taken by particles marking aspect, mood, evidential and other grammatical categories. Like all the other Tibeto-Burman languages, Nuosu Yi is extremely rich in the aspectual marking system (see Chen and Wu 1998, Hu 2001, Gerner 2003, and Wu 2009). In the following section we will illustrate that Nuosu Yi aspect markers do not form a homogeneous grammatical category.

2.1 Grammatical aspect markers vs. verb-level aspect markers

Nuosu Yi has two sets of aspect markers. One of them contains the grammatical aspect markers, and the other verb-level aspect markers. Among the grammatical aspect markers are the perfective, imperfective, inceptive, and some other aspect markers. Among the verb-level aspect markers are the continuous and frequentative aspect markers.[6] These two different types of aspect markers exhibit different syntactic behavior. The differences can be best illustrated by their in/ability to form polar interrogative sentences via reduplication. One prominent verbal

---

6 So far we have only identified the continuous aspect marker and the frequentative aspect marker in the set of Nuosu Yi verb-level aspect markers.

morphological process in Nuosu Yi is the formation of polar interrogatives which reduplicates the main predicate of a sentence,[7] as shown in (1a):[8]

(1) a. *nɯ³³ dza³³ dzɯ³⁴ dzɯ³³?*
         2sg   rice   eat   eat
         'Do you (want to) eat the rice?'

     b. *ŋa³³ dza³³ dzɯ³³.*
         1sg   rice   eat
         'I want (to) eat the rice.'

The main verb in (1a) is reduplicated and the resultant construction is a typical polar interrogative sentence, which can be answered by (1b). Like lexical verbs, the verb-level aspect markers can also be reduplicated to form polar interrogatives, but the grammatical aspect markers cannot, as shown in the contrast between (2) and (3):

(2) a. *tshɿ³³ dza³⁴ dzɯ³³ ta³⁴ o³⁴.*
         3sg   rice   eat   Cont SFP
         'He was eating the rice.'

     b. *tshɿ³³ dza³⁴ dzɯ³³ ta³⁴ ta³³ o³⁴?*
         3sg   rice   eat   Cont Cont SFP
         'Was he eating the rice?'

---

7 This morphological process is completely different from the one that derives the V-V form by deleting the negative morpheme in the A-not-A construction, a well-known phenomenon in some Hmong-Mien languages and Chinese dialects, because Nuosu Yi does not employ the A-not-A construction to express interrogatives. It still remains a puzzle why Nuosu Yi can use this reduplication means to form polar interrogatives. Notice there is a tone sandhi phenomenon here. The mid-level tone of the base verb becomes a high rising tone, and the reduplicant, regardless of the citation tone of the base, always assumes the mid-level tone. Our hunch is that the reduplication process may be triggered by the mid-level tone, which carries the interrogative force. More research is needed here to explicate the exact nature of this phenomenon. **8** Throughout this paper, the examples are presented in the following way: the first line is the transcription of the target language using standard IPA symbols. In presenting the tones, we adopt the tone letters devised by Chao (1930), where digits indicate the pitch value on a five-point scale, with 5 being the highest. Thus 55, 33, and 21 represent a high level tone, a mid level tone, and a low falling tone, respectively. The second line is word-to-word glossing. The third line is the English translation. For expository purposes, some times individual Yi words in the examples may be glossed in a separate line when they are highlighted in the discussion.

(3) a. *tshŋ³³ dza³⁴ dzɯ³³ o³⁴.*
>   3sg rice eat   Perf
>   'He has eaten the rice.'

  b. **tshŋ³³ dza³⁴ dzɯ³³ o³³ o³⁴?*
>   3sg rice eat   Perf Perf
>   'Has he eaten the rice?'

  c. *tshŋ³³ dza³⁴ dzɯ³⁴ dzɯ³³ o³⁴?*
>   3sg rice eat   eat   Perf
>   'Has he eaten the rice?'   (Wu 2009: 27)

In (2b) the continuous aspect marker *ta³³* is reduplicated to form a polar interrogative, but the perfective aspect marker in (3b) cannot be reduplicated. In the case of (3b), in order to form a polar interrogative sentence, the lexical verb should be reduplicated, as shown in (3c). From the contrast shown in examples (2) and (3), we can conclude that the verb-level aspect markers are more like integral components of the lexical verbs, which suggests that the Nuosu Yi frequentative aspect marker is derivational (rather than inflectional) in nature. They are sensitive to the morphological process of reduplication, whose operating domain is that of the main predicates (verbs or adjectives). Apart from using the reduplication morphological process as a test to differentiate the two types of aspect markers in Nuosu Yi, we can also use the negative morpheme as a diagnosis. Verb-level aspect markers can be negated by the negative morpheme, but grammatical aspect markers cannot. We will illustrate this point in the following section when we are discussing the morphosyntactic behavior of the frequentative aspect marker.

2.2 Nuosu Yi frequentative aspect marker

The frequentative aspect marker in Nuosu Yi is a verb-level aspect marker, which indicates that it can be reduplicated to form interrogative sentences:[9]

(4) a. *mu³³ ka⁵⁵ dɯ³³ dɯ³³ mu³³ la³³ ko³³ ʂɯ³⁴.*
>   Muga   often   come Freq
>   'Muga often comes.'

---

9 Notice when a base contains two or more syllables, only the last syllable is reduplicated.

b. *mu³³ ka⁵⁵ duɯ³³ duɯ³³ mu³³ la³³   ko³³ ʂɯ³⁴ ʂɯ³³?*
Muga   often   come Freq   Freq
'Does Muga often come?'   (Chen & Wu 1998: 178)

In the existing literature on Yi, the frequentative aspect marker is often categorized as a temporal adverb, especially when the preverbal temporal adverb is absent, as in (5b). The omission of the preverbal adverb does not render the meaning of (5a) and (5b) different. On the contrary, they have more or less the same meaning as judged by Nuosu Yi speakers. This leads to the belief that the postverbal particle *ko³³ ʂɯ³⁴* in (5b), responsible for the frequentative reading, is a frequency-denoting adverb (See Chen and Wu 1998).

(5)   a.   *mu³³ ka⁵⁵ duɯ³³ duɯ³³ mu³³ zo³³ duɯ³³ ko³³ la³³   ko³³ ʂɯ³⁴.*
Muga   often   school   LOC come Freq
'Muga often comes to school.'

   b.   *mu³³ ka⁵⁵ zo³³ duɯ³³ ko³³ la³³   ko³³ ʂɯ³⁴.*
Muga   school   LOC come Freq
'Muga often comes to school.'

This view, however, can be easily challenged. First, Nuosu Yi adverbs are expected to occur in the preverbal position. Second, Nuosu Yi adverbs are not expected to form polar interrogatives by reduplication. Moreover, it is puzzling why there is the need for two frequency-denoting adverbs to co-occur in (5a), if *ko³³ ʂɯ³⁴* is also taken to be a frequency-denoting adverb. This co-occurrence pattern has not received any explanation until recently; the postverbal particle *ko³³ ʂɯ³⁴* in (5b) has been analyzed as an aspect marker (see Hu 2001).

In Nuosu Yi, aspect markers occur in the postverbal position, and they are able to co-occur with preverbal adverbs.

(6)   a.   *tsho²¹ ko³³ tsi³⁴   dzɯ³³ kɯ³³ o³⁴.*
3pl   in-process eat   Prog SFP
'They are eating (their food).'

   b.   *tsho²¹ dzɯ³³ kɯ³³ o³⁴.*
3pl   eat   Prog SFP
'They are eating (their food).'

The progressive aspect marker co-occurs with a preverbal temporal adverb in (6a). Similar to the case of the frequentative aspect marker in (5), the preverbal temporal adverb in (6a) can be omitted without altering meaning, as shown in (6b).

Despite the similarities observed in (5) and (6), there exists a striking difference between the progressive aspect marker and the frequentative aspect marker. The difference lies in the fact that after the omission of the frequentative aspect marker ko^{33} $ṣɯ^{34}$ in (5a), the remaining sentence is still grammatical with the frequentative meaning unchanged, as (7a) below shows. However the omission of the progressive aspect marker $kɯ^{33}$ in (6a) renders the whole sentence ungrammatical, as reflected in (7b):

(7)　a.　mu^{33} ka^{55}　$dɯ^{33}$ $dɯ^{33}$ mu^{33} zo^{33} $dɯ^{33}$ ko^{33} la^{33}.
　　　　　Muga　　often　　　　　　school　　LOC come

　　　　　'Muga often comes to school.'

　　b.　*$tsho^{21}$ ko^{33} tsi^{34}　$dzɯ^{33}$.
　　　　　3pl　　in-process eat

　　　　　Intended meaning: 'They are eating (their food).'

This contrast shows that the frequentative aspect is an optional aspect marker, but the progressive aspect marker is an obligatory aspect marker. This contrast also reminds us of the preverbal adverb *zhengzai* in Mandarin Chinese.

(8)　a.　*tamen zhengzai　chi pingguo*. (*Mandarin*)
　　　　　3pl　　in-process eat apple

　　　　　'They are eating apples.'

　　b.　*$tsho^{21}$ ko^{33} tsi^{34}　$sɿ^{21}$ $ n̥i^{33}$ $dzɯ^{33}$ (*Nuosu Yi*)
　　　　　3pl　　in-process apple　　eat

　　　　　Intended meaning: 'They are eating apples.'

In the Mandarin example (8a), the adverb *zhengzai* indicates an event in progression, and this adverb can anchor the event in time and space; thus the sentence can stand alone without any additional aspect marker. In contrast, the adverb ko^{33} tsi^{34} in Nuosu Yi has to go together with the progressive aspect marker, but the adverb $dɯ^{33}$ $dɯ^{33}$ mu^{33} in Nuosu Yi is similar to the Mandarin adverb *zhengzai* in that it does not need to go with the frequentative aspect marker, as shown in (7a). How can we get the frequentative reading of (7a) in the absence of the frequentative aspect marker ko^{33} $ṣɯ^{34}$? We will come to this question in sections 3 and 4.

So far we have shown three different ways of expressing a frequentative event in Nuosu Yi: the first way is to use a preverbal temporal adverb, like the English *often* or the Mandarin *jingchang*; the second way is to use a postverbal frequentative aspect marker; the third way is to let the temporal adverb and the frequentative aspect marker co-occur in the same sentence. The corresponding examples are repeated here for ease of the ensuing discussion:

(9) a. *mu³³ ka⁵⁵ dɯ³³ dɯ³³ mu³³ zo³³ dɯ³³ ko³³ la³³*.
        Muga   often   school   LOC come

     'Muga often comes to school.

   b. *mu³³ ka⁵⁵ zo³³ dɯ³³ ko³³ la³³   ko³³ ʂɯ³⁴*.
       Mugas   chool   LOC come Freq

     'Muga often comes to school.'

   c. *mu³³ ka⁵⁵ dɯ³³ dɯ³³ mu³³ zo³³ dɯ³³ ko³³ la³³   ko³³ ʂɯ³⁴*.
       Muga   often   school   LOC come Freq

     'Muga often comes to school.'

In section 2.1, we have shown, with the diagnosis of reduplication, that the frequentative aspect marker is a verb-level aspect marker. We also mentioned another diagnosis regarding negation. In Nuosu Yi, the negative morpheme can be affixed to the verb root, as in (10a), but (10b) shows that the negative morpheme can also be affixed to the frequentative aspect marker, thus giving rise to different scopes of negation:[10]

(10) a. *mu³³ ka⁵⁵ zo³³ dɯ³³ ko³³ a²¹ la³³   ko³³ ʂɯ³⁴*.
         Muga   school   LOC Neg-come Freq

      'Muga doesn't often come to school.'

    b. *mu³³ ka⁵⁵ zo³³ dɯ³³ ko³³ la³³   ko³³ a²¹ ʂɯ³⁴*.
        Muga   school   LOC come Neg-Freq

      'It is not often that Muga comes to school.'

In (10a) what is negated is the event of *coming to school*, whereas in (10b) what is negated is the frequency of the event. While verb-level aspect markers can be negated, grammatical aspect markers, however, cannot be negated. This

---

10 The negative morpheme of Nuosu Yi is a prefix if the base is monosyllabic, but an infix if the base contains two or more syllables.

contrast can be seen in (11). This fact serves as additional evidence to prove that the frequentative aspect marker, different from grammatical aspect markers, is a verb-level aspect marker.

(11)   a. $ŋa^{33}$ dza^{34} dzu^{33} $a^{21} ta^{33}$ $ʑi^{21} sɿ^{33}$.
            1sg   rice   eat   Neg-Cont   yet

            'I am still not eating.'

      b. $^{*}ŋa^{33}$ dza^{34} dzu^{33} $a^{21} o^{34}$.
            1sg   rice   eat   Neg-Perf

            Intended meaning: 'I haven't eaten the rice.'

Besides its co-occurrence with the adverb $du^{33} du^{33} mu^{33}$ 'often', the frequentative aspect marker can also co-occur with another adverb $a^{21} nu^{33} mu^{33}$ 'ceaselessly', as shown in (12).

(12)   a. $tshɿ^{33}$ $a^{21} nu^{33} mu^{33}$ $ʑɛ^{55} ho^{21}$ $ʑɛ^{55}$ $ko^{33} ʂu^{34}$.
            3sg   ceaselessly   song   sing   Freq

            'He often ceaselessly sings songs.'

      b. $tshɿ^{33}$ $a^{21} nu^{33} mu^{33}$ $ʑɛ^{55} ho^{21}$ $ʑɛ^{55}$.
            3sg   ceaselessly   song   sing

            'He ceaselessly sings songs.'

Similar to $du^{33} du^{33} mu^{33}$, the adverb $a^{21} nu^{33} mu^{33}$ can appear with the frequentative aspect marker, as shown in (12a), or without the frequentative aspect marker, as shown in (12b). In both cases we can get the frequentative reading. So far, we have found that only these two adverbs can collocate with the frequentative aspect marker. We will explain why only these two adverbs can occur with the frequentative aspect marker in the following section. At the same time, we will explain why the frequentative aspect marker can pluralize events, thereby giving rise to the frequentative reading, and why the preverbal adverb can also invoke the frequentative reading.

3 Frequentative aspect and pluractionality

Van Geenhoven (2004) shows that the West Greenlandic frequentative aspect marker, which surfaces as -*tar*-, can be interpreted as a pluractional marker. When the frequentative aspect marker is left out, the sentence becomes semantically anomalous. (13a) and (13b) in the following examples illustrate the contrast (Van Geenhoven 2004: 157).

If the sentence "Nuka left (and returned) repeatedly the whole morning" is viewed as depicting a complex macro-event, then the macro-event can be decomposed into numerous sub-events. The repetitive meaning of (13a) can be formally schematized as in (13c), following Van Geenhoven (2005: 112). (13c) suggests that the frequentative aspect marker -tar- contributes three meaning components to a given sentence: repetitive, distributive, and cumulative.

(13) a. *Nuka   ullaap   tungaa   tamaat anisarpoq.*
          Nuka   ullap-p   tunga-a   tama-at ani-**tar**-puq
          N.ABS   morning-ERG   direction-3SG.SG.ABS   all-3SG

          leave-<u>repeatedly</u>-IND.[-tr].3SG
          'Nuka left (and returned) repeatedly the whole morning.'

      b. *Nuka   ullaap   tungaa   tamaat sanioquppoq.*
          Nuka   ullap-p   tunga-a   tama-at saniuqqut-puq.
          N.ABS   morning-ERG   direction-3SG.SG.ABS   all-3SG

          go.by-IND.[-tr].3SG
          'Nuka went the whole morning to pass once, very slowly.'

      c. There was a time t that lasts the whole morning and for every time t' that is part of t, at which Nuka went by, and there was a time t'' that is also part of t, at which he went by, and $t'' > t'$, and there is a time t''' between t' and t'' at which he did not go by, and ...

The repetitive meaning comes from the fact that there is a temporal hiatus between each two sub-events. Hence in (13c), t''' could be a hiatus between two time-spans of two sub-events, during which Nuka did not pass by.

The distributive meaning comes from the allocation of each sub-event, i.e. the time of each sub-event is distributed along the whole event time, which emphasizes that all the sub-events are not happening at the same time. To be more precise, the time axis of the whole event is a disconnected linear sequence of time slots, each of which is occupied by a sub-event.

The cumulative meaning comes from the conjunction of sub-events, which is responsible for the same atelic reading for both telic and atelic verbs with the frequentative aspect. Conjunction, by nature, yields a plural reading due to the combination of a series of sub-events.

The frequentative aspect, therefore, is a linguistic expression of a functional category which serves to pluralize events. Different languages may employ different grammatical strategies to realize such a function. Many languages make use of verb reduplication to express repetition, continuity, and frequency of actions (See Xu, this volume, for an overview of such phenomena in a variety of languages), thereby achieving the purpose of pluralizing events.

Van Geenhoven's (2004) analysis of treating the frequentative aspect as a pluractional marker has an advantage in accounting for the fact that telic verbs, if marked by the frequentative aspect, can be modified by the temporal *for* frame adverbials. This phenomenon would otherwise seem odd, if the pluractional operator is not taken into consideration in the analysis in order to capture the behavior of telic verbs.[11]

We will show in the following that this analysis of treating the frequentative aspect marker as a pluractional operator also applies to Nuosu Yi. We will use three different sets of data to demonstrate the situation in Nuosu Yi. The first set of data is concerned with the modification by the temporal *for* adverbial in sentences with the frequentative reading. The second set and the third set are concerned respectively with the singular/plural subjects and the singular/plural objects of such sentences.

3.1 Frequentative aspect with the *for* frame adverbial

In Nuosu Yi there are three different ways to express the frequentative meaning equivalent to the West Greenlandic example seen in (13a). Let us consider the examples in (14).

(14) a. ηa^{33} i^{21} ni^{21} $tshi^{21}$ ni^{33} su^{33} a^{21} nu^{33} mu^{33} a^{33} di^{55} bo^{33} ko^{33} $\underline{s}u^{34}$.
   1sg today a.whole.day   ceaselessly   there go Freq
   'I went there again and again for a whole day today.'

   b. ηa^{33} i^{21} ni^{21} $tshi^{21}$ ni^{33} su^{33} a^{21} nu^{33} mu^{33} a^{33} di^{55} bo^{33}.
   1sg today a.whole.day   ceaselessly   there go
   'I went there again and again for a whole day today.'

   c. ηa^{33} i^{21} ni^{21} $tshi^{21}$ ni^{33} su^{33} a^{33} di^{55} bo^{33} ko^{33} $\underline{s}u^{34}$.
   1sg today a.whole.day there go Freq
   'I went there for a whole day today.'

   d. ηa^{33} i^{21} ni^{21} $tshi^{21}$ ni^{33} su^{33} a^{33} di^{55} bo^{33}.
   1sg today a.whole.day there go
   'I spent a whole day going there.'

---

11 Telic verbs are known to occur in sentences depicting temporally bounded events, and are hence compatible with the *in* frame adverbials, e.g. John finished his project in (*for) two days.

(14a) contains a typical example expressing the frequentative meaning, where the frequentative aspect marker ko^{33} su^{34} co-occurs with a manner adverb a^{21} nu^{33} mu^{33} 'ceaselessly'. (14a) differs from (14b) and (14c) in that (14b) does not contain the frequentative aspect marker, while (14c) does not contain the temporal adverb. There is no repetitive reading in (14d) as it contains neither element.

From our Nuosu Yi consultants, we learned the following facts about the semantic differences between these sentences. (14a) and (14b) are really identical, but (14c) is a little bit different: both (14a) and (14b) emphasize that the sub-events of going there occur continuously, which means the hiatus between two consecutive sub-events is very short. In other words, the frequency of repeating the same event is very high. On the other hand, although the frequentative aspect marker in (14c) can give rise to the repetitive, distributive, and cumulative meaning, it does not imply that the frequency is very high, which means the hiatus between two consecutive sub-events depicted in (14c) might be either short or long. If the hiatus is short, (14c) will have the meaning identical to (14a) and (14b). If the hiatus is long, (14c) will have a slightly different meaning, i.e., the frequency of going is not as high as that in (14a) and (14b). If we delete the frequentative aspect from (14c), we will get (14d), which can be used in the scenario that the road condition or the weather might be so bad that the speaker may have to spend a whole day going there. No repetitive reading is available for (14d).

The verb phrase a^{33} di^{55} bo^{33} 'go there' in the above sentences, depicting an accomplishment situation, is semantically incompatible with the temporal *for* frame adverbial 'a whole day'. The unexpected grammaticality of (14a) and (14b) can be account for by the presence of the postverbal frequentative aspect marker ko^{33} su^{34}, which creates an unboundedness of the sub-events of *going there*. The verb phrase a^{33} di^{55} bo^{33} ko^{33} su^{34}, depicting a repetitive (atelic) macro-event, has no semantic conflict with the temporal *for* frame adverbial 'a whole day'. In the presence of the preverbal manner adverb a^{21} nu^{33} mu^{33}, the frequentative aspect marker can be omitted with the meaning unchanged, as in (14b). The preverbal manner adverb a^{21} nu^{33} mu^{33} can also be omitted, leaving the hiatus between two consecutive sub-events being either long or short, as in (14c). This indicates that Nuosu Yi differs from West Greenlandic in that the frequentative aspect marker -tar- is obligatory in West Greenlandic, but ko^{33} su^{34} can be optional in Nuosu Yi under one and only one condition: the preverbal adverbs du^{33} du^{33} mu^{33} as seen in Subsection 2.2. or a^{21} nu^{33} mu^{33} under discussion here must be present. The omission of the frequentative aspect marker in (14b) does not strip off the repetitive, distributive, and cumulative meaning from the sentence, as long as the above mentioned preverbal adverbs are present. In a nutshell, the examples in (14) show that the overt frequentative aspect marker can give the sentence a distributive, repetitive and cumulative meaning, and the preverbal temporal adverbs dui^{33} dui^{33} mu^{33} and a^{21} nui^{33} mu^{33} can also do so. We will explain why this is the case in Section 4.

3.2 Frequentative aspect with singular/plural subjects

The second piece of evidence pointing to the existence of a pluractional operator, which is able to generate the distributive, repetitive and cumulative meaning in Nuosu Yi, comes from sentences with plural subjects. It has been argued in the literature (e.g. Verkuyl 1996) that the number feature of arguments may contribute to the aspectual properties of a sentence. Van Geenhoven (2004) examines the English examples in (15) and argues that there exists a silent frequency marker sitting directly on the achievement verb *to explode*.

(15) a. *Bombs exploded for a long time.*

   b. *?A bomb exploded for a long time.*

According to such an analysis, (15a) describes a situation in which one bomb exploded, and then another one exploded, and then another one exploded, and so on. (15b) is grammatical only with the scenario that there was a toy bomb, which could be restored after each explosion. In a similar vain, such examples can also be found in Nuosu Yi, as shown in (16).

(16) a. $t\!\!\:şa^{21}$ ta^{21} $tsh\!\imath^{34}$ gui^{33} a^{21} nui^{33} mu^{33} bi^{55} ko^{33} $şui^{34}$.
    bomb   Dem   pl.Cl ceaselessly   explode Freq
    'These bombs exploded ceaselessly one after another.'

   b. $?t\!\!\:şa^{21}$ ta^{21} $tsh\!\imath^{34}$ ma^{33} a^{21} nui^{33} mu^{33} bi^{55} ko^{33} $şui^{34}$.
    bomb   Dem   sg.Cl ceaselessly   explode Freq
    'This bomb exploded ceaselessly again and again.'

Plural subjects often can get two different interpretations: a collective reading (e.g. 'the bombs exploded together') and a distributive reading, 'the bombs exploded one after another'. In (16a) with the frequentative aspect marker, the distributive reading wins out. It can only mean that the bombs exploded one after another. (16b) with a singular subject can be plausible only in the sense that the bomb is a toy bomb, which can be restored to its original state each time after explosion. This scenario is enforced by the postverbal frequentative aspect marker, because as a pluractional operator, the frequentative aspect will generate the distributive, repetitive and cumulative meaning. However, a bomb cannot explode more than once. Therefore, there is a semantic crash here. The only imaginable situation is that there was a toy bomb which could explode more than once. The semantic oddity (or rather the plausibility) shown in (16b) proves that the frequentative aspect marker can give a distributive, repetitive and cumulative meaning to the sentence.

3.3 Frequentative aspect with singular/plural complements

The last piece of evidence as proof for the existence of a pluractional operator comes from sentences with plural or singular complements.

(17) a. *tshɿ³³ a²¹ nɯ³³ mu³³ ʑɛ⁵⁵ ho²¹ tshɿ³⁴ gɯ³³ ʑɛ⁵⁵ ko³³ ʂɯ³⁴,*
       3sg ceaselessly   song   Dem pl.Cl sing Freq

       ɲi²¹ tsi³³ vi⁵⁵ ʑɛ⁵⁵ o³⁴.
       twenty times sing SFP

       'She sings these songs ceaselessly, and now already twenty times.'

     b. *tshɿ³³ a²¹ nɯ³³ mu³³ ʑɛ⁵⁵ ho²¹ tshɿ³⁴ so³³ ʑɛ⁵⁵ ko³³ ʂɯ³⁴,*
       3sg ceaselessly   song   Dem Cl sing Freq

       ɲi²¹ tsi³³ vi⁵⁵ ʑɛ⁵⁵ o³⁴.
       twenty times sing SFP

       'She sings this song ceaselessly, and now already twenty times.'

The frequentative aspect marker in (17a) pluralizes the event of singing these songs. Suppose there were five songs altogether. (17a) can be interpreted as she sang the five songs for the first time, and then sang the five songs again, and again, till altogether twenty times. Hence finally she must have sung 100 songs in total, twenty times for each of the five songs. What can be easily observed is the distributive (each time singing the five songs), repetitive (singing the five songs repeatedly), and cumulative (adding up all the times of singing the five songs) meanings in the sentence. The frequentative aspect marker in (17b) pluralizes the event 'sing this song'. It means she kept singing the same song twenty times. Again we can observe the distributive (each time singing the same song), repetitive (singing the same song repeatedly), and cumulative (adding up all the times of singing the same song) meanings the sentence conveys.

From the three sets of data, we can observe that what the frequentative aspect marker actually does is to generate a reading which is distributive, repetitive and cumulative. The frequentative aspect marker thus can be analyzed as a kind of pluractional operator, as proposed in Lasersohn (1995) and Van Geenhoven (2004, 2005).

4 Explicit and implicit pluractional operator

In the previous section, we have shown that the frequentative aspect marker in Nuosu Yi can, as a kind of pluractional operator, generate a reading which is distributive, repetitive, and cumulative. We have also shown in (14b) that the preverbal adverb can trigger such a reading in the absence of the frequentative aspect marker. Can the preverbal adverb be analyzed as a pluractional operator as well? If so, how can we account for the case where the preverbal adverb co-occurs with the postverbal frequentative aspect marker? How can a sentence contain two identical pluractional operators?

This question does not arise in West Greenlandic, English, or Mandarin. In West Greenlandic, the frequentative aspect cannot be omitted: it is obligatory. English and Mandarin do not have an overtly realized frequentative aspect marker. Both English and Mandarin Chinese use the frequency adverbs to express the pluractional reading. We assume that Nuosu Yi serves as an intermediate case. We have shown in (9), repeated below as (18), there are three different ways to express a frequentative event in Nuosu Yi, the use of an aspect marker in (18a), the use of a preverbal temporal adverb in (18b), or the use of both in (18c):

(18)   a. $mu^{33}\ ka^{55}\ zo^{33}\ du^{33}\ ko^{33}\ la^{33}\quad ko^{33}\ su^{34}$.

   Muga   school   LOC come Freq

   'Muga often comes to school.'

   b. $mu^{33}\ ka^{55}\ du^{33}\ du^{33}\ mu^{33}\ zo^{33}\ du^{33}\ ko^{33}\ la^{33}$.

   Muga   often   school   LOC come

   'Muga often comes to school.'

   c. $mu^{33}\ ka^{55}\ du^{33}\ du^{33}\ mu^{33}\ zo^{33}\ du^{33}\ ko^{33}\ la^{33}\quad ko^{33}\ su^{34}$.

   Muga   often   school   LOC come Freq

   'Muga often comes to school.'

Given that all the sentences receive more or less the same interpretation, we propose that there is a phonetically null postverbal aspect marker in (18b) which serves the function of a pluractional operator. This implicit pluractional operator, like the overtly realized frequentative aspect marker ko^{33} $șu^{34}$ in (18c), is also responsible for generating the distributive, repetitive, and cumulative reading. The null operator can only be semantically trigged into effect by the preverbal adverbs dw^{33} dw^{33} mu^{33} and a^{21} nw^{33} mu^{33}. The assumption that the function of the preverbal adverb in (18b) is to prime the null pluractional operator can be confirmed by the examples in (19).

(19) a. $tshŋ^{33}$ a^{21} nw^{33} mu^{33} $ʑɛ^{55}$ ho^{21} $tshŋ^{34}$ $șo^{33}$ $ʑɛ^{55}$.
      3sg   ceaselessly   song   Dem Cl sing
      'She sings this song ceaselessly.'

    b. $tshŋ^{33}$ a^{21} nw^{33} mu^{33} $ʑɛ^{55}$ ho^{21} $tshŋ^{34}$ $șo^{33}$ $ʑɛ^{55}$ ko^{33} $șu^{34}$.
      3sg   ceaselessly   song   Dem Cl sing Freq
      'She sings this song ceaselessly.'

To confirm our analysis, we performed the following investigation during our consultation with the Nuosu Yi informants. For (19a), we gave the following scenario to our consultants: suppose the song is very long, and she has to spend two days finish singing the song. We asked our consultants whether we could use (19a) to describe the situation that she was singing the song continuously. Our consultants could not get this interpretation for (19a). For them, (19a) could only have a frequentative reading, i.e., she sings the song again and again ceaselessly for many times, identical to the meaning of (19b) with the overt frequentative marker.

Now let us turn to the question why only the two preverbal adverbs dw^{33} dw^{33} mu^{33} and a^{21} nw^{33} mu^{33} can trigger the frequentative interpretation. We use the following formula as an event template to recapitulate the meaning of (19):

(20) Macro-event =
     $\{|\ e_1|\ldots|\ e_2|\ldots|\ e_3|\ldots|\ e_4|\ldots|\ e_5|\ldots|\ e_6|\ldots|\ e_7|\ldots|\ e_8|\ldots|\ e_9|\ldots|e_n|\}$

The sub-events (e_1, e_2, ..., e_n) represent 'singing the song'. The macro-event is the linear combination of all the sub-events. Suppose the time-slots occupied by each sub-event are constant, and the time span of the complete macro-event is also constant; then the frequency of the sub-events will be determined by the hiatus between each sub-event. If the hiatus is long, then the frequency will be relatively low, and if the hiatus is short, then the frequency will be relatively high. Both $dɯ^{33}$ $dɯ^{33}$ mu^{33} and a^{21} $nɯ^{33}$ mu^{33} bring to light a situation where the hiatus between two adjacent sub-events almost disappears by emphasizing the nonstop of actions within the macro-event. In other words, the two adverbs $dɯ^{33}$ $dɯ^{33}$ mu^{33} and a^{21} $nɯ^{33}$ mu^{33} are semantically most compatible with the frequentative event template in (20), and they are able to modulate or further specify the frequency of sub-events within the macro-event. This explains the close collocation (co-occurrence) between the two adverbs and the sentence-final frequentative aspect marker (be it overt or covert). The semantic association between the preverbal adverbs and the frequentative aspect is so strong that the *drop* of the frequentative aspect marker will not influence the semantic interpretation of the sentence. To put it differently, the presence of the preverbal adverbs in the sentences examined so far manifests that the events the adverbs modify must be frequentative by default. Therefore it can be concluded that sentences depicting such events contain a pluractional operator.

At this stage, we are not sure about the mechanism of the drop of the frequentative aspect marker. However, in light of Nuosu Yi's overall analytic morphosyntactic properties, and its intensive contact with Mandarin Chinese, chances are that Nuosu Yi further simplifies the morphological marking of its aspectual system. In fact, Nuosu Yi has already started to march on the grammaticalization path and the function of a grammatical marker may be finally taken by relevant lexical items as a result of these items gaining richer expressive power. The reason for the morphological change regarding the phenomenon we have encountered here is, in our opinion, partly due to the semantic association between the preverbal adverb and the postverbal aspect marker, and partly due to the influence of Mandarin Chinese. It is generally accepted that Nuosu Yi is a Tibeto-Burman language which has been greatly influenced by the Mandarin Chinese spoken in the Yi region and its vicinities, mostly the Southwest version of Mandarin known as *Xinan Guanhua*. This influence can be easily observed in the large-scale borrowing of Mandarin words into the Nuosu Yi lexicon. Almost all Nuosu Yi speakers, except for those elderly people living in very rural and mountainous areas, are fluent bilinguals of Nuosu Yi and Southwest Mandarin, and more and more Nuosu Yi people living in cities have shifted their first language to Mandarin, due to the rapid socio-economic changes taking place in China over the past decades.

With regards to the ways of expressing pluractionality, Nuosu Yi at the present stage is able to employ both morphological means (overt marking) and syntactic means (temporal adverbs), and it can be predicted that the syntactic means may eventually win out as a result of language-contact induced grammaticalization.

The discussion so far offers a nice morphological typology with regard to the marking of the frequentative aspect. There seems to be a typological continuum ranging from the agglutinating languages such as West Greenlandic with an obligatory frequentative morphological marker to the analytic languages such as Mandarin Chinese without such a morphological marker. Put it simply, there is a continuum ranging from syntheticity to analyticity. Nuosu Yi seems to be standing in between. In the presence of a preverbal adverb, the Nuosu Yi frequentative aspect marker can be left out. In this case, the preverbal adverb can prime a covert frequentative aspect to generate the frequentative reading.

5 Conclusion

In this paper we have explored the following questions:
  i) Do the preverbal adverbs du^{33} du^{33} mu^{33} and a^{21} nu^{33} mu^{33} have to co-occur with the frequentative aspect marker?
 ii) How should we understand the frequentative aspect marker as a pluractional operator, which is responsible for generating the distributive, repetitive, and cumulative meaning?
iii) How should we understand the semantic association between the preverbal adverbs and the postverbal frequentative aspect? Why can the preverbal adverb trigger the frequentative reading in the absence of the postverbal frequentative aspect marker?
 iv) How should we account for the three different ways employed by Nuosu Yi to express a frequentative macro-event?
  v) What kind of typological generalization can we capture after an examination of the frequentative aspect marking in West Greenlandic, Mandarin Chinese, and Nuosu Yi?

In Section 2, we first differentiate Nuosu Yi aspect markers into two sets: the grammatical aspect marker and the verb-level aspect marker, and explain why we treat the frequentative aspect marker as a verb-level aspect marker. In this section we also present data illustrating the different frequentative aspect marking strategies employed by Nuosu Yi. We have found that du^{33} du^{33} mu^{33} does not need to co-occur with the frequentative aspect marker, and the frequentative aspect marker can also co-occur with the adverb a^{21} nu^{33} mu^{33}. In Section 3, we give a semantic account of the frequentative aspect data based on the notion of unbounded pluractionality. Following Van Geenhoven (2004, 2005), we argue that the Nuosu Yi frequentative aspect marker is a pluractional operator, contributing the semantic components [+distributive, +repetitive, +cumulative]. Since there is a strong semantic association between the preverbal adverb and the frequentative aspect marker, the preverbal adverb may trigger a silent frequentative aspect marker into play, thereby contributing the frequentative meaning to the whole sentence. Based on this argumentation, in Section 4, we offer a unified account for the three different ways of expressing a frequentative macro-event in Nuosu Yi, arguing that there is an implicit pluractional operator, and this operator can be trigged into effect by the presence of a preverbal adverb. In the last part of the paper we also take a typological perspective to examine different frequentative aspect marking strategies employed by different languages such as West Greenlandic, Mandarin Chinese, and Nuosu Yi. The relatively flexible behavior of Nuosu Yi frequentative aspect marker, implicit or explicit, offers us a nice picture highlighting the grammaticalization path from expressing pluractionality via a derivational suffix to expressing pluractionality periphrastically via an independent adverb plus an implicit pluractional operator.

Appendix – List of abbreviations

1,2,3	person;
sg	singular;
pl	plural;
Cl	classifier;
Cont	continuous aspect marker;
Dem	demonstrative;
Freq	frequentative aspect marker;
LOC	locative marker;
Neg	negative;
Perf	perfective aspect marker;
Prog	progressive aspect marker;
SFP	sentence final particle.

References

Bar-el, Leora. 2001. Plurality in squamish salish: a look at reduplication. In *Proceedings of the First SULA Workshop: The Semantics of Under-represented Languages in the Americas*, Ji-Yung Kim and Adam Wehrle (eds.), 25: 1–7. University of Massachusetts Occasional Papers.

Chao, Yuen Ren. 1930. A system of tone-letters. *Le Maître Phonétique* 45: 24–27.

Chen, Kang and Wu Da. 1998. *Yiyu Yufa [Nuosu Yi Grammar]*. Beijing: Central University for Nationalities Press.

Dahl, Östen. 1985. *Tense and Aspect Systems*. Oxford: Blackwell.

Gerner, Matthias. 2004. Occurrence particles in the Yi group and their interaction with the occurrence types of a situation. *Lingua* 114: 1331–1366.

Golovko, Evgenij V. 1997. Iterativity in Aleut. In *Typology of Iterative Constructions*, In: Viktor S. Xrakovskij (ed.), 69–91. München: Lincom Europa.

Gruzdeva, Ekaterina. 1997. Plurality of Situations in Nivkh. In *Typology of Iterative Constructions*, In: Viktor S. Xrakovskij (ed.), 164–188. München: Lincom Europa.

Hu, Suhua. 2001. Yiyu dongci de timao fanchou [The aspectual system of Nuosu Yi]. *Minzu Yuwen* [Minority Languages] 4: 28–35.

Krifka, Manfred. 1989. Nominal reference, temporal constitution and quantification in event semantics. In *Semantics and Contextual Expression*, Renate Bartsch, Johan van Benthem and Peter van Emde Boas (eds.), 75–115. Dordrecht: Foris.

Lasersohn, Peter. 1995. *Plurality, Conjunction and Events*. Dordrecht: Kluwer Academic Publishers.

Lieber, Rochelle. 2010. *Introducing Morphology*. Cambridge: Cambridge University Press.

Smith, Carlota S. 1997. *The Parameter of Aspect*. Dordrecht: Kluwer Academic Publishers.

Van Geenhoven, Veerle. 2004. For-adverbials, frequentative aspect, and pluractionality. *Natural Language Semantics* 12: 135–190.

Van Geenhoven, Veerle. 2005. Atelicity, pluractionality, and adverbial quantification. In *Perspectives on Aspect*, In: Verkuyl Henk J., De Swart Henriette and Angeliek Van Hout (eds.), 107–124. The Netherlands: Springer.

Vendler, Zeno. 1967. *Linguistics in Philosophy*. Ithaca: Cornell University Press.

Verkuyl, Henk J. 1972. *On the Compositional Nature of the Aspects*. Dordrecht: Reidel.

Verkuyl, Henk J. 1996. *A Theory of Aspectuality: The Interaction between Temporal and Atemporal Structure*. Cambridge: Cambridge University Press.

Wu, Da. 2009. Liangshan Yiyu dongci de zhonglei jiqi biaoji [Verb types and verb markers in Nuosu Yi]. *Minzu Yuwen* [Minority Languages] 2: 20–28.

Xu, Dan. 2012. Reduplication in languages: A case study of languages of China. In Chapter 2, *This volume*.

Thomas Hun-tak Lee

10 Quantificational structures in three-year-old Chinese-speaking children[1]

Abstract: This paper demonstrates that existential quantifiers encoded in numeral phrases and additive focus structures, as well as universal quantifiers in the form of adverbs and affixes, are used spontaneously by two- to three-year-old Chinese children. Structures of existential quantification appear earlier than those of universal quantification, and adverbial and affixal quantifiers (A-quantification) are more accessible than determiner quantifiers. The expression of logical scope is evidenced in children's use of negation in relation to modals and other quantifiers. The paper explores the implications of these early logical structures for our understanding of language development and cognitive development.

Keywords: Existential quantification, universal quantification, quantifier scope, first language acquisition, cognitive development, early child Chinese, acquisition of Mandarin, acquisition of Cantonese

1 Introduction

Quantificational structures involve quantifiers and variables, and the binding of variables by logical operators. In first order logic or predicate calculus, the

---

1 Earlier versions of this paper were presented at the Workshop on Quantification and Number, Plurality, and Person in the Languages of Asia held on July 5, 2009, CRLAO, EHESS, Paris, and at invited talks at Shanghai International Studies University, Beijing Language and Culture University, Tianjin Normal University, and Nanzan University during 2009–2011. I would like to thank participants of these workshops for comments on my presentations, in particular Stephen Crain, Hua Dongfan, Keiko Murasugi, Ning Chunyan, Marie-Claude Paris, Alain Peyraube, Rosalind Thornton, and Xu Dan. I would like to express sincere thanks to the following colleagues for their contributions to the Chinese Early Language Acquisition (CELA) project, their help with the corpus data, and their comments on my progress reports: Xiaolu Yang, Fang Li, Fan Li, Song Gang, for the research on Beijing children; Ning Chunyan, Aijun Huang, Zeng Tao, Yajuan Hu for work on Hunan children; and Margaret Lei, Aijun Huang and Joey Li for work related to Hong Kong Cantonese children. Thanks are also due to the reviewer for valuable comments on the paper, and to Margaret Lei for suggestions for revision. The support of GRF grant #CUHK4470/08H is hereby acknowledged. This paper is dedicated to the memory of the late Professor Fang Li (1942–2010), colleague and friend, who shared with me a conviction in Universal Grammar and a long-standing interest in the early development of logical form in Chinese children.

quantifiers consist of the existential quantifier, the universal quantifier, negation, conjunction, and disjunction, symbolized in (1).

(1)   ∃, ∀, ¬, ∧, ∨

It is well-known that the tools of first order logic are inadequate for capturing natural language, which makes use of quantifier noun phrases with complex modifiers, count/mass distinctions, epistemic and deontic modals, as well as interrogative and imperative structures. The standard quantificational structures have been much expanded to describe restricted quantification, binding of sets and predicates, questions and various kinds of modality (Reichenbach 1947; Dowty, Wall and Peters 1981; Barwise and Cooper 1981; Higginbotham and May 1981; Keenan 1987, 1992; May 1989; Landman 1991; Partee, ter Meulen and Wall 1990; McCawley 1993). If the logical system only permits quantification over individuals and does not allow quantification over sets, it would be difficult to give an adequate description of cardinal numeral phrases, fuzzy plural phrases such as *many-N* in English or *zhū-NP* in Chinese (see Meisterernst, this volume), or quantifier noun phrases such as *most-N*.[2] Without question operators, a logical system such as predicate calculus will fail to account for the quantificational property of wh-phrases, as reflected in the scope ambiguity of sentences involving a wh-phrase and another quantifier phrase, such as *What did everyone buy?*.[3] Adhering strictly to first order logic will also prevent us from describing complex quantifiers such as *a-different-N*, whose meaning, as we see from Paris (cf. This volume), may have different lexicalizations in different languages.[4] In a

---

2 In expressing the meaning of *"Four students laughed"*, one would have to appeal to a logical representation such as '∃P = set of individuals such that the cardinality of P is 4 and ∀x, x is a student, and if x ∈ P, x laughed'. Similarly, for quantifier phrases such as *most-N*, in which intuitively a proportion is expressed between the sizes of two sets, one needs to use set relations. A sentence such as *"Most students are hardworking"* can be taken as true if and only if the intersection of the set of students and the set of hardworking individuals exceeds in cardinality the set of students who are not in the set of hardworking individuals.

3 It is generally accepted that the ability to enter into scope relation with another quantificational element is an indicator of quantifier status. The sentence *What did everyone buy?* could mean 'Which is the thing y such that for ∀x = person, x bought y', or '∀x = person, which is the thing y such that x bought y'. In the former reading, the wh-phrase has scope over the universal quantifier; in the latter, the universal quantifier has wide scope.

4 As explained in Keenan (1992), a sentence like *"Different pupils answered different questions on the exam"* would require matching the individuals in the set of pupils to entities in the set of questions, such that each of the questions answered by the group of students will be distinct. A clear statement of such a meaning will involve set quantification and goes beyond predicate calculus.

word, natural language quantification involves more complex quantificational devices than are included in first order logic. For an understanding of early development of language and cognition in the individual, it would be instructive to observe the extent to which natural language quantifiers, in particular those of first order logic, are acquired by children. Early incidence of abstract quantificational structures in child language would lend support to the nativist view that children are endowed with abstract linguistic knowledge (Chomsky 1965, 1971, 1981, 1986, 1988, 1993; Crain 1991; Lightfoot 1991). If quantificational structures are not used by children until they are well into the preschool years, such a developmental fact would favor a usage-based view of language acquisition which sees language acquisition as gradual and piecemeal, based on general cognitive abilities by which inductive generalizations are made from experience (Tomasello 2000a, 2000b, 2003).

In this paper, we investigate how existential quantification, universal quantification, negation and scope relations are realized in the language of Mandarin-speaking and Cantonese-speaking children from one and a half to three and a half years of age, and explore the implications of these cognitive structures for our understanding of language development and cognitive development. I will first make some observations on how the quantifiers are realized in Chinese, and then I will report on the child language data that provide evidence for these quantifiers.

2 Quantifiers in Mandarin and Cantonese

In languages like Mandarin and Cantonese, negation is straightforwardly expressed by the negative words: *bu4* and *mei2* in Mandarin, and *m4*, *mou5* and *mei6* in Cantonese. Existential quantification is instantiated by numeral phrases consisting of number words, classifiers and nouns. In the absence of the classifier, it is not possible to achieve existential quantification, since to quantify something presupposes individuating the referents of the noun, and counting them in terms of some units of measure. The role of the classifier is to both individuate the entities denoted by the noun, and to provide a unit of measure for counting them. The numeral denotes the cardinality of the set of entities being counted. The default number interpretation of the classifier in the absence of a numeral is singular (Greenberg 1972/1990: 171; Li and Liu 1978: 4–5; Au Yeung 2005). In the case of bare nouns, neither the variable to be individuated nor the number information is clear in the absence of the numeral and the classifier, and the nominal is ambiguous between count and mass readings and unspecified quantity (Borer 2005). This can be seen from the contrast in meaning between (2), in which numeral classifiers are present in the object nominal, and (3), in which only a bare noun object is found. Whether bare nouns in Chinese are encoded for individuation is not an entirely settled issue, as it has been argued that some nouns in Chinese are inherently individuated (Cheng and Sybesma 1998; Cheng, Doetjes and Sybesma 2008). The argument in Harbsmeier (this volume) is that in Classical Chinese, certain nouns such as *shu4* 树 'tree' are inherently count, and words like *mu4* 木 'wood' are inherently mass, and that some words like *wang2* 王 'king' are inherently singular, while other words like *guo2* 国 'state' are inherently plural. This would support the view that lexical encoding of the count-mass distinction and individuation may not be entirely implausible based on diachronic considerations.

(2) a. *zhuo shang you ge pingguo* (*Mandarin*)
 table on exist CL apple

 'There is an apple on the table'

 b. *zhuo shang you san ge pingguo*
 table on exist three CL apple

 'There are three apples on the table'

(3) *Zhuo shang you pingguo*
 table on exist apple

 'There is apple on the table / There are one or more apples on the table'

Existential quantification is also embedded in additive focus adverbs denoting 'also', such as *ye3*, *you4*, *zai4* (in Mandarin) and adverbs such as *dou1*, *jau6*, *zung6*, as well as verb affixes and sentence final particles such as *maai4* and *tim1* (in Cantonese) (Zhan 1958; Cheung [1972] 2007; Lee 2005; Leung 2005).[5]

---

5 Cantonese is a language that makes rich use of adverbs, verb affixes and sentence final particles for the purpose of quantification, what Partee (1991a, 1991b) calls A-quantification. Earlier analyses of A-quantification in Cantonese are given in Lee (1995) and Peyraube (1997). In this paper, the following abbreviations are used: asp = aspect marker, CL = classifier, N = noun, sfp = sentence final particle, q-sfp = question particle, NOM = nominalizer, encl = exclamation. *Jyutping* (Linguistic Society of Hong Kong 1997), the standard romanization system for Cantonese, is adopted throughout this paper. The digits after the romanization indicate the tone category, which will only be indicated for the morpheme under discussion and when identification of the morpheme may be unclear without the tone information. The age description 'm;n;p' represents respectively the number of years, months and days.

The logical representation of additive focus involves a presupposition of existential quantification and an assertion (Horn 1969; König 1991), as illustrated by the Mandarin sentence in (4), whose meaning can be represented by (4').

(4) **Zhangsan** *ye*   *shuo*   *Fayu*   (*Mandarin*)
     Zhangsan also speak French

(4') Presupposition: $\exists x$ = person,   x ≠ Zhangsan,   and x speaks French.

   Assertion: Zhangsan speaks French.

Universal quantification is expressed in Mandarin by quantifier determiners such as *mei3* 'every' and *suo2you3* 'all' in Mandarin, but more importantly by adverbs such as *dou1* 'all/each'. In Cantonese, in addition to using determiners such as *mui5go3* 'every' and *so2jau5* 'all' and adverbs such as *dou1* 'all/each', one also employs verb affixes to signal universal quantification, such as the verb suffix *saai3* 'all' which quantifies over individuals as well as events, and the verb suffixes *can1* 'every' and *gik6* 'ever', which quantify over events and are restricted to non-root contexts (Lee 1994, 2008; Tang 1996; P. Lee 2004).[6] The Cantonese sentences in (5) illustrate the use of verb suffixes to signal universal quantification.

(5) a. *di haaujau lei*   *saai3 laa3* (*Cantonese*)
         CL alumnus come all   sfp

      'All the alumni came'

   b. *keoi gei*   *can1 seon* *dou1 jung DHL*
       s/he send all   letter all   use DHL

      'Every time s/he sends letters, s/he uses DHL'

   c. **can1* seon*
       *keoi gei
       s/he send every letter

   d. *ngo haang gik6 dou1 m*   *gui*
       I   walk ever all not tired

      'However much I walk, I never get tired'

   e. **ngo haang gik6*
       I   walk ever

---

6 It should be noted that the adverb *dou1* 都 in Cantonese is ambiguous: it can function as a universal quantifier meaning 'all' or as an additive focus marker expressing the meaning 'also'. As will be seen later, the additive focus meaning is the stronger one.

In addition to its realization in the form of determiners, adverbs, and affixes that quantify over individuals and events, the universal quantifier in Mandarin and Cantonese is also found in structures for restrictive focus, signaled by adverbs such as *zhi3* in Mandarin, and *zing6hai6* in Cantonese. In the latter language, the meaning of 'only' can also be expressed by the verb suffix *dak1* (when the object quantified is a numeral phrase) and the sentence final particle *zaa3*. Restrictive focus requires exclusion of all alternatives to the one in focus, hence the necessity for invoking universal quantification (Horn 1969; Rooth 1985, 1992), as illustrated in the Mandarin example in (6), whose meaning is represented by (6′).

(6) *Xiaoming <u>zhi</u> shuo **Fayu** (Mandarin)*
     Xiaoming only speak French

(6′) Presupposition: Xiaoming speaks French.

   Assertion: $\forall x$ = language, and x ≠ French,
                    it is not the case that Xiaoming speaks x.

Apart from negation and the existential and universal quantifiers, natural language employs words to denote epistemic, deontic and dynamic modality, which call for operators that go beyond first order logic. The modal words encode the epistemic concepts of possibility and necessity, the deontic concepts of obligation and permission, and the concepts of volition and ability (Palmer 2001). The modal concepts are typically encoded in the form of auxiliary verbs and adverbs, but in the case of epistemic modality, it may be expressed in Cantonese through sentence final particles as well (Kwok 1984; Leung 2005; Lee and Law 2001). For example, in Mandarin, the epistemic modal *hui4* 'will' encodes possibility or prediction, the deontic modal *ke2yi3* 'may' typically expresses permission, and the modal *neng2* 'can' signals either ability or possibility. The particle *de* inserted between the verb and its complement signals primarily dynamic modality, with the negation of dynamic modality expressed by having the negative particle *bu4* replacing *de*.[7] The corresponding modal words in Cantonese parallel those in Mandarin in terms of usage: the auxiliary verb *wui3* 'will' conveys possibility or prediction, the modal auxiliary *ho5ji3* 'may' signals

---

7 Strictly speaking the modal *ke2neng2* 'possible' is not an auxiliary, but rather a verb in its own right, as it can function as the center of predication as well as an adverb. The same comment will apply to the Cantonese counterpart of this modal verb, i.e. *ho2nang4* 'possible'. The two words are included because semantically they are quantifiers, which enter into scope relations with other logical operators.

permission, and the postverbal particles *dak1* and *m4* mark dynamic modality. A rich system of sentence final particles is available in Cantonese, some of which encode degrees of possibility or certainty as epistemic markers. For example, *gwaa3* 'might' signals weak possibility, *ge3* marks an assertion as somewhat certain, and *wo5* is a quotative particle indicating a lack of commitment of the speaker to the truth of the statement.

One salient property of logical operators lies in their ability to enter into scope relations (Keenan 1971). Given two logical operators A and B, one may have two scope relations, with either A or B taking wide scope over the other. All of the quantifiers mentioned above exhibit scopal properties: negation, the existential and universal quantifiers, the additive and restrictive focus operators and the modal words. Thus in (7), the existential quantifier in subject position and the universal quantifier in object position can each have scope over the other, with the subject wide scope preferred, as in the two readings represented in (7′).[8] In (8), the additive focus operator *ye3* 'also' and the modal auxiliary *ke2yi3* 'may' interact with negation, with the scope order given by surface order. Thus in (8a), the additive focus particle has scope over negation; in (8b), the permission modal *ke2yi3* has scope over negation, and in (8c) when negation precedes the modal, it enjoys wide scope.

(7) you   *liang zhi* xiaomao tiao   guo *meige*   wuding (*Mandarin*)
    exist two CL   cat   jump asp every-CL rooftop
    'Two cats jumped over every rooftop'

(7′) a. There is a set of two cats, such that for each cat x of this set, for all
        rooftops y, x jumped over y   (subject wide scope)

     b. For all rooftop y, there is a set of two cats, such that for each cat x
        of this set, x jumped over y   (object wide scope)

(8) a. *Zhangsan ye   bu   qu* (*Mandarin*)
      Zhangsan also not go
      'Zhangsan also didn't go'

---

8 Despite scope isomorphism in Chinese (Huang 1982) – so that scope order generally follows that of surface structure c-command relations – thematic hierarchy has a strong effect on the possibility of inverse scope – so that object quantifiers bearing the location or goal role may take scope over the subject quantifier bearing the role of theme – as demonstrated in adult judgments reported in Lee, Yip and Wang (1999) and Lee (2003).

b. *Zhangsan keyi bu ban   zou   naxie zawu*
   Zhangsan may not move away those item

   'It is possible for Zhangsan not to move away those items'

c. *tamen bu keyi ban   zou   naxie zawu*
   they   not may move away those item

   'They may not (or are not permitted to) move away those items'

Chinese quantificational structures are of particular interest because of the abundance of adverbial and affixal quantification – what Partee (1991a, 1991b) and Jelinek (1993) have termed A-quantifiers – in addition to the use of determiner quantifiers (D-quantifiers). The preference for adverbial quantification in Chinese was earlier observed by Harbsmeier (1981) in the context of the historical development of Chinese syntax.

In the remainder of the paper, I document the range of quantificational structures that exist in early naturalistic child speech, drawing from both child Mandarin and child Cantonese. Essentially, I will show that existential quantifiers occur earlier than universal quantifiers, with respect to numeral phrases and universal quantifier determiners and adverbs, and also with respect to additive and restrictive focus operators. There is some evidence suggesting that children prefer A-quantification to D-quantification, and that quantifiers that are limited to non-root contexts appear later than those that are not so restricted. I will also show that while the principle for determining the relative scope of quantificational expressions may well be a late acquisition, children use sentences involving more than one quantificational expression relatively early to express scope relations, notably in the relative scope of negation, modality and focus. The paper will end with some thoughts on the significance of the early onset of quantificational structures for our understanding of language development and cognitive development.

3 Existential quantification in early child Chinese

From the study of determiner acquisition in languages such as English (Brown 1973), it is known that some aspects of the distinction between the indefinite article *a* and the definite article *the* are acquired by three and a half years of age, particularly the specific/non-specific distinction (in terms of accuracy of use in obligatory contexts). The classic study of article acquisition by Maratsos (1976) has confirmed Brown's observation by showing that children understand the difference between the definite and the indefinite articles in some contexts.

If one assumes that a nominal of the form 'article + N' invokes existential quantification, then we have reason to believe that children are in command of existential quantifiers by three and a half or earlier. This result is further confirmed by the controlled act-out comprehension study of Hanlon (1981), who tested 61 children aged 4 to 7 on sentences such as *Put some of the letters/cookies in a box.* Four-year-olds were able to perform accurately at a level of 90% or above. In longitudinal and controlled studies of Mandarin-speaking children and Cantonese-speaking children, we observe the use of existential quantification before three years of age in nominals as well as additive focus structures.

3.1 Existential quantification as reflected in numeral phrases

Various longitudinal studies indicate that the earliest nominals of Chinese-speaking children are dominated by bare nouns and null forms, with classifiers becoming productive only at a later stage. In the detailed longitudinal study of Mandarin-speaking children by Min (1994), for one of her subjects (Mengmeng) observed in detail from 1;3 to 2;8, around 60% or more of the nominals were bare nouns, and approximately 25% were null arguments; only 1% or less of the nominals contained a classifier. In another longitudinal study of Mandarin-speaking children, Lee (2010) examined the nominals of two Mandarin-speaking children growing up in Changsha from the time of their lexical spurt, around 1 year 5 months of age, to approximately two years of age.[9] It was also found that in the productions of both children, the first nominals consisted predominantly of bare nouns, proper names and demonstrative locatives, evidenced from 1;05. For one of the children (LSY), classifier-containing nominals did not become productive until 1;08;16, three months after the first observation session. For the other child (AJR), classifier-related nominals did not surface until around 1;08. The classifier-containing nominals consisted of four types: 'Dem-CL-(N)', 'Num-CL-(N)', 'CL-(N)', and 'Dem-Num-CL-(N)', with the last category occurring only negligibly (accounting for less than 2% of the total number of classifier-related nominals used in the period of observation). In Wong (1998), a study of noun phrase development in four Cantonese-speaking children, it was reported that

---

9 The two subjects were each observed and taped with audio recorders and audiovisual cameras, LSY (male) from 10 months to 2 years 11 months, and AJR (female) from 9 months to three years of age. Transcripts of 17 hour-long sessions were used for each child in Lee (2010), with one to two transcripts per month. The data for LSY covered the period 1;05;19–2;03;06, and those for AJR covered the period 1;05;13–2;02;12.

bare nouns are acquired at 1;11, but classifiers are not acquired until after 2;0.[10] The relative delayed occurrence of classifier-containing nominals in comparison to bare nouns, proper names and demonstratives, may be attributed to the fact that nouns in Chinese are individuated by sortal classifiers, which are obligatory for the purpose of enumeration. It probably takes children time to acquire the syntax of individuation, that is, the fact that the presence of a numeral calls for the placement of a classifier, as some number words must be in their command before they can learn the syntax of classifiers.

To illustrate the use of the bare nouns and the classifier-related structures by Mandarin-speaking children, let us observe the exchanges between LSY and his caretakers in (9)–(10).[11] In (9a), the boy essentially used the bare noun *tang* 'candy' non-referentially as a predicate nominal, in answer to an identifying question from his mother. In (9b), the bare noun was used as an argument without any specification of number. It should be pointed out that when we say that children have started using 'numeral-CL-(noun)' structures, we are not claiming that children have fully understood the meaning of the numeral. That they may not have done so is clear from the semantically untrue answers given by the child in the exchanges in (10), showing that the child had not grasped counting at two years of age. However, the child was expressing quantification correctly using words of the appropriate category and stringing them together in the right order.

(9) a. *LSY at 1;09;26*

      MOT: *na de   shi shenme dongxi?*
             take NOM be what   thing
             'What is the thing that (you) are holding?'

       LSY: *tang*
            candy
            'Candy'

---

[10] Wong (1998) adopted a stringent criterion for determining age of acquisition. She defined the age of acquisition as the first of three consecutive sessions in which the child used the category in three different syntactic positions.

[11] The data in (19)–(20) were taken from the transcripts of LSY on which the data analysis of Lee (2010) was partly based, but these exchanges are reported here for the first time, and not reported in that particular paper.

b. *LSY at 1;09;26*

> INV: *zhege shu shangmian hai you   shenme dongxi &a?*
>   this tree above also have what thing sfp
> 'What else is there on the tree?'

> CHI: *pingguo*
>   apple
> 'Apple'

(10) a. *LSY at 1;11;06*

> Adult: *gen ayi shuo ni ji   sui le?*
>   to aunt say you how-many year asp
> 'Tell aunt how old are you?'

> CHI: *san sui la*
>   three year sfp
> 'Three years old'
> (a moment later)

> INV: *duo da le?*
>   how big sfp
> 'How old are you?'

> MOT: *Simao   shi kuai ji   sui la?*
>   Simao (= child's name) be almost how-many year sfp
> 'How old is Simao going to be?'

> CHI: *kuai   liang sui le*
>   almost two year sfp
> '(I am) almost two years old'

b. *LSY at 2;00;06*

> INV: *na ni kankan   ayi you ji   zhi yanjing?*
>   so you take-a-look aunt have how-many CL eye
> 'So take a look, how many eyes does aunt have?'

> CHI: *san   zhi*
>   three CL
> 'Three (eyes)'

Now that we have established that Mandarin-speaking children begin to use classifier-containing nominals before two years of age, it would be important to next determine whether these are used for specific reference or non-specific reference. Based on the criterion used by Min (1994: 18), specific reference is said to be involved "when the speaker refers to particular individuals, which are distinct from all the other members of their class or of a group", and non-specific reference is involved "when there is no reference to particular individuals". It was observed earlier by Min that while 70% or more of the children's noun phrases involved specific reference, numeral phrases of the form 'numeral-classifier-noun' were first used for non-specific reference. Example (11) records an instance of specific use by one of Min's subjects at 2 years 9 months of age.

(11) *JJ at 2;9;11*

> CHI: *ta dai   yi   ge xiao houzi*
>   he bring one CL little monkey
>   'He comes with a little monkey'

The non-specific use of the 'numeral-classifier-noun' structure can be illustrated by data from Chang-Smith (2005), who observed a monolingual Mandarin-speaking child from 21 months to 27 months. As shown in (12), the numeral phrases used by the child BING were non-specific in nature, as these tokens were related to the number reading of the noun phrase. Further examples of specific and non-specific uses of numeral phrases can be found in (13) and (14) respectively, based on the productions of LSY. As reported in Lee (2010), the data from both of his subjects revealed that the earliest uses of 'Num-CL-(N)' and 'CL-(N)' phrases were non-specific in reference. In one of the children (LSY), the numeral phrase was first used for non-specific reference at 1;08;02, but was not used for specific reference until 1;8;30. For the other subject (AJR), the non-specific use of numeral phrases first appeared at 1;07;16, whereas their specific uses were not found until 1;09;02.

(12) a. *(BING at 1;8;22)*

> MOT: *ni   you-mei-you   gei   wo qianqian?*
>   you have not have give me money
>   (The mum asks Bing to pay)
>   'Have you paid me?'

> BING: *shi kuai qian*   (He pretends to pay)
>   ten   CL   money
>   'Ten dollars'

b. AUN: *ni   chi ji   ge?*   (The aunt is referring to the jellies)
you eat how-many CL
'How many pieces have you eaten?'

BING: *liang ge*
two   CL
'Two pieces'

(13) a. (*LSY at 1;08;16, watching a picture on the computer screen*)
CHI: *zai qianmian, zhe lao yeye,   yi   zhi daxiang zai zheli*
at   front   this old grandpa, one CL   elephant at   here
'Ahead, this old grandpa, here is an elephant'

b. (*LSY at 1;08;16, watching a computer screen, expecting to see an elderly man that he had seen earlier*)
CHI: *yi   ge lao yeye   kan bu jian &la*
one CL old grandpa see not seen sfp
'Can't see an old grandpa'

(14) a. (*LSY at 1;08;16. The child takes the paper and the pencil and is ready to draw on paper*)
CHI: *hua yi   ge, hua yi   ge pangxie!*
draw one CL, draw one CL crab
'Draw a crab'

b. (LSY at 2;01;04)
CHI: *hai meiyou   hua ge da binggan*
still not-have draw CL big cookie
'(I) still haven't drawn a big cookie'

The earlier occurrence of non-specific uses of numeral phrases can be understood in light of the fact that children are first exposed to number words probably used to indicate quantity and cardinality. This fact of nominal development in Chinese would lead one to question the claim of Jackendoff (1983) that noun phrases by default are used to denote specific referents, and that [+referential] is the unmarked value of noun phrases. On the contrary, our data would support the hypothesis of Hornstein (1984) that the default status of quantifier phrases is [+operator] reading, given that cardinal numeral phrases are a type of quantifier phrase, and a non-specific reading of the numeral phrase can be taken as a narrow scope reading.[12] Our data would also lend support to the idea that nominals with an empty numeral phrase are assigned a non-specific interpretation as a default reading (Cheng and Sybesma 1999).

3.2 Existential quantification as reflected in additive focus structures

As observed earlier, existential quantification is embedded in additive focus structures expressing the meaning of 'also'. These structures are subject to variation in lexical encoding across languages, well-illustrated by the case of Cantonese, which employs four different additive particles differing in the direction of quantification and the constituent with which the focus particle can associate.

We have good evidence that Chinese-speaking children begin to use these additive particles between two to three years of age. The recent study of Liu (2009) has demonstrated clearly that Mandarin-speaking children are able to use the additive focus particle *ye3* 'also' shortly after two years of age, in both experimental and quasi-naturalistic settings.[13] *Table 1* shows the first spontaneous uses of some additive focus particles: *ye3* 'also', *hai2* 'also', *you4* 'again', *zai4* 'more/again' in the Beijing Chinese Early Language Acquisition (CELA) database documenting the language of four Mandarin-speaking children growing up in Beijing.[14] It can be seen that all of the children began to use these additive focus

---

12 In an opaque context such as the *want*-context, the non-specific reading of a numeral phrase is often accounted for as a narrow scope reading of the phrase with respect to a modal operator (cf. Karttunen 1976): for example, the non-specific reading of the noun phrase *a novel* in *I want to read a novel this weekend*.

13 In a game play situation in which two balloons were each placed on a car, the experimenter pointed to one of the cars and asked the child what was on the car. After the children gave the expected answer *you yige qiqiu* 'there is a balloon', the experimenter pointed at the other car and asked *zhege ne?* 'How about this?' It was found that all of the five child subjects aged between 2;00 and 2;06 were able to produce the expected answer using the additive focus particle: *ye2 you3 yige qiqiu* '(there is) a balloon too'. In picture tasks involving 21 children aged between 2;6 and 3;10 (mean age 3;06), all of the children used the additive focus particle *ye3* 'also' appropriately. Liu (2009) also showed that two-year-olds were able to use the additive focus particle *you4* 'also/again', as in *Ta you reng le yige qiu* 'S/he tossed a ball again/tossed another ball'.

14 The four BJCELA children were all audiotaped and videotaped: CY, a girl, from 10 months to 2 years 4 months in 66 sessions; SJQ, a girl, from 1 year 2 months to 1 year 11 months in 30 sessions; ZHZ, a girl, from 1 year 4 months to 2 years 5 months in 50 sessions; and ZTX, a boy, from 11 months to 2 years 6 months in 52 sessions.

particles at or before two years of age. Some examples of their use of additive particles are given in (15), in which the additive focus particle *ye3* 'also' is associated with the subject (15a) and the verb phrase (15b).

Table 6: First spontaneous uses of some additive focus adverbs in four Mandarin-speaking children in Beijing

Child	*ye3* 'also'	*you4* 'again'	*hai2* 'also'	*zai4* 'more/again'
CY	1;10;04	2;00;28	1;09;07	1;09;07
SJQ	1;10;09	1;10;09	1;09;18	1;10;05
ZHZ	1;10;06	0;11;17	1;10;06	1;10;20
ZTX	1;10;13	1;09;01	1;09;15	1;09;22

(15) a. *CY at 1;10;04. The child and her mother are looking at a picture in which a child is pressing a button of the lift. After mother tells her that the child is pressing a button, the child subject moves close to the picture and uses her finger to press the button.*

    MOT: *dianti   xianshi yi,   er,   san,   si,   wu,   liu,   qi,*
              elevator show   one, two, three, four, five, six, seven,

              ba,   jiu,   shi
              eight, nine, ten

              'The elevator shows: one, two, three, four, five, six, seven, eight, nine, ten'

    CHI: *wo ye   an*
           I   also press
           'I am also pressing'

    MOT: *ni   ye   an   na?*
            you also press sfp
            'You are also pressing?'

    b. *SJQ at 1;10;09. The child and her mother are talking about whether the child likes the sea*

    MOT: *ni   xihuan dahai   ma?*
            you like   ocean sfp
            'Do you like the ocean?'

    CHI: *&xi1*
           like
           'Yes, (I) like (the ocean)'

> MOT: *na ni zai   da yidian mama dai   ni   qu dahai li hao bu hao?*
> so you more big a-little mom bring you go ocean in ok-not-ok?
> 'So when you grow bigger, mom will bring you to the ocean, OK?'

> CHI: *keyi xi zao*
> can take-bath
> '(We) can take a bath (there)'

> MOT: *dui,   keyi xizao   keyi youyong*
> right, can take-bath can swim
> 'Right, (we) can take a bath and swim (there)'

> CHI: <u>*ye*</u>   *keyi youyong*
> also can swim
> '(We) can also swim (there)'

Like Mandarin-speaking children, Cantonese-speaking children begin to use additive focus particles in their various lexical manifestations before three years of age, illustrated in (16) (Lee 2005).[15] One of the CANCORP children (LTF) was capable of using the focus adverb *dou1* 都 'also' to focus on the subject, the adverb *zung6* 仲 'also' as well as the sentence final particle *tim1* 添 'also/too' to focus on the verb phrase. Another child CGK was able to use the verb suffix *maai4* 埋 'also' to focus on the object noun phrase. For four of the CANCORP children (CGK, CKT, MHZ, LTF), the age of first occurrence of the additive adverbs *zung6* 仲 'also' and *jau6* 又 'also/again' was around 2 years 2 months. The additive adverb *dou1* 都 'also' appeared at around 2 years 3 months for two of the children, and at around two and a half for the other two children. The naturalistic longitudinal data show clearly that the additive particles *dou1*, *zung6*, *jau6* were used spontaneously before three years of age.

(16) a. *LTF at 2;08;24. tells the investigator what she is afraid of*

> CHI: *ngo5 geng1 mou4po4 gaa3   ngo5*
> I   fear   witch sfp   I
> 'I am afraid of witches'

---

15 The Cantonese data reported here are drawn from the transcripts of several of the children of CANCORP (Lee and Wong 1998): CGK, CKT, MHZ, LTF and LLY, audio-recorded for 19, 25, 26, 16 and 20 hour-long sessions respectively, each for approximately a year. The age at which these children were recorded ranged from 1;05 to 2;08, and the age at which the observation sessions ended varied between 2;07 and 3;08.

INV: *ngo5 m4 geng1 gaa3*
    I   not afraid sfp
    'I am not afraid (of witches)'

CHI: *maa1 mi4 <u>dou1</u> m4 geng1*
    mom   also not afraid
    'Mommy is also not afraid (of witches)'

b. *LTF at 2;02;10. LTF and investigator are playing with toy babies. The child is taking the toys to eat various things*

INV: *nei5 daai3 bi4bi1 heoi3 sik6 mat1je5 aa3?*
    you take baby to   eat what   sfp
    'What are you taking the baby to eat?'

CHI: *&Ei6, syut3gou1, <u>zung6</u> jau2 gwo2zap1,*
    excl. icecream, also   have juice,

    syut3tiu2,   *hai6 m4 hai6?*
    icecream-stick be   not be
    '(Eat) icecream, also juice, icecream bar, right?'

c. *LTF at 3;01;21. LTF and the investigator pretend that a toy robot is a television and they switch it on. They talk about the programs that will be shown, including the Snow White story*

INV: *bei5 mou4po4 zuk1 zo5 aa3*
    let witch   catch asp sfp
    '(Someone) will be caught by the witch'

CHI: *tung4maai4 jau5 wong4hau6 cat1   go3 siu2ngai2jan4 <u>tim1</u>*
    and   have queen   seven CL dwarf   also
    'And there will be the queen and the seven dwarfs as well'

d. *CGK at 2;07;11. CGK is playing with a toy set, offering to help the investigator comb her hair*

CHI: *bong1 nei5 so1*
    help you comb
    '(I'll) help you comb (your hair)'

INV: *nei5 bong1 ngo5 so1   &aa4?*
    you help me   comb q-sfp
    'You want to help me comb?'

> CHI: *ngo5 bong1 <u>maai4</u> nei5 ziu3 geng3*
>   I   help   also   you look mirror
>   'I'll also help you look at yourself in the mirror'

3.3 Pre-requisites for quantification: Learning to individuate with classifiers

As mentioned earlier, the view we take of bare nouns in Chinese is that they are unspecified with respect to individuation and number. Given that individuation is a pre-requisite to quantification, and sortal classifiers (but not mensural classifiers) function to individuate nouns, Chinese children have to be familiar with the semantic properties of different types of classifiers in order to master quantification. All classifiers bear the function of quantification, but they have different properties vis-a-vis individuation. For example, in Mandarin, individual classifiers (also called 'sortal classifiers') like *ge* (general classifier) and *tiao* (classifier for long and slender objects) individuate the noun denotation, while container classifiers such as *tong* 'bucket' and *bei* 'glass' do not. Thus, the noun *xiangjiao* 'banana' preceded by the sortal classifier *ge/tiao* denotes individuated bananas (17a), but the noun preceded by the mensural classifier *tong* 'bucket' does not (17b). While the classifier *tong* 'bucket' provides a unit of measurement for grouping the bananas, it nonetheless does not require the bananas to be conceptualized as individuated entities: *liang tong xiangjiao* 'two buckets of banana(s)' can denote two buckets containing whole bananas or banana chunks.[16]

(17) a. *zhuo shang you liang ge/tiao xiangjiao (Mandarin)*
          table on   have two CL_{sortal} banana

          'There are two bananas on the table'

      b. *Zhuo shang you liang tong   xiangjiao*
          table on   have two $CL_{mensural}$ banana

          'There are two buckets of banana(s) on the table'

---

16 Huang (2009) and Huang and Lee (2009) propose a taxonomy of classifiers based on the description of types of classifiers in (1968) taking into account two factors: the individuation requirements of classifiers, and whether the classifier denotes discrete units.

In the experimental studies of Huang (2009) and Huang and Lee (2009), children were asked to judge whether a given test sentence correctly describes a picture. The pictures show whole objects or pieces of objects, and the test sentences include bare nouns, as well as classifier-noun and numeral-classifier-noun structures. It was found that when presented with a picture depicting a plural set of objects, over 90% of children between three and a half and five years of age accepted it for bare nouns phrases, but only 12% of them accepted it for the numeral phrase *yi-ge-N* 'one-CL-noun' or *ge-N* 'CL-N'.[17] This indicates that children of this age range are already sensitive to the quantificational difference between bare nouns and (numeral)-classifier-noun structures; they also understand that the default number reading of 'CL-N' structures is unitary. The study also found that while children understand the individuation function and the quantifying function of sortal classifiers, their interpretation of the unit of individuation may differ from the adults'. Children accepted nominals containing sortal classifiers for describing partial object situations, unlike adults.

4 Universal quantification in early child Chinese

When children begin to use the universal quantifier is of great interest, since this quantifier is linked to the expression of scope relations and distributivity. One would need to be sure that children have grasped the meaning of universality of the quantifier before one can proceed to ascertain their ability in handling scope relations. The act-out comprehension study of Hanlon (1981) has shown that for English-speaking children, universal quantifiers such as *all* are acquired by 4 years of age, with the youngest child subjects (the four-year-olds) performing at 100% accuracy. Other universal quantifiers such as *each* seem to be more difficult, with children performing at less than 60% accuracy on the task.[18]

4.1 Universal quantification expressed by determiners, adverbs and affixes

Earlier experimental studies have shown that Mandarin-speaking children have mastered the universality meaning of the universal quantifier *dou1* 'all' before 4

---

17 The children who accepted a picture depicting two objects when a singular numeral phrase was used may have been assigning an 'at least one' reading for the noun phrase.
18 We searched the transcripts of Adam and Eve in the Brown corpus (Brown 1973) and found that *every* was not used as productively as *all* by these children, and was limited by and large to instances of *everybody*, *everything* and *everywhere*.

years of age (Lee 2008). Our longitudinal data indicate that they begin to use the quantifier in naturalistic production much earlier. Mandarin-speaking children have started using *dou1* 'all' in their spontaneous utterances at or before two years of age: at around 1;8 for three of the BJCELA children, and at 2 years of age for the other child. The spontaneous use of the quantifier adverb is illustrated in (18). On the other hand, the determiner universal quantifiers *mei3* 'every' and *suo2you3* 'all' were not evidenced in our longitudinal data even at the end of our observation period, at two and a half years of age.

(18) a. *CY at 1;08;30*, interacting with her aunt, and counting some boxes that were made to stand upright on the floor

> CHI: *li4   qilai*
>   stand up
>   'Stand (this) upright'

> AUN: *yige   li4   qi*
>   one-by-one   stand up
>   'Stand (this) up one by one'

> CHI: *&Lai4 qi*
>   come-up

> AUN: *li4   qilai*
>   stand up
>   'Stand (this) upright'

> AUN: *ai*
>   interjection

> CHI: *dou li   qilai*
>   all stand up
>   'Stand (all of them) upright'

The restrictive focus adverb *zhi3* 'only', which encodes the meaning of universal quantification, was evidenced only in one of the four children at two and a half years of age toward the end of the observation period. The episode in (19) illustrates the spontaneous use of *zhi3* 'only' by the child at 2 years 5 months of age. The context suggests that the child has grasped certain dimensions of the meaning of restrictive focus at this stage.[19]

---

19 In reporting on use of the quantifier by the child, we are merely saying the child is using it in seemingly appropriate ways. Whether the child has fully grasped the meaning of the quantifier will need to be ascertained by controlled methods. As pointed out in Lee (2005), children seem to be using the restrictive focus particle as a contrastive marker at the initial stage, a possible interpretation one may adopt for (19) as well.

(19) *ZTX at 2;05;03, talking with the investigator about whether the child's father and mother would return home at noon*

CHI: *mama huilai*
     mother return
     'Mother come home'

INV: *mama huilai a!*
     mama return sfp
     'Mother come home!'

CHI: *baba baba   shang ban*
     father father at   work-duty
     'Father is at work'

CHI: *baba liu   ban*
     father stay work-duty
     'Father stays at work'

INV: *na ni   gei*
     so you give...

CHI: <u>*zhi*</u> *you   mama yi   ge ren   huilai*
     only have mother one CL person return
     'Only mother comes home by herself'

Like their Mandarin-speaking counterparts, Cantonese-speaking children show early grasp of the adverbial and affixal elements expressing universal quantification. *Table 2* (based on Lee and Lei 2011) shows clearly that Cantonese-speaking children have started using *saai3* 'all' productively before three years of age, mostly by two and a half years of age. Unlike its counterpart in Mandarin, the adverb *dou1* in Cantonese is polysemous between an additive focus reading and a universal quantification reading, the former being the stronger one. This is reflected both in the later appearance of *dou1* (in its universal quantifier sense) and in its lower frequency of use by children, as compared with *saai3*. The CANCORP data do not show any use of the universal event quantifiers *can1* and *gik6*, which are limited to subordinate contexts. Some examples of children's use of *saai3* and *dou1* are given in (20a)–(20b) and (20c)–(20d) respectively.

Table 7: Cantonese-speaking children's use of the universal quantifier *saai3* and *dou1*

Child (Period of observation)	Age of first occurrence of *saai3* (no. of tokens)	Age of first occurrence of *dou1* (universal) (no. of tokens)
CKT (1;05;22–2;07;22)	2;01;08 (16)	n/a (0)
MHZ (1;07;00– 2;08;06)	2;00;16 (28)	2;06;04 (1)
LTF (2;02;10– 3;02;18)	2;02;10 (29)	2;08;24 (4)
LLY (2;08;10– 3;08;09)	2;09;28 (37)	3;01;30 (10)

(20) a. *CKT at 2;03;17*

    INV: *gaa gaa ce dou waai   zo2 &a4?*
           CL CL   car all   broken asp q-sfp
        'Was every car broken?'

    CHI: *xxx waai saai &a3*
           broken   all   sfp
        '…all broken'

  b. *LLY at 3;03;26. The investigator is drinking something*

    INV: *ha?*
         'what?'

    CHI: *cyunbou jam   saai keoi &a1 &he1*
           whole   drink all   it   sfp sfp
        'Drink all of it'

  c. *LTF at 2;10;18*

    INV: *&E6, fangaau &lo1*
           excl. sleep   sfp
        'Sleep'

    CHI: *keoi mou   meimaai ngaan ge3*
           s/he not-have close   eye   sfp
        'S/he has not closed his/her eyes'

    INV: *hai6 wo3, mou5   meimaai ngaan &wo3*
           Right,   no-have close   eye   sfp
        'Right, (s/he) has not closed his/her eyes'

CHI: *gogo doul meimaai ngaan &a3*
CL CL all close eye sfp
'All have closed (their) eyes'

d. *LTF at 3;02;18*

INV: *tai jizai &ga3 &lol*
look ear sfp sfp
'Take a look at the ear(s)'

INV: *tai ha zek jizai gon m gonzeng &lol*
look asp CL ear clean not clean sfp
'Take a look at whether the ears are clean or not'

INV: *jau mou sai gonzeng zek3 jizai &a3 siu pangjau?*
have not wash clean CL ear sfp little child
'Have (you) washed (your) ears clean, little child?'

CHI: *ngo mui jat doul sai &ge3*
I every day all wash sfp
'I wash (it) everyday'

4.2 Universal quantification expressed in restrictive focus markers

As we observed earlier, universal quantification is not only expressed in the form of determiners, adverbs and affixes, but is also embedded in the meaning representation of 'only'. In the experimental study of the acquisition of Mandarin focus particles *cai2* and *jiu4* (Yang 2000), it was found that four- to six-year-old children tended to associate *zhi3* 'only' and the restrictive use of *jiu4* with the verb phrase, even if these particles precede the subject. In other words, pre-school Mandarin-speaking children may interpret a sentence such as *zhi3/jiu4 xiaonuhai nazhe yusan* 'Only the girl is holding the umbrella' as if it meant *xiaonuhai zhi nazhe yusan* 'The girl is only holding the umbrella', corroborating the earlier findings of Crain and Conway (1994) for English-speaking children. The recent study of Mandarin-speaking children's use of focus particles (Fan and Song 2011) has observed spontaneous restrictive uses of *cai2* and *jiu4* at around two and a half years of age, in utterances such as *cai san ci ne*, only-three-CL-time 'only three times' and *jiu mai liu ge*, just-buy-six-CL 'only buy six (of these)'.

One generalization that has been proposed on the acquisition of focus (based on child Cantonese) is that restrictive focus particles appear later than additive focus particles (Lee 2005). As shown in *Table 3*, the Cantonese-acquiring children from CANCORP all started using an additive focus particle (e.g. *dou1* or *zung1*) shortly after they reached two years of age. On the other hand, they did not begin to use any restrictive particle until two and a half or three years of age. This pattern of acquisition is also supported by the Mandarin data. All four subjects from the BJCELA corpus started using additive focus particles by 1 year 9 months of age. However, only two of them started using restrictive focus particles at around two and a half years of age.[20] For these two children, the restrictive focus particles lagged behind additive focus particles for about half a year in terms of time of first spontaneous occurrence. The later appearance of restrictive focus markers in comparison to additive focus markers may be related to the relative semantic complexity of the two types of particles: while additive focus involves existential quantification, restrictive focus involves both universal quantification and negation (exhaustivity and exclusion). An example of Cantonese-speaking children's expression of restrictive focus in the form of the focus adverb *zing6hai6* and *zaa3* is given in (21).

Table 8: Additive and restrictive focus particles in Cantonese-speaking and Mandarin-speaking children.

Cantonese-speaking children	Age of first use of additive focus particles	Age of first use of restrictive focus particles
MHZ	2;02;26	2;06;04
CKT	2;01;08	——
LTF	2;02;10	2;11;16
Mandarin-speaking children	**Age of first use of additive focus particles**	**Age of first use of restrictive focus particles**
CY	1;09;07	——
SJQ	1;09;18	——
ZHZ	1;10;06	2;04;17
ZTX	1;09;01	2;05;03

---

20 Some of the children – CKT in the Cantonese corpus and CY and SJQ in the Mandarin corpus – did not show any use of restrictive focus particles during the period of observation.

(21)   *LLY at 3;3;26. The investigator is showing the child the mosquito bites on her arms. The child comments that these are moles. Then they start counting the 'moles' on their legs*

INV: *tai   haa nei go   zek sin1,*
       look-at asp you that CL   first,

       nei bei ngo tai   haa nei go   zek
       you let me look-at asp you that CL

       'Look at your (leg) first; you let me look at yours'

INV: *jau   mou   mak2?*
       have not-have mole

       'Are there moles?'

CHI: *ngo zing6hai6 zek goek nidou jau*
       I   only   CL   leg   here have

       'I only have (moles) here on my leg'

5 The marking of scope relations in early child Chinese

Earlier studies of scope acquisition by Chinese-speaking children have focused on nominal quantifiers, testing children aged four years and older with experimental tasks on sentences such as *meige xiaohai dou nazhe yiba yusan*, every-CL child ALL hold-asp one-CL-umbrella 'Every child is holding an umbrella'. Various scholars have shown that preschool children aged 4–6 are perfectly capable of handling such relations of scope dependency, even though they differ from adults in tolerating greater scope ambiguity (Chien and Wexler 1989; Lee 2003; see Lee 2008 for a review).[21] The question is whether these abstract logical structures are used by children at all in their early naturalistic speech, and whether children have any communicative need of these structures in their early cognitive development.

---

21 Other studies of children's scope interpretation have also reported adult-child differences with respect to the scope of negation and the universal quantifier (Fan 2007; Zhou and Crain 2008).

In our Chinese early language data, quantifier scope relations of the text-book type involving two nominal quantifiers are not attested.[22] The earliest quantificational structures that involve two quantifiers have to do with negation interacting with modals and quantifier adverbs. As reported in Lee and Fan (2009), children need to express these logical scope relations in daily interactions, and must order the logical operators correctly to express the intended meanings. The study found that Mandarin-speaking children before two years of age are capable of negating modals with the negator in preverbal position or infixed between the verb and the complement in a verb compound, and do so productively.[23] In (22), the child ZTX positions the negator before the modal *ke2yi3* 'be allowed to' and *neng2* 'can' in denying permission or ability. In (23), the child ZHZ infixes the negator in a verb compound between the verb root and the complement, expressing denial of ability.

(22) a. *ZTX at 1;09;29*

    CHI: *bu keyi na zou*
        not may take go
        '(It) may not be taken away'

  b. *ZTX at 1;10;27*

    CHI: *bu neng xia lai*
        not can down come
        '(I) can't come down'

  c. *ZTX at 2;03;08*

    CHI: *zhe liang ge mantou bu neng chi*
        this two CL steamed-bun not can eat
        'These two steamed buns can't be eaten'

(23) a. *ZHZ at 1;07;19*

    CHI: *cha bu jin*
        plug not in
        '(The building block) can't be plugged into (the car)'

---

22 Data from Adam in the Brown corpus (Brown 1973) reveal some instances of use of multiple quantifier sentences around four years of age, with the child Adam producing utterances such as "*Did everyone see a fish fly?*" (3;8;14) and "*Everyone was on a horse*" (4;02;17).
23 Lee and Fan (2009) found that Mandarin-speaking children have started using the negators *bu4* and *mei2* from around one and a half productively, and use them in simple clauses as well as complex sentences involving complementation, relative clauses and adverbial clauses before two and a half years of age.

b. *ZHZ at 2;00;22*

  CHI: *zhao   bu   dao   mama le*

      look-for not arrive Mom   sfp

      '(The duck) can't find (its) mother'

c. *ZHZ at 2;04;17*

  CHI: *ta kou   bu   chu lai*

      he dig-out not out come

      'He can't dig (it) out'

To understand how Chinese children interpret the scope of negation and the universal quantifier, we note that while no spontaneous utterance containing a universal quantifier determiner was found in our child Mandarin data before two and a half years of age, the universal quantifier adverb *dou1* has begun to be used productively between 1 year 10 months and two years of age.[24] This reflects the primacy of A-quantifiers over D-quantifiers in Chinese in ontogenetic development. Two of the children expressed the scope relation of negation and the universal quantifier, in the 'all-neg' scope order, exemplified in (24).

(24) a. *ZHZ at 2;05;01*

    CHI: *xxx shu,   dou bu   neng kan le*

        xxx book all   not can   read sfp

        'Book. All can't be read'

  b. *ZHZ at 2;03;21, turning to the last page of a book*

    CHI: *dou mei   le   ba?*

        all   not (have) sfp sfp

        'No more pages (I've finished reading all the pages)'

We saw earlier that existential quantification in the form of numeral phrases appear early in Chinese child language before two years of age. However, utterances expressing the scope of negation and the existential quantifier were infrequent, with only two of the four BJCELA child subjects using such utterances approximately half a dozen times or less before two and a half years of age. The examples in (25) indicate that unlike the case of the universal quantifier,

---

24 The age at which the relevant quantifier has been used spontaneously in three distinct linguistic contexts is considered the age at which the quantifier has been used productively by the child.

the existential quantifier was typically used in the scope of negation in terms of meaning.

(25) a. *ZTX at 2;05;17*

CHI: <u>*liang fen qian*</u>   *bu*   *neng*
two CL money not can
'Two *fens* aren't (enough to buy it)'

 b. *ZHZ at 2;04;11, answering the question Haiyou duoshao qian a?*
'*How much money is left?*'

CHI: <u>*mei you*</u>   *yi fen qian*   *ba*   *mao le*
not have one CL money eight CL   sfp
'There isn't one *fen* eight *mao*'

Our Mandarin-speaking children have started using some of the quantificational adverbs (on some of their meanings) to express scope: for example, the use of *ye3* to mean 'also', and the use of *you4* and *zai4* to signal the meaning 'again', illustrated in (26).

(26) a. *CY at 1;10;18*

CHI: *xiaoniaor ye*   <u>*bu*</u> *wanr le*
bird   also not play sfp
'Birds don't play either'

 b. *ZHZ at 1;10;06*

CHI: *luyinji*   *ye*   <u>*bu*</u> *pa*
recorder also not fear
'(I) don't fear the recorder either'

 c. *ZTX at 1;10;27*

CHI: *zhe*   *ye*   <u>*mei*</u> *suo* *men*
here also not lock door
'The door here is not locked either'

 d. *ZTX at 1;09;01*

CHI: <u>*you*</u>   <u>*mei le*</u>
again not sfp
'(The toy) disappeared again'

Our data indicate that children as young as two years of age need to express affirmation or negation of modality. In addition, they need to express the relative scope of negation and quantifiers. They talk about negation in relation to exhaustivity, encoded by the universal quantifier. They communicate about negation in relation to inclusion, signaled by the additive focus marker. The child language patterns highlight a prominent fact about scope order in Chinese: the word order of a quantificational adverb and negation is typically fixed, permitting generally only one scope order within a clause (Teng 1983).[25]

6 Early emergence of quantificational structures: Implications for the study of cognitive development

Our review of current findings in child Mandarin and child Cantonese has revealed that while children may not have grasped the full meanings of the quantifier expressions, they start using these expressions and have a need for such use by three years of age. In this section, I would like to discuss the implications of these findings within the broader context of quantifier acquisition and its relevance to our understanding of cognitive development.

The study of quantifier acquisition is important for our understanding of children's understanding of set relations. As remarked earlier, the meanings of natural language quantifiers involve relations between sets or classes. "*Some student laughed*" means that the intersection of the set of students and the set of persons who laughed is not a null set. To say that "*Every student laughed*" is to assert that the set of students is a subset of the set of persons who laughed.

---

25 Given two quantifiers, two scope orders are logically possible, but the relative accessibility of the two scope orders may be different. As reported in Fan (2007), even children as old as seven years of age found the 'neg-*dou*' order (as in [a]) more difficult to interpret than the '*dou*-neg' order (as in [b]) in picture verification tasks.

(ia) *xiaotuzi men* <u>bu</u> <u>dou</u> *zai   chi huluobu*
    rabbit   pl   not all PROG eat carrot
    'The rabbits are not all eating carrots'

(ib) *xiaotuzi men* <u>dou</u> <u>bu</u> *zai   chi huluobu*
    rabbit   pl   all not PROG eat carrot
    'All the rabbits are not eating carrots'

To express the idea of "*Some student cleaned every classroom*" would involve pairing members of the set of students and the set of classrooms.

There have been conflicting findings on how early children acquire logical structures whose meanings involve set relations. Psychologists like Jean Piaget have put forward the view that children below the age of 7 or 8 are generally deficient in interpreting sentences containing universal quantifiers, which is reflected in children's failure to correctly respond to questions such as "*Are all the circles black?*" when presented with an array of figures (consisting, for example, of three black circles, one black square and one white square) (Piaget 1953; Inhelder and Piaget 1964; Piaget and Inhelder 1969). This deficiency has been attributed to the lack of the cognitive operation of reversibility. When a set is decomposed into two subparts, children cannot relate the subparts to the original un-decomposed set. While attempts have been made to demonstrate children's ability to handle these sentences using more friendly designs, the fact remains that these sentences pose problems for preschool children (Neimark and Chapman 1975; Donaldson 1977; McGarrigle, Grieve and Hughes 1978; Siegler 1998).

For linguists, these results from cognitive psychology pose a puzzle, since one may assume that the ability to deal with these logical structures is unique to humans, and structures such as logical connectives and variables must be part of Universal Grammar, i.e. our biological endowment (cf. Chomsky 1993; Fodor 1980). If logical structures constitute part of innate knowledge, why should they emerge so late? We have also seen that Chinese-acquiring children produce quantifiers such as *all* well before three years of age, and use them singly as well as in combination with other quantifiers (e.g. negation) at an early age. The findings from child language need to be reconciled with those from cognitive psychology.

While it is true that children do not behave exactly like adults in their quantifier interpretation, linguists have opted to explain this discrepancy by arguing that children are not cognitively deficit, but rather that they have a slightly different grammar or different logical representations than adults. In a seminal study by Roeper and Matthei (1975), it was found from picture selection tasks that children seemed to interpret a sentence like "*All the circles are black*" as 'All the circles are all (wholly) black', with the quantifier in the determiner position spreading to the preverbal position.[26] Around 90% of their subjects

---

[26] Roeper and Matthei investigated around 200 children between 3 and 9 years of age, with 15 to 35 subjects in each age group.

selected a picture depicting circles that were wholly black, but none of them chose the picture in which all the circles were half black. The authors conjectured that "all children will pass through a phase where they will interpret a single quantifier as if it occurred in two positions with the scope unique to each position". The fact that children may postulate a different grammar than adults has also been proposed by Philip (1995) in his analysis of preschool children's symmetric interpretations of sentences such as "*Every boy is riding a pony*". In a situation in which there are three boys and five ponies, with each boy riding a pony, preschool children would tend to reject the sentence. On the other hand, if the situation depicts three boys and three ponies, with each boy riding one, then the child will accept the sentence as true of the situation. Philip argues that children tend to give symmetric responses because they are quantifying over event variables rather than individual variables. In other words, children interpret the sentence "*Every boy is riding a pony*" as 'For all events e in the relevant situation, e is an event of a boy riding a pony'. Thus, if there are ponies that are not being ridden, or boys who are not riding ponies, or other characters present (e.g. a girl) that are not riding a pony, the child will consider the sentence false.[27] The linguistic analyses have enriched our understanding of the complexity of quantifier development as an important aspect of children's cognitive development.

With respect to existential quantification and numeral phrases, experimental research on Chinese children's understanding of classifier-related nominals (Huang 2009; Huang and Lee 2009) has shown that four-year-olds may interpret *san ge pingguo* 'three apples' as three apple pieces rather than three whole apples. This suggests that while children grasp the quantificational dimensions of classifier syntax early, it may take them longer to master the individuation properties of various types of classifiers. Such a finding corroborates much earlier findings on the assumptions of children acquiring a non-classifier language (i.e. English) about default units for counting and quantification. A number of studies of cognitive psychology have demonstrated that four-year-old English-acquiring children may accept pieces of an object as well as whole objects as units for enumeration, so that they may include, for example, umbrella handles along with complete umbrellas in a count of umbrellas (Shipley and Shepperson

---

27 The ability of young children to postulate logical structures in which operators quantify over individual variables has been evidenced in various studies reported in Crain *et al.* (1996). This argues against the claims of Philip (1995), though the latter study can be taken to hypothesize that children make use of event quantification structures as well as structures with operators binding individual variables.

1990; Sophian and Kailihiwa 1998; Brooks, Pogue and Barner 2011). Such convergence of findings will point to underlying similarities between number marking and obligatory classifier use in the syntax of individuation across languages (cf. Borer 2005).

Studies of quantifier acquisition from the perspective of Universal Grammar (UG) have deepened our understanding of children's early cognitive competence by demonstrating the possibility of innate knowledge of specific logical structures, as can be illustrated with acquisition studies on negation and disjunction. In some languages such as English, the syntax of disjunction directly mirrors De Morgan's law so that a structure of the form 'not (A or B)' is generally understood as '(not A) and (not B)'. Recent research has shown that children by four years of age interpret a sentence like "*None of the pirates found the jewel or the necklace*" as 'None of the pirates found the jewel and none of the pirates found the necklace' (Gualmini and Crain 2002). In some languages, however, the syntax of disjunction may not reflect De Morgan's law in a straightforward manner, so that a natural language expression such as "*John does not eat butter or cheese*" may mean 'John does not eat butter or John does not eat cheese' rather than 'John does not eat butter and John does not eat cheese'. This is the case with Chinese and Japanese, illustrated with the sentences in (27). These examples indicate that in the two languages, for simple clauses involving two conjuncts in the verb phrase in the two languages, *NP1-neg-verb-NP2-or-NP3* means 'NP1 neg verb NP1 or neg verb NP2' and not 'NP1 neg verb NP1 and NP1 neg verb NP2'.

(27)   a.   *Milaoshu   meiyou   juqi zhouzi huozhe dianshiji*
            Mickey-Mouse not-have lift table or   TV

            'Mickey Mouse did not lift the table or did not lift the TV'

       b.   *John-wa   aisu   ka keki-wo   tabe-nakat-ta*
            John-TOP ice cream or cake-ACC eat-neg-past

            'John didn't eat ice cream or didn't eat cake'

Studies of Japanese (Crain, Goro and Thornton 2006; Goro 2007) show that contrary to the pattern of disjunction in the adult input, four-to-five year-old Japanese-speaking children will observe De Morgan's law at the initial stages of acquisition, and interpret (27b) as 'John didn't eat ice cream and didn't eat cake'. This result has been replicated for Mandarin Chinese (Jing, Crain and Hsu 2005). Mandarin-speaking children's sensitivity to the syntactic conditions governing the interpretation of disjunction in the language is also demonstrated in Su and

Crain (2009) and Su (2011).[28] This early sensitivity to De Morgan's law in the absence of positive evidence from the target language lends support to the hypothesis that children are endowed with abstract logical structures and operations. These findings will pose severe problems for the usage-based claims of Tomasello (2000a, 2003) on the nature of early language development.

A deeper understanding of issues such as innateness and universality of quantificational structures would benefit from considerations of diachronic development of classifiers, even though it is generally true that ontogeny does not recapitulate diachrony (see Feng, as well as Lin and Peyraube, this volume). Does the historical development of Chinese suggest that explicit linguistic encoding of a marker of individuation, either in the form of number marking or classifiers, confers advantages for language processing? If the language does not opt for number marking, there will be pressures for the language to develop categories like classifiers. But if classifier development was triggered by prosodic factors, the cognitive motivation for the emergence of classifiers would be weakened. Our understanding of the cognitive aspects of quantification would also benefit from typological studies of how number and quantity are expressed in natural language (Comrie 2011; Bisang, this volume). If in a particular language, existential quantification is instantiated only in a limited numeral system, for example a language such as Pirahã, reported in Gordon (2004), with only the words for 'one', 'two' and 'many', and no words for universal quantification, would this imply that the quantifiers of predicate calculus and generalized quantifiers are cultural inventions rather than biological givens?[29] Or should we understand the early logical competence demonstrated in Chinese-speaking

---

28 The studies of Su and Crain show that Mandarin-speaking children will interpret the disjunction marker conjunctively if it is within the scope of a universal quantifier, as in (a), but may not do so if it falls outside the scope of the latter, as in (b).

(iia) *Meige*   [*dian le*   *bingjilin*   *huozhe dangao de*   *xiaohai*]
     every-CL order asp ice-cream or   cake   NOM child

     dou dedao le   *diezi*
     all   get   asp plate

     'Every child who ordered ice-cream or cake got a plate'

(iib) *Meige*   [*dedao le*   *diezi de*   *xiaohai*]
     every-CL get   asp plate NOM child

     dou dian le   *bingjilin*   *huozhe dangao*
     all   order asp ice-cream or   cake

     'Every child who got a plate ordered ice-cream or cake'

29 Gordon (2004) reports experimental findings indicating that Pirahã speakers experienced difficulty in determining cardinality for sets of sizes greater than two or three.

and English-speaking children as cognitive potentialities which are innately available to human beings but which may not be exploited by every language community? These are all complex issues on which acquisition findings on quantification should have a bearing.

7 Conclusions

In this paper, we have reviewed longitudinal evidence from the naturalistic speech of Mandarin-speaking children and Cantonese-speaking children before four years of age, demonstrating in detail the various quantificational structures used by children from the earliest stages of their syntactic development. We have provided copious evidence indicating that two- and three-year-old children have a need to express the relative scope of quantifiers, and are in command of the lexical and syntactic means for achieving such a purpose.

Some generalizations about the emergence of quantificational structures can be made based on the Chinese acquisition studies we have reviewed. First, existential quantification structures appear earlier than those for universal quantification, as reflected in the early use of numeral phrases and the later emergence of universal quantifiers (adverbs or affixes), as well as in the earlier occurrence of additive focus markers compared to restrictive focus devices. Secondly, our developmental findings highlight the greater accessibility of adverbial and affixal quantification (A-quantification) than determiner quantification in Chinese. While all our Chinese-speaking subjects had started to use the universal quantifier adverb or the universal quantifier verb suffix at or before two years of age, their use of the universal quantifier determiner was not evidenced until much later.

Thirdly, we have observed that despite evidence for abstract logical structures in early child Chinese, children's logical representations may differ from the adults', as reflected in their assumptions about the units for enumeration in classifier-related structures when expressing existential quantification, in their interpretation of the relative scope of nominal quantifiers, or in their understanding of the scope of negation and disjunction.

Our documentation of the early onset of quantifier structures in Chinese children's naturalistic speech, coupled with other experimental findings demonstrating Chinese children's early sensitivity to the logical scope of quantifiers, is consistent with the assumptions of UG. These results would, however, pose severe problems for usage-based theories of language acquisition, which reject early abstract linguistic structures in the face of considerable empirical evidence in favor of these structures, the data from Chinese constituting part of it.

References

Au Yeung, Wai Hoo. 2005. An interface program for parameterization of classifiers in Chinese. Ph.D. diss., The Hong Kong University of Science and Technology.

Barwise, Jon and Robin Cooper. 1981. Generalized quantifiers and natural language. *Linguistics and Philosophy* 4: 159–219.

Borer, Hagit. 2005. *Structuring sense*. Volume I: *In name only*. Oxford: Oxford University Press.

Brooks, Neon, Amanda Pogue and David Barner. 2011. Piecing together numerical language: Children's use of default units in early counting and quantification. *Developmental Science* 14 (1): 44–57.

Brown, Roger. 1973. *A first language*. Cambridge, MA: Harvard University Press.

Chang-Smith, Meiyun. 2005. *First language acquisition of functional categories in Mandarin nominal expressions: A longitudinal study of two Mandarin speaking children*. Doctoral dissertation, Australian National University.

Chao, Yuen Ren. 1968. *A Grammar of spoken Chinese*. Berkeley: University of California Press.

Cheng, Lisa L.-S., Jenny Doetjes and Rint Sybesma. 2008. How universal is the universal grinder? In *Linguistics in the Netherlands*, 50–62.

Cheng, Lisa L.-S. and Rint Sybesma. 1998. *Yi-wan tang*, *yi-ge tang*: Classifiers and massifiers. *The Tsing Hua Journal of Chinese Studies*, New Series 28 (3): 385–412.

Cheng, Lisa L.-S. and Rint Sybesma. 1999. Bare and not-so-bare nouns and the structure of NP. *Linguistic Inquiry* 30 (4): 509–542.

Cheung, Samuel H.N. [1972]. *Xianggang Yueyu yufa de yanjiu (zengding ban)* [Studies on the grammar of Hong Kong Cantonese (enlarged revised edition)]. Hong Kong: Chinese University Press.

Chien, Yu-Chin and Kenneth Wexler. 1989. Children's knowledge of relative scope in Chinese. In *Papers and Reports in Child Language Development* 28, 72–80.

Chomsky, Noam. 1965. *Aspects of the theory of syntax*. Cambridge, MA: MIT Press.

Chomsky, Noam. 1971. *Problems of knowledge and freedom: The Russell lectures*. New York: Vintage.

Chomsky, Noam. 1981. *Lectures on government and binding*. Dordrecht: Foris. 26.

Chomsky, Noam. 1986. *Knowledge of language*. New York: Praeger.

Chomsky, Noam. 1988. *Language and problems of knowledge: The Managua lectures*. MIT Press.

Chomsky, Noam. 1993. A minimalist program for linguistic theory. In *The View from Building 20*, In: K. Hale and J. Keyser (eds.). Cambridge, MA: MIT Press.

Comrie, Bernard. 2011. *Typology of numeral systems*. Lecture given on July 19, 2011 at Language Engineering Laboratory, Chinese University of Hong Kong.

Crain, Stephen. 1991. Language acquisition in the absence of experience. *Behavioral and Brain Sciences* 14: 597–612. Reprint, in *Language Acquisition: Core readings*, In: Paul Bloom (ed.). 1994. Cambridge, MA: MIT Press.

Crain, Stephen and Laura Conway. 1994. Learning, parsing, and modularity. In *Perspectives on sentence processing*, In: C. Clifton, L. Frazier and K. Rayner (eds.). Hillsdale, NJ: Lawrence Erlbaum.

Crain, Stephen, Takuya Goro and Rosalind Thornton. 2006. Language acquisition is language change. *Journal of Psycholinguistic Research* 35 (1): 31–49.

Crain, Stephen, Rosalind Thornton, Carole Boster, Laura Conway, Diane Lillo-Martin, and Elaine Woodams. 1996. Quantification without qualification. *Language Acquisition* 5 (2): 83–153.

Donaldson, Margaret. 1977. *Children's minds*. London: Fontana.

Dowty, David, Robert Wall and Stanley Peters. 1981. *Introduction to Montague semantics*. Dordrecht: Reidel.

Fan, Li. 2007. *Ertong he chengren yufa zhong de fouding he fouding xiayu* [Negation and its scope in Mandarin Chinese]. Hefei: Anhui University Press.

Fan, Li and Gang Song. 2011. *Ertong zaoqi yuyan zhong de jiaodian* [Focus in early child language]. Paper presented at the 2011 Annual Research Forum of the Linguistic Society of Hong Kong, December 3, City University of Hong Kong.

Fodor, Jerry. 1980. Fixation of belief and concept acquisition. In *Language and learning: The debate between Jean Piaget and Noam Chomsky*, M. Piattelli-Palmarini (ed.). London: Routledge and Kegan Paul.

Gordon, Peter. 2004. Numerical cognition without words: Evidence from Amazonia. *Science* 306 (5695): 496–499.

Goro, Takuya. 2007. *Language-specific constraints on scope interpretation in first language acquisition*. Doctoral dissertation, University of Maryland.

Greenberg, Joseph. 1990. Reprint. Numeral classifiers and substantival number: Problems in the genesis of a linguistic type. In *On language: Selected writings of Joseph H. Greenberg*, In: Keith Denning and Sazanne Kemmer (eds.). Stanford, CA: Stanford University Press. Original edition, In *Working Papers on Language Universals* 9: 1–39, 1972.

Gualmini, Andrea and Stephen Crain. 2002. Why no child or adult must learn De Morgan's laws. In *Proceedings of the 26th Boston University Conference on Language Development (BUCLD26)*, 243–254. Summerville, MA: Cascadilla Press.

Hanlon, Camille. 1981. The emergence of set-relational quantifiers in early childhood. In *Child language: An international perspective,* In: P. Dale and D. Ingram (eds.). Baltimore, MD: University Park Press.

Harbsmeier, Christoph. 1981. *Aspects of classical Chinese syntax*, 27. London: Curzon.

Higginbotham, James and R. May. 1981. Questions, quantifiers and crossing. *The Linguistic Review* 1: 41–80.

Horn, Larry. 1969. A presuppositional approach to *only* and *even*. *Papers from the Fifth Regional Meeting*, 98–107. Chicago: Chicago Linguistics Society.

Hornstein, Norbert. 1984. *Logic as grammar*. Cambridge, MA: MIT Press.

Huang, Aijun. 2009. *Count-mass distinction and the acquisition of classifiers in Mandarin-speaking children*. MPhil thesis, Chinese University of Hong Kong.

Huang, Aijun and Thomas Hun-tak, Lee. 2009. Quantification and individuation in the acquisition of Chinese classifiers. In *Proceedings of the Tenth Tokyo Conference on Psycholinguistics,* Yukio Otsu (ed.). Tokyo: Hituzi.

Huang, C.-T. James. 1982. *Logical relations in Chinese and the theory of grammar*. Doctoral dissertation, MIT.

Inhelder, Bärbel and Jean Piaget. 1964. *The early growth of logic in the child*. New York: W.W. Norton.

Jackendoff, Ray. 1983. *Semantics and cognition*. Cambridge, MA: MIT Press.

Jelinek, Eloise. 1993. Languages without determiner quantification. In *Proceedings of the 19th Annual Meeting of the Berkeley Linguistic Society*, J. Guenter *et al* (eds.). Berkeley, CA: Berkeley Linguistic Society.

Jing, Chunyuan, Stephen Crain and Ching-fen Hsu. 2005. The interpretation of focus in Chinese: Child vs. adult language. In *The Proceedings of the Sixth Tokyo Conference on Psycholinguistics*, In: Yukio Otsu. (ed.) Tokyo: Hituzi Syobo.

Karttunen, Lauri. 1976. Discourse referents. In *Syntax and semantics 7: Notes from the linguistic underground*, J. McCawley (ed.). New York: Academic Press.

Keenan, Edward. 1971. Quantifier structures in English. *Foundations of Language* 7 (2): 255–284.

Keenan, Edward. 1987. Unreducible n-ary quantifiers. In *Generalized quantifiers*, Peter Gärdenfors (ed.), 109–150. Dordrecht: Reidel.

Keenan, Edward. 1992. Beyond the Frege boundary. *Linguistics and Philosophy* 15 (2): 199–221.

König, Ekkehard. 1991. *The meaning of focus particles*. London: Routledge.

Kwok, Helen. 1984. *Sentence particles in Cantonese*. Hong Kong: Center of Asian Studies, University of Hong Kong.

Landman, Frederick. 1991. *Structures for semantics*. Dordrecht: Kluwer.

Lee, Po Lun Peppina. 2004. *Affixal quantification: A syntax-semantics mapping approach to Cantonese suffixal quantifiers*. Doctoral dissertation, City University of Hong Kong.

Lee, Thomas Hun-tak. 1994. *Yueyu saai3 de luoji tedian* [The logical properties of *saai3* in Cantonese]. In *Proceedings of the First International Conference on Yue Dialects*, In: Chow Yiu, Sin (ed.), 131–138. Hong Kong: Modern Educational Publishers.

Lee, Thomas Hun-tak. 1995. *Postverbal quantifiers in Cantonese*. Paper presented at the 10th Workshop on Asian Oriental Languages, May 16–17. Centre de Recherches Linguistiques d'Asie Orientale, Paris.

Lee, Thomas Hun-tak. 2003. Two types of logical structure in child language. *Journal of Cognitive Science* 3: 155–182.

Lee, Thomas Hun-tak. 2005. The acquisition of additive and restrictive focus in Cantonese. In *POLA Forever: Festschrift in honor of Professor William S-Y. Wang on his 70th birthday*, 71–114. Taipei: Institute of Linguistics, Academia Sinica, Taiwan.

Lee, Thomas Hun-tak. 2008. *Hanyu ertong dui shuliang mingci duanyu xiayu guanxi de renshi* [Children's knowledge of the relative scope of quantifier noun phrases]. In *Dangdai yuyaxue lilun he hanyu yanjiu* [Contemporary linguistic theory and studies of Chinese], In: Yang Shen and Shengli Feng (eds.). Beijing: Commercial Press.

Lee, Thomas Hun-tak. 2010. Nominal structure in early child Mandarin. In *Chinese matters: From grammar to first and second language acquisition*, In: Chris Wilder and Tor Åfarli (eds), 75–109. Trondheim: Tapir Academic Press.

Lee, Thomas Hun-tak, and Li Fan. 2009. *Negation and its scope in child Mandarin*. Paper presented at the Center for Research on Chinese as a Second Language, April 16, Beijing Language and Culture University.

Lee, Thomas Hun-tak, and Ann Law. 2001. Epistemic modality and the acquisition of Cantonese final particles. In *Issues in East Asian language acquisition*, In: Mineharu Nakayama (ed.), 67–128. Tokyo: Kuroshio Publishers.

Lee, Thomas Hun-tak, and Margaret Ka-yan Lei. 2011. *Acquisition of the postverbal universal quantifier affix in Cantonese*. Paper presented at the Seventh Conference of the European Chinese Linguistic Association (EACL-7), September 13–15, Università Ca' Foscari, Venice, Italy.

Lee, Thomas Hun-tak and Colleen Wong. 1998. CANCORP-The Hong Kong Cantonese Child Language Corpus. *Cahiers de Linguistique Asie Orientale* 27 (2): 211–228.

Lee, Thomas Hun-tak, Virginia Yip, and Chuming Wang. 1999. Rethinking isomorphism as a scope principle for Chinese and English. In *Proceedings of the Tenth North American Chinese Linguistics Conference*, 169–186. Graduate Students in Linguistics: Department of Linguistics, University of Southern California.

Leung, Chung-sum. 2005. *Dangdai Xianggang Yueyu yuzhuci de yanjiu [A study of the utterance particles in Cantonese as spoken in Hong Kong]*. In *Monograph series in computational and linguistic analysis of Asian languages* 2. Language Information Sciences Research Center: City University of Hong Kong.

Li, Jinxi and Shiru Liu. 1978. *Lun xiandai Hanyu zhong de liangci* [On classifiers in Modern Chinese]. Beijing: Commercial Press.

Lightfoot, David. 1991. *How to set parameters*. Cambridge, MA: MIT Press.

Linguistic Society of Hong Kong Jyutping Editorial Group. 1997. *Guide to LSHK Cantonese romanization of Chinese characters*. Hong Kong: Linguistic Society of Hong Kong.

Liu, Huijuan. 2009. *Additive particles in adult and child Chinese*. Doctoral dissertation, City University of Hong Kong.

Maratsos, Michael. 1976. *The use of definite and indefinite reference in young children*. London: Cambridge University Press.

May, Robert. 1989. Interpreting logical form. *Linguistics and Philosophy* 12 (4): 387–435.

McCawley, James. 1993. *Everything that linguists have always wanted to know about logic, but were afraid to ask*. Second edition. Chicago: University of Chicago Press.

McGarrigle, James, R. Grieve, and M. Hughes. 1978. Interpreting inclusion: A contribution to the study of the child's cognitive and linguistic development. *Journal of Experimental Child Psychology* 26: 528–550.

Min, Ruifang. 1994. *The acquisition of referring expressions by young Chinese children*. Doctoral dissertation, The Catholic University of Nijmegen.

Neimark, Edith and Robin Chapman. 1975. Development of the comprehension of logical quantifiers. In *Reasoning: representation and process in children and adults*, In: R. Falmagne (ed.). Hillsdale, NJ: Lawrence Erlbaum.

Palmer, Frank. 2001. *Mood and modality*. Second edition. London: Cambridge University Press.

Partee, Barbara. 1991a. Adverbial quantification and event structures. In *Proceedings of the Seventeenth Meeting of the Berkeley Linguistic Society*, In: L. Sutton, C. Johnson and R. Shields (eds.). Berkeley, CA: Department of Linguistics, University of California at Berkeley.

Partee, Barbara. 1991b. Domains of quantification and semantic typology. In *1990 Mid-America Linguistics Conference Papers*, F. Ingeman (ed.). Department of Linguistics, University of Kansas, Lawrence.

Partee, Barbara, Alice ter Meulen, and Robert Wall. 1990. *Mathematical methods for linguistics*. Dordrecht: Kluwer.

Peyraube, Alain. 1997. Cantonese post-verbal adverbs. In *In Memory of Mantaro J. Hashimoto*, In: Anne O. Yue and Mitsuki Endo (eds.), 303–313. Tokyo: Uchiyama Shoten.

Philip, William. 1995. *Event quantification in the acquisition of universal quantification*. Doctoral dissertation, University of Massachusetts at Amherst.

Piaget, Jean. 1953. *Logic and psychology*. Manchester, UK: Manchester University Press.

Piaget, Jean and Bärbel Inhelder. 1969. *The psychology of the child*. New York: Basic Books.

Reichenbach, Hans. 1947. *Elements of symbolic logic*. New York: MacMillan.

Roeper, Thomas and E. Matthei. 1975. On the acquisition of 'some' and 'all'. *Papers and Reports in Child Language Development* 9: 63–74.

Rooth, Mats. 1985. *Association with focus*. Doctoral dissertation, University of Massachusetts at Amherst.

Rooth, Mats. 1992. A theory of focus interpretation. *Natural Language Semantics*. 1: 75–116.

Shipley, Elizabeth and Barbara Shepperson. 1990. Countable entities: Developmental changes. *Cognition* 34: 109–136.

Siegler, Robert. 1998. *Children's thinking*. Third edition. Upper Saddle River, NJ: Prentice Hall.

Sophian, Catherine and Christina Kailihiwa. 1998. Units of counting: Developmental changes. *Cognitive Development* 13: 561–585.

Su, Yi (Esther). 2011. *Disjunction and downward entailment in child Mandarin: An experimental investigation into the acquisition of semantic universals*. Doctoral dissertation, MacQuarie University.

Su, Yi (Esther) and S. Crain. 2009. Disjunction and universal quantification in child Mandarin. In *Proceedings of the Tenth Tokyo Conference on Psycholinguistics*, In: Yukio Otsu (ed.). Tokyo: Hituzi.

Tang, Sze-wing. 1996. On lexical quantification. In *UCI Working Papers in Linguistics* 1, In: B. Agbayani, K. Takeda and Sze-Wing Tang (eds.), 119–440. Department of Linguistics: University of California at Irvine.

Teng, Shou-hsin. 1983. Quantifier hierarchy in Chinese. In *Studies in Chinese syntax and semantics – Universe and scope: Presupposition and quantification in Chinese,* In: T. Tang, R. Cheng, and Y. Li (eds.). Taipei: Student Books.

Tomasello, Michael. 2000a. Do young children have adult syntactic competence? *Cognition* 74: 209–253.

Tomasello, Michael. 2000b. The item-based nature of children's early syntactic development. *Trends in Cognitive Sciences* 4 (4): 156–163.

Tomasello, Michael. 2003. *Constructing a language: A usage-based theory of language acquisition*. Cambridge, MA: Harvard University Press.

Wong, Sin Ping. 1998. *The acquisition of Cantonese noun phrases*. Doctoral dissertation, University of Hawaii at Manoa.

Yang, Xiaolu. 2000. *Focus and scales: L1 acquisition of CAI and JIU in Mandarin Chinese*. Doctoral dissertation, Chinese University of Hong Kong.

Zhan, Bohui. 1958. Yue fangyan zhong de xuci *cin1, zhu4, fan1, maai2, tian1* [The function words *can1, zyu6, faan1, maai4, tim1* in Cantonese]. *Zhongguo Yuwen* [Chinese Language] 1958 (3): 119–122.

Zhou, Peng and Stephen Crain. 2008. Scope assignment in Chinese: Why children and adults differ. In *The Proceedings of the Ninth Tokyo Conference on Psycholinguistics*, In: Y. Otsu (ed.). Tokyo: Hituzi Syobo.

Author index

Subject index

www.ingramcontent.com/pod-product-compliance
Lightning Source LLC
Chambersburg PA
CBHW070022100426
42740CB00013B/2577